THE LETTERS OF CHARLES HARPUR AND HIS CIRCLE

CHARLES HARPUR.

Sydney Studies in Australian Literature
Meg Brayshaw, Series Editor

The *Sydney Studies in Australian Literature* series publishes original, peer-reviewed research in the field of Australian literary studies. It offers engagingly written evaluations of the nature and importance of Australian literature, and aims to reinvigorate its study both locally and internationally.
SUP thanks Professor Robert Dixon, Founding Editor.

THE LETTERS OF
CHARLES HARPUR
AND HIS CIRCLE

Selected and edited by

PAUL EGGERT
and
CHRIS VENING

SYDNEY UNIVERSITY PRESS
sydney.edu.au/sup

First published by Sydney University Press 2023
© Paul Eggert and Chris Vening 2023
© Sydney University Press 2023

Sydney University Press
Fisher Library F03
Gadigal Country
University of Sydney NSW 2006
Australia
sup.info@sydney.edu.au
sydneyuniversitypress.com.au

 A catalogue record for this book is available from the
NATIONAL LIBRARY OF AUSTRALIA National Library of Australia.

ISBN 9781743329498 hardback
ISBN 9781743329283 paperback
ISBN 9781743329290 epub
ISBN 9781743328897 pdf

Cover. 'A Veiw [i.e. view] of the River Hawkesbury N.S. Wales' (*c.* 1810), J. W. Lewin

Front cover. Charles Harpur (probably early 1868), photographer A. Lomer

Half-title page. 'Charles Harpur' (engraving of 1874), engraver unknown

We acknowledge the traditional owners of the lands on which Sydney University Press is located, the Gadigal people of the Eora Nation, and we pay our respects to the knowledge embedded forever within the Aboriginal Custodianship of Country.

CONTENTS

ILLUSTRATIONS

Cover: 'A Veiw [i.e. view] of the River Hawkesbury N.S. Wales' (*c.* 1810), artist J. W. [John William] Lewin, 46.4 x 58.8 cm (State Library of New South Wales, DG VIB/3).

Front cover: 'Harpur', photograph portrait of Charles Harpur (probably early 1868), photographer A. [Albert] Lomer, 10.5 x 6.3 cm (State Library of New South Wales, PI/716).

Half-title: 'Charles Harpur' (engraving 1874), engraver unknown, from photographic image of early 1868, 14.6 x 13.2 cm, in *Australian Town and Country Journal*, 14 March 1874, p. 413.

1. Untitled photograph portrait of Charles Harpur, Poet (probably early 1868), photographer A. [Albert] Lomer, 11.9 x 8.6 cm (National Library of Australia, PIC Box PIC/7082 #PIC/7082). *page xviii*

2. Untitled portrait of Charles Harpur (June 1892), artist unknown, reworked (inkwash) opalotype (i.e. milkglass) transfer of magnified photographic image of early 1868, 38 x 29 cm (State Library of New South Wales, P*88). *xxvi*

3a. 'A View of Part of the Town of Windsor in New South Wales' (1813), artist P. [Philip] Slager, engraver W. [Walter] Preston, 24.3 x 38.7 cm (image), *c.* 30.5 x 44.8 cm (engraved block, dated 'June 4th 1813'), in series *Views in New South Wales* (Sydney: A. [Absalom] West, 1812–14: *Copy*: State Library of New South Wales, ML SAFE/F981/W). *xxviii*

3b. 'A View of Hawkesbury, and the Blue Mountains. New South Wales' (1817, with the ruins of the wharf at Windsor damaged by the 1816 flood; from 1815 watercolour), artist James Wallis, engraver W. [Walter] Preston, 32.5 x 54.0 cm (image), 41.3 x 56.5 cm (engraved block), in [James Wallis], *An Historical Account of the Colony of New South Wales and its Dependent Settlements; in Illustration of Twelve Views...* (London: R. Ackermann, 1821: *Copy*: State Library of New South Wales, PX*D 65). *xxix*

4. 'Henry Parkes From an Engraving by H. S. [Henry Samuel] Sadd, 1854', 9.0 x 7.0 cm, reproduced in 1892 as frontispiece to Parkes, *Fifty Years in the Making of Australian History* (London: Longman, Green). *xxxi*

PREFACE

Despite a near continuity of scholarly interest in the writings of the colonial poet and essayist Charles Harpur since the 1940s, we still only partially know him. This book's parent project, the digital Charles Harpur Critical Archive (CHCA), aimed to fill the documentary gap by providing images, transcriptions and automated comparisons of the versions of all of the poems that survive in manuscript or printed form – printed, in fact, mainly in newspapers of the 1840s–1860s. This archival phase of the CHCA was published online in 2019 at charles-harpur.org. But before the second, editorial phase could be properly undertaken we realised we needed to know more, and in a more systematic way, about the personal, cultural and political background of the poetry. J. Normington Rawling's diligent Harpur biography of sixty years ago quoted many unpublished letters; but ultimately, if we were to proceed with establishing the reading texts of the poems, together with reliable annotation and textual commentary, we needed to have the letters themselves, preferably those of Harpur *and* his circle.

Some readers are content to think of literary works as self-contained things; others, to understand them as discursive effects. But editors who ask very particular questions about texts and their genesis do not have either luxury. They soon learn that the material object matters, and the questions it immediately and then more generally begs cut across existing, broader lines of enquiry. So it is that the letters perform something like a geological cross-section through Australian colonial culture. A denser, thicker description of its overlapping strata is a principal outcome of this book, even for those who, like us, fancied they knew that culture tolerably well.

A much clearer sense of a writing life, lived, is the other principal outcome. This is because, when dealing with the letters of a poet – in eliciting their often elusive testimony – biographical questions inevitably come first, and with bibliographical ones not far behind. The latter, in Harpur's case, have required much sorting out because the poetry of this inveterate reviser typically underwent multiple stages of revision, and the titles he gave the poems (over 700 of them) often changed from version to version and from printing to printing. Cross-reference to the CHCA has made specification possible. It allows the reader immediately to consult the poem-version under mention or comment in the letter and to see it *in situ* if desired, whether in manuscript form or as a newspaper printing – where it would typically compete for attention with the miscellaneous contents of the newspaper. Poetry was a respected literary form and had a much more significant role to play, culturally and politically, than today. Harpur's satires could be especially barbed; and they sometimes sat cheek-by-jowl with news reports of the very public figures at whom they were aimed. Harpur was an essayist too, and he wrote prose notes to his poems, which are often more extensive in scale than the poems themselves and are attuned to the changing social environment. And they are similarly versional: the textual problem recurs with them and it is resolved in the same way.

We were aware of only about three dozen letters written by Harpur when we began this compilation: no previous scholar had seriously tried to identify, locate and publish – let alone annotate – them all, instead digging into the archive only as far as their immediate purpose required. We thought at first that the job would be straightforward. Several years later, and more than a little wiser, we found we had accumulated about 400 letters and another 30-odd life-documents (invoices, sales figures, receipts, personal references etc.). The consequent shift in our understanding of Harpur's life or, more precisely, of aspects of it, is recorded in the Introduction. Ultimately, however, this is an edition of a representative selection of the letters: many insights, often unexpected ones, are on offer, but not yet a rounded life-narrative. A fully satisfactory biography of Harpur is yet to be written: we hope this selected edition of the letters will pave the way and that the forthcoming *Supplementary Letters* volume containing the remainder of the known letters (see Abbreviations for details) will further assist in this and other endeavours.

Because we have come to believe that Harpur, born in Windsor, NSW, in 1813, was the most important poet of the Australian colonial era, the effort has felt continuously rewarding. Watching the successive phases of colonial life – including, in particular, its evolving print culture – open up before our eyes, and then feeling the obligation to explain in detailed annotation what we were seeing, have given us confidence that the materials we offer will benefit understanding of mid-century colonial writing.

Unexpected also when we started was the method of production of the present book. The Word file handed to our publisher was a copy-edited form of one automatically generated from an online working environment developed for the CHCA. One pleasing result is that the simultaneously published digital forms of the letters and their printed counterpart, although identical in wording and layout, have different affordances. The principal one is the live-linking in the e-book and PDF both to contemporary newspaper printings of Harpur's works (his poems, notes, essays, letters to the editor) as well as to the news articles, often political ones, to which he was reacting.

There are hundreds of such links and, in addition, a great many others take the reader inside the CHCA. The reader-user of the e-book or PDF who clicks on linked citations can engage with primary evidence, face to face and in serendipitous ways, rather than remaining at one interpreted remove from it. This is a not unimportant matter. Even newspaper advertisements have their humble role to play in bringing to life the culture to which Harpur's writings responded and endeavoured to shape. The reader of the *printed* book will find it does what printed books have always done when readers have turned to them for pleasurable and informed literary encounters. Harpur's world is a very different one from ours, if also, at times, oddly familiar and in disconcertingly direct communication. The scholarly edition offers another mode of entry to that world, another way of apprehending it, by staying close to the primary sources, their chronology and their materiality.

In working towards this end we have been assisted and supported by many people: our families, who have borne with our strange obsession with good grace; library and archive staff who have dealt helpfully and expertly with our stream of enquiries and requests – in particular, those at the Mitchell Library, State Library of New South Wales; Museums of History New South Wales – State Archive Collection; the National Library of Australia; the State Library of Victoria; Trinity College Library at the University of Melbourne; and the State Library of South Australia. The sustained, ongoing contribution of CHCA technical designer and programmer Desmond Schmidt and that of Meredith Sherlock, digital archivist for the CHCA until 2016, had dividends for our work on this book, as did the prior bibliographical work of Elizabeth Holt and Elizabeth Perkins. In our editing we have also benefited from the combined efforts of previous Harpur and Australian colonial-poetry scholars such as Cecil Salier, poet Judith Wright, school teacher J. Normington Rawling, as well as, from more recent times, academics such as Adrian Mitchell, Michael Ackland and our CHCA adviser Elizabeth Webby, together with many other scholars of Australian colonial poetry and print culture more generally, whether cited in this book or not. A professor of optometry at the University of Melbourne, Marianne Coleman, also kindly advised us on Harpur's sight problems. The CHCA itself was funded principally by the Australian Research Council, with significant contributions also from the University of New South Wales Canberra, and Loyola University Chicago.

16 June 2023   *Paul Eggert and Chris Vening*

CHRONOLOGY

Entries refer to Charles Harpur ('CH') except if indicated.

23 January 1813	Born at Windsor, NSW, son of Joseph Harpur and Sarah Chidley.
November 1829	Harpur family leave Windsor for Parramatta and Sydney.
Summer 1829–30	Probable early excursion to Hunter Valley.
11 May 1833	'The Grave of Clements' by 'C.H.' appears in *The Currency Lad*.
October 1833	Possible appearance on Sydney stage.
February 1835	Verse drama 'The Tragedy of Donohoe' published in *Monitor*.
1 February 1836	Appointed letter sorter at Sydney Post Office.
December 1837 – February 1838	Poems under pseudonym 'Stebii' in Tegg's *Literary News*.
10 October 1839	Resigns from Post Office.
July 1842	Quits Sydney to join his brother Joseph at Singleton, Hunter Valley.
August 1842 – August 1843	Poems from Hunter locations appear in *Australasian Chronicle*.
September 1842 – March 1844	Active in Temperance movement at Singleton, Jerry's Plains and Maitland.
August 1843	At Jerry's Plains, begins correspondence with Henry Parkes.
August 1843 – June 1844	Poems appearing in *Maitland Mercury*.

From 1844	Poems appearing widely in Sydney newspapers. *Songs of Australia* broadside (Sydney: D. L. Welch).
August–December 1844	At Parramatta.
January 1845 – July 1846	Living at Pyrmont, Sydney.
February–December 1845	Contributes over 50 poems to W. A. Duncan's *Weekly Register*, Sydney.
October 1845	*Thoughts. A Series of Sonnets* (Sydney: W. A. Duncan).
June–July 1846	Quarrel with R. K. Ewing of the Sydney *Spectator*.
After 16 July 1846 – March 1850	Proxy postmaster and pound keeper at Jerry's Plains. Poems in *Maitland Mercury* recommence. Living in various parts of Hunter Valley until 1859.
8 April 1847	Reapplies unsuccessfully for a government post.
September 1847	Farming cattle and horses with his brother Joseph.
From January 1849	Poems in E. J. Hawksley's *People's Advocate*, Sydney.
April 1850	Plans to publish collection 'Wild Bee of Australia'.
2 July 1850	Marries Mary Ann Doyle at Great Lodge, Jerry's Plains.
August 1850	Keeping small private school at Jerry's Plains.
31 March 1851	Washington Harpur born at Jerry's Plains.
June 1851	Teaching at temporary National School, Black Creek/Anvil Creek (Branxton).
c. October 1851 – May 1852	Teaching at Presbyterian denominational school, Muswellbrook.
c. June 1852	Probable first meeting with Daniel Deniehy, Sydney.
From April 1853	Farming sheep at Granbelang, west of Singleton.
12 April 1853	*The Bushrangers: A Play in Five Acts, and Other Poems* (Sydney: W. R. Piddington).
15 June 1853	Charles Chidley Harpur born.

c. March 1855	Plans to take a squatting run on the Namoi River.
18 February 1856	Harold Harpur born.
By March 1856	Has relocated to Lowsfield, near Doyle's Creek, Jerry's Plains, farming sheep.
April 1857	Attempts to raise subscriptions to publish poems. Begins corresponding with N. D. Stenhouse.
29 August 1857	Ada Harpur born.
23 November 1857	Deniehy's lecture on the poetry of CH, Sydney.
March–July 1858	Literary squabble with Frank Fowler and *The Month*.
29 August 1859	Appointed Sub-Commissioner of Gold Fields and magistrate, Southern District.
29 September 1859	Lectures on poetry in Sydney.
c. 14 October 1859	CH with family arrives in Braidwood (in Southern Tablelands)
24 October 1859	Lectures on poetry in Braidwood.
c. 31 October 1859	Relocates with family to Araluen goldfield, near Braidwood.
3 October 1861	Mary Araluen Harpur born.
12 December 1861	Is transferred to The Gulph (Nerrigundah) goldfield.
By 31 December 1861	'A Rhyme' and 'Coleridge's Christabel' published in pamphlet form, Braidwood.
January 1862	Friendship with Henry Kendall commences.
4 March 1862	Purchases a farm on Tuross River at Eurobodalla near Bodalla.
c. November 1862	'A Poet's Home' and 'The Poet' published in pamphlet form, Sydney.
By 1 January 1863	Euroma homestead completed.
c. April 1863	Family moves into Euroma homestead.

1 April 1863	Promoted to Assistant Gold Commissioner, Southern Goldfields.
1865?–68	Revising poems for book publication.
November–December 1865	'The Tower of the Dream' published in *Australian Journal*, Melbourne, and then issued as pamphlet.
9 April 1866	In pursuit of bushrangers following raid on Nerrigundah.
30 June 1866	Retrenched from Gold Commissioner service.
2 March 1867	Charles Chidley Harpur killed in shooting accident.
November 1867	Seeks help of Thomas Mort to publish in England.
c. mid-late January–February 1868	In Sydney for medical advice; photographed by Albert Lomer; first meets Kendall.
10 June 1868	Dies at Euroma.
From February 1871	Subscription plan for publishing CH's poems (by Stenhouse and John Dunmore Lang); it fails.
September 1875	Parkes proposes publishing poems, letters and life of CH; nothing eventuates.
April 1881	Mary Harpur opens her campaign, backed by Kendall, to publish poems by subscription.
August 1883	*Poems* (Melbourne: George Robertson), edited by H. M. Martin and assistant, financed largely by Mary Harpur's kinfolk.
2 June 1899	Mary Harpur dies.

ABBREVIATIONS

The following short-title and other abbreviations are used in editorial matter, textual commentary and biographical and historical notes.

ML	Mitchell Library, State Library of New South Wales
NLA	National Library of Australia
NSWSA	Museums of History New South Wales – State Archives Collection
SLV	State Library of Victoria

Ackland	Michael Ackland. *Henry Kendall: The Man and the Myths.* Melbourne: The Miegunyah Press, 1995.
ADB	*Australian Dictionary of Biography.*
ATCJ	*Australian Town and Country Journal.*
Bushrangers	Charles Harpur. *The Bushrangers. A Play in Five Acts, and Other Poems.* Sydney: W. R. Piddington, 1853.
CHCA	Charles Harpur Critical Archive. charles-harpur.org
'Daughter's Memories'	Mary Araluen Baldwin. 'Charles Harpur. First Australian-born Poet. A Daughter's Memories'. *Sydney Morning Herald,* 24 August 1929, p. 11.
Hatbox Letters	*The Hatbox Letters: The Story of the Migration to South Australia of the Families of Edward Montgomrey Martin and Francis Clark 1850/51.* Norwood, SA: The Martin/Clark Book Committee, 1999.

Holt   *The Poems of Charles Harpur in Manuscript in the Mitchell*
                    Library and in Publication in the Nineteenth Century: An
                    Analytical Finding List. Ed. Elizabeth Holt and Elizabeth
                    Perkins. Canberra: Australian Scholarly Editions Centre,
                    UNSW at ADFA, 2002.

Jordens   Ann-Mari Jordens. *The Stenhouse Circle: Literary Life in Mid-*
                    Nineteenth Century Sydney. Melbourne: Melbourne University
                    Press, 1979.

McLaren   Ian F. McLaren. *Henry Kendall: A Comprehensive Bibliography.*
                    Parkville: University of Melbourne Library, 1987.

Martin, *Parkes*   A. W. Martin. *Henry Parkes: A Biography.* Melbourne:
                    Melbourne University Press, 1980.

NSW   New South Wales.

OED   *Oxford English Dictionary.*

'Old   Henry Kendall. 'Old Manuscripts'. *Freeman's Journal,*
   Manuscripts'   17 November 1877, pp. 17–18.

PA   *People's Advocate.*

Rawling   J. Normington-Rawling. *Charles Harpur: An Australian.*
                    Sydney: Angus and Robertson, 1962.

Returns of the   Returns of the Colony ('Blue Books'), 1822–1857 and Public
   Colony   Service Lists, 1858–1870 and 1871–1960. NSWSA: NRS-1286
                    (accessible via Ancestry.com).

SA   South Australia *or* South Australian.

SMH   *Sydney Morning Herald.*

Suppl. Letters   *The Letters of Charles Harpur and his Circle: Supplementary*
                    Letters. Ed. Paul Eggert and Chris Vening. Charles Harpur
                    Critical Archive, forthcoming. charles-harpur.org/publications/
                    supplementary-letters.pdf

Thoughts   Charles Harpur. *Thoughts. A Series of Sonnets.* Sydney: W. A.
                    Duncan, 1845.

NOTE ON EQUIVALENCES

Currency

The unit of currency in use in the Australian colonies in the nineteenth century, and then in Australia after Federation in 1901, was the pound (£), divided into twenty shillings (*s.*), each of twelve pennies (*d.*). The guinea was a nominal amount equivalent to 21*s.*; it was used to express the price of luxury items. A half-guinea was 10*s.* 6*d.* – or '10/6' in handwriting – and similarly '10/-' or '10/.' for 10*s.* The sixpence (6*d.*) and threepence (3*d.*) were small silver coins, and the half-crown (equivalent to 2*s.* 6*d.*) a large one. The penny, halfpenny and farthing (one-quarter of a penny) were copper (hence, coppers). In 1901, £100 could be earned in the equivalent of 46 weeks: a 50-hour week produced an average male wage of £2 3*s.* 6*d.* The equivalent in May 2021 was $1837. Taking general inflation into account (and decimalisation of the currency in 1966), £100 equated to $15,800 in 2021 prices.

Length and area

Units of linear measurement in the imperial system in use in the Australian colonies and after Federation included the foot (ft), equal to 30.5 cm and divided into 12 inches (in.), the yard (3 ft) and the mile (1,760 yards or 1.6 km). An acre is 0.405 hectares.

Dates

The terms *ultimo* (abbreviation *ult* or *ulto*) and *instante* (*inst*), both from the Latin, were conventionally used in correspondence to indicate *last month* and *this present month*.

1. Charles Harpur (probably early 1868), photographer A. Lomer

INTRODUCTION

Various approaches to nineteenth-century Australian colonial poetry and to colonial literature more generally have been put forward during the last four decades. They have usually been characterised by historical awareness and theoretical pointedness. Both aims have tended to broaden the prior, more intently aesthetic literary-critical concentration on individual poets and their works, a focus that had been fed, throughout the twentieth century, by a steady stream of anthologies of colonial and later Australian poetry. The influence of Romanticism on colonial poets was newly configured; their writings were seen as addressing the problem of literary origins in a new antipodean society that was having to build itself from scratch. The forced displacement of the Aboriginal peoples by early colonists looking further and then further afield from the original site of colonisation complicated the picture. A Romantically conditioned sense of newness and awe at the landscapes and fauna was countered by half-acknowledged or repressed awareness of the violence that attended the displacement. So, too, under the expanded purview, the establishment in the colonies of new educational, religious and governmental institutions along existing British and Irish lines became relevant – as did, in Westminster, the gradual elaboration of political policy on representative government. Colonial poetry was an active player in the concurrent emergence in the 1840s and 1850s in New South Wales of a discourse of radical republicanism, one that would seek to cut ties with Britain and thereby, it was bravely hoped, establish an 'Australian' identity (when no equivalent political entity existed, and would not until 1901). The widespread crisis in religious faith was explored by colonial poets, Harpur among them and repeatedly; and, later in the century, the discourse of imperial adventure, together with the anxiety of racial degeneration that it answered or repressed, penetrated and inspired colonial prose fiction; but it affected poetry as well. It went together with the (countervailing) emergence of a localised vernacular 'bush' poetry and the persistence of an oral story-telling tradition.[1]

Each of these new emphases was shedding light on the phenomenon of colonial poetry, just as bibliographical projects (such as the AustLit database), scholarly editions of colonial works (such as the Academy Editions of Australian Literature), and the digitisation of colonial newspapers (gathered in Trove) were mapping, in their different ways, the literary contours of the colonial period.[2] Apart from the bibliographical and archival projects, the new perspectives were mainly discursive in focus. They have more recently been complemented by a parallel but oppositely inspired cultural-historical inquiry into the material vehicles of those discourses. Study of the area that has come to be known as print culture has drawn attention to the significance of such things as the establishment of regular and relatively fast sailing and then steamship routes from Europe to the Australasian colonies, the parallel development there of coastal shipping services – the standard way of getting around before the introduction of the railways – and of more reliable postal services. These factors gradually facilitated the efficient importation and distribution of books, magazines and weekly newspapers, and the stocking of the subscription libraries set up in the new mechanics' institutes, athenaeums and schools of arts. The evolution of weekly then daily newspapers in the cities, and the remarkable proliferation of weekly counterparts in the country towns, large and small, together with the establishment of (often short-lived) literary and general magazines especially from the 1850s onwards, created a demand on the part of newspaper editors and an appetite on the part of newspaper readers for conveniently short-form literary works (poems, stories) and, later, for serialised fiction. A literary culture was being normalised. The widespread habit of excerpting and reprinting literary gossip taken from overseas and city newspapers, together with the popularity of literary parody, added to the brew. Important for the present volume were the printing and reprinting of poetry, including that produced by local poets.[3]

These various dimensions of an evolving print culture bear on and are elucidated by the present edition's documentation. Explanatory notes capture the print-cultural phenomenon on the hop, as it were: they detail things that, to the letter writer and recipient, went without saying but need elucidation now. The role of informal literary coteries and friendships in encouraging the writing of poetry, essays and literary criticism also comes into sharper relief in the present edition even though some have been studied before: the circle of the lawyer-litterateur Nicol Drysdale Stenhouse, gathering, from the early 1850s, in his splendid personal library at his home on the shores of Sydney Harbour;[4] and the surprising cluster of poets on the staff of the Surveyor General's and then the Colonial Secretary's offices in Sydney (the young Henry Kendall, Henry Halloran and Henry Parkes, who had been friend, supporter and political comrade to Harpur from the 1840s and would later become colonial secretary and premier of New South Wales).[5] Again, the facilitating role of Sydney newspaper proprietors such as W. A. Duncan (of the *Weekly Register*), Edward Hawksley (of the *People's Advocate*) and Henry Parkes (*The Empire*) rises to the surface in this edition. Each provided a crucial incentive for Harpur. No matter the strength of his vocation as poet, Harpur's capacity to reach an audience and achieve a reception depended on them.[6] Kendall, from 1862, would serve as Harpur's unpaid literary agent in Sydney, giving him advice on the appropriate outlets for his poetry and essays, placing them himself and also acting as commentator on his friend's works, published and unpublished, and on that of their important contemporaries in Britain. Ann-Mari Jordens in her study, *The Stenhouse Circle*, biographers of Kendall and Harpur, bibliographers of colonial poetry and scholarly editors have drawn attention in the past to networks of friendship, assistance and influence such as these; they receive a new and differently nuanced witnessing here.[7]

The mechanics of book production in the colonies, the terms, costs and the dispiriting unviability of poetry collections, achieve a quite precise definition in the letters and notes. The books by Harpur that were never produced ('Wild Bee of Australia' in 1857 and a posthumous collection in 1871)[8], as well as the one that *was* – *Poems*, in 1883, fifteen years after his death in 1868 – all depended on the promises of subscribers: that is, sales preceded publication; if they were insufficient, publication did not go ahead. *Poems* appeared only because two relatives of Harpur's widow Mary Harpur stepped in with personal guarantees to cover the outstanding costs.[9] Earlier in Harpur's career, two other books had appeared, the first a mere sixteen pages paid for by W. A. Duncan.[10] Being a poet – especially being recognised as a potentially major one – meant becoming independent of the transience of newspaper publication. Harpur gradually realised this, but it was a hard row to hoe in colonial Australia. The failure of his attempt to publish the 'Wild Bee' collection and the production of *Poems* are captured in detail in the letters in this book, as is the interventionist role of the editor of *Poems*, Henry Maydwell Martin and his paid assistant; the latter did most of the work, and here, for the first time, a probable identification of her is made.[11] The letters show how the poems were selected and editorially burnished or abridged to suit the tastes of the day – to Mary Harpur's great chagrin and with misleading effects on the texts of those chosen for anthologising for the next hundred years.

Departures from the texts of Harpur's manuscripts raise questions of a text-critical kind. This intersection of print culture with textual studies can often be revealing, and so it is here. Harpur's deeply engrained tendency to remake his works by means of thoroughgoing revision presupposed an understanding of the colonial newspaper medium on his part that, once he revised his poems or extended them significantly, they could ordinarily be offered, in good faith, for republication. Thus the print context facilitated Harpur's lifelong inclination to revise and thereby to become, in practical effect, a versional poet; and all of this happened without payment. In the last years of his life, after he had foresworn newspaper publication, the habit continued but with the revised forms now oriented towards book-form publication in England.

The process is captured in the explanatory notes to this edition. Links to the original newspaper printings of the poems (the great majority available via Trove) and to their manuscript images and transcriptions, version by version (available in the Charles Harpur Critical Archive), allow a honing-in on the evidence of a literary life, lived, in all its retrievable details. Together they open out for momentary but revealing inspection the print-cultural and other pressures and expectations of the day, as well as complicating the broader discursive perspectives described above. This result is possible only because scholarly editing resolutely privileges the materiality of the primary documents, the agency of their texts, and the chronology of their inscriptions.[12]

A writer's life necessarily has other dimensions and facets that, in principle, biography aims to capture. Henry Kendall has been the recipient of several biographies but Harpur only one: that of 1962 by J. Normington Rawling. An edition of letters such as the present one is not a biography but it points the way towards one and raises expectations by the unfiltered nearness to the life, especially to the literary life, that the letters offer. What was previously unknown, or known only as an isolated piece of information, can assume a new importance when its context is reconstructed (which is what the explanatory notes in the edition are aimed economically at doing). A biography in fragments could be said to be what an edition of letters offers, for it remains up to the reader or to the future researcher to complete the canvas, to join the dots. In order to kick-start that process, and to give some initial guidance to the reader by providing the letters with some general context, a summary, with analysis, of what the editors believe they have learned, so far, about that life is given below.

This, then, is the first collection in print of the letters of arguably the most important poet of the Australian colonial period, Charles Harpur; it also includes relevant letters of those in his circle. It consists mainly of letters uncovered over several years through a systematic search of manuscript and newspaper collections. A little over 430 letters and biographical documents were discovered; 200 have been selected for this volume. Only about three dozen had previously been published.[13]

The volume contains nearly all of the surviving letters written by Harpur, his correspondents' replies where available, and letters concerning him between contemporaries and his family especially after his death. The sets of correspondence with Kendall and Parkes are especially impressive, and the one with Stenhouse not far behind. Together, they document Harpur's life in a previously unavailable way. The edited transcriptions of the letters, presented in chronological order, are accompanied by explanatory notes that identify the people, literary works and events mentioned in the letters, as well as the political movements of the day, in which Harpur intervened with characteristic vigour.[14]

The letters and notes also reveal the intriguing struggle of a high-minded young man to pursue a serious vocation as a poet amidst the unpromising contours of early–mid colonial New South Wales society. Despite bearing the taint of a convict family background, Harpur took his vocation with utmost seriousness and had much to endure before he would find recognition as a poet, mainly in colonial newspapers. They, not books, were the principal site of colonial literary culture. Immersion in that culture, and awareness of its successive phases, is encouraged in the digital forms of the present volume: the links in the explanatory notes to the digitised newspaper printings, as well as the links to other online resources, are live. The aspect of colonial print culture relevant to the particular letter may thus be encountered unfiltered, with what is at first a disconcerting but then a reassuring immediacy. Normal citations allow the reader of the print form of this book to achieve the same effect if desired, though a little more slowly.

Biographical fragments: How Harpur presented to others

We begin with some biographical fragments before attempting a more integrated, if still provisional, life-narrative.

Fragment 1

On 7 April 1838 at the inaugural meeting of the Literary and Debating Society in the centre of Sydney, a young Harpur, aged 25, seems to have had a falling-out with the young James Martin (1820–86), who would, much later, become premier and chief justice of New South Wales. This scenario, proposed by Harpur's biographer J. Normington Rawling in 1962, is suggested by Martin's *Australian Sketch Book*, which appeared some months later on 25 September 1838. In an essay in allegory form called 'The Pseudo-Poets', various versifiers in thinly veiled disguise are parodied when judged by Apollo. So Charles Tompson (who had published a volume of verse in 1826) has his poet's licence refused; and Henry Halloran, who worked at the Surveyor General's office and published verse in the local newspapers, is judged to have shown some gleams of talent but they are obscured by his laziness in composition. Local 'would-be poets', most of them 'tender-hearted, love-sick swains', are ticked off as a group for concentrating too much on the writing of love poems.[15] There was some justice in this jibe as regards Harpur's earlier poems, but his scope was already expanding. Extracts from an early version of what would become his play *The Bushrangers* (1853) had appeared in 1835 in the Sydney *Monitor* as 'The Tragedy of Donohoe'.[16]

The figure based on Harpur – whose talent for poetic composition is not denied – is ridiculed for his lack of cultivation and for his vanity. Martin describes the young Harpur as 'a tall, blear-eyed, pert-looking, cockscombish person, [who] strutted boldly forth, and walked consequentially towards the temple'. Despite the satirical intent, this scrap of description is at least a start if we are to get a sense of Harpur's physical appearance and his presence – as he appeared to others – since there is no pen-portrait of him and only one photograph has survived. A newspaper account from 1833 of a young 'Mr Harpur' (either Harpur or his brother Joseph) describes 'a soft-bearded native [i.e. Australian-born] youth'; and another from 1834 describes him as 'a youth of an open and ingenuous countenance' with a 'modest but firm steadiness of feature'.[17] These are hints, even pointers, but that is all.

Fragment 2

Rawling also generates a description of Harpur in the 1840s, before his marriage, as 'a man of serious purpose' who 'had no small talk', who had 'Honesty and sincerity ... in his eyes, which never flinched or wavered before any others', and who 'scorned to proffer himself as anything but what he was'.[18] Many of the letters support this interpretation, including those when Harpur was forced to solicit for subscriptions for the publication of his 'Wild Bee' collection in 1857. The social ineptness, the standing on his dignity despite his mendicant role, ill-at-ease, are palpable.

Fragment 3

A more self-confident if wayward Harpur is captured in the account of Martin Brennan, the policeman in charge of the southern goldfields at Araluen, where Harpur would find employment from late 1859. In 1909 Brennan remembered Harpur as not always having been in charge of his emotions or personal appearance: 'his hair fell carelessly on his shoulders, he was indifferent as to costume, and disclosed in his eccentricity and exhilaration on occasions a slice of that madness peculiar to genuine bards'.[19]

Fragment 4

The well-known photograph of Harpur (reproduced at page xviii) is a standard studio shot.[20] It was probably taken in Sydney in January–February 1868, evidently intended to serve as a keepsake or *carte de visite*. In it, Harpur stands straight-backed, broad and clear of brow, the hair slightly receding, the beard splayed across the chest, the tired eyes, intelligent and kindly, levelled at the camera, gazing at and through us the viewers, as if listening to a distant voice. It was probably this photograph that Harpur's widow referred to in 1882 in a letter to a relative as taken in 'the last stage of consumption'. Harpur's beard, which looks grey, even white in the photo, was, she said, previously 'quite yellow as was his hair', by which presumably she meant blond but with a distinct golden tinge.[21] Her comment registers her memory of Harpur's sudden aging from March 1867 when their second son was killed in a shooting accident, soon exacerbated by the virulent onset of Harpur's last illness.

Fragment 5

In October 1869 Henry Kendall described Harpur from his memory of when they first met in early 1868: 'He had the frame, and must have had in younger years, the strength of a giant. The man was a noble ruin – one that had been scorched and wasted, as it were, by fire. His face looked as if it had been through the hottest furnaces of sorrow'.[22] In Kendall's moulding, Harpur was becoming a Romantic giant, a seer clarified by fire. This interpretative direction was filled out in 1874 in the well-known woodcut, prepared from the 1868 photograph, for a retrospective on Harpur published in the *Australian Town and Country Journal* (see this volume's half-title page).[23] A more rugged, gritty, unaccommodating Harpur emerges: the image must have had its effect on the literary critics and historians of the 1940s and 1950s who hailed him as a quintessentially manly poet. Contradictorily, however, a coloured opalotype – probably from 1892 and also adapted from the 1868 photograph – shows a younger, more ingenuous, clearer-browed man: but it has had little effect as it remained within the Harpur family until 1973 and was first published in 1995.[24] (See Illustration 2, overleaf.)

The unnamed writer of the article that accompanied the woodcut evidently knew the young Harpur well; his brother Joseph (d. 1878), himself a writer, is a candidate:

> [Charles] had to improve the education he had received, as well as he could, by his own reading and study. In this he was indefatigable; and to such an extent that in early manhood his sight was seriously impaired for a time by close application to the only kind of works which his limited means enabled him to obtain – the cheap popular editions of standard authors, in small type.

Martin's 'blear-eyed' Harpur of Fragment 1 takes on another meaning in this light, just as the print culture of early Sydney comes into better focus.[25]

Biographical outline[26]

Exploring fragments of evidence is one thing; balancing them against the evidence in public documents and in Harpur's writings – *all* of them – is another. The writings cannot be deemed irrelevant to the biographical question since, in a most palpable way, Harpur's writing *was* his life: his writing, that is, together with the reading and thinking that preceded and succeeded each writing event. The question is too large to address here, although the notational overview provided by the Chronology should be of assistance, especially in its amplified form in the CHCA's online biographical Timeline.[27] In an edition of letters, the best that explanatory notes can do is to point to the relevant evidence. The best an Introduction can do, having acknowledged the unavoidable fragmentariness of that evidence, is to try a

2. Untitled portrait of Charles Harpur (June 1892), artist unknown

second tack – a biographical excursus – this time in narrative pursuit of the elusive quarry. Analysis, however provisional, can then meaningfully follow.

Born in 1813 in colonial New South Wales only twenty-five years after European settlement to an English mother and an Irish father, both ex-convicts, Charles Harpur was Australia's first important native-born poet.[28] He was not the very first, however, for others preceded him. William Charles Wentworth was one, if being born at sea in 1790 between Sydney and Norfolk Island qualifies him for the honour. Also in question is the extent to which Wentworth may be considered a poet. His well-known poem 'Australasia', written in 1823 while a student in Cambridge, seems nearly to have exhausted his muse. Colonial politics beckoned and would consume him.

Charles Tompson was born in Sydney in 1807, six years before Harpur. The AustLit database records his first poem as being published in 1823. In 1826 he published his chief work, *Wild Notes from the Lyre of a Native Minstrel*, the first volume of verse written by a native-born poet to be published in Australia. Both Harpur's father and his brother-in-law subscribed for two copies of it.[29] A copy could have come into Harpur's hands from either source; certainly, both he and his brother Joseph Jehoshaphat Harpur (born in 1810) would become poets. Tompson himself prudently accepted the rewards of a post in the public service and, in 1832, 100 acres of land from Governor Brisbane in recognition of his efforts.

Early life and then Sydney

No such generous public acknowledgement of his contribution to colonial society was in store for Charles Harpur. Poetry would have to be its own reward. He was born at Windsor on the Hawkesbury River, some 60 kilometres north-west of Sydney. The township was (and is) picturesquely located on the fertile plains below the Blue Mountains, which loom to the west. Harpur enjoyed what might be called the Wordsworthian advantage, with a boyhood spent amidst unspoiled natural beauty. (See Illustrations 3a and 3b, overleaf.)

It is equally important to remember that Harpur was of the second colonial generation. The first settlers after 1788 could not but be alive to the Aboriginal presence, as contemporary documents confirm, and paintings and etchings of the time remind us.[30] Harpur must, as a boy, have been well aware of Aboriginal people around Windsor and would write the first version of the profoundly compassionate 'An Aboriginal Mother's Lament' in 1845 and 'Ned Connor', who is haunted by his own violence, in 1846. Yet, like many native-born white Australians of his generation, Harpur was seized of a passion to build, institutionally, materially and culturally – despite the devastating cost to the Aboriginal peoples, especially on the shifting frontiers. Harpur himself would become entranced by some of the aspirations and possibilities of this new colonial society; and he would become embroiled in its political and other contestations. In addition, he would become, at first, a learner-driver of the print-cultural apparatus that underwrote the broader colonial project. It was a big tent, in which he would, in due course, become a fully fledged participant.

In this, he had the benefit of a schoolmaster-father who, although himself an ex-convict, must have looked to his son's education. The young Harpur must also have had access to some good private library, perhaps that of the successful if controversial colonial figure, the Reverend Samuel Marsden, who owned land in Windsor. But it was not simply the case for young second- and later-generation colonists that the European and specifically British culture that the first generation had brought with them could be taken up unchanged, but rather that they had actively to adapt it to local conditions, to a limited extent to hybridise it. At least, the most alert of them did; and amongst them we must count Harpur.

By the time he came to live in Sydney in 1833, probably after one or more periods on the Hunter River to the north where members of various Windsor

View of PART of the TOWN of WINDSOR, in New South Wales.
Taken from the BANKS of the RIVER HAWKESBURY.
Drawn and Engraved by R. Harper, Sydney

3a. 'A View of
Part of the Town
of Windsor in
New South
Wales' (1813),
artist P. Slager,
engraver
W. Preston

3b. 'A View of
Hawkesbury,
and the Blue
Mountains. New
South Wales'
(1817),
artist James
Wallis, engraver
W. Preston

families had gone to take up land, he was sufficiently well read to be able to take part almost immediately in the nascent literary culture of the day, one that would begin to flourish in the 1840s. He began contributing poems to the Sydney newspapers from 1833, and he secured a job in the post office as a letter-sorter and later as a clerk. He would not have had access to books in the expensive and exclusive Australian Subscription Library and Reading Room, Sydney's first significant public library, which opened in 1827 with 1,000 volumes. But the library of the new Sydney Mechanics' School of Arts, established in 1833, would have been available to him.[31]

Harpur's vocation, outlook and politics
The young Harpur's falling out with people that Fragment 1 exposes became something of a habit: it was an important aspect of his character to his contemporaries, and it is dealt with at more length below. Even in his twenties he was a proud and upright man, with a prickly dignity that grew from his devotion to his vocation as he saw it. He was jealous of the importance for a young colony of the literary tradition into which he had read his way and of which he would soon become an intelligent critic. Inevitably adopting inherited literary attitudes and diction until he could find his own, Harpur's poetry would be deeply in tune with the contemporary taste for wild nature and the sublime. Although he would never become a radical original in his poetry, he was easily able to master eighteenth-century verse forms. He was equally at home with the blank verse of the Romantics, with its flexible imitation of the tones of the speaking voice and the inner rhythms of the thinking mind. These talents he put to work to give poetic voice to the shared colonial experience of a natural antipodean world; he would carry his readers with him. This would be his vocation, about which he was and would remain both serious and high-minded.

But he was not only high-minded. Although he was heavily influenced by English and, from the 1840s, American book culture, his years in Sydney meant that, in the newspapers, he became adept at scrapping in verse with his opponents, especially those he despised. He could be witheringly satirical and, at times, quite amusing. Of Emancipist (ex-convict) stock himself, he was the natural enemy of the Exclusivists who separated themselves from those with the convict taint. Harpur would take particular delight in skewering the pretensions of the large landholding squatters as well as his political opponents, especially in the 1850s.

Harpur's evolving prose notes to his poems are significant here. Over the years, he republished, as we have seen, many of his newspaper poems in other newspapers, but often adding notes to the new printing, or revising the existing ones. The notes are sometimes more intriguing than the poems themselves. They constituted an attempt on his part to key the poems into the changing political and cultural agendas of the day.

In today's terms his colony made up a small society indeed. In 1838 the total non-Aboriginal population of New South Wales was only about 100,000. Thirty years later, by the time of Harpur's death in 1868, it had grown almost fivefold, but it had still not quite reached half a million: just a little bigger than Canberra's population today. In the same year, the population of the newer, sister colony of Victoria was about forty-five per cent larger, inflated by immigration to its rich goldfields. As far as is known, however, Harpur never left New South Wales.

Henry (later, Sir Henry) Parkes, himself a poet, arrived in Sydney in 1839, the year in which Harpur resigned his government post. Parkes seems not to have met Harpur until 1844. The latter was, from mid 1842, working at his older brother Joseph's farm at Patrick's Plains (at Singleton in the Hunter Valley) and then, by June 1843, once again with his brother who had found employment as poundkeeper and then postmaster at nearby Jerry's Plains. Both places are about 200 kilometres north of Sydney, located (once again, for Harpur) on fertile river-plains overlooked by surrounding hills.

4. 'Henry Parkes From an Engraving by H. S. Sadd, 1854'

5. 'A View of Jerry's Plains' (1856), artist James A. C. Willis

On 11 August 1843, following the appearance of a poem by Parkes in the *New South Wales Magazine* entitled 'To Charles Harper, Author of a Series of Beautiful Poems in the "Australasian Chronicle"', Harpur wrote to Parkes with thanks, initiating what would become one of his most valuable correspondences. Seven months later, Parkes sent him a multi-volume copy of Percy Bysshe Shelley's complete poems, in the edition of 1839 edited by Mary Shelley.[32] Harpur seems to have taken this as a sign – a recognition of his talent and an endorsement of his chosen direction in life. W. A. Duncan, who had already published many Harpur poems in the *Australasian Chronicle*, went on to establish the *Weekly Register* in 1843; it would become the principal outlet for Harpur's poetry throughout 1845 when Harpur was living in Pyrmont in Sydney. Duncan, Parkes and (after they first met, probably around June 1852) the younger Daniel Deniehy would be Harpur's natural allies, located at the radical end of the spectrum in the turbulent political discourse of the day.

During the 1840s and 1850s Harpur became involved in several of Parkes's agendas. These included opposition to proposals to revive the transportation of convicts to the Australian colonies; the campaign to liberalise the land regulations in order to open up to poorer, would-be small landholders the land occupied by the squatters; and the terms of the proposed (limited) self-government being granted by Westminster to New South Wales. At a time when the term 'Australia' was, officially, only a geographical denominator, Harpur gave the name a more freighted meaning. An Australian patriot, he was soon preaching republican, as opposed to monarchist, politics in the vain attempt to secure independence from Britain for the still-young colony. He signed more than one of his manuscript collections resonantly: 'Charles Harpur / An Australian'.

In his republican endeavours Harpur was joined in the early 1850s by Deniehy and the Reverend John Dunmore Lang. No correspondence between Harpur and either of them has been found, but it is clear that Harpur became close to Deniehy, who would lecture on Harpur's poetry to the Sydney Mechanics' School of Arts in November 1857. Harpur's native capacity for abstract thought drew him towards this political ideal. He was living, as he saw it, in a corrupt society in which rewards were periodically doled out, but rarely to those from convict stock and especially not to one like himself who could not help but rock the boat.

Harpur's satires, squibs and rhyming criticisms evidently gave play to this side of his personality. Always witty, they parade a scorn that half-reveals and half-suppresses an underlying seriousness of purpose. How this young society was going to define itself politically, culturally and socially was a burning debate, one that would allow Harpur to give expression to his natural role as poet in a period when the rhetorical power and social cachet of poetry were still acknowledged, and all the more so given its accustomed appearance in the same newspapers that carried the political debates of the day.

Harpur's evident aim to be recognised as the poet as public figure was an aspiration that his dealings with N. D. Stenhouse probably encouraged: the pair began corresponding in 1857. In 1859 Stenhouse invited Harpur to come to Sydney to give a lecture on poetry at the Sydney Mechanics' School of Arts. Though still sheep-farming on the Hunter on a leased property, Harpur promised to do so. His lecture, given on 29 September 1859 and entitled 'The Nature and Offices of Poetry', showed his familiarity with a wide range of poetry across the centuries and evinced a practitioner's inwardness with its forms and rhythmic possibilities. The published reports of his lecture suggest that he could easily have become the foremost literary critic of his day in the colonies.[33] A number of other essays and notes on Chaucer, Shakespeare, Andrew Marvell, Milton, eighteenth-century poets, the Romantics, and blank verse reinforce the impression, as does the squabble he became involved in with suave newcomer Frank Fowler when, in his magazine *The Month* (established in 1855), the latter offered to adjudicate the worth of Australian poetry to date. Parkes's *Empire* was soon at war with *The Month*; and, in 1857 and 1858, Harpur took up the cudgels on Parkes's side.[34] His correspondence in the 1860s with Kendall, in which Harpur's poems and their revised forms are freely discussed, shows how hyper-attentive Harpur was to the effects of scansion and rhythm in verse.[35] But he did not have the leisure to pursue this secondary vocation much further, and to date there has been no concerted effort to gather and edit his collected prose in a way that would permit a fully informed evaluation of his contribution.

In any case, his poetry came first. It would traverse a wide historical terrain, which in turn meant addressing broader questions of ethics, aesthetics and political philosophy. The ambitiousness of his poetry, especially in light of his circumstances, is striking.

Marriage and later life

Harpur met his wife-to-be Mary Doyle in 1843 on the Hunter. Some memorable love poems written to her survive, the first of which was published by the *Maitland Mercury*, which would be a consistent supporter of Harpur over the years. This support was not insignificant: Maitland was, until the population influx due to the goldrushes of the 1850s, the second largest town in the colony after Sydney. Harpur proposed to Mary in 1847, but her family would not countenance a marriage until the unworldly poet could support her. This finally happened in July 1850.[36] From around then until May 1852 Harpur found employment as a schoolteacher at a series of small schools in the Hunter Valley. Then, in mid 1853 after two months in Sydney, he returned to the Hunter and took up sheep farming, first leasing Granbelang near Singleton, and then, by early 1856, Lowsfield at Jerry's Plains. An attempt in the mean time to borrow sufficient money from Parkes to set up on a property of his own on the Namoi River had met with failure.[37] Finally in August 1859, through the good offices of politician John Robertson – another Hunter Valley farmer who would, as Secretary for Lands, be responsible for the famous Land Acts of 1861 that finally unlocked the lands for selection by poorer farmers – Harpur secured employment as Sub-Commissioner of Gold Fields and magistrate, Southern District. Located at the Araluen goldfield, he would be assistant to the gold commissioner at nearby Braidwood, a town set amongst the bleakly beautiful high tablelands of south-eastern New South Wales.

During his years on the Hunter, Harpur had worked at his political causes through various interventions in the public sphere; his poetry, as well as his prose writings, played their part in this. His radicalism grew, and by the end of 1853 he was, at least temporarily but fearlessly, supporting the need for armed revolution.[38] On 31 March 1855 Harpur, in a squib, satirised the donors to the Patriotic Fund set up to aid the widows and orphans of the British soldiers fighting in the Crimea, and in a letter to the editor in April he implicitly took aim at one of the prominent donors, Henry Parkes.[39] Both items appeared in the *People's Advocate* owned by Edward J. Hawksley, not in the *Empire*, edited by Parkes during 1850–58 and to which Harpur had contributed since 1851.[40] It was an unpopular position to take, and it signalled a partial break with a close friend and political ally. The break had begun the previous year when, as an incoming member of the New South Wales Legislative Assembly, Parkes gave a speech according some honour to his predecessor, the arch-conservative W. C. Wentworth, much despised by the radicals for his proposal of an upper house of newly created colonial aristocrats; in this, Harpur was joined by Deniehy and Lang.[41] But armed revolution was never really an option; and, as the new constitution was finalised, Harpur's public role retreated to that of disillusioned but still idealistic republican commentator.[42] Thereafter, the radical edge came off his political opinion-making; perhaps he came to consider that his new government position and duties were incompatible with its public expression.

For the last months of 1859 Harpur lived in Braidwood with his family. His salary was set at £275 per annum. There were by now three sons and a daughter: Washington (born 1851), Charles Chidley (1853), Harold (1856) and Ada Emily (1859); Mary Araluen Harpur would be born in 1861.[43] For the discharge of his official duties, Harpur first moved 27 kilometres south to Araluen and its goldfield; then, at the end of 1861, to the Gulph goldfields around Nerrigundah well to the south. Finally, in 1863, the family moved, not far away, to the Tuross River near Bodalla. Each lush setting enjoyed the prospect of imposing mountains just to the west. It was at the Tuross River that Harpur built the family home 'Euroma'. He was fifty.

In this same year he was promoted to Assistant Commissioner, adjudicating disputes amongst gold miners over their claims. His salary rose to £350. The two posts would be his first and, as things turned out, his only well-remunerated ones. He would die in 1868, broken in health following the death

Arulan Diggings.

6. 'Arulan [Araluen] Diggings' (c. 1879–89), photographer unknown

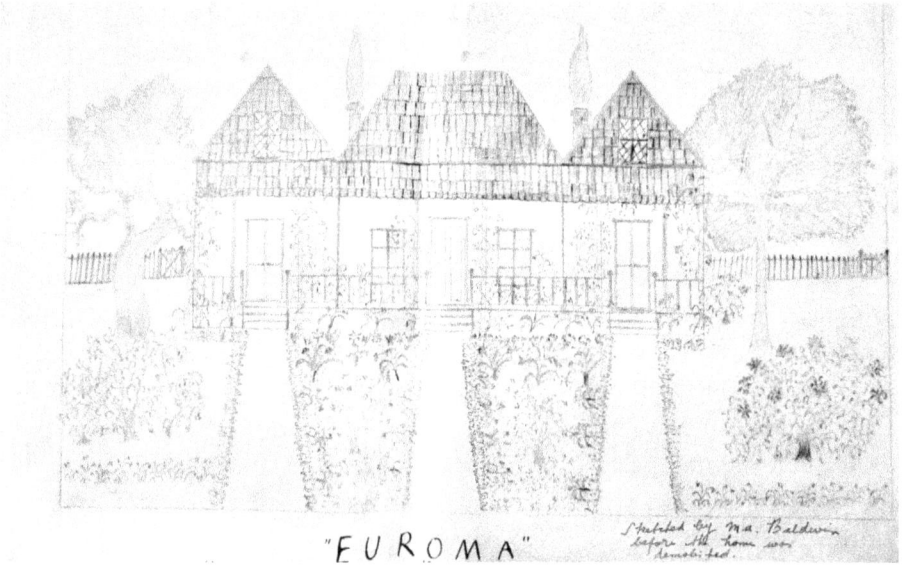

7. '"EUROMA" The home of Charles Harpur, Poet.
Sketched by M. A. Baldwin before the home was demolished [in 1933]'

of his second son in a shooting accident the previous year and after having fought a humiliating battle for financial relief following his retrenchment from government service in 1866 during a budgetary crisis.

Analysis: Character

Narrative biography can take us so far with Harpur, but the editor-biographer is acutely aware of how vulnerable the integration actually is. One of the frustrations of dealing with a correspondence of 400 letters rather than, say, 4,000 is the difficulty of inferring what is going on beneath the surface that would explain what is reported, professed or implied. Ascertaining what happened *between* the extant letters is another problem. Harpur's character lies beneath it all. One way of understanding it is to come to grips with the debilitating flaw that, over the years, was occasionally referred to by those who knew him. It was supposed to explain certain oddities in his behaviour such as those remarked by James Martin and Martin Brennan (in the Fragments). It seems to have been, in short, a misgiving that he was not fully socialised, as we might put it today. Harpur had, until late 1859, worked largely by himself, unsupervised, ever since he had rashly resigned from the Post Office in Sydney in 1839.

On 6 September 1845 Parkes responded to a letter from fellow poet Henry Halloran, quoting him: 'I, like you, cannot "respect his [Harpur's] personal character" … I have often had occasion to blame his conduct, and I have done so more severely to himself, than I need do, to others' (Letter 8). Halloran's letter is not extant, and Parkes does not further specify the offence. In a letter to Parkes of 4 December 1848, Harpur defends himself against a charge of his being 'thin skinned' at (it seems) criticism from Parkes (Letter 15). And in 1866, when explaining to Harpur why he could not expect to be exempted from the general retrenchment of government officials, Parkes told him of certain 'freaks' – 'minor matters of morals & manners', according to Harpur – 'as being all known in Sydney'.[44]

But what were they? There had been objections – made within six months of his entering duty in October 1859 – by his superior (Commissioner Peter Cloete) to 'the mode in which Mr Sub-Gold Commissioner Harpur has deported himself since his appointment'. This led to proposed disciplinary action (his removal to the Hargraves goldfield near Mudgee), narrowly averted by Harpur, and ongoing tension.[45] Cloete was replaced by James Harrop Griffin in October 1861;[46] soon there was another move proposed for Harpur (to the goldfield at Adelong, to be once again under Cloete); but his request, directly to the Lands Minister, John Robertson, on 2 December 1861 to move instead to the Gulph goldfield at Nerrigundah, was granted. It came with the rebuke that all correspondence should go through Griffin in future.[47] Harpur had prevailed, although there is no evidence he was able to have his family with him at Nerrigundah. Still at Araluen, 95 kilometres away by rough bush track, they would join him at 'Euroma' in April 1863 once he had purchased some fertile, riverside farming land and built the house.

At Nerrigundah, Harpur found he still had detractors, but defenders as well. News in June 1862 'that representations have been made to head-quarters tending to the derogation of our esteemed commissioner, Charles Harpur, Esq.' and that a local court might be established that would take over his duties as magistrate led to a protest by the miners and a spirited defence by the newspaper's local correspondent that cited Harpur's 'unassuming habits, his ready tact in dealing with mining disputes, his determination to hear both sides of the question, and his invariably just and judicious decisions'.[48] On 1 April 1863 Harpur was promoted to Assistant Gold Commissioner, so evidently things had turned around and he had settled into his role. Indeed, the miners at Nerrigundah came to think highly enough of his interventions to organise a public meeting in February 1866 and a petition to the Colonial Secretary to retain his services when the cutbacks were bruited.[49]

The specificity of the rest of Brennan's well-written 1909 account of the Araluen goldfield (from which Fragment 3 comes) gives some reason for confidence in his memory of Harpur, despite the passage of time. The account of a man given to 'eccentricity and exhilaration on occasions' suggests that Harpur's emotions lay close to the surface, were intensely felt and thus more liable, on occasion, to break out in freakish ways; that is, in ways incompatible with conceptions of restrained gentlemanly behaviour of the day.

But there may have been another cause. By his own frank admission – at least to the page on which he recorded it – the young Harpur sometimes drank to excess, uncontrollably. In a note to a poem about harmless carousing with friends ('Stanzas Good Night &c.') he described its addictiveness memorably:

> I once remarked a mounted Policeman on the Jerry's Plains race course—who kept expressing himself greatly disatisfied with the feats of the horses though it was acknowledged on all other hands that they performed them ["]splendaciously". "Why", asked one of his comrades, "are you so displeased with the horses? they do their work well." "Yes", he replied,—they run *well*—capitally—first rate!—I can't deny that, mate: but then,—somehow or other, I want to see them *go faster*.
>
> Even thus I find it with myself in the matter of strong drink. I cannot enjoy at a moderate pace; I am disatisfied and restless, like the Policeman, even under the most rapid degree of excitement, and want to see every thing *go faster*—and *faster still*. Hence accrues my peculiar peril. Sot respectably, like a prudent profess[or ....] I cannot.

This confession ends towards the foot of the page – in fact, an official Post Office form that was evidently the only piece of stationery Harpur had to hand when inspiration struck. The paper is now damaged so that the text is not fully recoverable. But on the verso the text continues:

> to be as wild as I generally am when under its influence—wild as a mountain pard, is nearly as low and brutal, and far more perilous. And so I *must* give up, and *have* given up henceforth for ever, the liberty of drinking any and every intoxicating beverage—

He then dates it '24th day of March, 1850' and, in a much larger hand, immediately below, he adds dramatically: 'God help me'.[50] Such self-enquiring, even self-inquisitorial honesty was typical of Harpur, and as always it was his alertness to the oddities and felicities of idiomatic language (here, the policeman's) that gave him the key to unlocking the problem. Very little was off-limits for him, although the note was never published: he probably grew cautious as he got older.

By 1850, Harpur had been on the road to reform for some years: he played a prominent part, along with his brother Joseph, in the temperance and teetotal societies of the Hunter Valley from 1842. Although access to the society of young ladies also taking part in this popular but respectable movement may have been an attraction (late-night dancing often finished off the 'tea-parties'), and although furthering temperance aims afforded the idealist in him another convenient channel of expression, his participation was probably, in large part, an attempt to dampen the rage for alcohol he sometimes found within himself. In 1847 he diagnosed the problem and in 1851 he published it: 'the want of

[love], I say, as in the case of the long unmarried, must naturally originate a vague craving for social compensation, the more insidiously unfavourable, from its very vagueness, to constancy of conduct'.[51]

By then he had married, on 2 July 1850 – much in love, as his sonnets to 'Rosa' show. Perhaps the satisfactions that came with marriage and then with children – in whom, in correspondence, he regularly expressed great pride – at first took the edge off his addiction and gradually removed much of the temptation.[52] The marriage seems to have been a happy one, despite the couple's hard financial struggle in the early years.[53] According to his daughter, Harpur would always admire his wife and remain fond of her; and the letters show that his memory inspired decades of ongoing loyalty from her after his death, as she strove to get his poems published in book form and then promote them, even though not fully literate herself. Her view of the drinking problem was that she had not witnessed it: 'From my mother's account Charles Harpur was neither a teetotallor nor a "tippler" ' but instead a social drinker, reported her daughter in 1945 (Letter 200).

It is possible, nevertheless, that occasional break-outs of hard drinking recurred in his years as a gold commissioner and magistrate, and that it was a response to depression, which itself was the burden of the poet. At least, that is how Kendall diagnosed it, and he was no stranger to depression himself. Roughly quoting Elizabeth Barrett Browning's verse-novel *Aurora Leigh* (1856), he wrote to Harpur on 22 October 1865:

> I am very sorry to hear of your illness—hope you are all right at the present date. Of course you must expect to suffer being possessed of that "great sad gift the poet's twofold life". Poets are as it were, *cursed* with a peculiar temperament which renders them wholly vulnerable to that perpetual fiend *Melancholy*. Let it be even as it is. It is better to be a racehorse than a rock. No man can realize the world till he sees the Sea. And in a like manner, I say, no man can comprehend life who is not set face to face with the boundless joys and sufferings of the "pardlike spirit" you speak of. The poet is the only Master of Life. (Letter 94)

Kendall was reaching, here, for the Romantic type of the poet, based on John Keats, for whom Shelley's long poem of 1821, *Adonais*, was an elaborate elegy. The spirit of the legendary leopard-like beast embodied by Adonais is the power and exhilarating insight of the hyper-sensitive soul, but one which is doomed to pay its compensatory dues.[54]

If in Harpur's case the form that the compensation took was, less poetically, occasional bouts of depression and drunkenness, that would help account for the official complaints and equally would help explain the loyalty of the miners who rallied in support when Harpur's position was in jeopardy:

presumably they would not have objected to his display of a shared failing, to a common humanity. But the problem cannot have been only the drink, which may in any case have been more symptom than cause: Harpur's was an unusual and complex personality. His intensity of feeling, coupled with a sharpness of vision, an insatiable, open-minded curiosity and a habitual uncompromisingness of statement – to all of which the letters attest – meant that he cannot have been an easy man to deal with, although Kendall found the key.

Harpur's brother Joseph, who was in a position to know, told Mary Harpur in a letter of 9 June 1871 (Letter 147) that her husband's 'faults as you know, were faults of temper. I suffered from them as well as you did'. Perhaps he had in mind the recriminatory letter of 23 February 1868 that he had received from his brother Charles. Gravely ill and, by now, utterly cleaned out ('there is not in my house enough cash to procure for me a coffin and a shroud. They would have to be got on *tick*'), Charles was in desperate need of financial assistance but had been ignored (Letter 138).

Being easily roused to anger and quick to take offence are testified to again and again in the extant letters, although generally it is around the question of his writings not being accorded the respect he believed they were due. In 1874, W. A. Duncan (who published Harpur's *Thoughts. A Series of Sonnets* in 1845) recalled Harpur's exhibiting 'the *genus irritabile*' of the creative mind when he angrily confronted Duncan (who had paid for the publication) with the accusation that he, 'a thirteenth rate writer', had dared to alter the title and text of one of the sonnets (a poem in honour of Duncan) by removing his name from both (Letter 149). Harpur's letters to editors were sometimes blistering, and his invective became almost an art form in itself – as witness his letter of September 1867 to Samuel Bennett, editor of the *Empire* from 1859 following Parkes's forced relinquishment of its ownership and editorial role (Letter 126). Fortunately for Harpur, Kendall intervened and prevented delivery. Again, in a letter written many years after her husband's death, Mary Harpur remembered her husband's being 'stamping mad' when confronted with careless typos in his newspaper poems; but he also aired this grievance at other times himself in public and in a comic mode.[55]

In 1851 Harpur described himself in a letter as 'constitutionally moody' – a 'desouled condition of feeling'; and in September 1866, in a poem, he described 'this winter of the heart—when / Its chords are all unstrung, / And the very birds seem not to sing / As long ago they sung!'[56] There were times, Kendall remarked of Harpur in 1869, when 'the devil of despondency had got him by the throat'; but, at all other times, 'One could not be ten minutes in his society without having cognisance of his genius. He had fitful flashes of enthusiasm, during which he never failed to give utterance to memorable things'.[57]

Harpur periodically brooded on the wrongs he believed done him and broke out at times, venting the indignation in letters. But the reverse is also true: some of his letters and many more of his poems, especially the satires, are full of joy, impishness and bravado. There is ample evidence, despite the evident mood swings, that he was characteristically of an open-hearted and optimistic outlook, an idealism that fed directly into his nature poetry but that led him, as Kendall tellingly put it in his last letter to Harpur on 16 October 1867, to 'overrate newspaper people by expecting them to see the great beauty and the genuine power of your writings' (Letter 132). His widow commented in 1875 that 'Poor C. knew not all, and expected too much' (Letter 151). His poverty throughout his manhood until about 1855 (when the Harpurs had sufficient income from sheep-farming to take on a servant) militated against his optimism and idealism.[58] The anger that he had sometimes to suppress or divert into irony was, as it were, another payment for an extraordinary openness to his subject matter and for the appealing honesty about the feelings it unleashed in the course of writing.

He was too dignified a man to dally in self-pity for long: although starved for most of his adult life of company on an intellectual level comparable with his own, he knew how to put the dilemma into unself-pitying context;[59] and his exchange of letters with his principal correspondents provided another support and solace. His scholarly pursuits – his translations and adaptations, his reading, and his various notes and essays on politics and poetry – were evidently also steadying factors in a life otherwise much preoccupied with the chores of farming from 1853 and then with official duties on the southern goldfields from 1859 until 1866. In a letter of 2 July 1859 he described his situation, carrying 'a book about with me, in my pocket, for a fortnight at a stretch, without being able to snatch time enough to glance over even so much as a page of it … You, my dear Sir, can have no idea of the care required and the labor imposed by sheep, on an indifferent run in a bad season' (Letter 57). This was in the age before the widespread adoption of barbed-wire fences when it was necessary to tail around after the sheep all day long. Some of Harpur's manuscript books in the Mitchell Library are in bindings that are heavily worn, presumably from being constantly in and out of his pockets as occasion permitted.[60]

Above all, writing poetry settled him.[61] It gave him an arena for coherence that, with effort, he could control, and allowed him to develop his exquisite sympathies with the natural world in a country that he, with others, was endeavouring to write into conscious being. He was never in any doubt that he was and must act as a gentleman, even at his poorest, and that his poetic project must be outward-looking and truthful, sometimes searingly so, in its admissions and self-enquiries. His letters reflect this orientation, which could become an incautious one in circumstances such as Parkes complained of.

Even towards the end of his life, after his official career had been terminated, leaving him 'very lonely' (Letter 121), and as consumption must have been slowly devastating his lungs, he could write almost ironically of his condition: 'In the words of Browning I have had "enough for one", and begin to look grave-ward with a grim satisfaction' (Letter 124).

Analysis: Career

In his high ambition to become known as the singer of a nation-in-the-making, Harpur was unsuccessful, at least as judged by the appearance of his works in book form. The only significant exception was Harpur's play *The Bushrangers*, published in Sydney in 1853 in a volume that also contained some of his poems. The poems were well received but the play itself was not. W. R. Piddington was the publisher. Subscribers were sought, an effort led by Deniehy and William Pennington, a leader-writer for the *Empire*, with Parkes apparently guaranteeing to make up any shortfall (Letter 42). When Harpur tried once more in 1857 to publish a collection of his poems to be called 'Wild Bee of Australia', the plea for subscriptions, as we have seen, fell flat and the plan lapsed. Evidently no guarantor stepped forward; certainly Parkes was in no position to do so (see Letter 48).

Besides *Bushrangers*, only a handful of pamphlets and broadsheets by Harpur appeared, including *Songs of Australia, First Series* printed by D. L. Welch in Sydney, probably in 1844.[62] Preserved in the Mitchell Library, this unique copy – which was either a broadsheet or a galley sheet, subsequently torn into segments for re-use – is pasted face down (it is not known by whom) to show what Harpur would newly write on the blank versos, which are face up. Unable to be read until computerised techniques were brought to bear on the documents for the CHCA project, the item typifies the larger problem in coming to grips with Harpur's works, a problem that has been, until very recently, both materially based and interpretative at once.

The following year Duncan published Harpur's *Thoughts. A Series of Sonnets* (16 pages); and, in late 1861, the *Braidwood Dispatch* produced a four-page pamphlet containing his 'Rhyme' and 'Coleridge's Christabel'. The latter was duly picked up for republication by the *Empire* in Sydney. In 1862, its printers Hanson and Bennett also published, in pamphlet form, *A Poet's Home*, a new 240-line version of the poem of the same name. Finally, in 1865, Clarson, Shallard, & Co., Printers, of Sydney and Melbourne, reprinted Harpur's long poem 'The Tower of the Dream', which the firm had recently printed for its appearance in the *Australian Journal*. It made 24 pages including front matter. Such ephemeral publications must have been welcome but, by their very nature, could do Harpur's longer-term reputation only limited service.

His failure to achieve his longstanding aspiration for publication of his poetry in book form is unsurprising.[63] In fact, no one in the Australian colonies is known to have been successful in carving out a professional literary career until near the end of the nineteenth century, and even then it was exceedingly rare. The London book trade dominated the colonial literary and bookselling scene, especially from the 1860s once large-scale book-distribution arrangements were put efficiently into operation in Melbourne and Sydney. There was little if any place locally for literary book-publishing unless financed by advance subscription or by the author. In 1874 George Robertson of Melbourne paid Marcus Clarke £50 for the copyright of *His Natural Life*, and there were other, similar experiments, although the evidence is thin. But when, in the mid-1890s, Angus & Robertson of Sydney introduced as a norm royalty-based or half-profits publishing where the publisher took the financial risk, it was widely hailed as a breakthrough for local authors.[64]

Harpur's reception in his contemporary colonial print culture was nevertheless real. Over 900 appearances of poems by Harpur in colonial newspapers have now been identified. He published mainly in Sydney newspapers but also in those in the country areas in which he lived, including Maitland, Braidwood and Moruya and also, indeed, much further afield in Melbourne, Geelong, Adelaide, Tasmania and New Zealand. There were almost certainly more appearances of his poems than we shall ever identify, as newspapers were not systematically collected by the fledgling public libraries of the time. A round-figure estimate of 1,000 such appearances may not be wide of the mark.

By 1866, Harpur had despaired of his colonial reception and turned his attention instead to preparing for the long-hoped-for book publication of his Works, but now in London.[65] He was an obsessive reviser of his poems, and not always for the better, as Kendall would occasionally but tactfully point out. Harpur copied the poems out afresh and rearranged them in manuscript books. Those fair copies would then, in turn, become the site of further revision.

But the intended publication was never to be; and Harpur died, from consumption, in the bitter knowledge of defeat. A report published in the Melbourne *Argus* the following year, its details clearly sourced from somebody at the scene, brings together a number of the observations made above:

> To the last the poor fellow kept up his heart. In certain trying moments, when his mind was wandering, he appeared to be under the impression that his writings were in course of publication. Frequently he perplexed his wife with inquiries for 'proof sheets.' But sanity and repose returned an hour or two before death. On the afternoon of the 9th June he told a faithful watcher that his 'sensations were those of a dying man.' He then instructed

his wife to write to three Sydney friends whom he named; and his final sentence was a request that he might be carried out into the verandah. His wish was acceded to. He died in the mild brightness of a clear moonlight three hours afterwards.[66]

To have the self-control, in extremis, to describe his own shockingly debilitated condition in impersonal terms – rather than (forgivably) pleading for sympathy for his bodily collapse – shows, again, the dignified trust in language, in the poet's ongoing project and in the clarity it brought with it, to which Harpur had committed himself from the start and carried to the grave.

Notes

[1] The successive recent histories reflect the developments: see and compare *The Oxford History of Australian Literature*, ed. Leonie Kramer (Melbourne: Oxford University Press, 1981): organised by genre (see section on poetry); *The Penguin New Literary History of Australia*, ed. Laurie Hergenhan (Ringwood, Vic.: Penguin, 1988): see essays by Elizabeth Webby, Robert Dixon, Elizabeth Perkins and Ken Stewart; *The Oxford Literary History of Australia*, ed. Bruce Bennett and Jennifer Strauss (Melbourne: Oxford University Press, 1998): essays by Adam Shoemaker, Delys Bird, Perkins, Dixon and Susan K. Martin; and *The Cambridge Companion to Australian Literature*, ed. Elizabeth Webby (Oakleigh, Vic.: Cambridge University Press, 2000): essays by Penny van Toorn and Webby. See also Vijay Mishra, 'Charles Harpur's Reputation 1853–58: The Years of Controversy', *Australian Literary Studies*, 8 (1978), 446–56; and Michael Ackland, *That Shining Band: A Study of Australian Colonial Verse Tradition* (St Lucia: University of Queensland Press, 1994). FOR MID-CENTURY REPUBLICANISM, see Ackland, 'Charles Harpur's Republicanism', *Westerly*, 29 (1984), 75–88; *Our First Republicans: John Dunmore Lang, Charles Harpur, Daniel Henry Deniehy: Selected Writings, 1840–1860*, ed. David Headon and Perkins (Leichhardt, NSW: Federation Press, 1998). FOR THE PROBLEM OF LITERARY ORIGINS, see Leonie Kramer, 'Imitation and Originality in Australian Colonial Poetry: The Case of Charles Harpur', *Yearbook of English Studies*, 13 (1983), 116–32; Dixon, *The Course of Empire: Neo-Classical Culture in New South Wales 1788–1860* (Melbourne: Oxford University Press, 1986); Paul Kane, 'Charles Harpur and the Myth of Origins', *Australian Literary Studies*, 13 (1987), 146–60; Ackland, 'Innocence at Risk: Charles Harpur's Adaptation of a Romantic Archetype to the Australian Landscape', *AUMLA*, 70 (1988), 239–59; Philip Mead, 'Charles Harpur's Disfiguring Origins: Allegory in Colonial Poetry', *Australian Literary Studies*, 14 (1990), 279–96; Kane, *Australian Poetry: Romanticism and Negativity* (Melbourne: Cambridge University Press, 1996); and Thomas H. Ford and Justin Clemens, *Barron Field in New South Wales: The Poetics of Terra Nullius* (Carlton, Vic.: Melbourne University Publishing, 2023). FOR THE CRISIS IN FAITH, see Perkins, 'The Religious Faith of Charles Harpur', *Quadrant*, 23 (1979), 29–35; and Ackland, '"Though Urged by Doubt...": Charles Harpur and the Nineteenth Century Crisis of Faith', *AUMLA*, 64 (1985), 154–74. FOR THE IMPERIAL ADVENTURE, see Dixon, *Writing the Colonial Adventure: Race, Gender and Nation in Anglo-Australian Popular Fiction, 1875–1914* (Cambridge: Cambridge University Press, 1995).

[2] austlit.edu.au; trove.nla.gov.au; asecentre.org/completed_projects. See also the bibliographies listed in n. 7 below

[3] Indexing for AustLit shows that, in 1838 (five years after CH began to publish his verse in Sydney newspapers), there were 38 newspaper and magazine titles in the Australian colonies; in 1868, when CH died, there were 223: see www.austlit.edu.au/austlit/page/5960612. Work in the general area has included: Gavin Souter, *Company of Heralds: A Century and a Half of Australian Publishing by John Fairfax Limited and its Predecessors 1831–1981* (Carlton, Vic.: Melbourne University Press, 1981); Michael Ackland, 'Publishing Practice

and Poetic Reputation: The Case of Henry Kendall', *BSANZ Bulletin*, 15.1 (1991), 21–31; Wallace Kirsop, *Books for Colonial Readers: The Nineteenth-Century Australian Experience* (Melbourne: BSANZ, 1995); Graeme Johanson, *A Study of Colonial Editions in Australia, 1843–1972* (Wellington, NZ: Elibank Press, 2000); Rod Kirkpatrick, *Country Conscience: A History of the New South Wales Provincial Press, 1841–1995* (Canberra: Infinite Harvest, 2000); Elizabeth Morrison, *Engines of Influence: Newspapers of Country Victoria, 1840–1890* (Carlton, Vic.: Melbourne University Press, 2005); Victor Isaacs, *How We Got the News: Newspaper Distribution in Australia and New Zealand* (Andergrove, Qld: Australian Newspaper History Group, 2008); Jennifer Alison, *Doing Something for Australia: George Robertson and the Early Years of Angus & Robertson, Publishers 1888–1900* (Melbourne: BSANZ, 2009) – see chapter 1; Katherine Bode, *Reading by Numbers: Recalibrating the Literary Field* (London: Anthem, 2012); and Kirkpatrick, *Dailies in the Colonial Capitals: A Short History* (Newmarket, Qld: self-published, 2016). FOR MECHANICS' INSTITUTES, see the general history: Martyn Walker, *The Development of the Mechanics' Institute Movement in Britain and Beyond: Supporting Further Education for the Adult Working Classes* (London: Routledge, 2016); Bronwyn Lowden, *Mechanics' Institutes, Schools of Arts, Athenaeums, Etc.: A Checklist* (Melbourne: Lowden Publishing, 2012); and Pam Baragwanath and Ken James, *These Walls Speak Volumes: A History of Mechanics' Institutes in Victoria* ([Ringwood North, Vic.]: self-published, 2015).

[4] See Jordens.

[5] For the poets at the Surveyor-General's Office from August 1863, see p. 127 n. 8; from 1866 at the Colonial Secretary's Office (and as satirised in *Sydney Punch* as 'The Three Jolly Poets'), see p. 181 n. 7. During November 1861 – April 1863 the solicitor and poet James Lionel Michael had employed Kendall as a clerk in North Grafton: see p. 127 n. 10. The appointment of writers, as gentlemen of education, to government positions (including as teachers) seems to have been not uncommon.

[6] For the three newspaper proprietors, see p. 8 n. 4, p. 45 n. 8 and p. 4 n. 2.

[7] BIOGRAPHIES: three by Agnes Marie Hamilton-Grey: *Facts and Fancies about 'Our Son of the Woods' Henry Clarence Kendall and his Poetry* (1920); *Poet Kendall: His Romantic History (from the Cradle to the Hymeneal Altar)* (1926); *Kendall our 'God-Made Chief'…A Continuation of 'Poet Kendall' Making a Complete History from Cradle to Grave* (1929): all, Sydney: John Sands, Printers; *Henry Kendall his Later Years: Notes by his Son Frederick C. Kendall: A Refutation of Mrs. Hamilton-Grey's Book Kendall our 'God-Made Chief'* (Glebe, NSW: Simmons, Printers, 1938); Ackland; Adrian Mitchell, *Where Shadows Have Fallen: The Unhappy Descent of Henry Kendall* (Mile End, SA: Wakefield Press, 2020); and unpublished D. Litt. thesis: Thomas Thornton Reed, 'The Life and Poetical Works of Henry Kendall' (University of Adelaide, 1953); and, for CH: Rawling. BIBLIOGRAPHIES: Elizabeth Webby, *Early Australian Poetry: An Annotated Bibliography of Original Poems Published in Australian Newspapers, Magazines & Almanacks Before 1850* (Sydney: Hale & Iremonger, 1982); Ian F. McLaren's *Comprehensive Bibliography* of Adam Lindsay Gordon (1986), Henry Kendall (1987) and James Lionel Michael (1989), all: Parkville, Vic.: University of Melbourne Library; Lurline Stuart, *Australian Periodicals with Literary Content 1821–1925: An Annotated Bibliography* (Melbourne: Australian Scholarly Publishing, 2003); and Holt. SCHOLARLY EDITIONS: e.g. *The Collected Verse of Mary Gilmore*, ed. Jennifer Strauss, 2 vols, Academy Editions of Australian Literature (St Lucia: University of Queensland Press, 2004–07): see Introduction, vol. 1; 'Oliné Keese' (Caroline Woolmer Leakey), *The Broad Arrow; Being Passages from the History of Maida Gwynnham, a Lifer*, ed. Jenna Mead (Sydney: Sydney University Press, 2019); and *Eliza Hamilton Dunlop: Writing from the Colonial Frontier*, ed. Anna Johnston and Elizabeth Webby (Sydney: Sydney University Press, 2021).

[8] See p. 48 n. 1; Letter 28 and p. 58 n. 1; p. 93 n. 3; and Subscription List for an Edition of Charles Harpur's Poetry, 1 February 1871 (Letter 145).

[9] See Letter 165 and p. 283 n. 3. A large number of unbound copies, evidently left unsold, were reissued in 1899 in paperback format by the Sydney bookseller-publisher William Dymock, following a campaign over several years by Harpur's loyal widow Mary Harpur to achieve republication. Earlier, in 1890, she had also tried to secure fresh publication in London. ML C381 contains a 'List of Poems Copied into Manuscript' (pp. 290, 315–21). Against 17 of the

20 numbered manuscripts is the annotation (apparently in Mary's hand) 'England' or 'To England' or 'Sent to England'. Above the first annotation is the date '1890'. In a letter to her aunt Mary Harpur on 3 October 1891 (in *Suppl. Letters*), Lilian Isabella Parnell refers to 'the parcle of Uncle's manuscripts' sent to Elizabeth Barnston Parnell, née Everest (1837–1913), widow of Lilian's uncle William Charles Parnell, grazier. Elizabeth returned to Britain after her husband died in 1880. She had evidently undertaken to approach prospective publishers, but nothing came of it.

[10] See Letter 149.

[11] See p. 254 n. 1 and p. 254 n. 5.

[12] The practical implementation of these imperatives is described below in Editorial Approach.

[13] Principally in *Charles Harpur*, ed. Adrian Mitchell (Melbourne: Sun Books, 1973); *Charles Harpur: Selected Poetry and Prose*, ed. Michael Ackland (Ringwood, Vic.: Penguin, 1986); *Henry Kendall: Poetry, Prose and Selected Correspondence*, ed. Ackland (St Lucia: University of Queensland Press, 1993); and Ackland. Letters have also been excerpted or quoted in biographical, bibliographical and literary-historical studies, most notably in Rawling's 1962 biography; his papers are preserved in ML. A volunteer transcription project at ML also made another 39 letters (from ML MSS 947) available online in *c.* 2011, but it is clear the transcriptions were not rigorously checked.

[14] Facsimile images of the manuscript and other original forms of letters – both those selected here and those not selected – are available in the CHCA at charles-harpur.org. The through-page-numbering of the CHCA facsimiles of the manuscript books in the Charles Harpur Papers at ML, used in citations here, does not always match the sometimes erroneous penciled numbering added by librarians. The CHCA also contains images and transcriptions (but not yet edited or annotated texts) of CH's complete poetry: this archival phase of the project was published in 2019. The imaging of the manuscript books, arranged by SLNSW, was originally carried out for the CHCA, which then processed the images for functionality. SLNSW preserves a copy of the original imaging. For the anthologies mentioned below, see charles-harpur.org/Sources/Anthologies/.

[15] James Martin, *The Australian Sketch Book* (Sydney: James Tegg, 1838), p. 150; for the day of publication, see *Australian*, 25 September 1838, p. 3.

[16] *The Bushrangers* would be reworked in 1867 as 'Stalwart the Bushranger' (ML A94): ed. Elizabeth Perkins (Paddington: Currency Press, 1987).

[17] Martin, *Australian Sketch Book*, p. 169. 'Harpur vs. Levey', *Sydney Monitor*, 18 December 1833, p. 2. [Edward Smith Hall], 'Australian Literature', *Sydney Monitor*, 10 May 1834, p. 2.

[18] Rawling, pp. 90–1.

[19] [Martin] Brennan, 'Looking Backward over Fifty Years: The Golden Valley of Araluen', *Freeman's Journal*, 30 September 1909, p. 57. It may be that Brennan was conflating CH with a half-memory of the minstrel – with 'His flashing eyes, his floating hair!' – at the end of Coleridge's 'Kubla Khan' (published 1816) – who has 'drunk the milk of Paradise'. And it was probably the editor of *People's Advocate*, E. J. Hawksley who appealed to the same, special category in referring to Harpur's 'wayward and erratic genius' in a headnote to his 'To an Echo on the Banks of the Hunter', 20 January 1849 (h602c – version c of the Harpur poem numbered 602 in CHCA).

[20] Several copies survive. The original of the reproduction at page xviii is sepia-toned, oval in shape and mounted on a rectangular board 11.9 x 8.6 cm; it has provenance to Mary Araluen Baldwin, née Harpur (at NLA PIC Box/7082 #PIC/7082). Another copy of the photo (NLA MS 3605) bears a signature and date (6 November 1859), both in CH's hand; but they have been clipped from some other source, presumably from the foot of a signed and dated poem, draft letter or other document no longer extant, and pasted to the board. The dating, probably posthumous, cannot be trusted. In November 1859 the Harpurs were in Braidwood; but 'A. LOMER SYDNEY' is printed in blue on the board of the two sepia-toned copies at ML P1/716. (the battered and faded one reproduced on the front cover of this book is one of them). Albert

Lomer set up in Sydney in 1865. This fact, together with CH's visit to Sydney in early 1868, probably his first since 1859, and the first mention of CH's giving away a portrait being on 11 March 1868 (Letter 139), exposes the sophistication as serving some other function, perhaps an experiment relating to the production of *Poems*: 'it might be well to have the required number of copies printed by photography from either the engraving or such other portrait as you may prefer, and afterwards attached to each book with the autograph below' (Henry Martin to Mary Harpur, 17 June 1882, in *Suppl. Letters*). It was not used. For another possible explanation (relic hunting), see Jules Henerie to Mary Harpur, 27 September 1898 (ibid.). Some other copies of the photograph survive (a sepia-toned one bearing a CH signature but no date at DLMS 169, SLNSW), and some later, black-and-white, probably 20th-century re-photographings.

[21] Letter 169; in October 1867, CH noted that 'my beard is grey, or nearly so' (Letter 129).

[22] Henry Kendall, 'About Some Men of Letters in Australia', *Australian Journal*, 1 October 1869, pp. 84–5 [p. 84].

[23] The wood-block engraving (14.6 x 13.2 cm), taken from one of the photograph copies of 1868, was prepared (engraver unknown) for an unsigned retrospective entitled 'Charles Harpur' in *ATCJ*, 14 March 1874, p. 413.

[24] This opalotype (38 x 29 cm, at ML P*88) is a particularly light image on a milk-glass stock; it is a mixed-media sketch applied to the surface created by the white frosting on the glass. It was apparently based on projection of light through a glass plate (created from the 1868 photograph) onto the back of the milk glass thus permitting a considerably enlarged portrait to be applied to the front. CH has been deliberately made to look more youthful about the face. Parkes's letter to Mary Harpur of 15 June 1892 (*Suppl. Letters*) dates it: he will 'endeavour to have the photograph [of CH] filled out a little with pencil or brush, and reproduced' for a 'Book' that he wants to 'begin' in 'July'. In his next letter of 29 June 1892 (ibid.), Parkes returns it, saying he has had an enlargement made. This letter is now stuck onto the back of the photograph in NLA MS 3605. For Parkes's projected 'Book' (never published and presumably never completed), see further, p. 296 n. 2. On the back of the opalotype a card reads: 'Donated by / Mrs. Doreen Duff, great granddaughter / of Charles Harpur. April 1973'. The image was first published in Ackland, p. 131.

A photographic glass-slide negative at NSWSA (NRS-4481-4-22- [AF00184368]) shows a portrait of CH, dated 25 January 1925 on the back. It was probably taken from the portrait now at ML P2/132 (41.4 x 31.8 cm), which hung on the walls of the ML Reading Room until 1933. Like ML P*88 (the opalotype) the latter is a colourising and extensive retouching of an enlarged photographic transfer of one of the photograph copies of 1868. On the back of P2/132: 'Don.[or] Mrs. M A Baldwin ? 1917'; a reproduction of it (not of P*88) later appeared in Cecil W. Salier, 'The Life and Writings of Charles Harpur', *Royal Australian Historical Association Journal and Proceedings*, 32.2 (1946), 89–105 [p. 91]. The negative may have been the intervening step, or one of them, since it bears the same patterns of foxing, worse than on P2/132 itself.

[25] For CH's 'impaired' sight, see further Letter 42 and p. 83 n. 3.

[26] This section of the Introduction is an extension and adaptation of the one in CHCA (2019), which, in an earlier, abbreviated form appeared also in 'Charles Harpur: The Editorial Nightmare', *Journal of the Association for the Study of Australian Literature (JASAL)*, 16.2 (2016), 1–14 (article pagination; no issue pagination).

[27] charles-harpur.org/Biography/Timeline/

[28] Barron Field (1786–1846), who came to Sydney in 1817, claimed to be the first 'Austral Harmonist' in his collection of two poems ('Botany Bay Flowers' and 'The Kangaroo') published by the government printer in Sydney in 1819, *First Fruits of Australian Poetry*. A second expanded edition appeared in Sydney in 1823; Field returned to England in 1824. See further, Ford and Clemens, *Barron Field in New South Wales*, pp. 58–63.

[29] Sources for biographical details may be found in the CHCA Timeline (in this instance, see entry for October 1826).

[30] See, e.g., Grace Karskens, *The Colony: A History of Early Sydney* (Crows Nest, NSW: Allen & Unwin, 2009); and see Illustration 3b (1817).

[31] See CHCA, Timeline entries for 1829, early 1830, April 1833 and 1 February 1836.

[32] See p. 5 n. 7. For Henry Halloran's parallel recognition of CH, see CHCA, Timeline entry for May 1843.

[33] *Southern Cross* (edited by Deniehy and possibly drawing on CH's own lecture notes), 8 October 1859, pp. 10–12 ('Mr. Charles Harpur on the Nature and Offices of Poetry'); *Empire*, 3 October 1859, p. 2. CH gave another poetry lecture in Braidwood on 24 October 1859 (reported in *Southern Cross*, 5 November 1859, pp. 4–5).

[34] See p. 97 n. 4 and Letters 54 and 56.

[35] E.g., Letter 109.

[36] See further, CH's two notes, dated 1847 and 1850, to 'The Lass of Eulengo' (CHCA, h283c).

[37] See Letters 41–2 and p. 79 n. 7.

[38] See the revised version of his poem 'A War Song for the Nineteenth Century' (h670e) in *PA*, 7 January 1854, p. 5; and see CHCA, Timeline entry for 7 January 1854.

[39] 'The Great Gun of the Patriotic Fund Brought to a Queer Test' (CHCA, h163b); Letter 44. See also CHCA, Timeline entry for 31 March 1855.

[40] CH had been a frequent contributor of poems to *PA* from January 1849 but there had been nothing since July 1854; he would continue to contribute during the rest of 1855, and 1856 saw by far the highest number of his contributions, including essays.

[41] See CHCA, Timeline entry for 5 September 1853, p. 51 n. 9 and p. 81 n. 5.

[42] See CHCA, Timeline entries for 23 February and 15 November 1856.

[43] Washington was named after the revolutionary president; cf. 'The Name of Washington' in Letter 42 (h152a in CHCA).

[44] Letter 105; see also Letter 106 and p. 187 n. 9.

[45] Under-Secretary for Lands Michael Fitzpatrick to Peter Lawrence Cloete, 30 April 1861 (in *Suppl. Letters*); and see further, p. 119 n. 6.

[46] See p. 128 n. 2.

[47] Fitzpatrick to CH, 10 January 1862 (in *Suppl. Letters*).

[48] 'The Gulf Diggings', *Empire*, 30 June 1862, p. 8.

[49] See *Empire*, 22 February 1866, p. 8.

[50] ML A87-2, pp. 765–6; the poem itself (h156a) is copied in ML A92, p. 18. Cf. CH's letter to Parkes, 4 December 1848: 'Even when my means are a little flush, I never exceed in any respect' (Letter 15).

[51] From a note, added in 1847 in ML C382 (h703b), to 'The World's Victims', and published with variation (h703c) in *PA*, 12 April 1851, p. 8. Frustrated by the opposition of his fiancée's family, marriage was on his mind, and in 1849 he talked about going to California, where 'at all events, one might have Hope for a companion' (Letter 19). For dancing at the tea-parties, see, e.g., *Maitland Mercury*, 14 January 1843, p. 3. On 7 October 1842, CH had given 'a speech of great eloquence and power' to the Patrick's Plains Temperance Society in favour of total abstinence: *Teetotaller and General Newspaper*, 26 October 1842, p. 1; and he spoke again at another meeting in 1843, when 'About 250 persons sat down to tea': *Maitland Mercury*, 22 April 1843, p. 2. CH wrote a long essay 'Teetotalism' (ML C382, pp. 109–31; no publication traced) and would publish many poems in the temperance *Australian Home Companion and Band of Hope Journal* during 1858–61.

[52] See CHCA, Timeline entry for *c*. March 1858.

[53] See Letter 36, including CH's modest comment on the enclosed poem, 'The Song of the Poet Shepherd's Wife'.

[54] 'A pardlike Spirit beautiful and swift— / A Love in desolation mask'd;—a Power / Girt round with weakness;—it can scarce uplift / The weight of the superincumbent hour; / It is a dying lamp, a falling shower, / A breaking billow': from Shelley's *Adonais: An Elegy on the Death of John Keats, Author of Endymion, Hyperion etc.* (1821), XXXII. 280–5.

[55] Letter 160; see also Letters 3, 43, 112 and 115.

[56] Letter 24; 'A Song of Sorrow', C381 clipping from *Moruya Examiner*, dated 'Sept. 1866', p. 83.

[57] Kendall, 'About Some Men of Letters', p. 84.

[58] See CHCA, Timeline entry for 5 January 1855.

[59] E.g., see Kendall to CH, 2 June 1867 (Letter 122): the 'sympathy intellectual and otherwise, which you have not known since the death of poor Deniehy'. Cf. 'On Leaving x x x, after a residence there of several Months' (CHCA, h352a); 'x x x' is Pyrmont, Sydney. See also the notes of 1847 to 'To the Lyre of Australia' (h629d) and 'To the Spirit of Poesie' (h625a).

[60] For descriptions and images of the MSS, see charles-harpur.org/Sources/Manuscripts/ Those still in original bindings include A93, A98-1, B78 and C380.

[61] See Letter 24.

[62] See CHCA, Timeline entry for 1844.

[63] It was first announced in 1847: see Letter 14.

[64] See further, Paul Eggert, *Biography of a Book: Henry Lawson's 'While the Billy Boils'* (Sydney: Sydney University Press, 2013), p. 50 n. 11, p. 79 n. 15, p. 215 n. 49; and, for the literary income of Henry Lawson and Rolf Boldrewood in the 1880s and after, pp. 207–21.

[65] See Letters 104 and 133.

[66] *Argus*, 25 May 1869, p. 6 (author unknown).

EDITORIAL APPROACH

Charles Harpur died in 1868. After his widow Mary Harpur's death in 1899 their daughter Mary Araluen Baldwin sold her father's papers to the collector David Scott Mitchell, and by this route they made their way into the collections of the Mitchell Library, State Library of New South Wales, Sydney. It was not until they were unearthed again in the 1940s, first by Cecil Salier, that it was realised that the anthologised texts of the well-known poems did not derive from Harpur's own versions. That began a long scholarly journey of discovery, which saw Rawling's biography appear in 1962, Elizabeth Perkins's edition of *The Poetical Works of Charles Harpur* in 1984, and the ongoing Charles Harpur Critical Archive ('CHCA', 2019–), of which the present edition of the selected letters is an offshoot.[1]

Discovering and editing the letters

The bulk of the letters in the CHCA are holograph manuscripts and have not been published previously. The major sources are, in descending order, the Harpur, Kendall and Parkes papers in the Mitchell Library (State Library of New South Wales – SLNSW), the Museums of History New South Wales – State Archives Collection (NSWSA), colonial newspapers, the National Library of Australia, the State Library of Victoria, the G. W. Rusden collection at Trinity College, University of Melbourne, and the National Archives of Australia. Difficulties of conducting thorough searches in colonial government records preserved at NSWSA mean some official correspondence may have been overlooked. Any more letters that come to light will be included in the CHCA.

Texts of letters as sent or received are editorially preferred here and in the forthcoming *Supplementary Letters* (see Abbreviations). Where such letters are no longer extant or unable to be traced, drafts of letters (evidently retained by Harpur as a record of letters sent), later typed or printed copies of letters (such as letters to the editor or to a third party via the editor or newspaper) have also been used. Given that Harpur's hand is usually a clear one and that deletions and additions are relatively uncommon, it may be that his practice was to prepare a draft or partial draft beforehand and then subsequently discard it. However, the surviving evidence suggests that he did so mainly in important or official circumstances, such as the letters he sent out containing requests to circulate subscription lists or his fierce letter of rebuke to the editor of the *Empire*, Samuel Bennett, in September 1867 (Letter 126). Copying from drafts always involved, as might be expected, some development of the wording, so we cannot assume that the text of those drafts we fall back on would have been identical to that of the letters actually sent.

In a very small handful of cases in *Supplementary Letters*, transcriptions have been made by scholars in the past but the letters or documents themselves can no longer be found. Mostly this is associated with the gradual transfer of NSW government records from SLNSW to NSWSA from the 1960s. Whether published or not, such transcriptions, being the closest to the originals, are used and the source noted. NSWSA also preserves Registers of letters sent or received, usually summarising them. Such records are noted if a scholar's transcription has been relied on. Where we have nothing but a Register entry or only a scholar's summary of the contents of a letter, this will be found as a letter-substitute.

Almost inevitably, the bulk of the surviving correspondence comes from the final three decades of Harpur's life, but with another efflorescence in the early 1880s as his *Poems* (1883) was arranged, edited and published. This is frequently the case with literary figures from the past. Usually the early decades are hardly represented at all – as is often the case with immediate family members, with whom there was little or no need for correspondence. These are the limitations within which the process of selection of letters for the present edition has taken place. The surprising thing is that so many were found from which to choose at all. Harpur often apologised for his dilatoriness as a correspondent.[2]

Selecting the letters

This book is a selected edition of the correspondence of Harpur and his circle, letters in and out where available. Although Harpur's letters are necessarily at the centre of the enterprise, not all of his extant letters are represented here. Those not present include letter fragments where the letter itself is mostly missing or all that remains is a report of it. Official correspondence (letters in and out), usually concerning routine matters and always couched in a formal bureaucratic register, are mostly passed over. They concern Harpur's early employment by the Post Office in Sydney, his employment by the Board of National Education in the early 1850s, and as a gold commissioner in the 1860s. Some official letters are nevertheless included, chosen either because they record important changes in Harpur's life (e.g. in his employment) or because they are conveniently representative of one or more others concerned with some significant issue. Many letters after Harpur's death in 1868 deal with, among other topics, the production of his *Poems* in 1883.

Readers wishing to engage with the complete documentation may consult the CHCA (at charles-harpur.org), where facsimiles of all the extant letters and life-documents (e.g. invoices or receipts for services or goods, royalty and sales calculations) may be found. In due course, the initial archival transcriptions of the letters that lie behind the present volume's edited reading texts will also be made available online in the CHCA, accessible individually. The same will be true for letters not selected for the present volume; their edited and annotated versions will be published by the CHCA as *The Letters of Charles Harpur and his Circle: Supplementary Letters*, edited by Paul Eggert and Chris Vening. The book will be presented in a searchable, typeset format on the CHCA website, freely available for printing or downloading. (See Abbreviations for its online address.) This supplementary volume, together with the present selected one, constitute the works of reference for the Harpur correspondence. Corrections and new discoveries will appear in the CHCA.

Topics that are more fully documented in *Supplementary Letters* include: Harpur's father's attempts to gain a government pension after his retirement as a school teacher at Windsor; the handwritten documents giving the names of recipients of printed subscription lists for Harpur's intended collection 'Wild Bee of Australia' in 1857; Harpur's broader contemporary reception (often in newspaper letters to the editor: e.g. Joseph Sheridan Moore to *Sydney Morning Herald*, 26 September 1863; Henry Kendall to *Empire*, 26 July 1865); the campaign, mainly amongst relations and their friends and neighbours, to raise subscriptions for *Poems* during 1880–82, attended by much news, gossip and the recalling of family history; the falling-out between Mary Harpur and Henry Martin, the editor of *Poems*, after early reviews began to appear and the extent of the editorial interference became plain; the broader reception of *Poems*, including in England; dealings with David Scott Mitchell to buy the Harpur poetry manuscripts and other papers during 1895–99; and literary scholar Cecil Salier's dealings with Mary Araluen Baldwin in the 1940s.

Postage

The widespread adoption of envelopes did not start until 1845 when the folded 'diamond' envelope appeared in Britain, with a folding machine patented by Warren De La Rue and Edwin Hill (the brother of the founder of the penny post Rowland Hill). Before this, letters were typically made up of a single sheet (a 'letter sheet') folded once to create two leaves, that is, four page surfaces. After the writing, a wax seal completed the operation. Usually, the verso side of the second leaf carried the address and official postage-cancellation. The last such letter sheet in the present collection is dated 10 July 1853 (Letter 36). New South Wales had pioneered prepaid letter sheets with embossed stamps in 1838, when Harpur was clerking at the Sydney Post Office; and the first adhesive postage stamps appeared in NSW in 1850.

The length of the letter seems often to have corresponded with the space available: that is, there was an expectation that it should be filled so that receivers would think that they had received full measure. Nevertheless, the letters can be surprisingly short, especially if written on small-format letter sheets – an effect exacerbated by the adoption or cultivation of large handwriting.

With the exception of the printed letters published in newspapers and a typed letter of 11 April 1943 (Letter 199), the originals of all letters in the present volume are in manuscript form. Some survive from the 1880s because they are letterbook copies. The document is a reproduction of a top-copy letter, which would be immediately placed, after writing and with the ink still wet, under a leaf of absorbent copying paper in a bound letterbook. Under pressure, an image of the writing-in-reverse would be transferred to the leaf above it. As one turns the leaves of the letterbook, one looks *through* the translucent leaf from the top side, thus seeing a positive image – though one that is blurrier, sometimes very much so, than the original letter.

Annotating the letters

Notes identifying a person or place are normally provided only once, at first mention, or at first writing or receipt of a letter; but new material in a later letter sometimes warrants additional annotation. Cross-reference to the initial note is sometimes provided; otherwise the Index should be consulted.

The digitised colonial and later newspapers available via Trove have been a main primary source of historical information. Biographical and other notes draw largely on open-access online sources, especially the *Australian Dictionary of Biography*, Obituaries Australia, Design and Art Australia Online, AustLII, Australharmony, AustLit and, for its late-nineteenth-century perspective on prominent British and Irish figures, the *Dictionary of National Biography, 1885-1900* (as well as its Supplements of 1901 and 1912, corrected where necessary by the *Oxford Dictionary of National Biography*, 60 vols. 2004–). Where available, live links to these sources are provided in the e-book and PDF forms of this volume. In each case, the presence of a link – normally attached to the full name of the person glossed in the note – can be exposed by hovering the cursor over the name.

Word definitions are drawn predominantly (and normally without further citation) from the *Oxford English Dictionary* as well as *The Macquarie Dictionary*. The Internet Archive is the main source for images of out-of-copyright works and historical documents referenced in the notes; and the HathiTrust Digital Archive and Google Books provide several more. Where such resources exist they are noted, as well as being live-linked in the e-book and PDF. The NSW Returns of the Colony or 'Blue Books,' 1822–1857, held at NSWSA at NRS 1286, provide information on early colonial officials and governance; they are cited in their archival form but are accessible online by subscription at Ancestry.com. AustLit, mentioned above, is also by subscription; in a handful of cases, linking is done here to its top-level name searches, which are open access.

In order to provide immediate material and historical context, links are provided to printings of poems, letters and essays by Harpur and of some other contemporaneous items in those newspapers, gazettes and magazines digitised in Trove as of May 2023. They include *People's Advocate* (abbreviated as *PA*), *Sydney Morning Herald* (as *SMH*), *Australian Town and Country Journal* (as *ATCJ*), *Weekly Register, Sydney Chronicle, Australasian Chronicle, Maitland Mercury, Atlas, Empire, NSW Government Gazette, Month* and *Bulletin*.[3]

Presenting the letters

With some exceptions, the letters were not written for publication. Varying degrees of formality or intimacy would have been understood by the letter writers and recipients. Accordingly, fidelity to the letters' textual idiosyncrasies is observed – but not a slavish representation of the exact layout: the facsimiles in the CHCA provide that better than any transcription could do.

The letters are presented here not as diplomatic transcriptions with their deletions and additions but as edited reading texts in which various textual difficulties in the original documents and prints have been resolved and the final state of the texts preferred. Deleted or superseded wordings may be inspected in the CHCA; occasionally, they are the subject of a note. Draft forms of letters existing in two documents appear in *Supplementary Letters*.

The broader policies are as follows, and the detailed conventions are listed in Note on the Texts:

THE LETTER TITLE (sender, recipient, date) is followed on the next line by a source statement; see Abbreviations for the acronyms used. The bulk of the letters, as previously mentioned, are holograph manuscripts. If the source is a printed one, a citation is given. In the absence of a date on the letter itself, the date of the postmark on the addressed or stamped surface of the letter (or on the envelope, if present), or the date of the publication, supplies the 'by' date; the problem may be discussed in a note. The address given on the stamped surface is not transcribed. An image of the envelope, if extant, is provided with the letter in the CHCA. As a general policy, dates or parts of dates of letters that are inferential are enclosed in square brackets.

THE POSITION OF DATES AND ADDRESSES in manuscript and typed letters is regularised, as is the positioning of the complimentary openings and closes.

The addressee's name, often placed at the foot of the first manuscript page, is given instead in the letter title; the address may be given or discussed in an explanatory note. Page numberings by the letter writer and catchwords at the ends of pages (and, similarly, 'over', and 'Continued' in lists), used to direct the recipient to the correct following page, are silently discarded.

LETTERS TO OFFICE HOLDERS are titled by the personal name of the office holder. Letters to the editor of newspapers are by the name of the publication except where the letter is addressed to a third party via the editor.

ORTHOGRAPHY. Harpur was not an especially accurate speller but his idiosyncratic spellings (e.g. 'recieve'), which sometimes have historical warrant, are respected, along with his sometimes inadequate punctuation. Similarly, his abbreviations, capitalisations, hyphenations and his very occasional aberrant grammar are respected – unless, in all categories, a significant impediment to reading would result. The context will guide most readers to the intended meaning intuitively; but some readers may initially go down the wrong track. So, for instance, 'birth' in 'With regard to Mr Boyd's service &c. I think almost any respectable birth under him would suit me well' (Letter 6) is emended to 'b[e]rth'. This is a judgement call, a limit case that could have gone either way, but was influenced by the –er– spelling's being the predominant form in Australian newspapers in the first half of the nineteenth century (witnessed in Trove) – although, on the basis of *OED* citations, apparently not in the eighteenth in Britain. Normally, the need for emendations is more obvious, including printed typos (e.g. 'ssem' for 'seem' in printed Letter 39). Each emendation is presented in square brackets, and the original reading may be ascertained in the CHCA. For some characters Harpur's lower and upper case forms are almost interchangeable (e.g. 'k'/'K'); in these cases, the context is allowed to decide the intended form. Random marks or rests of the pen, meaningless in context, are ignored: for example, a dot in the middle of a sentence that might otherwise be interpreted as a full stop, as in: 'furnish me forthwith. with a clear and straightforward statement' (Letter 42). For a few less-lettered correspondents (e.g. James H. Doyle), the rest-marks may have been functioning as breath pauses. But there is no system in evidence: the facsimile images in the CHCA must suffice for any readers interested in the matter.

ILLEGIBLE OR NEARLY ILLEGIBLE TEXT is especially a problem with letters taken from letterbook copies. If a suggestion of a missing character can be discerned, it is treated as being present. Editorial interventions deemed necessary are presented in square brackets, as are editorial completions of missing characters or words caused by failures in the carrying surface or by library mounting and tight binding of manuscripts. Images of letters in the CHCA occasionally chop off the ends of words on the righthand edges of pages where the continuation goes on to the lefthand edge of the adjacent page in the folded leaf: such continuations are treated as being present on the transcribed page.

CROSS-REFERENCES are expressed, for example, as 'see Letter 158'; *or* 'see p. 123 n. 3' for a reference to the note alone; *or* in combination for both letter and note. As life-documents are presented in the same numerical sequence, they are, for simplicity, cross-referenced in the same way, for example, 'see Letter 145', even though this item is a subscription list.

CITATION OF LETTERS: Many of the letters are in the Charles Harpur papers at ML; only the call number is given (e.g. ML A87-2). Where such citations occur in notes, live-links to the collection are also provided in the e-book and PDF forms of this publication. One then navigates to the given page number. Where letters are from other collections at ML, NLA or SLV, this is normally stated by surname (e.g. Stenhouse, Parkes or Kendall papers), together with the call number.

POSTSCRIPTS, AS WELL AS HEADNOTES AND MARGINAL NOTES IN OTHER HANDS (as on letters officially received and processed by government departments), are rendered at the end of the letter; their meaning, where the administrative practice can be ascertained, is interpreted in explanatory notes. For example, the annotation '39/11,307' is an example of the use of the annual running number (or 'top number') used to enumerate letters received by the Colonial Secretary's Office; it means, in this case: item 11,307 for the year 1839. The high number may surprise, but this department was at the centre of colonial government in New South Wales. Non-official annotations by holders of the letters, where present, are also recorded and interpreted where possible. Children's scribblings and jottings are among them; although trivial, they serve as a reminder of what conditioned the survival of these personal, family and historical documents down the decades – and what they silently endured.

Citation of Harpur poems

Charles Harpur had a lifelong commitment to revision: most Harpur poems exist in multiple versions, sometimes with titles varying between versions. Citations of poems in this volume use the 'hNumber' system developed for the CHCA. Thus 'h123' indicates the poem by Harpur numbered 123 in the CHCA, while 'h123a' indicates version 'a' of that poem. In the e-book form of the present publication, such citations of poems are live-linked to the CHCA. Hovering the cursor over the citation and clicking brings up the image and transcription. Clicking in turn on the facsimile of any manuscript form of a poem brings up the complete MS collection at the point at which the original is located.

Notes

[1] For an account of post-World War II editorial, biographical and bibliographical scholarship on Harpur, see Eggert, 'Editorial Nightmare', cited above in Introduction, n. 26; and, for a list of the Harpur selected editions, see charles-harpur.org/Sources/Editions/.

[2] E.g., to William Pennington (Letter 24), Bernard McMahon (Letter 32) and Henry Kendall (Letter 90).

[3] Links were all accessed during 2017–22 and checked in May 2023, but their ongoing validity cannot be guaranteed. *Month* and *Bulletin* are linked via Trove Magazines and Newsletters, the others via the familiar Trove Newspapers and Gazettes.

NOTE ON THE TEXTS

Texts of the letters are taken from the source declared immediately below the letter title and date. General policies of presentation are described in 'Presenting the letters' on pages liv–lvi. The following conventions covering matters of detail have been implemented silently; wherever editorial changes (enclosed in square brackets) have been made, images of the originals may be consulted in the Charles Harpur Critical Archive (CHCA) at charles-harpur.org. On the rare occasions that letter writers themselves use square brackets they are converted into parentheses.

1. Where a reading is inferable even though the MS is torn or defective – often obliterated by a fold of the paper or by library mounting – it is provided in square brackets, with a question mark if uncertain. If not inferable, the lacuna is indicated by [...]: three dots for one word or part of one word; four dots for two to four words, five dots for five to fifteen words, and six dots for sixteen to thirty words. Where text is illegible or nearly illegible – whether because of a smudge or other damage or because the source is a fuzzy reproduction of a top-copy letter preserved by wet-ink transfer in a letterbook – it is represented using the same convention. If a suggestion of a missing character can be discerned it is treated as being present.

2. Errors are faithfully copied unless a significant impediment to reading would result, in which case an editorial emendation is provided in square brackets. In the case of inadvertent dittography (e.g. 'longed particularly to to see it'), the redundant word is removed; *sic* is not used.

3. Non-contemporary page or item numbering (usually the result of official filing) is ignored, as are annotations by library staff or researchers. Pagination and catchwords provided by the letter writer are ignored when present, as are seals and postal date stamps if present (although the latter may be taken into account in the dating of the letter). Contemporary marginalia, item numbering and notes, usually added by a hand other than the letter writer's and often running along the top of the first page, are presented in grey type and placed at the end of the letter.

4. End-of-line hyphenations of compound words are resolved by the letter writer's ordinary practice so far as it can be ascertained; again, the facsimiles in the CHCA may be inspected by interested parties. There they will find end-of-line

hyphens variously presented and positioned: whether as a colon or an equals sign (=); or sometimes placed at the beginning of the next line; or they may be missing altogether (as typically in Mary Harpur's letters, and occasionally in printed letters).

5. Paragraph indentations are regularised; and text that, in the original, continues on the same line from the salutation (as often in printed letters) is presented as a new paragraph.

6. In manuscript letters, the abbreviations st, nd, rd (*as in* 1st, 2nd, 3rd), Mr, Mrs, Jany, Octr, Jas [*for* James], Chas [Charles], recd [received], etc. are usually rendered in the manuscripts by a superscript positioning of the final character(s), with some underscoring (or a dot or two) under the raised characters. Usually there is no additional fullstop such as printed practice of the period typically added: Mr., Mrs., etc. For manuscript texts, the practice adopted here is to lower the raised letters but not to provide the extra full stop unless clearly intended as an additional element of the presentation. In surnames 'M'' is reduced to 'Mc'. Harpur's idiosyncratic use of the colon for abbreviation, especially of his own name (Chas: Harpur), is retained.

7. Other common abbreviations, intended to be understood *as* abbreviations, such as 'Yrs faithfy' for 'Yours faithfully', are rendered as they stand, whereas a flourish at the end of a word clearly intended to represent, say, 'ing', but where the 'n' is only notionally present, is expanded.

8. The long s (ſ) in manuscript letters is rendered as s.

9. Italics substitute for manuscript underlinings. Double underlinings occasionally appear on the manuscript letters; only when they appear in a context intended for print are they converted to their typographical meaning of small capitals rather than merely emphasis.

10. The handwriting habits of the document writer are taken into account before following unconventional capitalising of characters.

11. Manuscript, typed and printed dashes are rendered as unspaced em dashes (*word—word*). Varying lengths of manuscript dashes are ignored except if a very long dash is clearly intended (usually, to indicate an unfinished sentence or thought), in which case a two-em dash is used: *word——*.

12. Failures to leave a clear space between adjacent words, or the provision of redundant spaces, whether in manuscript, typescript or print, are made good. Errors in print unlikely to be the letter writer's (such as turned characters, e.g. *u* for *n*) are silently corrected.

13. Handwritten abbreviations for ditto (two small vertical strokes) are represented by two commas. Similar vertical markings for divisions of £ s d monetary amounts are represented by two fullstops. The presentation of costings is regularised.

14. The abbreviation for 'et cetera' is sometimes a near-random squiggle, but the nineteenth-century convention normally at work is followed here: &c (*or* &c.).

15. Rules between sections of a letter, flourishes and decorative material are ignored, as are general column headings in newspapers ('Original Correspondence', and the like); but headings afforded the individual letter are reported.

End-of-line hyphenations

Of the compound words that are hyphenated at the end of a line in the reading texts, only the following forms should be retained in quotation:

Letter 18 (p. 40): Charley-Harpurian-honey

Letter 35 (p. 67): botch-nondescript

Letter 37 (p. 73): dodo-like

Letter 47 (p. 91): super-human

Letter 52 (p. 99): half-an-hour

Letter 56 (p. 111 col. 1): re-enclose

Letter 113 (p. 191): thunder-storm

Letter 150 (p. 234): long-past

THE LETTERS

8. Harpur's powder flask and seal used to dry the ink and seal letters.

1. Charles Harpur to James Raymond, 12 October 1839

Text: NSWSA: NRS-905 [4/2472.2], 39/11307

Cumberland Street,[1] 12th October, 1839.

Sir,[2]

I beg leave to inform you, that, as my present declining state of health[3] must frequently interfere with that regularity of attendance which the due performance of my official duties indispensably demands; and being persuaded that a Situation in the country requiring less confinement, would, consequently, be a very desirable and necessary change; I have made up my mind with considerable reluctance in a pecuniary point of view, to give up the situation I now hold[4] in your department; and I now most respectfully tender to you my resignation accordingly—trusting, however, that you will have the goodness to add to the many obligations that I feel myself under to you already, that of forwarding my views in obtaining a situation in the interior,[5] and of furnishing me with testimonials of character.

Thanking you, Sir, most sincerely, for the many instances of disinterested kindness, which I have experienced at your hands, during the three years which I have had the honor to serve under your immediate direction in the General Post Office,

I beg to subscribe myself,
Your most obedient,
and Humble Servant
Chas Harpur

39/11307.[6]

---

[1] CH was probably writing from the home of his sister Mary Palmer in The Rocks, Sydney.

[2] James Raymond, Postmaster-General of NSW 1835–51.

[3] CH does not elaborate on the state of his health in his early correspondence. In later years he suffered, and would finally succumb to, tuberculosis.

[4] He worked as a letter-sorter at the General Post Office in Sydney, February 1836 – October 1839.

[5] CH would not move north to farm in the Hunter Valley for another three years. In the interim, he apparently worked as a journalist in Sydney: see Letter 12.

[6] Departmental correspondence number for the year 1839, added after receipt of the letter.

2. Charles Harpur to Henry Parkes, 11 August 1843

Text: ML Ah131

Jerry's Plains,[1] 11th August, 1843.

Dear Sir,[2]

I have just had sight of your beautiful sonnet[3] addressed to me as author of a series of poems in the "Australasian Chronicle."[4] To attempt to express the feeling of gratification and pride with which I read it, were about as vain in me as to aim at rivalling the generosity of which it is a noble manifestation. Indeed, to enwreath the brow of one so clouded up in obscurity, with so fragrant and blooming a garland, merely because you believed him to possess poetical merit, is what could only be expected of one imbued with the rarest spirit of human kindness: and believing this, I do, and shall ever, set a higher value on your applause and kind wishes, than upon those of any other literary man in the Colony.

I would mention also, how flattered I was by your having addressed the sonnet simply to "Charles Harpur."[5] This substantiates in my mind the fact of your thinking highly of me. If a name be any thing in itself, what need is there for prefixing "Mr" or adding "Esq." to give it weight? Who, for instance, with any soul, ever thinks of Byron as having been a Lord—of Shelley as a man of fortune—or of Milton as Latin Secretary to a Government?[6] I know you will not attribute these remarks to mere vanity. In making them I am only elucidating what appears to be a principle of feeling in myself—and in you.

Again thanking you for your most generous notice of me and my *Harp*,

I beg to subscribe myself
yours fervently,
Charles Harpur.

[1] Agricultural settlement on the Hunter River 40 km west of Singleton. CH's brother Joseph was poundkeeper and postmaster there 1843–50, and CH would act as his proxy.

[2] Henry Parkes (1815–96), poet, was at this time working as a tide-waiter (customs inspector of ships) on Sydney Harbour. He would become a merchant, journalist, newspaper proprietor and editor, parliamentarian, colonial secretary and finally premier of NSW.

[3] 'To Charles Harper, Author of a series of beautiful poems in the "Australasian Chronicle"', by H. Parkes, in *New South Wales Magazine, or, Journal of General Politics, Literature, Science and the Arts*, 1.7 (July 1843), p. 366.

[4] During August 1842 – August 1843, CH had 30 poems published in the *Australasian Chronicle*, which for half of that time was edited by his friend (and Parkes's) W. A. Duncan. See Letter 8.

[5] True, but printed as 'Harper'.

[6] Three of the great English poets: the ten-year-old George Gordon Byron (1788–1824) became sixth Baron Byron of Rochdale on the death of a great uncle in 1798; Percy Bysshe Shelley (1792–1822) received allowances and settlements with the death of his grandfather Sir Bysshe Shelley in 1815; and John Milton (1608–74) served during 1649–60 as Secretary for Foreign Tongues ('Latin Secretary') under Oliver Cromwell and the Commonwealth, translating official communications from foreign governments.

3. Charles Harpur to Henry Parkes, 21 March 1844

Text: ML Ah131

Jerry's Plains, 21st March, 1844.

My dear Sir,

I hasten to acknowledge your kind present of Mrs Shelley's edition of her illustrious husband's poems,[7] which has only just come to hand. The letter accompanying the books, for which I am also sincerely thankful, is dated, I perceive, as far back as Novr in last year. The delay in the conveyance which has evidently taken place, makes me very anxious lest you should attribute my silence since to any other than the true cause—my not being aware of your having again manifested in so flattering and substantial a manner your disinterested regard for a brother poet whom you have never seen,—and merely because you believe him to be a true child of Song. I say *substantial* above with reference to the beauty and rareness of your present,—but assure you, at the same time, that even a pin from you, given in token of good will, would be as gratefully received—aye, and as highly prized, in as far as the commercial value of articles constitute a consideration. In nothing do I feel more honored and assured of my merit as a poet, than in the respect and attention with which you have from time to time gladdened my solitude. Accept then in return, all that I have at present to offer, the grateful friendship of a heart, which, though something less warm and trusting perhaps than it has been, is yet, I believe, true in its affections, and unspotted by the selfishness of the world.

As far back as in Jany. last, with a view of re-filling the "cup of kindness" that had passed between us, I composed the following Sonnet[8] to you, intending to publish it in the "Register";[9] and I delayed to do so only, because my pieces latterly have been so fearfully misprinted therein, that I have felt quite savage while glancing them over—and I would not for a good deal that this Sonnet to you should meet a similar fate. However lamely expressed, I know you will give me credit for sincerity in the feeling it unfolds.

---

[7] Probably *The Poetical Works of Percy Bysshe Shelley. Edited by Mrs. Shelley*, 4 vols. (London: Edward Moxon, 1839), along with *Essays, Letters from Abroad, Translations and Fragments, by Percy Bysshe Shelley. Edited by Mrs. Shelley*, 2 vols. (London: Edward Moxon, 1840). CH recalled the gift of the six volumes in a manuscript footnote to 'The Dream by the Fountain' (h101e: for this naming system, adopted from the CHCA, see Editorial Approach, 'Citation of Harpur poems', p. lvi). Mary Harpur's letter to Parkes of 18 September 1875 (Letter 151) recalled CH's rapture at receiving the gift. Sydney bookseller James Tegg was advertising 'Shelley's Poetical Works, edited by Mrs. Shelley 4 vols' in *Colonist*, 23 November 1839, p. 3.
[8] For later versions of this much revised poem, see h610 in CHCA.
[9] See p. 8 nn. 4, 5.

Sonnet to Henry Parkes.

Dear Henry, though thy face I ne'er have seen,
    Nor heard thy voice—albeit that beams, I know,
    With goodness, and that this at times can flow
Melodious as a mountain stream—between
The waters of Port Jackson,[1] and the scene
    Where now I muse, of rich, poor, high or low,
    There dwells not one that I so far would go
To talk with through the evening hours serene.
And when we yet shall meet, say, shall not we
    Be as old friends at once? and sit, and pour
Our souls together? which, so mixt, shall be
A brimming draught of thought-thick poesie—
    Even such as young Keats reel'd with, gazing o'er
The wondrous realms of Homer's minstrelsy.[2]

You will see by the above that I was not willing that the kindly feelings which had sprung up between us should pass away with the blossoms of the Spring. No: I trust that they will ever continue to strengthen—and whenever my regards are turned Sydney-ward, I love to promise myself that they shall furnish the fruit of many an intellectual feast throughout the summer, and even the winter of our mortal days.

I am exceedingly gratified by the selection you have made in your present. Shelley is a great favorite of mine; and besides I never saw the whole of his poems before. I had heard that Mrs Shelley was giving or had given to the world a complete edition of her husband's works, and longed particularly to see it—guess then the pleasure I was master of, or rather was mastered by, on recieving this same work in testimony of a friendship I value so much—and which evinces to me the fact, that disinterested literary kindness departed not the world with that most benevolent of men.—I love Shelley intensely; and yet I am not blind to his faults. If we would attain to highest excellence we must exercise the judgment with a rigid and resolute will, maugre our feelings to the contrary. Shelley has great faults, or rather great wants. His poems, though brilliant and beautiful as the splendors of sunset, are, I fear me, as unsubstantial as those fleeting hues. Not that I complain of their extreme visionariness; but that there is not enough of solid humanity wrought up with it to add strength and flavor. Even in the "Revolt of Islam" the human interest is damaged by the airy-nothingness of the characters, and the impossibility

---

[1] Sydney Harbour, where Parkes worked as a tide-waiter.
[2] 'On First Looking into Chapman's Homer' by John Keats (1795–1821) was written in October 1816 when Keats was 21, after a night of poring over Chapman's translation with his friend and mentor Charles Cowden Clarke.

of many of the incidents. Modern Ideality and Wonder, however wandering and willing, are yet, when over tasked, very apt to grow skittish, and to fly off at a tangent, with an appeal to Reason.[3] Still Shelley is perhaps *my* greatest favorite; and though I may seem just now to be much "critic-bitter", I have been throwing out such objections as I *apprehend*, rather than such as I *feel*. As a proof of this, it is scarcely an hour since I was gloating over the pages of your fine present with inexpressible satisfaction.

The generous object of your letter is, I take it, to incite me to renewed efforts. I also found a pen in the packet, which I understand to mean *write away*. I will obey in as far as I can; but I have to care so much for the mere crusts of life, that I am not often now in right tune for song. Your letter has, however, somewhat revived the "bard in my bosom."[4] Whether any thing worth reading will be the result I cannot pretend just now to say. But we shall see.—I sometimes feel it hard to have written so much as I have already written with the power of publishing so little. Those sustained efforts upon which I would peril my poetic claims with considerable confidence I have not been able to give to the light at all. But perhaps all is for the best.

I hope you have not abandoned the Muse. I promise myself a trial, when I shall some day *forgather* with you, in pouring over the MSS of your late and more sustained pieces. Let me not be disappointed. You have the power if you have the will.

In conclusion, accept again my pledge of friendship, and allow me to solicit yours. Let us determine from this day, to be resolute so as to overcome whatever may tend to chill or diminish the brotherly feelings and kind wishes that have grown up so singularly between us. This is my firm resolve, and I assure myself that it will be yours—and

I subscribe myself therefore
Your friend and brother
Charles Harpur.

Excuse haste!

---

[3] 'The Revolt of Islam; a Poem, in Twelve Cantos' (1817) is a political epic, a parable on liberation and revolutionary idealism set in fictional Argolis under the tyrant Othman. The parallels with the French Revolution and its aftermath are obvious and deliberate. The heroes Laon and Cythna, martyred revolutionaries, lack substance and many plot devices are fanciful. See *Poetical Works*, Vol. I (London: Moxon, 1839; online at Internet Archive). In 'Shelley's Poetry' (*SMH*, 3 October 1866, p. 3), CH would comment: 'Taking the whole mass of his poetry together, it is chiefly to be esteemed as composing a vast chamber of imagery, intensely poetic and gorgeously primeval, but having too little of rational purpose and actuality to be permanently valued by solid-thoughted readers...[T]he human can only heartily sympathise with and appreciate the human—not the angelic.'

[4] 'And the bard in my bosom is dead': Byron, 'To the Countess of Blessington'.

4. Charles Harpur to Henry Parkes, 16 August 1844

Text: ML Ah131

Parramatta,[1] 16th August, 1844

Dear Henry,

Having some little matters to do for my sister,[2] which may detain me here for four or five days, should any communication touching my play, &c.[3] reach you between this and Tuesday or Wednesday next, will you have the kindness to drop me a note by the post, directed to "Mrs Harpur's, Hunter Street, Parramatta."—So much for *business*—if I may be allowed to designate my laggard and paltry concerns by a term so bustling and important: and now I will see if I can make this note something like an equivalent for the postage, by copying out (of my head) the following sonnet, which I composed last night in bed—being watchful and restless; perhaps to little purpose. I am afraid it is not so good as ought to be, considering the Subject; but I did my best in it, to embody in the form you love, my sense of Mr Duncan's merits as a public writer. You must get it into the Register. The worthlessness of any praise of mine, and Mr Duncan's modesty will, I fear, stand in the way of your doing so—but you must get over both these stumbling stones—that is, if you can.— But to the Sonnet.

To W. A. Duncan Esq.[4]
On—(what shall we say? I leave this to your better judgment)

> In these unprosperous days of this crude State,[5]
>> When needy jobbers in the public weal
>> Are at the helm, and few who ought can feel,
> Through private care, for the disastrous fate

---

[1] Township 23 km west of Sydney on the Parramatta River, and founded shortly after it to raise crops for food for the infant colony. CH's mother lived in Hunter-street, and CH probably stayed with her during his time in the town in 1844.

[2] Possibly Mary Palmer, whose husband Walter, insolvent, had disappeared to Chile four months previously.

[3] *The Bushrangers.* It would not appear until 1853: see p. 67 n. 10.

[4] William Augustine Duncan (1811–85), liberal Catholic journalist, newspaper owner and editor and public servant. His *Weekly Register of Politics, Facts and General Literature* (1843– 45) showed him to be 'an intelligent critic and the patron, publisher and friend of colonial poets', notably CH and Parkes (*ADB*); see also p. 233 n. 9. For the fate of the poem, see p. 233 n. 7.

[5] The high property qualification for electors ensured that the new Legislative Council of 1843 was dominated by wealthy landowners and squatters (chief among them W. C. Wentworth), who stymied reform. Duncan's liberal *Weekly Register* urged the growth of representative institutions, advocated universal public education and opposed the privilege and power of the big pastoralists. CH's 'unprosperous days' may also allude to the simultaneous drought and economic depression of the early 1840s.

Thence threatening the sick land,—'tis comfort great
 To all who love their country, thee to find
 Its champion still! in mail of thine own mind
Lapp'd well, and early in the cause and late.
And Duncan, still—still be it thine to bear
 Forward unblenchingly! alone, yet bold
In Wisdom's piety and fraternal care!
 "Be just and fear not", said the Bard[6] of old;
And Truth the precept hath engraven fair
 On thy true heart—a lump of her own gold.

15 August, 1844.

I like the "lump of her own gold"—do you? At all events, it is closing, according to the proverbial canon, with a "key of gold."[7]

I have nothing to tell in the shape of news worth telling; and will only add, that I am yours

Sincerely—gratefully—now and forever,
Charles Harpur.

Give my respects to Mrs Parkes[8]

5. Henry Parkes to William Augustine Duncan, 20 August 1844

Text: ML MSS 947

To W. A. Duncan Esq.[9]

In these unprosperous days of this crude State,
 When needy jobbers in the public weal
 Are at the helm; and few who ought can feel,
Through private care for the disastrous fate
Thence threatening the sick land,—'Tis comfort great
 To all who love their country, thee to find
 Its champion still! in mail of thine own mind
Lapp'd well, and early in the cause and late.

---

[6] '[B]e just, and fear not. / Let all the ends thou aim'st at be thy country's, / Thy God's, and truth's; then if thou fall'st, O Cromwell! / Thou fall'st a blessed martyr' – Shakespeare, *Henry VIII*, III.2.447–9.

[7] I.e., the key that can open (and, by extension, close) any door, as in Milton's *Comus* (1634): 'that golden key / That opes the palace of Eternity'.

[8] Clarinda Parkes, née Varney (1813–88). In 1845 CH inscribed to her a copy of *Thoughts* (held at ML C378) in token of 'his gratitude for much kindness received at her hands'.

[9] See p. 8 n. 4.

And Duncan, still—still be it thine to bear
   Forward unblenchingly! alone, yet bold
In Wisdom's piety and fraternal care!
   "Be just and fear not," said the Bard of old;
And Truth the precept hath engraven fair
   On thy true heart—a lump of her own gold.

Charles Harpur
August 15th. 1844.

Dear Sir,

   The above noble sonnet addressed to you I received yesterday in a letter
from Mr Harpur now at Parramatta. We have frequently spoken of you as being
the only political writer in this country whose single aim has been the public
good uninfluenced by any underground expectations or desires. On one of
these occasions I asked him to write a Sonnet on your political championship
(conceiving the sonnet which Wordsworth has made the trumpet tongue of
Liberty,[1] as the most appropriate form for the subject) and he sent this to me
yesterday as I have stated. In his letter containing it, he says ["]I did my best
to embody in the form you love my sense of Mr Duncan's merits as a public
writer. You must get it into the Register. The worthlessness of any praise of
mine, and Mr Duncans modesty will, I fear stand in the way of your doing
so—but you must get over both these stumbling stones—that is if you can."
I am sure you will not deem as worthless the praise of this young fine spirited
and highly gifted Australian—a man who, with the same accidents of wealth
and station, would throw the Wentworths and Macarthurs[2] of his country
into the shade, and stand foremost of her sons in her cause, and in the glorious
work of humanity. I have a strong hope also that you will not let any delicacy
restrain you from publishing it in accordance with the author's wish; though
I would beg to suggest it is deserving a more prominent place than the niche
which you usually allot to poetry. You may have occasion ere long to make some
reply to the stupid ingrates who, perverting what they cannot comprehend in
your advocacy of their real interests, seize every opportunity and any success
to turn from you the public esteem; and with any such article of your own this
manly and beautiful eulogy of your conduct might (so I venture to think) be

---

[1] Sequence 'Sonnets Dedicated to Liberty' in *Poems, in Two Volumes* (1807) by William
Wordsworth, English Romantic poet (1770–1850) and a major influence on CH, who indited
several poems to him (h640, h472, h695) and to whom CH dedicated his own sonnet collection
Thoughts (1845). Parkes reviewed it effusively: 'As a sonnet-writer, in particular, we think Mr
Harpur excels so far, that we are inclined to question whether from Wordsworth's "Sonnets
dedicated to Liberty" there could be taken any twenty-three consecutively arranged, superior,
"all in all," to the twenty-three before us' (*Weekly Register*, 22 November 1845, p. 243).
[2] Bywords for dynastic wealth and power in the colony: William Charles Wentworth (see
p. 41 n. 5) and James Macarthur (1798–1867), innovative and successful pastoralist.

happily and well incorporated. The sonnet itself, I think, is very rich; the fine last words are worth five reams of average modern poetry and all through it has the robust beauty of thought and the fulness and strengths of expression which essentially belong to this grand form of verse. Pardon my poor attempt to "gild this *lump* of refined *gold*"

I am Dear Sir
your most respectful and
obedient Servant
Henry Parkes

Augst 20th / 44

(Copy)[3]

6. Charles Harpur to Henry Parkes, 1 October 1844
Text: ML MSS 947

Parramatta 1st October, 1844—

Dear Parkes,

I received yours today; and am exceedingly sorry to learn from it that Mrs Parkes is unwell—but I console myself with the hope that by this time she is quite recovered, and that when I see her again she will be in all things as well as all who are sincere in their admiration of womanly worth must wish her—all I mean who know her. Express all this and more to her on my part—

With regard to Mr Boyd's service[4] &c. I think almost any respectable b[e]rth under him would suit me well for two reasons—first, my hopes of employment are blanked, or nearly so, in every other direction; and second: in so extensive a concern as his, to get but a footing were something; as by good conduct, ability, and so forth, I should have a pretty good chance of working myself up afterwards—. And for the kindness—the fraternal solicitude manifested by you in my behalf, in this and in every instance—but I cannot speak my thanks—I *feel* them.

I did not get back the MS. of the "Bushrangers" I called again at Lazar's[5] the day I left for Parramatta, and after being kept standing in the doorway for half an hour at least, I was told by Lazar's son that his father could not find the MS. and that I *must* call again. Finding the matter thus, I had no course

---

[3] Parkes retained copies of much of his outward correspondence, but this copy, preserved in a collection of CH letters to him (ML MSS 947), is not part of the main Parkes collection at ML.

[4] Probably Benjamin Boyd (1801–51), entrepreneur, banker, shipowner, whaler and one of the largest landholders and graziers in NSW.

[5] John Lazar (1801–79), actor, stage manager and, until August 1844, manager of Sydney's Royal Victoria Theatre. He may have been considering staging the play.

but to request that when found, it might be left with Mr Duncan, with whom I afterwards left a note stating the case as it stood, and requesting him—as I was going out of town for, perhaps, a fortnight—to have the kindness to call upon Lazar for it, in the event of its not being left with him within five or six days. Lazar is not engaged at the Theatre, and will be off to Hobart or Port Philip very speedily, and this it was that led me to make the above request of Duncan. I do not think it was asking too much of him; and if he fails to comply—he and I have done with one another. No loss to him perhaps,—nor to me. But more than enough of this!

I have not sold the bone ware[1] yet; nor shall I sell them, I am afraid even though I come down to the wholesale Sydney prices. The dealers here do not complain that they are dear, but decline the bargain, because they should not be able to sell a doz. of the gem rings, for instance, in a twelvemonth. You may judge from this, how it is with Parramatta. Unless I can get the Sydney wholesale prices for the articles, of course I shall bring them back.

You ask me about the country—and "lovely things,

> Flowers, waters, forests, glancing wings"[2]—:

there is much of all this within a mile of me—but by God, I can't enjoy it.—I have no place in the land and cannot enjoy its beauty. I cannot write of these things.

I have employed myself much since I have been here in giving Keats a thorough reading. The following is the only thing I have done in the poetical way.—Is it good? it is true.

To Robert Sydney Parkes,[3] aged 10 Months.

Ay, crow, rogue, crow! Thy little Being thrilling is
    Like an embodied carol of a bird!
    Thine eyes are like two fountains, under-stirr'd
By their own gush—and a new-minted shilling is
Not brighter than thy face, as full up at me
    'Tis lifted oft, with a most gamesome meaning,
    Giving much merry roguery to my gleaning,
Till hinder'd by thy bold attempts to pat me:

[1] Although Parkes was at this time a tide-waiter he was by trade a bone and ivory turner, and would soon set up in this trade and as an importer of fancy goods. CH may have been testing the market for him at Parramatta.

[2] From 'The Prisoner of Ghent' by Irish poet Bartholomew Simmons, *Blackwood's Edinburgh Magazine*, 51 (January–June 1842), p. 99.

[3] Son (1843–80) of Henry and Clarinda Parkes. For later versions of the poem see h626.

When from thy sterning mood, methinks, a spirit
    Of lion-mettle and yet mild withal,
Looks out, prophetic of thy future merit,
    And pith of manhood.—May it so befall,
Even so, dear Boy! And all who know thy father,
A garland of like hopes for thee must gather.

My Sister[4] is highly gratified with your present, and desires me to convey to you her thanks and best respects—and for myself, my dear friend,

believe me sincerely yours
Charles Harpur.

7. Charles Harpur to Henry Parkes, 25 August 1845

Text: Parkes papers, ML A68

To Mr Henry Parkes,

On Board the American Ship "Robert Pulsford",[5]
Sydney Harbour.

Dear Henry, your Letter has just come to hand;
And as to a Pilgrim o'er Arabie's sand,[6]
Some Fountain, unlooked for, fresh bounty might roll,
The wave of its kindness gusht over my soul.
For ever a chat with, or letter from you,
Has freshened my Life as with Friendship's own dew;
And for hours, thereafter, with Hope I could smile,
And Misery's presence felt genial awhile.

By this you have found from the portion that ended
My Tale of the Bush,[7]* that you misapprehended
The drift of the Thing—and to this I advert,
Just to say, that so far from thereby feeling hurt,
I am flattered; because the Mistake was the fair
Though premature child of much brotherly care.

---

[4] CH's sister Elizabeth Rotton had given birth at Parramatta in July 1843, but the sister here was possibly Mary Palmer (see p. 3 n. 1).

[5] Out of Boston, a regular visitor to Australian and New Zealand ports in the 1840s and 1850s, with general cargo ranging from spirits and tobacco to pine boards, ham, sarsaparilla, crackers and wheelbarrows. Parkes was on board as a customs officer.

[6] Pilgrim to Mecca across the deserts of Arabia.

[7] 'The Creek of the Four Graves. A Tale of the Bush' was serialised in *Weekly Register*, 9, 16 and 23 August 1845 (see h080a).

Your Poem came also to hand with the Letter,[1]
And the more that I read it, I like it the better.
In vain for the Worldling all beauty and grace
Flushes Nature's, as Love does a frank human face;
But e'en bodiless splendors that Poets behold,
By the wand of their souls are made solid as gold:

And hence you have built from that grand morning past,
A Temple of Poesie ever to last.
I read—and each phrase as it streams through my voice,
So apt in its richness, so carelessly choice,
Seems coined just as wanted, with "double milled" edges,[2]
From the "flamy dust"[3] mentioned, all fused into wedges
Of Beauty's own bullion.

                And when 'mid this blaze
Of glorious Things, my own name met my gaze,[4]
Recurring to what you had said in the Letter,
As to blanking the same, if I thought it were fitter,
In my pride I said plumply—Why should I, forsooth?
No; there it shall stand as eternal as Truth,
Although not a fragment of mine should remain
To speak of the Love that once throbbed in my brain!
And then, lest friend Duncan* might think I was vain,
A desp'rate intention of "starring" the place[5]
Grew strong in my fingers, but pale in my face;
And as my pen's nib, I preparingly blew it,
Friendship spoke from the Past—'Twere ungracious to do it!
And so dear to my heart is all mention by you,
That Gratitude pleaded against the thing too:
Besides in the web of your musings it seemed
So thoughtfully woven—so richly indreamed,

---

[1] Parkes's 'Sunrise': CH apparently received a MS copy. A spectacular Pacific sunrise is used to foretell the rise of Australia and freedom.

[2] Twin rows of fine serrations along the edge of a coin to prevent clipping or counterfeiting.

[3] From Henry Parkes, 'Sunrise', lines 9–13: 'Long banks of gold and purple, far between / Whose glorious rents, in lines of liquid green / Besprent with flamy dust, like paths of sky, / Where many angels late had journeyed by, / The Eastern realms of Heaven opened to mortal eye.'

[4] Ibid., lines 48–55: 'I thought how many a bard of hers will watch / The sunrise of her summer morns, to catch / New glimpses of the wonderful; and weave / The splendours into song, all fit to leave, / Unfearing, to posterity. I thought, / Harpur, of thee—the rich things thou hast bought / With the world's modicum of happiness: / Alas, that Nature would not sell for less!'

[5] Inserting asterisks (stars) in the place of a name.

That I felt, through a foretaste most vital of Fame,
It were like doing murder upon my own name.
And so to the Register's next publication
I have sent it in full for poetic ovation.[6]

To conclude: How has Jonathan[7] used you? I wis
He has "guessed" you an excellent fellow by this;
And a true-hearted, strong-headed creature of Song;—
If the contrary—damn him! he "calculates" wrong:
And in that case, I wish him (no worse) the next time
He trades to our Port—just a *cargo of Rhyme*!

Charles Harpur.

Pyrmont,[8] 25 August, 1845.
*Poem published in the *Weekly Register*   *Editor of the *Weekly Register*

8. Henry Parkes to Henry Halloran, 6 September 1845

Text: Parkes papers, ML A931

Ship "Robt. Pulsford"[9] Saturday Night 6th Sept / 45

My dear Sir,[10]

I received your letter of the 4th instant[11] this morning; and thank you for a kindness I value as highly as anything that breaks the monotony of my humble life. I again thank you from my "heart of hearts" for your good opinion of my poems; though I should not consider these things worth the trouble to ascertain any man's opinion concerning them, were they not, for the most part, faithful transcripts of my inmost nature. The lines in last Register[12] were more hastily written, I think, than any verses of mine of equal length. I never read the "Endymion" of glorious young Keats,[13] although, shame for me, it

[6] Parkes's 'Sunrise' would appear in *Weekly Register*, 30 August 1845 p. 101; CH's poem to Parkes first appeared in *PA*, 7 April 1849, p. 7 (see h609b) with the two asterisked notes, which are neither in CH's hand nor Parkes's.
[7] The stock Yankee sailor of popular culture usually called 'Brother Jonathan' (as in a New York weekly of the same name with wide circulation, from 1842) – here, the crew of the American ship that Parkes, as customs officer, had been inspecting; ' "guessed" ' and ' "calculates" ' were quintessentially American to the British and Australian ear.
[8] CH's mother Sarah Harpur lived at John Street, Pyrmont, then a suburb of scattered stone cottages, wharves and sandstone quarries across Darling Harbour from town. Poems and letters are signed from there during part of 1845–46; CH was evidently staying with her.
[9] See p. 13 n. 5.
[10] Henry Halloran, public servant and poet (1811–93). A friend of Parkes, he would serve him as Under-Secretary in the 1860s.
[11] See Halloran to Parkes, 4 September 1845 (in *Suppl. Letters*).
[12] H. Parkes, 'Sunrise', *Weekly Register*, 30 August 1845, p. 101.
[13] Long poem (1818) on a classical theme by English Romantic poet John Keats (1795–1821).

has been in my possession for two or three years. I would now speak of Harpur.

I also know not much of Mr Harpur, but enough to fill my heart, when I think of him, with "sorrow and commiseration"; nor am I conscious of cause for shame in such feelings. It is part of my sorrow that I, like you, cannot "respect his personal character". A poem entitled the "Vision of the Rock",[1] in the Australasian Chronicle, first made me acquainted with his name, I think about three years ago. Some time afterwards I published a Sonnet to Mr Harpur,[2] in a Sydney periodical, which elicited from him a letter, followed by an interchange of other letters, and, on my part, a present of a book.[3] When he came to Sydney, some sixteen or eighteen months ago, he called upon me; and hence arose our acquaintance. My opinion of his powers as a poet is far higher, it would appear, than yours, but I am sure your manliness will allow me to hold an opinion in such matter even in opposition, as I freely confess, to a more competent judge. In some things, at least, I think Harpur has "written for posterity." But I could wish I had never known him other than by his poetry,—I have often had occasion to blame his conduct, and I have done so more severely to himself, than I need do, to others. I regret having been so unguarded as to betray my particular feelings towards him in my letter; but we will name the matter no more. I thank you, my dear Sir, for the good opinion you are pleased to express towards me personally; and sincerely hope that, when you come to know me better, I shall not be tumbled down from my "starry place" in your esteem. As to my "elegant art", I must send you and Mrs. Halloran specimens of that, some of these next days. I must reserve any remark of mine on "New Zealand matters"[4] till I see your poems, beyond that I agree with you the Moari Wallace[5] must have a queer opinion of our consistency and good intentions.

Your spirited rebuke of Mr Poet-and-Lawyer-and Editor-and-Senator Lowe, on the Levee, I saw, and much admired, and said at the time was yours.[6]

---

[1] See h665a, in *Australasian Chronicle*, 1 September 1842, p. 2.

[2] See Letter 2 and p. 4 n. 3.

[3] The 'letter' was Letter 2; the 'present' was a set of the *Poetical Works of Percy Bysshe Shelley* – see p. 5 n. 7.

[4] Halloran's 'Three Sonnets about New Zealand Matters' would appear anonymously in *Weekly Register*, 13 September 1845, p. 126; it protested the unchristian violence of the war being waged on the Māori tribes of the Bay of Islands in 1845–46.

[5] The chief Hōne Wiremu Heke Pōkai, or Hōne Heke (1807?–50), leader of the Māori resistance in the so-called Flagstaff War, here likened to the 13th-century Scottish national hero William Wallace.

[6] *Atlas* had attacked Governor Gipps and his Downing Street policies in language so extreme that the loyalty of its editor Robert Lowe was questioned by many, particularly when he called for a boycott of the Governor's levee and annual reception for the Queen's birthday (see *Atlas*, 10 May 1845, p. 278). Halloran's 'rebuke', in the form of a poem 'The Queen', subtitled 'Lines written in honour of the Anniversary of the Birthday of Her Gracious Majesty Queen Victoria', appeared anonymously in *SMH*, 26 May 1845, p. 2.

I never saw the other lines referred to in your letter; the Southern Queen[7] is more unknown to me than Queen Victoria, for her Majesty of England I once had the honour to see. Speaking of the late warfare of rhymed missiles, I, too, had a shot or two at the enemy,—"The Association in Council," "A 'Lesson' for the 'Patriots',", in answer to the "Tyrant's Lesson" in the second number of the Atlas, and "Ye Senators of Sydney," were mine;[8]—I wish they had been keener weapons. They were printed in the Register; if you saw them, tell me how you liked them, for they constitute all in this way I ever perpetrated.

I thought of asking in our talk about Sonnets whether you remembered reading an article in prose (a sounding designation!) in the Australasian Chronicle some years ago, entitled "Beautiful Sonnets,"[9]—that was a lucubration of mine; I name it more particularly, as it contained an opinion of you as a poet, though briefly expressed, which may go some way towards proving the sincerity of my admiration of your high abilities. One other word concerning my self: I have written, since confined on board this ship, a sort of rambling, gossiping criticism on the American Poets,[10] which is now in the hands of Mr Duncan. If it is published in the Register, be pleased to favour me with your opinion thereon.

I am exceedingly sorry to hear of your children's sickness,[11] the more so, because I can almost believe you deserve to be exempted from domestic affliction. I trust however they will soon be restored to rosy health, and you and their mother to perfect happiness. As soon as you have time, be pleased to write to me again. I remain, my dear Sir,

yours most sincerely
H. Parkes.

P. S. I have a word to say in my next on your "reason for not publishing." I would here express my abomination of Harpur's attempt in prose,—the

---

[7] Halloran's address to 'The Spirit of Freedom' had appeared in *Southern Queen*, organ of the Church of England Lay Association.

[8] 'The "Association" in Council. A Parody', signed Byron Junior, *Weekly Register*, 19 October 1844, p. 200; 'A "Lesson" for the "Patriots." (Inscribed to the Poets of the ATLAS.)', unsigned, *Weekly Register*, 21 December 1844, p. 309; and 'Ye Senators of Sydney', unsigned, *Weekly Register*, 14 December 1844, p. 291. 'The Tyrant's Lesson', an attack on Governor Gipps, signed Machiavelli but undoubtedly the work of the paper's editor Robert Lowe, appeared in *Atlas*, 14 December 1844, p. 27. Parkes's 'enemy' was the powerful squatters' Pastoral Association, opponents of Gipps's proposed squatting regulations and backers of the *Atlas*.

[9] In this article (signed 'Falconbridge', a variant or misspelling of his mother's maiden name, Faulconbridge), Parkes quotes and discusses sonnets by nine British and American poets, then Halloran's 'On My First Poetical Aspirations' – see *Australasian Chronicle*, 3 May 1842, p. 2.

[10] See unsigned two-part article 'American Poets', *Weekly Register*, 27 September 1845, pp. 149–51 and 4 October 1845, pp. 161–3.

[11] Halloran's sons Henry and William were ill with whooping cough; both recovered.

"Importance of a Rhyme",[1] don't he call it?

Confidential[2]

Copy

9. Henry Parkes to *Spectator*, 30 June 1846

Text: Spectator (Sydney), 4 July 1846, p. 285

LECTURES ON MODERN POETRY.

MR. SPECTATOR,[3]—

My attention has been directed, by my valued friend Mr. Halloran, to the notice of Mr. Ewing's lectures[4] in your last Saturday's journal, wherein my name is somewhat ungraciously in[tr]oduced.

I, too, would fain say a few words on the subject of "Colonial Poetry," with which it appears I am so far identified as to obtain mention, in this instance, with "Sparta's worthier sons."[5]

As I should not have complained, if Mr. Ewing had really given me a "severe castigation" for my evil doings in verse, I do not, of course, complain of your assertion that I "richly merit" one. All I would say of myself, with reference to this matter is, that to whatever censure of my poetic efforts which may arise from a sincere desire to protect and nourish true poetry in this, the dear and beautiful land of my adoption, whencesoever it may come, I will bow

[1] CH's sole published short story, 'The Importance of a Rhyme. A Story of the Old Dock-Yard', recounting the struggle of Micky Devine with his Muse, appeared in *Weekly Register*, 30 August 1845, pp. 101–2 immediately below Parkes's 'Sunrise' – which may help account for his displeasure. It adapts an old yarn: see, e.g., 'Irish Blunder', about Paddy Divine of Tralee, in *Sydney Gazette*, 29 November 1836, p. 4, copied from *The Mirror of Literature, Amusement and Instruction* (London, 1836), where it is credited to 'W.G.C.'

[2] Parkes's cautious '*Confidential*' is understandable: first, the recipient was a public servant, at this point chief clerk with the Surveyor General's Department, and this letter's political content was not for the eyes of his colleagues; and, second, it reveals doubts about CH that Parkes must have wanted kept from him.

[3] Short-lived Sydney weekly funded by entrepreneur Benjamin Boyd and his banker partner Joseph Robinson to advocate the land interests of the squatters. It did not survive the fulfillment of their demands in late 1846. Its editor, Richard Thompson (1810–65), served on other papers with similar interests: *Atlas* and Boyd's latter-day *Australian*. *ADB* describes him as 'a skilful though unoriginal poet and an able editor'.

[4] On 23 June 1846 schoolmaster and minister Robert Kirkwood Ewing (1823–99) gave the third in his series of lectures on 'Modern Poetry', in part devoted to colonial poets. According to *Spectator*, 27 June 1846, pp. 270–1, Ewing 'rather cruelly lingered over a most severe, though highly merited, castigation' of CH, provoked by *Weekly Register*'s (actually Parkes's) comparison of CH with Milton. A spat would ensue between CH and *Spectator* editor Richard Thompson: see Letters 10 and 11.

[5] Parkes is facetiously adapting Byron: 'And be the Spartan's epitaph on me,—/ "Sparta hath many a worthier son than he."' ('Childe Harold', Canto IV, itself recalling Plutarch's attributing the sentiment to Argileonis, mother of the slain Brasidas, in *Moralia: Sayings of Spartans*).

my heart unto thankfulness, and kiss the chastener's rod.[6]

It is due to Mr. Duncan to explain that he is in no way guilty of "comparing Harpur with Milton." The article in the *Register*[7] (a notice of *Thoughts*, by Charles Harpur, and *Marmont*, by G. F. Poole) to which evidently allusion was made by Mr. Ewing, I alone am answerable for. It was written by me at Mr. Duncan's request, but that gentleman, I remember, so far from being chargeable with any opinions it contained, expressed himself to the effect that it was a piece of extravagance to compare Harpur with Wordsworth, which was done, however, in a limited degree.

The sum of my 'absurdity' and 'sin' which afforded the Pitt-street audience[8] so much "laughter" is contained in the following sentence—"Mr. Harpur is a poet not unworthy to be named with those august sons of genius (Milton, Shakspeare, Wordsworth, &c.,) *though he may never attain to their universal fame*" With this explanation, I must leave Mr. Harpur to take care of his own reputation, which, I doubt not, he is well able to defend. Leisure is not allowed me at present, even if I were competent, to discuss his merits as a poet.

As you have expressed your intention to follow Mr. Ewing through his series of lectures, I trust you will not omit, in your extracts, that portion devoted to Colonial Poets; especially as I fear those of our "tuneful tribe" who were severely dealt with by the lecturer, will not otherwise be able to benefit (in "turning from the evil of their ways") by his condemnation.

Desirous, as I believe you to be, for the healthful growth and well-being of Literature in this Land, I do hope you will accede to my request in publishing, entire, Mr. Ewing's examination of our Poets' respective claims to public attention, feeling certain that good must accrue to the writers from any candid and sincere, though condemnatory criticism.

With regard to myself, as I have said, Mr. Ewing is welcome to snuff out my little rushlight[9] of fame, if thereby the clear stars above me can be more steadily gazed upon. My heart is, and if I had a purse, that too should be, in the cause of Australian Literature, believing that where sweetest bloom the flowers of Poesy, there ever, strongest and hardiest, will grow the tree of Freedom.

Holding this belief, I thank Mr. Ewing for whatever notice he may have

---

[6] Submit to divine will, a usage common in mid-19th century verse.

[7] See *Weekly Register*, 22 November 1845, pp. 243–4, reviewing CH's *Thoughts. A Series of Sonnets* (Sydney: W. A. Duncan, 1845) and *Marmont; or, Suffering without Guilt. A Tale, in Six Cantos* by chemist George Frederic Poole (Sydney: W. A. Colman, 1845), two volumes representing, according to the reviewer, 'by far the best, and decidedly the worst, sample of "poetry" which the colony has yet produced'.

[8] Ewing's lectures were given at the theatre of the Sydney Mechanics' School of Arts, Pitt-street.

[9] A rush candle; figuratively, something weak, feeble or insignificant.

bestowed upon the poets of Australia in his lectures; and I would also tender to you, Mr. Spectator, my best thanks for the attention you appear to give our infant literature in your journal, and for your choice and valuable selections from the Poets of Europe.

I beg to remain, Sir,
Your obedient servant,
H. PARKES.

25, Hunter-street,[1] 30th June, 1846.

10. Charles Harpur to *Spectator*, [4–11 July 1846]

Text: ML C376

Appendix.[2]

The "Temple of Infamy"[3] was the result, in part, of the Spectator's refusal to insert the following the Letter and Squib, elicited by a spiteful attack made by a Schoolmast of the name of Ewing[4] upon the author's poetry in the concluding Lecture of a Series delivered by him at the "School of Arts."

To the Editor of the Spectator.

Sir,

Having long since buckled myself in a quiet "grin and bear it" sort of resolution, and the conclusion, that he who would attain to any literary distinction in the present times of Australia, by straightforward and manly means alone, has but little of fair play to expect from the decisions of the Newspaper scribes of Sydney; I shall not be greatly disappointed, and not at all dejected, should you refuse insertion to these remarks, and the annexed squib at Lecturer Ewing, in return for the "cruel" one which you say he has played off upon that unlucky and uninspired (aboriginal?) lassie whom, it would seem, I have been hitherto in the habit of mistaking, in my lonely

---

[1] In 1846 Parkes set up shop as a bone and ivory toymaker and importer of fancy goods, at 25 Hunter-street, Sydney, soon shifting to 20 Hunter-street. Another address, ignored here, is given below this one; it should have headed the next item, a notice from Colonial Secretary Edward Deas Thomson.

[2] The letter is CH's copy, apparently intended as an appendix to 'The Temple of Infamy' (h580a). It must date from the week between 4 July 1846 (see CH's reference below to the *Spectator*'s report of Ewing's distinction between poetry and prose in 'your last') and the paper's reference to rejecting the letter in its issue of 11 July.

[3] In the 1860s subtitled in manuscript 'A Satire', the poem was by then 'the first step in an attempt to expose, and root up if possible, the "thousand and one" Infamies that are everywhere depraving the morals and debasing the intellects of the rising generation of this Colonial Public' (see h580b); it would not be published in its entirety until 1984. The title is from Alexander Pope's *The Dunciad*, where, in a footnote, the attorney William Arnall is described as amply deserving of 'a niche in the Temple of Infamy'.

[4] See p. 18 nn. 3, 4. For Ewing in 'The Temple of Infamy', see h580b, footnote 8.

wanderings about my native land, for an accompanying Muse. I shall not be greatly disappointed, I say; albeit I do believe, Sir, that, by disposition, *you* are more inclined to literary justice than any other *one* of the Editorial Brotherhood (of Sydney I mean) whose […] and nature I can just now call to mind.

In proof of the propriety of my denying to Mr Ewing the requisite critical ability to judge justly of poetical merit, it is only necessary, I think, to refer your *impartial* attention to the passage in his opening lecture (given in your last), in which he attempts to mark the difference between Prose and Poetry:[5] than which indeed, nothing more senseless could have emanated even from Samuel Prout-Hill[6] himself, in the act of flaying alive both the one and the other. You will therein find this philosophical lecturer on poetry talking about "Idea siezing upon Imagination"—making such a mistake as a child might upon its supposing that *the mouse had siezed the cat*; and such a mistake therefore, as were *pardonable only in a child*. If you will but please to make such a reference as I suggest, it strikes me mightily, that you will thereupon ejaculate (to yourself) somewhat after this fashion. "Well! I must needs confess that Harpur in this matter, however much astray when rhyming, has hitten the right nail on the head. Yes: lest the very spirit of Charlatanism descend upon *me* also, as a judgment for intellectual faithlessness. By the Lord, Prout himself then, could hardly have dished up any thing in the way of a definition much more preposterously!"

I will only remark further, that, if I understand myself at all, I am very little interested at this present writing as to the quality of my own published effusions. If this be good, they will take care of themselves; if the contrary, they will perish as they should do. But I am much interested in the general issue of the question "What is Poetry?" which this Lecturer has attempted to answer with so much self sufficiency, and in which attempt he has so signally failed; and I would assert therefore, in its beha[lf], that he is most manifestly an incompetent authority. It is just possible, however, that *you* may think differently;—and, at all events, the insertion of these my retorts in the Spectator, must be a matter entirely dependent upon your editorial favor—at the feet of which (to speak like a poor chap-fallen poet) I must ever leave them,

and subscribe myself
Yours very respectfully.
Charles Harpur.

---

[5] See Ewing's argument in *Spectator*, 4 July 1846, pp. 281–2. The paper misreported the words to which CH objected here, but corrected in its issue of 11 July 1846, p. 297: 'In place of "it is the power of poetry. Idea seizes upon the Imagination;" it should have been "it is the power of poetry, and seizes upon the Imagination." ' CH would dispute that this was simple misreporting: Thompson and Ewing had 'laid heads together upon the matter' (Letter 11).
[6] Poet, lecturer, painter and public servant (1821–61), Samuel Prout Hill was secretary and librarian of the Sydney Mechanics' School of Arts, the venue for Ewing's lectures.

The following is the Squib which was annexed to the above, with this note appended, in reference to that part which reflects upon Mr Ewing's countryship. "All scots of real sense and refinement, will perhaps excuse this 'rub national,' when informed that there exists at present in Sydney, a conspiracy amongst a set of *small Scotch* wits, the sun and centre of which is or was Mr John Rae,[1] against everything intellectual of such an order as may eclipse their own pygmy efforts."

What Next!

'Twas Ewing's to ask t'other night at the Lecture,
What's Poetry, Ladies and Gents?—Let's inspect her.
Then straightway, by wholesale, from Johnson[2] he picked, Sir,
Such words!—each as long as a boa-constrictor.
But his *meaning* hopped off, like an uncaughten ball,
And the *answer* in sense was—Just nothing at all!

Then, Sir, his Classification how level!

11. Charles Harpur to *Spectator*, 16 July 1846

Text: Spectator (Sydney), 18 July 1846, p. 309

To the Editor of the Spectator.

SIR,—

A single glance at your notice in the last *Spectator*, of my communication with reference to Mr. Lecturer Ewing,[3] was quite conclusive, to my own mind at least, that he and yourself had laid heads together upon the matter; and moreover, that he had succeeded with you in begging himself off. You *did* not therefore, nor *do* you intend to publish that communication.

As to the *correction* of the nonsense[4] with which I had therein charged Mr. Ewing's definition, and which prefaces impudently enough the notice above adverted to, the very structure of the passage as it originally stood, belies the pretence of his having written it otherwise. The subterfuge is gross as the nature of a hog, and vile as the odour of a fox: and the cowardly meanness of his thus evading the blow I had fairly directed at that bladder of folly and fume which he has mistaken for a critical capacity, is just as contemptible as

---

[1] Aberdeen-born public servant, author, painter and bibliophile, John Rae (1813–1900) lectured at the Mechanics' School of Arts on various subjects: Taste, Elocution, the English Language, the poetry of Robert Burns etc. His account in mock-heroic verse of the fancy dress ball of 1844 held by the Mayor of Sydney (his then employer) earned him some ridicule.

[2] Dr Samuel Johnson produced his renowned *A Dictionary of the English Language* in 1755; see further, p. 211 n. 9.

[3] See p. 20 n. 2.

[4] See p. 21 n. 5.

the editorial dishonesty by which he has been prompted and enabled to do so. And, besides, can you not perceive, Sir, that in helping him out of the ditch of ignorance, you have most miserably bemudded your most sapient self? In other words, you have just made yourself chargeable with the intolerable nonsense for which your friend Ewing were otherwise justly whipable, even though he wore yet his corderoys.[5] But, admitting that the stupidity pointed out in this instance, is indeed a mental bye-bantling[6] of your own, yet, is not every other passage you have given from the lectures in question, every whit as preposterous and ignorant as the one in which it was detec[t]ed? If you have but one gleam of common sense, with the smallest amount of candour that may be, you must answer—Yes.

You speak of my communication as being an angry one. Had you published it, I do not think a single reader of your paper would have been of the same opinion. For myself, I can truly affirm that I never laughed more merrily in my life than I did while writing it; and even *now*, I am *only indignant*—to find MEN so paltry.

Another word or two, and I shall have done for the present. I am *now* glad that you did not insert my letter and squib. Had you done so, it is very likely, that, being a merciful man in the main, I should have then whistled the affair at once out of mind. But now it shall cost me a phamphlet:[7] in which, I promise you, I will give both yourself and Mr. Ewing, with some others, a lustier idea of a literary castigation than has ever yet rattled, like a peal of thunder, athwart the self-conceit of either you, him, or them: for, as brother Jonathan[8] would say, "When rubbed ag'in the hair, I *ar'* a screamer."[9]

One word more, on the strength of an after-thought. If you possess a single spark of intellectual spirit, you will *dare* to give insertion to *this* and my prior communication,—and then have at them like a thresher! But you dare not. Should you, however, succeed in screwing up your courage to the necessary sticking place for venturing thereupon, you had as not well resort to any such magnanimous tricks as *misprinting* and so forth; because the manuscripts have been read by several persons of education, who, in that event, will be able and

---

[5] Trousers of corduroy, a coarse, thick-ribbed cotton stuff: 'to attempt to inflict pain through the thick corderoys of a boy's trowsers is labour lost' – J. J. H. Harris, *The School-Room: Part II. Its Discipline and Supervision* (1849), p. 92.

[6] A bantling is a young or small child, a brat: hence 'poetical bantlings' (1808, *OED*): here, frivolous thought.

[7] A misspelling of 'pamphlet', not unique to CH.

[8] See p. 15 n. 7.

[9] Slang for a person or thing of exceptional size, intensity or attractiveness. *OED*'s first citation is 1846 (US).

willing to certify as to their *true* contents.

I remain, Sir,
Yours in all reason,
CHARLES HARPUR.

Pyrmont, July 16, 1846.

* It will be remembered that Mr. Ewing strongly objected to Mr. Charles Harpur taking rank with MILTON as a Poet, and that we were base enough to acknowledge that we had laughed heartily at the comical association of ideas created by the lecturer's allusion to the comparison.[1]

12. Charles Harpur to Sir Charles Augustus FitzRoy, 8 April 1847

Text: NSWSA: NRS-905 [4/2770.2], 47/3194

To His Excellency, Sir Charles Augustus
Fitz Roy,[2] Knight, Captain General and
Governor in Chief of New South Wales and
its Dependencies. &c—&c—&c.

May it please your Excellency.

In applying for employment under your Excellency's Government, I beg your Excellency will be graciously pleased to peruse the ensuing Statement.

I am a native of the Colony, and received in 1838 the Government Appointment of Clerk in the General Post Office, from Sir Richard Bourke,[3] being then about twenty years of age.[4] The duties of this Situation I discharged satisfactorily for nearly three years; when I resigned it, in order to devote myself more strenuously to Literature[5] than these duties permitted. It is almost needless to add, that such an exchange of pursuit, in a colonial community, was every way for the worse, and the youthful enthusiasm which prompted to it any thing but wise. For after working, or rather battling, out a very hard subsistence for some years through the Newspaper Press of Sydney, I became disgusted, and sought employment in the Country, where, for the most part, I have since remained: and what chiefly urges me to make the present application, is a certain delicacy of bodily constitution,—

---

[1] This footnote is Richard Thompson's (see p. 18 n. 3), not CH's; no location in the text is indicated. The *Spectator*'s hearty laugh is recorded in its report on Ewing's lecture, 27 June 1846, p. 271 – except the Australian poet is misidentified as Parkes, corrected in the same issue to CH (p. 273).

[2] Sir Charles Augustus FitzRoy (1796–1858), Governor of NSW – vice-regal representative of the British Crown and the Colony's chief executive officer 1846–55.

[3] Sir Richard Bourke (1777–1855), Governor of NSW 1831–37.

[4] CH misremembered the details. He was in fact 23 when appointed a Letter Sorter (3rd Class) on 1 February 1836 – see Returns of the Colony, 1837. He consistently under-reported his age.

[5] Contrast his explanation to James Raymond in 1839 (Letter 1).

superinduced I believe by my early studies and pursuits,—which somewhat incapacitates me for the rugged usages and employments of a Bush life. It may be proper, however, to observe here, that my literary attainments, though profitless enough in a worldly regard, have yet elicited honorable mention from many gentlemen in the Colony of taste and learning: amongst whom I may just name Mr Robert Lowe, Mr Hastings Elwin, and Mr Duncan late Editor of the Weekly Register.[6]

As to my qualifications,—I write, as your Excellency will perceive, a good official hand, and am not deficient in English scholarship: and should your Excellency be graciously pleased to confer upon me any such office as Clerk in one of the Departments in Sydney, or of Petty Sessions[7] in the Country, I doubt not but that I shall discharge my duties efficiently, both for my own credit, and in testimony of my gratitude to your Excellency.

With regard to my moral character, I may state in conclusion, that I do not believe even my enemies can charge me with the commission of any thing essentially dishonorable during the whole course of my life.—And humbly hoping that your Excellency will excuse the mode of this Application—any informality of it being a consequence of my desire to trespass as little as possible on your Excellency's time,

I have the honor to be,
Sir,
Your very obedient and
respectful Servant,
Charles Harpur,

Jerry's Plains, April 8th 1847

47/3194—17th April, 1847. Charles Harpur Applying for Employment

Is any thing known of Mr Harpur? or is he a fit person to be placed on the List of Candidates for public Employment?

16th Sept [CAF?[8]]

See within

20th

---

[6] For Robert Lowe, see p. 26 n. 3. Hastings Elwin (1776–1852), lawyer, former member of the NSW Legislative Council and translator of the Italian poet and librettist Metastasio, is a surprising inclusion, as CH would reserve a niche for him in his 'Temple of Infamy', still in manuscript – see h58ob. By this time W. A. Duncan had left journalism to take a government post as sub-collector of customs at Moreton Bay (Brisbane).

[7] In Courts of Petty Sessions, magistrates (usually local justices of the peace) could convict for such offences as theft, drunkenness, disorderly or dishonest conduct, disobedience of a master's orders, running away from work etc. They were held in Sydney and 19 country centres, and staffed by a government-appointed clerk.

[8] The annotation is Governor FitzRoy's.

Inform Mr Harpur that I will have his name placed on the List of Candidates, but that I can hold out no hopes to him, of immediate Employment.

[CAF?]
22d Apl

Mr Harpur 23 April 1847

13. Charles Harpur to *Atlas*, [by 19 June 1847]
Text: Atlas, 19 June 1847, p. 296

THE NEW SQUATTING ACT.

Mr. ATLAS—

This fourteen years' lease affair,[1] if carried into effect, will be the future perdition of the colony. The complexion of the squatting question was frightful enough before, seeing that the squatters were actually in the habit of considering themselves as in permanent possession of their runs, even up to the land debate in the Council. Nay, even the *Herald*, reviewing this debate,[2] went so far in affirmation of the fact, as to ask—Who would purchase these squattages seeing they would have to *fight* for their possession afterwards? If such was the aspect of this question *then*, surely, *now*, every right-minded colonist should rally round Mr. Lowe,[3] in the event of his giving sturdy battle to the villainous impositions of the above denounced act. Fourteen years' leases, will put the whole of the squatted lands beyond the boundaries, into the hands of their present holders *for ever:* and, Good God! are *we*, then, (the colonists generally,) and our children, to be thus robbed of whole provinces by

[1] The Waste Lands Acts of 1842 and 1846 passed by the British parliament governed alienation of crown lands in the Australian colonies at a purchase price of £1 per acre. An Order in Council in 1847 divided NSW for land-tenure purposes into three categories: settled, intermediate and unsettled. In the unsettled districts leases could be granted for 14 years, and a pre-emptive right of purchase gave current lessees first right to purchase the freehold of the land they occupied ('the squatted lands', below). Democrats, CH among them, saw high land prices, long leases and pre-emption as victories for the squatters' lobby, locking the 'small man' out of his fair share of the land: cf. CH's note to 'The New Land Orders' (h358b), in *Sydney Chronicle*, 30 October 1847, p. 4.

[2] 'The Debate on Crown Land Occupancy' in *SMH*, 1 June 1847, p. 2 and 2 June 1847, p. 2, responded to the speech of Robert Lowe to the Legislative Council of 27 May. Lowe would issue an edited version: *The Impending Crisis: An Address to the Colonists of New South Wales, on the Proposed Land Orders* (Sydney: Daniel Lovett Welch, 1847; online via NLA).

[3] Robert Lowe (1811–92), brilliant lawyer, journalist, editor and politician, the future Viscount Sherbrooke. In 1844–45 Lowe had sided with squatters in their demands for local control of waste lands, but now viewed with alarm their increasing power and influence. Elected to a seat in the Legislative Council in July 1845, he opposed W. C. Wentworth and the pastoral interests. Backed by Parkes and other progressives (who organised his re-election in 1848), he would agitate against the renewal of the transportation of British convicts.

a few adventurers, who occupied them in the first instance for mere purposes of private gain? Is the mere going into the bush, under motives no nobler than such as point to the bettering an individual fortune, a merit of such magnitude, that it should be rewarded with an infant principality? and this too, to the detriment of unborn millions? The scribes of the *Herald*, will not look at the question in this light; their feeling being, very evidently—that it matters little how the immense tracts are held, nor by whom, so long as plenty of wool is grown upon them—such political earthworms always identifying social progression with the vulgar "go-a-head" principle.[4] But let them not be trusted. Even in Australia, and at present, we are going a-head too fast; and in the particular of large landed estates especially. Immense inequalities of this kind are the arch curses of the Old World. A splendid is never a happy land. Wherever there are palaces there are hovels. It should be our wisdom then in Australia, to have as few of either as possible. Wherever mansions are numerous, and gentlemen (in the useless sense of the term) as "plenty as blackberries," there also, poor houses abound, and paupers starve in heaps. Such universally, is the condition of the Old World: and our present and future legislators should perpetually propound to themselves the question— Whether the same national mockery—patrimonial pomp on the one hand, and hereditary destitution on the other—is to be extended into this portion of the new? By keeping this constantly at heart, they will assuredly grow up to something better. I say above, *this portion of the New World*, because America, having fallen from her first love, is but a second edition of European polity, with the royal frontispiece blusteringly expunged. A land of mere worldly impulses—of mere go-a-head selfishness—is unworthy of the graves of a Washington, a Henry, and a Channing.[5]

C. H.

---

[4] The principle of economic progress, money-making.

[5] Three prominent Americans whose lives, sayings or writings inspired CH. George Washington (1732–99): statesman, military leader in the War of Independence, a 'Founding Father' and first president of the United States; CH would name his first son in his honour. Patrick Henry (1736–99): statesman and orator, known for his declaration 'Give me liberty, or give me death!' William Ellery Channing (1780–1842): Unitarian preacher and liberal theologian; his *Self-Culture* (1838) was influential.

Dear Parkes,

I told you in my last, that I had at length a prospect of doing reasonably well. It is this. I have taken a station in connexion with my brother, who still holds the Pound and Post-Office, with the view of taking in horses at so much per head per annum, and horned cattle on the halves. The scheme promises to answer exceedingly well, as we have already got about thirty horses at 10/ and 15/ each yearly, and 400 head of cattle on the halves. You will see from this, that, with any thing like ordinary luck, I can hardly do amiss. And on this head, by the bye, I want you to turn me a stock whip handle out of mahogany, ebony, or rosewood (the latter if possible) of the following dimensions. But first let me draw its shape.

Its entire length is to be 14 inches, an inch in diameter at the but and a quarter of an inch at the whip end. A piece of hard brass, or iron, an inch solid is to be screwed into and turned on to the but; from which (including it) to the first of the three beads, 4 inches, the stock is to taper to three quarters of an inch in diameter; then 4 inches from the first of these beads, two other beads are to occur, and in this compartment the stock is to taper to half an inch in diameter; then from the first of these two beads to the whip end the stock is to taper to one quarter of an inch.

When it is finished, (capitally mind) wrap it up in paper and address it to the "Postmaster, Jerry's Plains", and ask Mr. Hunt of the Gen: Post Office to have the goodness to put in the mail bag for the Postmaster, which he will do as a matter of course. If you make it as I know you can, I'll warrant that there's not a sprig in

9. Letter, Charles Harpur to Henry Parkes, 26 September 1847

14. Charles Harpur to Henry Parkes, 26 September 1847

Text: ML MSS 947

Dear Parkes,

I told you in my last, that I had at length a prospect of doing reasonably well. It is this. I have taken a station in connexion with my brother,[1] who still holds the Pound and Post Office,[2] with the view of taking in horses at so much per head per annum, and horned cattle on the halves.[3] The scheme promises to answer exceedingly well, as we have already got about thirty horses at 10/- and 15/- each yearly, and 400 head of cattle on the halves. You will see from this, that, with any thing like ordinary luck, I can hardly do amis. And on this head, by the bye, I want you to turn me a stock whip handle[4] out of mahogany, ebony, or rosewood (the latter if possible) of the following dimensions. But first let me draw its shape.

Its entire length is to be 14 inches, an inch in diameter at the but and a quarter of an inch at the whip end. A piece of hard brass, or iron, an inch solid is to be screwed into and turned on to the but; from which (including it) to the first of the three beads, 4 inches, the stock is to taper to three quarters of an inch in diameter; then 4 inches from the first of these beads, two other beads are to occur, and in this compartment the stock is to taper to half an inch in diameter; then from the first of these two beads to the whip end the stock is to taper to one quarter of an inch.

When it is finished, (capitally mind) wrap it up in paper and address it to the "Postmaster, Jerry's Plains", and ask Mr Hunt of the Gen: Post Office[5] to have the goodness to put [it] in the mail bag for the Postmaster, which he will do as a matter of course. If you make it as I know you can, I'll warrant that there's not a sprig[6] in the district who shall visit Sydney in future without giving you an order for a similar one: and as to the *damage*,[7] I shall be in Sydney about Christmas, when of course I will settle it. So much for a whip handle—a matter of some importance you see in these parts.

[1] CH presumably meant that, together with his brother Joseph, he had taken a lease on a rural property.
[2] See p. 4 n. 1.
[3] For equal shares of the profits and natural increase.
[4] Parkes was by trade a bone and ivory turner, at this time in business in Sydney.
[5] Robert A. Hunt was principal clerk at the Sydney General Post Office, then in George-street (see Returns of the Colony, 1847).
[6] A youth or young man; also used humorously to mean a scion or offshoot of a family or class.
[7] Cost, expense (colloquial).

You give me a rub for having Newspapered it again. I have sinned. But you will never see a line of mine in a Newspaper again—not at my own instance.[1] I intend to occupy my leisure, with collecting into one M.S. all my poems, and annotating myself. That is, I intend to keep up a running discharge of anecdotes of their heros and heroines, with revelations of the circumstances and feelings under which they were severally written, mingled with nice critical chit chat, to the extent of about as much prose as there will be verse; and I do flatter myself, that of the whole, in this way, I shall make a gloriously singular book—to be published—say, ten years hence![2] What think *you?*

Now tell me all about your own thinkings and doings. Recollect, you are not *Parkes the ivory turner* to me, but *Parkes the Poet.*[3] I have written a letter to Halloran in rhyme.[4] Perhaps you will see it. On what terms are you and he at this present? Enliven my solitude with some earnest chit chat—that which you can tip so well when in the mood. Spin me a long yarn about yourself— about any thing in short. What has become of Strang?[5] and is long Hart as long as ever? and what of my friend Prout Hill? and of that scape grace, Desborough?[6]—do I spell his name right. There! It will be odd if you cannot find something to chat about.

[1] Newspapers and magazines were the sole means by which a 19th-century Australian poet might reach the local reading public unless able to meet the costs of publishing independently or by subscription. Newspapers paid nothing, and often marred contributions with misprints. CH's later correspondence is littered with resolutions like this one.

[2] A lifelong intention – see, e.g., Letters 22, 42 and 54 to Parkes; Letter 49 to Donaldson; Letters 113, 127 and 131 to Kendall; and Letter 133 to Mort. CH would not live to see a collected edition.

[3] Parkes was a well-established poet: see *Stolen Moments: A Short Series of Poems* (Sydney: James Tegg, 1842: online via NLA). Most of the poems had already appeared in periodicals. W. A. Duncan printed over 50 in *Australasian Chronicle*, 1840–42, and 19 in his *Weekly Register*, 1842–45. Occasional pieces had also appeared in *NSW Magazine* and Robert Lowe's *Atlas*.

[4] For the rhyme (perhaps in abbreviated form), see h223a. In a note preceding the verses (ML C382, pp. 186–8), CH explained that they were his reply to Halloran's 'Lines Written on the perusal of a poem called FINALITY, by Charles Harpur, which was published in the ATLAS of 21st August, 1847' – see *Atlas*, 28 August 1847, p. 417. CH thanked Halloran for his notice, but 'an imputation of moral weakness in the spirit of the compliment' rankled, as well as 'some thing ... unpleasantly humurous in Mr H's allusion to our comparative worldly trials'.

[5] W. J. Strang appears in the list of subscribers to Parkes's first volume *Stolen Moments* (1842); and Parkes is described as agent of W. J. Strang, 'at present in China', in a notice in *SMH*, 12 August 1847, p. 1. Martin, *Parkes* (p. 40) calls this figure W. E. Strong, then acting as Parkes's agent in Hong Kong purchasing oriental fancy goods for the Hunter-street shop. See p. 80 n. 2.

[6] Identity of Desborough is uncertain; 'long Hart' is possibly the minor poet A. B. Hart, whose verse appeared in *Sydney Times* and elsewhere (see Martin, *Parkes*, p. 40). CH had mocked Prout Hill in 1846 (see p. 21 n. 6), included him (as 'H–ll') in the 'Temple of Infamy' (see h580b), and dismissed him as a 'witling' in an 1848 squib, 'To S. P. Hill Esqr Author of "Tarquin the Proud" and other equally splendacious and never-to-be-forgotten pieces' (see h627a), unpublished until 1984.

Remember me to Mrs Parkes and the youngsters,[7] and to all enquirers—and believe

Yours ever truly
Charles Harpur

Am not I getting into a vile method of scrawling? But I mean to correct it forthwith: for evidence of which vide[8] my next letter. C.H.

Jerry's Plains 26 Sept/47

15. Charles Harpur to Henry Parkes, 4 December 1848

Text: ML MSS 947

Jerry's Plains, Decr 4th 1848.

My dear friend,

What could possess you to think me positively offended with *you*—and to talk about being the "first to humble"? To me? God forbid! If there be any sin against the spirit of friendship between us, *it must be on my part*.

The truth is, where I love much, I am somewhat disposed *to jealousy*—I cannot help it: and under some morbidity of this sort I wrote to you a letter which I would fain have recalled the moment I had despatched it. But it was *too late*—and you replied to it a *little reproachfully*. Still all you said was just—I felt that it was; and intended to have answered you immediately in a becoming and atoning spirit; and have been delayed doing so by the sole fact, that my wandering foot has been ever since lifted as it were, in the act of paying you a visit in person. Have I said enough? I trust I have; and that the price of womanish jealousy *on my part* above confessed to—being forgiven, will forever henceforth be but a "by-gone" between us.

Believe me, there is nothing in fortune could afflict me more, than to have to look back upon your friendship as amongst the good things I have lost: some through my own folly, and some through the folly of others; some wantonly, and some fatally.

Do you know that for the last 18 months I have been living the life of a hermit—utterly alone, day and night, in a sad looking house, with Mount

---

[7] At this point, 'Menie' (Clarinda Sarah), born at sea off NSW, 1839, and Robert Sydney, born 1843. CH had dedicated a sonnet 'To Robert Sydney Parkes, aged 10 Months' in 1844 (h626a). Menie would become a journalist, poet and novelist, publishing in the Sydney papers in the 1860s and 1870s as 'Patty Parsley', 'Alethea' and 'Ariel'.

[8] See (Latin).

Kobanbonia in the distance,[1] and a [lass?]less, gainless, hopeless, bookless solitude all between and around me. I see my brother about once a week, if so often, and two or three other persons on post office or pound business[2] (more pigs) twice or thrice in the same time. I wash, bake, cook, and mend &c for myself, the profits of my agency not yielding more than what will bearly clothe me. Can I be so very thin skinned then? *Hardly*; and could I but once stand fairly before my countrymen,[3] I could well submit ever afterwards even to such a condition as this. I should be quite content, could I but once say to them, in my entirety, through the press, "I am a solitary prarie tree, but I have borne fruit in my solitude: behold it; gather it; taste; and *know me aright.*"[4]— But I must jump out of this egotism.

I read your little Leader in the Atlas,[5] and liked both the spirit and style of it. And I am glad to hear the Atlas is now in such worthy hands. I had not failed both to perceive and admire a very marked improvement in it for some time.

I saw notices in the papers of the association[6] you speak of. There can be no question but that such an association is greatly needed; and I should like to see similar ones forming in every populous district: for in the present state of society, your only efficient political battering-ram, is an *Association.*

Leigh Hunt's answer to "What is Poetry?"[7] is all right. What a firm old

---

[1] The Jerry's Plains post office (usually also the postmaster's residence) is said to have been a single-room stone building on the banks of the Hunter, on a property later known as Ball's Farm, east of the present village. It would be washed away in the flood of 1857. In a note to 'Have Faith' (h170b) in *Sydney Chronicle*, 20 November 1847, p. 4, CH said Kobanbonia was 'the aboriginal name of a singular double-coned mountain, south of Jerry's Plains (Comenaroy), and overlooking the Vale of Wambo'.

[2] Joseph Jehoshaphat Harpur (1810–78), journalist, radical reformer, future Parliamentarian. He was official poundkeeper and postmaster at Jerry's Plains 1843–50.

[3] I.e., by publishing his annotated collected works (see p. 30 n. 2).

[4] Evoking the colonial wilderness of the early Quaker William Penn, founder of Pennsylvania and reputed author of *Some Fruits of Solitude in Reflections and Maxims* (1693), widely read in the nineteenth century. See also 'The Loneness of Sorrow' (h271a; 1858).

[5] Leading article (editorial) in the newspaper backed by the squatters' Pastoral Association, established in 1844 and edited at first by Robert Lowe (see p. 26 n. 3). The *Atlas* stood for local control of lands and against direct colonial rule from London. By 1848 it was no friend to the landed interests that originally sponsored it, and was printing contributions from the likes of G. W. Rusden (see p. 60 n. 2) and Parkes, who in 1848 organised a tradesmen's committee that successfully promoted Lowe for a seat in the Legislative Council.

[6] In November 1848 Parkes joined radicals in the Constitutional Association that developed out of the Lowe committee to agitate for franchise extension, representative government and land reform: see advertisements ('notices') in, e.g., *SMH*, 16 December 1848, p. 1.

[7] Leigh Hunt (1784–1859), English critic, essayist, poet and centre of the Hampstead-based 'Hunt circle' that included William Hazlitt and Charles Lamb. 'An Answer to the Question What is Poetry? Including Remarks on Versification' appeared as an introductory essay in his *Imagination and Fancy; or Selections from the Best English Poets* (London: Smith, Elder, & Co., 1844 – second edition, 1845, online at Internet Archive). CH's copy, a third edition of 1846, was given him by Parkes in 1851; it is held at ML at shelf-mark 821.08/H. CH has signed and dated the title-page '1851'.

fellow it is! with his spirit still as bright as the face of the Beautiful, and his heart as fresh as a rose bud. I cannot help fancying, how the heart of the old boy must sometimes indulge in a pleasant laugh at the expence of his grey head—being itself so juvenile. What would I not give to shake hands with him, and sit in his actual presence, as at the feet of my poetical Gamaliel,[8] *once* at least, before he is called out of Time, to join the Immortals in Eternity. But that cannot be.—

You will be glad to hear that I am very temperate. Even when my means are a little flush,[9] I never exceed in any respect. That is, I have not exceeded, for a long time. "Wisdom", you know, "(curse on it) will come soon or late." I am actually getting wise!—that is to say, (perhaps), *wiser.*

I have a world-full of questions to ask you—but I defer them, first, for want of space (as you see), and secondly, because I intend (God willing) to visit you about Christmass. I cannot positively say that I will see you at Christmass, but about that time, or shortly after, I certainly will, God willing, as I said before. I suppose you will be more at leisure then than usual—and won't I dose you?

Remember me to Mrs Parkes, and to Clarinda the younger, and to Sydney the first, whom I calculate to be a bouncing rogue[10] by this time—And believe me yourself, yours wholly,

Chas: Harpur.

Recd Dec. 9/48

---

[8] A leading authority in the Sanhedrin (rabbinical court) in the early first century AD; in Christian tradition, a Pharisee doctor of Jewish law and teacher of Paul – who declared: 'I am verily a man which am a Jew, born in Tarsus, a city in Cilicia, yet brought up in this city at the feet of Gamaliel' (Acts 22.3).

[9] Plentifully supplied (with money).

[10] See p. 31 n. 7. CH's sonnet 'To Robert Sydney Parkes, aged 10 Months' in 1844 (h626a) commenced: 'Ay, crow, rogue, crow! Thy little Being thrilling is / Like an embodied carol of a bird!' CH was apparently unaware of Mary Edith, born 3 March 1848.

16. Charles Harpur to Board of National Education, [January 1849]

Text: NSWSA: NRS-613 [1/382], f.74

The Memorial[1] of Heads of Families
and other Inhabitants of Jerry's Plains
to the National Board of Education:[2]

Humbly Sheweth,

That in the District of Jerry's Plains there are about fifty children:

That amongst the parents and guardians of these children there are persons of no less than three different religious denominations—namely, Anglicans, Presbyterians, and Roman Catholics:

That many of the children are witheld from the present Public School, and thereby deprived of all means of instruction, for the reason (amongst other reasons) of its being a denominational one:[3]

That at Several Public Meetings, which were attended by nearly all the householders of the district, certain resolutions in favor of the National System of Education (and consequently *against* the denominational one) were unanimously adopted:

That moreover, the masters provided for the denominational school now obtaining in the district, have been all along notoriously incompetent, uneducated men, and thrust into the Situation without respect to the interests of the Inhabitants generally, as parents and guardians, and in contempt also, in the instance of the last appointment,[4] of their unanimous recommendation of a more competent Individual:

That under these circumstances, your Memorialists, though too poor to raise immediately a sufficient sum of money to enable them even with the

---

[1] An undated draft or copy of a memorial, signed by CH, dating between the residents' meeting of 30 December 1848 where CH's brother Joseph proposed there be an application 'for government aid towards the establishing of a school under the general system of education at Jerry's Plains' (*Maitland Mercury*, 6 January 1849, p. 2) and 14 January 1849, when a favourable response from the Board of National Education was reported (*Maitland Mercury*, 17 January 1849, p. 2).

[2] The Board of National Education in Sydney, responsible for administering the NSW National School system introduced in 1848. The Board granted aid (see below) normally only to schools with a minimum of thirty pupils and was responsible for the appointment of teachers, teacher training and the inspectorial system.

[3] From 1848 schools in NSW operated by the four main religious denominations – Anglican, Catholic, Presbyterian and Wesleyan – were supported by government grants through the Denominational School Board. At local level each school was under the control of a Local Board nominated by the relevant church authority. The school at Jerry's Plains was run by the Church of England.

[4] The schoolmaster at the denominational school at Jerry's Plains in 1848–49 was John Elliot – see Returns of the Colony, Return of the Number of Schools, &c., 1848 (p. 568) and 1849 (p. 614).

proferred aid of your honorable Board,[5] to build a National School House, are yet willing to contribute their quota towards the rent and furnishing of a premises now vacant and very convenient for the purposes of tuition:

That your Memorialists beg finally to submit to the judgment of your honorable Board, the propriety (under all the facts above stated) of at once extending to their district the boon of the National System of Education.

And your Memorialists, in the event of the compliance of the Board with this (they believe) their very reasonable request, will, as in duty bound, ever pray &c. &c.

Chas: Harpur.

17. Charles Harpur to Henry Parkes, 28 June 1849
Text: ML MSS 947

Jerry's Plains, 28 June, /49.

Dear Parkes,

I thank you for the papers you have occasionally sent me—and in short for being in any way remembered by you.—But to come at once to the main purpose of this note—it is intended, mind, as nothing more, the long letter full of all sorts of loveables which I intend writing *immediately* being altogether another thing. Besids were I ever so inclined to pour out the wine of my heart just now, I lack the time.—But to the main purpose hinted above. There is a packet in the office[6] addressed to me in your hand—containing I think tobacco—and charged 14s/8d postage. Of course I have declined releasing it till I hear from you; when if its contents are of less value than the postage, I shall have nothing to do but *refuse* it. It will be then returned to the general Post office and enclosed in a cover addressed to you as the writer or first owner. On this cover, however, "Returned Letter" will be printed, and when presented to you, you will know by the size and feel and, above all, by the amount of postage (14/8) the packet to be the same, and being at perfect liberty to do so,—*refuse it also*: and in this way we shall both escape a serious loss,[7] the hardness of the levies considered.

In conclusion—for the present—how are you? And how is Mrs Parkes, Bob, Clarinda, and all?

---

[5] The aid was intended to help finance the erection and fitting out of the premises and the acquisition of schoolbooks and other supplies. The local community was expected to contribute at least one-third of the capital costs of establishing and maintaining its school, to offset part of the cost of the teacher's salary by the payment of school fees, and to form a school committee of 'local patrons' to manage the affairs of the school.

[6] The Jerry's Plains post office.

[7] CH's strategy backfired – see Letter 18.

Suppose here all the questions that one who esteems you and yours as much—perhaps more,—than he does any other of his friends, ought to ask—

And believe me
Yours ever truly
Chas: Harpur.

Excuse haste.

18. Charles Harpur to Henry Parkes, 26 July 1849

Text: ML MSS 947

Jerry's Plains, July, 1849.

Dear Hal,[1]

"Prepend," as bold Pistol saith[2]—and that is nearly all the prose, I think, you will get out of me in this letter—which, mind you, is not the "long one" I promised you the other day;[3] though it will be quite long enough of itself very likely.

To Henry Parkes, on re-reading his
Sonnet beginning "Who would not be a Poet?"[4]

"Who would not be a Poet?"—thus I read
In thy proud Sonnet, my harmonious Friend;
And then the streamy lines still led
My utterance on—but at the end
The question made me ponder, and let pass
The Poet; seeing that for aye, alas!
A Man of Sorrows he is doomed to be.
Yet thus far my assent was given:
There is not under the dome of heaven
Aught happier in itself than the witch Poesie.

---

[1] Henry Parkes. CH also used 'Hal' (a diminutive form of 'Henry') as an endearment for Henry Kendall (Letter 84) – perhaps alluding to 'bluff King Hal' in Walter Scott's *Marmion* (1808) and thus implying frank, good-natured (see *OED*, *bluff* 2b); and also here, given the next reference, Hal, the future Henry V, in Shakespeare's history plays.

[2] I.e., *perpend*, to ponder or consider: 'Perpend my words, O Signieur Dew, and mark' – Pistol to French Soldier, in Shakespeare's *Henry V*, IV.4.8.

[3] See Letter 17.

[4] CH transcribes here the text of a poem he had revised extensively, apparently for the occasion: see h611. Parkes's 'Sonnet' had appeared in *Australasian Chronicle*, 1 June 1841, p. 1 and subsequently in his *Stolen Moments* (1842), p. 131.

What is not spell-touched by her wingèd Powers?
See those happy creatures, flowers,
Even where they sweetest be
Blest into beauty by the genial hours—
There, as they breathe into the day
Their soul of fragrance, should but we
Name them in verse, Or are not even they
Then sweeter for the breath of rapturous Poesie?

    Yea, Love itself is earthy, till betimes,
Upon the bosom of her mystery
We lay it, like a wayward child,
Hushing its nature wild
With honey-flowing but truth-tempered rhymes,
Distilled from all things sweet that be,
And wrought from all that most sublimes
In Nature hand in hand with passionate Poesie!

    But "who'd not be a Poet?"—there I pause
Forebodingly; because,
To see "all beauty with his gifted sight,"[5]
To love like him with all the soul,
To be where life is bright
The very creature of Delight—
Delight beyond control!
Is ever still to be,
Even in the same degree,
Too sensitive of loss and images of dole.

    There was an earnest-thoughted Boy, that still
Had to himself proposed thy question, till
His swelling heart and throbbing head
Flowed with the tunefulness he coveted.
He loved to stray alone, this studious Creature,
Yet was not solitary, but apart;
For to his eye and ear and heart,
Each prospect, tone, and trick of Nature,
Was still a grand, or sweet, or lovely feature;
And temperingly with these,
Her veriest simplicities,
Even with his body's growth, nourished his spirit's stature.

---

[5] See Parkes's 'Sonnet', line 10.

And thus accomplished only, to the fight
Of life's dishonest battle did he come;
To meet instead of Valor mean Despite;
To see unblushing Fortune doom
To some repute unholy,
Or to some miserable estate,
All such as would not trample on the lowly,
Or glorify the falsely great;
Or for a hireling's sordid pay
Defend the oppressor and belie the opprest:
And so at last he turned from *all* away,
Even those he loved the best,
To brood with a proud bitterness apart,
O'er dead yet lovely hopes—a quick yet broken heart.

Tell me at length what you think of that. And now, are you yet quite aware, think you, of what a d—d many-sided son of a gun, your humble servent, my own sweet self, is in reality? Let us see.

To the Same.[1]

I sometimes wish my Muse a Monthly Nurse,[2]
Or something else—or even something worse!
For here I'm still "Poor Jack"—*without* "the shiners",[3]
And thence unwelcome to all sorts of diners!
Whilst others clip their fleecy flocks, and store
Bright gold, I've only so much verse the more!
Gainless, however gainful be the times;
Even you turn ivory[4]—I nought but rhymes!
A vagrant—and the cause still, all along,
This damn'd unconquerable love of song!

I'll cut it yet, though! and, the mans devising,
Can't we get up an Act 'gainst poetising?
I'll cut it—yes! as all my advisers bid me,
And get as rich as any Jew in Sydney.

---

[1] See h608, not published until 1984.
[2] A nurse who attends a mother during the first month after childbirth.
[3] From the old broadside ballad 'Jack Returned from Sea': 'Here I am Poor Jack, / Just come home from sea, / With shiners [i.e., money] in my sack, / Pray what do you think of me' (example at National Library of Scotland).
[4] See p. 29 n. 4.

That is, I mean to turn an Auctioneer,
And take to buying cheap and selling dear.
Gods! how I'll puff[5] the "lots" I'll have to class—
Even Stubbs[6] shall stand astonished at my *brass*!
Stale cheese shall be ambrosia, and sour Cape[7]
The blessèd vintage of any heaven-grown grape
Filched by Prometheus, and for which Jove's ire
Was thundered at him—*not for filching fire*:[8]
Nay, even Gin half yellow[9] to the eyes
Shall be the very cream of Paradise!
And when I think of what I'll do for Rum
However hell-fire-ish—but all that's to come.
Then lands beneath my hammer, which a rat
Would starve, shall wax than Lombardy more fat;
Shall utter forth a murmurous song of streams,
And glow with verdure!

          Are not *those* the dreams
To foster? Is not *that* the one design
For which 'twere well to cut the coinless Nine?[10]
Being the *sole one* that 'mongst Australia's sons can
E'er make me great: they're all such *Number Ones*,[11] man.

    I'm serious.—Henceforth I'm a son of pelf!
But honest: hark, how I advise myself:
"Let no low trick of Trade, Charles, be *thy* trick;
Nor cut out aught that makes men "cut their stick",[12]
And then, "their lucky"—if they've luck to do it;
If not, the[y're] sure unluckily to rue it:
Though quite the dealer, always *cut* the sharper;
Or Parkes, thy friend, will have to *cut*

                        "Charles Harpur".

---

[5] Praise, extol or commend extravagantly or unduly.

[6] Thomas Stubbs (1802–78), the leading auctioneer in Sydney of the 1840s.

[7] Wine of poor quality imported from the Cape of Good Hope, South Africa.

[8] The Titan Prometheus defied the gods by stealing fire and giving it to humankind. For this transgression Zeus had him bound eternally to a rock, where each day an eagle gorged upon his liver, which grew back at night.

[9] Cheap gin was often adulterated with substances, some noxious, to enhance its taste.

[10] The nine Muses.

[11] 'Number one' is oneself (as in 'to look after number one') – used in the refrain of 'The Great Guns of Squatocracy' (1845, h564a).

[12] Take their departure, be off; 'the idea being that of cutting a staff for one's journey': Eric Partridge, *A Dictionary of Slang and Unconventional English* (London: Routledge and Kegan Paul, n.d.; via Internet Archive), p. 201.

Now trusting that you have been a good and attentive boy thus far, I will even treat you to such a sufficing mouthful of the real native Charley-Harpurian-honey as you have not had this many a long day. It is a drop from my "Wild Bee of Australia"[1]—in lieu of which title a lady suggested the other day (in all sincerity) that I should call it "The Book of Wisdom Love and Beauty". What do you think of that? But enough of nonsense—and what do think of this?

How I woo'd and won my true love.[2]

I sung her bright songs, not of splendor and fashion,
But of Love, when his nectar he sips;
And still as I sung them, I acted the passion;
[Till] I [knew] it [was] secretly big at her heart[3]—
Till I saw it flash forth in her glances, and part
Like a ripe double cherry her lips.

Then gently I drew her still nearer and nearer,
When she made—O the aptest of slips!
And I felt as we neared, that each grew to each dearer;
Till daring the worst, like a madman, I prest
The rosiest, balmiest mouth ever kissed!—
And her heart came away with my lips.

If that has n't made your mouth moistish, I don't know what would be likely to do it—nay, it must be as dry as a brick. But it has.

[continued next page

---

[1] See p. 58 n. 1.
[2] See h258, retitled 'Love Budding' in later versions; not published until 1984.
[3] A fold in the paper in MS along the middle of this line makes these emendations uncertain, but they reflect the next version's deleted readings replaced by revised ones: see h258b.

(For the People's Advocate[4])

Wentworth.
(from an unpublished Satire.[5])

First come the Magnates[6]—lo, their Leader—he,
The would-be Tell of the Fraternity.[7]
His state is that, so infamously sad,
When Talent has through selfishness run mad.
In his well-masked displays of by-gone years,
With democratic wrath he tore the ears
Of Sydney's wealthiest groundlings—being then
Thwarted and snubbed by Darling's party-men:[8]
But *now*, behold him, in his native hue,
The bullying, bellowing champion of the Few!

A Patriot?—*he* who hath nor sense nor heed
Of public ends beyond his *own* mere need!
Whose Country's ruin to his public fear
Means only this—the loss of Windermere![9]
And by the same self-legislative rule,
Australia's growth the growth of Wentworth's wool

[4] See p. 45 n. 8.

[5] William Charles Wentworth (1790–1872), explorer, author, barrister, newspaper proprietor, squatter and statesman, a prominent figure in the early history of the colony. Native-born, son of a convict mother, Wentworth in the 1820s and 1830s was the champion of emancipists and small settlers. His powerful advocacy for a free press, trial by jury and representative government made him a popular hero. But as his wealth grew he became more conservative, siding with pastoral vested interests. Radicals such as CH and his brother Joseph became disgusted at what they deemed Wentworth's betrayal. The following lines would form part of 'The Temple of Infamy: A Satire' (h580b). 'Wentworth' (h713b) would be published, with its footnote, in *PA*, 18 August 1849, p. 6. CH elaborated on Wentworth's 'greatness' in a manuscript footnote to this poem dated September 1849 (ML C376, h713d). See also 'A New Song to a Queer Tune' (h332a), 'Is Wentworth a Patriot?' (h536a), 'Wentworth Again' (h545a), 'Wentworth's Council Dream' (h550a), 'The Great Guns of Squatocracy' (h564a) and 'Wentworth's Constitutional Myth' (h673a).

[6] The rich and powerful pastoralists, who effectively controlled the part-elected Legislative Council, of which Wentworth was the de facto leader.

[7] I.e. the brotherhood of the legendary 14th-century Swiss folk hero William Tell, slayer of the tyrant Gessler, his act supposedly inciting the rebellion which led to the foundation of the Swiss Confederacy. Tell emerged as a symbol of resistance to aristocratic rule in the revolutions of 1848–49 against the Habsburgs.

[8] Supporters of Ralph Darling (1772–1858), Governor of NSW 1824–31. Attempts by the military-minded Darling to curb an outspoken press ignited a feud with Wentworth, then publisher of the *Australian* and the colony's leading agitator for civil liberties.

[9] Wentworth's country estate between Maitland and Singleton on the Hunter River, leased from his friend and business associate Thomas White Winder.

Her rights—her liberties—for Number One,
A universal ten-pound right of Run![1]
Who now his emptied purse, a second time,
Would store through the base sweat of British crime![2]
Crime that, transplanted here, would make the brand
Of "Felonry" indellible on the land!

A Patriot?—*he* from whose statistic care,
All that his Country's general homes should bear
Of mind and happiness, is thrust by that
(Wer't men, no matter,) which, when boiled, yields fat;[3]
And which, when given Europe-ward to swim,
May purchase pomps for dunghill lords like him!

Such is yon Man, and not a whit belied!
A Patriot?—let him "doff that lion's hide",[4]
And being, *seem* the scandal of his race,
Venal in soul as vulgar in his face!
Let him read these—and wincing, feign a laugh;
No matter:—they'll outlast his epitaph! ✕

C.H.

✕ It has always been a puzzle to really large-minded, full-hearted men, by what *outre* and antipodean combination of circumstances, this man could ever have been lifted into prime political eminence. As an orator, he is a mere blearer.[5] As a statesman, he is crudity personified. A[s] a lawyer, he is but so so; consistency he has none: and for *patriotism*—but listen to Doll Tearsheet's dissertation on the words *Captain* and *occupy*. "Captain! thou abominable damnëd cheater, art thou not ashamed to be called—captain? ✕✕✕ You a captain, you slave! for what? ✕✕✕ A Captain! these villains will make the word captain as odious as the word *occupy*; which was an excellent good word

---

[1] Depasturing (or squatting) licence for an area of grazing land upon payment to the government of £10 per annum.
[2] From his seat in the Legislative Council in 1846–47 – and after the measure was proposed by London – Wentworth led the argument for the reintroduction of transportation of British convicts to NSW as a source of cheap labour. The policy was abandoned following mass demonstrations in Sydney.
[3] When the price of wool tumbled in the economic depression of the early 1840s many graziers were saved from ruin by boiling down their animals for tallow, used for candles. Wentworth was a pioneer of the process, at his estates Vaucluse in Sydney and Windermere (see his advertisement in *Maitland Mercury*, 24 August 1844, p. 1).
[4] 'Thou wear a lion's hide! doff it for shame, / And hang a calf's-skin on those recreant limbs' – Shakespeare, *King John*, III.1.128–9.
[5] Deceiver, hoodwinker: Wentworth was a powerful and pugnacious orator.

before it was ill sorted: therefore *captains* had need look to it."[6] Now, the word patriot is undergoing a process precisely analogous to this at the dirty hands of our Pistolian "Billy Winfords",[7] who will eventually make it as disreputable as the term "white washing", which was a good one enough before it was roguishly applied:[8] therefore *patriots* had need look to it.

P.S. The above lines were written two or three years since—all but the four in italics, which were recently introduced; and the occasion of which has set the author upon tracing out, in plain but pounding prose, the brassy career of our so called great Australian Patriot! Of his private character, of course, as he cares nothing, we shall say nothing. It is that huge blind boil, the legislative part of him,—that alone which he has to lay open to the pestilent core. (And a nasty job it is!) It is his political consistency—or rather inconsistency that he has to compel into the broad daylight—as a big-blustering but surely detected felon is dragged, say, into the Sydney Police Court—with, however, Jemmy Martin[9] to plead for him. Long-eared Jemmy, who butters Wentworth to his face, descriptively, as "that great man!" But lord, it's quite natural. The veriest pimple of a human head—even Jemmy's own—is a mountain to a louse: and the two together are perfectly and analogically suggestive of the reason whereby it comes that "Billy Wentworth" is really a *great* man to Jemmy Martin.

C.H.

No more at present for I must turn to and make up the Mails—Let me hear from you soon

   Oh: I had nearly forgot the packet[10]—damn it! But the tobacco was prime— but then the postage sticks in my gizzard, and in yours too I apprehend.

---

[6] See Shakespeare, *2 Henry IV*, II.4.149–61. The word 'Captain' is 'contaminated by the vile nature of the person it designates…any word can become an insult if it is "ill sorted" and becomes pregnant with negative connotations': Nathalie Vienne-Guerrin, *Shakespeare's Insults: A Pragmatic Dictionary* (London: Bloomsbury Academic, 2016), p. 93.

[7] Nickname for William Charles Wentworth, used by CH and others. Also appearing as 'Windford', it perhaps derived from a combination of Wentworth and Winder. In the poem 'Wentworth' (h713b) it is printed as 'Winfends' (*PA*, 18 August 1849, p. 6).

[8] Clearing a person from liability for debts, especially by judicial declaration of bankruptcy. The NSW *Insolvent Act* of 1841, made necessary by the recession, saw insolvencies proliferate, with some unscrupulous debtors using the provisions of the so-called 'whitewash act' to avoid their creditors.

[9] James (later, Sir James) Martin (1820–86), politician and future chief justice of NSW. An ambitious, able and successful lawyer, Martin was an ally of conservatives Wentworth and William Bland in the colony's first elections of 1843. Hence 'Long-eared', i.e., like a donkey: cf. the later poem 'Marvellous Martin' (h280b). He had ridiculed CH in his allegorical satire 'The Pseudo-Poets' in his *Australian Sketch Book* (1838) – see above, p. xxiii.

[10] Parkes had sent CH a gift of tobacco leaving him to pay postage of 14s.8d., a cost he could barely afford – see Letters 17 and 18.

You should have let me sent it back and refused it also in turn. Fourteen & eightpence! By the lord! I have not myself had so much money, over and above my daily necessities,—not any time these two years! Remember me to all friends, and

believe me, Hal, yours
With all my heart,
Chas: Harpur.
26th July 1849[1]

19. Charles Harpur to Henry Parkes, 20 November 1849

Text: ML MSS 947

Jerry's Plains, 20th Novr /49.

Dear Parkes,

I am in receipt of your last: and with regard to the matters first mentioned in it—viz: the enclosure of the £1,[2] and the starting of the Dwarf,[3]—I did not allude to those things, because ever since the receipt of that letter (and indeed for long before) I expected to be tramping Sydneyward, where I should be able to discuss all matters of overstanding interest that might be between us (the above included) face to face: being fully determined to leave this part for many reasons—and for Sydney; because even though I should not be able to get any permanent employment there, I could yet (at the worst) suit myself to a shepherd's berth or what not, much more readily through the Registry Offices,[4] and more to my satisfaction as to locality &c. in Sydney, than I could in this most hateful and miserable district. The truth is, no man out of an ironed gang[5] has lived a more lonely, profitless, uncomfortable and hopeless life than I have for the last twelvemonth. So much for my condition here.

---

[1] CH's complimentary close, signature and date were at some point removed from this letter and pasted onto one of two leaves tipped-in before the title-page in a copy of CH's *Poems* (1883) signed by D. S. Mitchell and now held in ML at DSM/a821/H295/5A1.

[2] Possibly reimbursement for the postage CH had to pay on Parkes's gift of tobacco.

[3] A reference in *SMH*, 15 July 1850, p. 3 to 'Our Dwarf's Anticipatory Report' shows the term was at first a journalist's byline in *Representative: A Daily Journal of the Election*, issued by Parkes and David Blair during July 1850 to support the election to the Legislative Council of the Reverend John Dunmore Lang. But the meaning evidently shifted to refer to Parkes's *Empire* as a whole, e.g., 'The day [the Anniversary Regatta of 1851] will doubtlessly be observed as a general holiday by all in Sydney, except the Dwarf and Giant Daily papers' (*Empire*, 27 January 1851, p. 3).

[4] Privately run registry offices in the towns recruited servants – including shepherds, hutkeepers and farm hands – for up-country settlers. A typical advertisement is in *Bathurst Advocate*, 24 February 1849, p. 3.

[5] Also 'iron gang', a party of convicts kept in iron chains, usually employed in road-building.

A word as to my Californian project.[6] Of course I do not think it "all gold that glitters *even* there."[7] But there, at all events, one might have Hope for a companion. But here, I at least am denied the questionable benefit of being even cheated by Hope—for I cannot entertain her at all.

With regard to an engagement at the Advocate Office,[8] I should prefer, if it could be so arranged, to enter it at first as a sort of Jack of all work—an occasional contributor, corrector of the Press, labeller of newspapers,—any thing in short: nor would I care about being hard worked in such a capacity; and for remuneration I should only expect what would roughly lodge feed and clothe me. Such an apprentiship I think would be almost necessary to my thoroughly understanding the position I was eventually to fulfil as a regular writer for the paper.

But could you start the Dwarf, and let me be *your* man Jack?[9] Let it be half literary half political—and then see if *we together* cannot astonish the natives!

Let me hear from you again as soon as convenient, and

believe me
Yours truly
Chas: Harpur.

What of the Warragl—the wild dog?[10] Shall I bring him if I come?

---

[6] With the discovery of gold in California in 1848 (preceding the first Australian rush by three years) adventurers and whole families flocked across the Pacific to try their luck. CH was evidently tempted.

[7] Reversing the proverbial phrase 'all that glitters is not gold'.

[8] The *People's Advocate and New South Wales Vindicator* (abbreviated in notes as *PA)* was established in 1848 by chartist Edward John Hawksley (1807–75) and Francis Cunninghame. It was the organ of the Constitutional Association established by Parkes and his radical friends after they had achieved the election in June 1848 of Robert Lowe. Published December 1848 – late 1856, it was edited or co-edited by Hawksley. Parkes contributed leaders and political verse during its first year, and presumably had influence there. It is not known if CH was ever employed by the paper but he was a regular contributor of poems and letters over the next eight years.

[9] The average or common person, as in 'every man jack' (*OED*), echoing 'Jack of all work' (as above) or 'all trades' – a person able to do many different types of work.

[10] The dingo, *Canis familiaris*, a dog native to Australia (now usually spelled 'warrigal', from Dharug *warigal*, dingo). See footnote *d* in second set of footnotes to 'The Kangaroo Hunt' (h209-cc).

20. Charles Harpur to Henry Parkes, 23 February 1850

Text: ML MSS 947

Jerry's Plains 23rd Feby. 1850.

Dear Parkes,

The request I am about to make (a request long delayed in the vain hope that something would turn up here to prevent the need that occasions it), I wish you to comply with only in case that your means are such as *perfectly* to justify your doing so: for I hold with poor Burns, that

"A frien' may wish a body weel,
Yet hae na cash to spare him."[1]

But to my request. I am utterly aground; and in this strait, purpose opening a day-school at Singleton,[2] but want an outfit. About five pounds would help me to right ship, and can you advance me as much; trusting to my honor for repayment of the amount the moment my means may enable me to do so.?

When I settle myself, I will write to you of many things, which ask for friendly utterance and sympathy.

Meanwhile, believe me yours truly,

Chas: Harpur.

P. S. The Mastership of the Public school here[3] becoming vacant a short time since, I applied for it, supporting my application by a Recommendation signed by *the head of every family in the district*. Still the berth was refused—and upon what grounds, think you? Why, because I was not a constant attendant at church, and was supposed or said to hold radical opinions! And this is fraternity and public justice in Australia. But wait awhile.

C. H.

---

[1] Misquoted from 'Epistle to a Young Friend' by Scottish poet Robert Burns (1759–96): 'A man may tak a neebor's part, / Yet hae nae cash to spare him.'

[2] Joseph Harpur's time as postmaster and poundkeeper at Jerry's Plains would end in March 1850. CH, his proxy there, was evidently on the lookout for fresh employment, but there is no evidence he started a school at the nearby town, Singleton.

[3] Church of England denominational school at Jerry's Plains, the board of which was chaired by local chaplain the Reverend Joseph Cooper. The mastership, which paid £30 a year, was awarded to Richard Harrison (see Returns of the Colony, Return of the Number of Schools, &c., 1850 and 1851). By mid-year CH had set up a small private school of his own at Jerry's Plains (see the community's reference for CH, 24 May 1851, in *Suppl. Letters*).

21. Charles Harpur to Henry Parkes, 1 April 1850

Text: ML MSS 947

Jerry's Plains, 1st April 1850.

My dear Parkes,

I am surprised, pained, and disappointed, at not having at least heard from you in reply to my last, in which, as you requested, I explained fully my present condition.

Still, I can no more believe your professions of friendship hollow, than I can believe that God is a *Jesuit.*

In that letter I told you that I was endeavouring to get the General System of Education[4] extended to this district, with an eye to the Mastership. But after drawing up a Memorial for that purpose, and getting it well signed, it was useless to send it in, as looking to the people to do [a]ny more—that is, though heartily ready to put down [their?] names, they had no h[e]art (being indeed very poor—that's my case) to [put?] up their quota,—a third, the Board giving two thirds,[5]—of [the] expense of establishing t[he] School.[6] Thus, in that direction also, I am now aground. I must now try my luck [on?] some other: and [to that end?], will you read [sign?] then seal and cause the enclosed letter to [be?] delivered to Na[tion?] the Printer.

I remain yours, truly.
Chas Harpur.

Excuse poverty, and haste.[7] A line by return of Post will be gratifying.

P.S. I have not enclosed, as I intended, the letter for Nation,[8] not having paper just now fit to copy it on. It is simply an offer to give him the entire profits

---

[4] The NSW National School system, established in 1848 and modelled on the Irish national system.

[5] See p. 35 n. 5.

[6] National School agent and inspector G. W. Rusden, visiting Jerry's Plains on his tour of the Hunter, noted: 'Mr C Harpur to give memorial to me', and 'Jerry's Plains failure & reasons. Memorial re renting' (Diary entry, 8 April [1850], Rusden papers GWR061, Trinity College, University of Melbourne). Jerry's Plains would wait until 1881 for its public school.

[7] CH wrote his letter on a blank official form used for monthly returns of impounded cattle sold at the pound – see *NSW Government Gazette*, 11 July 1840, p. 667.

[8] Presbyterian printer William Nation (1818–1903), publisher of the short-lived *Layman's Prompter* where only two of CH's poems appeared, both as 'A Leaf from Charles Harpur's "Wild Bee of Australia" ': the sonnet 'Andrew Marvel' (8 January 1850, h010c) and 'Rhymes to a Lady, with a Copy of Love Poems' (8 March 1850, h477c – and see CH's fragmentary letter to Parkes of 12 March: in *Suppl. Letters*).

of my "Wild Bee"[1] if he will publish it, say, in Numbers, and give myself employment afterward during my necessary superintendence of the publication—just enough employment otherwise, at any thing, to keep me alive. I believe, if I could once come fairly before my Country, in that work, I could do well enough afterwards. At all events, I believe, that when once in possession of it, my Countrymen would not "willingly let *it* die"[2]—whatever they might will with regard to *myself.*

Yours &c C.H.

22. Charles Harpur to Henry Parkes, 22 August 1850

Text: ML MSS 947

Jerry's Plains, 22 August / 50

Dear Parkes,

Had I "followed suit"—that is, imitate[d] the introductory coldness of your own last letter, I should have headed this "Dear Sir"—and not as usual, "Dear Parkes". That was the *first letter* I ever recd from you that was not initiated with the words "Dear Harpur". *Dear Sir* instead! How frosty!—but enough of that.

I did not before acknowledge you[r] remittance (£2) which came very seasonably,—because as it was contained in a "Registered" Letter, I supposed my rect[3] for it to the Post office qui[te] enough for awhile—until something besides should turn up worth writing about.

I have just read of you[r] great second meeting at the Circular Wharf for the purpose of damning Fitzroy's most infamous Dispatch and himself together.[4] It was glorious.

---

[1] 'Charles Harpur's Wild Bee of Australia', a collection of poems, some with prose notes, written or revised 1849–53, which CH intended for book publication. Two bearing the collective title would appear in *Layman's Prompter* and over 20 in *PA*; the remainder stayed in manuscript (ML C376).

[2] Echoing John Milton: 'that by labour and intent study (which I take to be my portion in this life), joyn'd with the strong propensity of nature, I might perhaps leave something so written to aftertimes, as they should not willingly let it die' – *The Reason of Church-Government Urged against Prelaty*, Preface to Book II (1642).

[3] Rec[eip]t for a registered letter. This would be returned to the General Post Office, Sydney, to confirm delivery.

[4] In fact, the third such demonstration. On 11 June 1849 a mass anti-transportation protest at Circular Quay in Sydney greeted the convict ship *Hashemy*. Parkes had figured prominently in organising and addressing it and penning the remonstrance. A second 'meeting' was held the following week. When the text of Governor FitzRoy's despatch to London was revealed in *SMH*, 9 August 1850, p. 3 – he dismissed the protesters as idlers and their leaders as agitators – Parkes and the radicals organised a mass meeting on 12 August at Circular Quay and the gates of Government House calling for the abolition of transportation, the removal of FitzRoy, and responsible government for NSW.

It is needless to say that I admire the political conduct of yourself and the liberals of Sydney—being myself on "Auld Lang's side".[5] But you must be wary, I tell you. The more of Responsible Government you get just yet—will only be just so much more of evil—that is, will only strengthen the devilism of our Present Wool-Kings.[6] In a Note to my Tree of Liberty, I have said with reference to any great governmental change, what you will find to be the fact: "Preparatory to any such issue, we must have an entirely new set of leading men;—men to whom sheep and wool, and oxen and tallow, and wages down at the Zero of Serfdom,[7] are not every thing worthy of account in this our virgin Land of Australia—this so meet cradle for a new birth of Liberty." And where *now* is this new set of leading men? *Lang?* He's a host in himself certainly—but that won't do. We must "wait a little longer." Still, perhaps, if I saw from a nearer point of view, how the political elements are working in Sydney, I might think more hopefully.

But are there, think you, five thousand men in Sydney who would be willing to fight upon a pinch? If there are not—we may talk largely and all that, but our burthens will still lump our shoulders for many years to come. We shall see.

Now of myself. I am married—and to Rosa;[8] and were I a little better

[5] John Dunmore Lang (1799–1878), Presbyterian clergyman, journalist and politician, had proclaimed his republicanism in lectures in April 1850 and soon after, with Parkes (at the height of his radicalism), James Wilshire and others, founded the Australian League, dedicated to the independence of the Australian colonies and their federation into the 'United Provinces of Australia'. In July 1850, when Lang was elected to represent Sydney in the Legislative Council largely thanks to the efforts of Parkes as campaign secretary, his supporters toasted him and roared 'Auld Lang's Side' (Martin, *Parkes*, p. 65) in parody of Burns's famed 'Auld Lang Syne'.

[6] The powerful pastoralists who dominated NSW politics and on whom CH reflected in a note to a manuscript version of 'The Tree of Liberty' in 1849: 'But though utterly a republican in my politics, speculatively, I yet believe, that it will be best for Australia to continue during the present century (at the very least) a part of the British monarchy. For even the state-botches of Downing Street are full fifty years in advance of our present half educated wool-kings; and such forms of Government therefore, as they may from time to time fabricate for us, though upon the most thread bare models, will be altogether preferable to any things of the kind which the latter would or could tinker up in the event of a premature separation' (ML C376, h644d). While the poem had been published in 1845 without a note (h644a), words very close to those next quoted can be found in the 1849 version.

[7] A settler could recoup much or all of the wages he paid his workers by selling them at inflated prices the food, clothing and provisions they needed: see letter from 'H. B., One of the Working Classes' (*SMH*, 20 March 1844, p. 4).

[8] CH and Mary Ann Doyle, daughter of Edmund and Frances Doyle of Eulengo and Montrose Park, Jerry's Plains, were married on 2 July 1850 at Great Lodge, Jerry's Plains, the estate of the Doyles's neighbour Richard Hobden, by the Reverend James Smith White, Presbyterian Minister of St Andrew's Church, Singleton. Their courtship had been a long one: CH's first love poems for Mary had appeared in 1843 ('The Lass of Ulengo', h283a; 'On First Seeing Rosa', h418a). The 'Rosa' sonnets were written 1843–50, some of them, Parkes claimed, when CH was staying with him in Sydney (see his annotation in Clarinda Parkes's copy of *Thoughts*, ML C378); they would be gathered by C. W. Salier as *'Rosa': Love Sonnets to Mary Doyle by Charles Harpur* ([Melbourne]: Hutchinson, 1948).

circumstanced I should be perfectly happy. I am keeping a small school here, by which I can just make ends meet, and barely. Do you know of any thing better in Sydney? Do you think I could do any thing, with your assistance in the matter of engaging subscribers, towards publishing a volume of Poems[1]—a well selected collection? I say "with your assistance", in particular, because you seem to have a great deal of influence in Sydney in other matters;[2] and any exercise of the same influence in my favor could not but essentially serve me—and would certainly be serving as well,—you know not perhaps to what degree,—the good cause of Australian freedom and popular intelligence. You would be thereby serving also, I believe speak[in]g generally the interests of Truth: for the following closing par: from a General Preface which I have prepard for my first publication of any extent, is as truly a part of my nature, as is the blood in my very heart.

"And with thus much premised, I have launched forth upon the stormy waters of the world my poetical Argo—not so much in quest of the golden fleece[3] of its material favor, as to test by the verdict of its best heads, the validity of the belief I have hitherto most studiously cherished, and upon the altar of which I have sacrificed nearly all the gains and pleasures and appearances which most men alone value,—the belief that it is in my destiny if I *will* it, to do something worthily for the mind and heart of my Country, and for the intellectual advantage of Man. Finally, I would say to all—Read my Book; but cautiously—thinkingly: for if I know myself at all, I would neither mislead nor be misled. May that only of its contents which is true to the Good and the Beautiful, to Humanity and Nature, to Virtue and Liberty;—may that only survive its perusal. *That* only, at all events, is all that can ultimately survive."[4]

I have exhausted my space: and I write this with a wretched steel pen.[5] So you must make all necessary allowances for the various kinds of short comings in this—until you hear from me again—which shall be immediately on my

---

[1] See p. 30 n. 1.

[2] By late 1850 Parkes was deeply involved in radical and liberal causes. He was a regular contributor to newspapers, the organising force behind the elections to the Legislative Council of Robert Lowe in 1848 and John Dunmore Lang in 1850, advocate of universal male suffrage through the Constitutional Association of 1848 and of independence and federation through the Australian League, and prominent in the mass anti-transportation protests of 1849–50. By December 1850 he had established his own newspaper, the *Empire*, 'destined to be the chief organ of mid-century liberalism and to serve as the rallying and reconciliation point for the sharpest radical and liberal minds of the day' (*ADB*). In early 1852 he would pass his Hunter-street fancy goods shop to his nephew Thomas, dedicating himself to a life of journalism and politics.

[3] Jason, leader of the Argonauts, set out in his ship the *Argo* to retrieve the Golden Fleece – recounted by Apollonius of Rhodes in his 1st-century BC epic the *Argonautica*.

[4] This paragraph is a quotation from the Preface of 'Wild Bee of Australia': see Letter 28 and p. 105 n. 2.

[5] A pen with a steel nib. These began to replace quill pens in the 1820s, and were being mass-produced in Birmingham by the 1840s.

hearing from yourself.

Remember me kindly to Mrs Parkes, and tell her I should like of all things to introduce her to "my Mary."

Hoping that all your little ones[6]—how many are they now?—are well; and that you yourself are also as well in every respect as I have always wishe[d] you to be

I am yours truly
Chas: Harpur.

23. Charles Harpur to *People's Advocate*, [by 7 September 1850]

Text: People's Advocate, 7 September 1850, p. 6

A WORD MORE OF MR. WENTWORTH.[7]
To the Editor of the People's Advocate.

SIR,—

In the postscript to certain satirical lines of mine, which were published some time since in your journal,[8] I promised to "trace out in prose the brassy career of our so-called *great* Australian Patriot." This design, however, I have since dropped, thinking the subject not worth the powder. Still, as to Mr. Wentworth, a word or two more, at this juncture, "once for all." It is still contended that he is a *great* man—the "Great Son of the Soil," and so forth. Even my friend, Henry Parkes (a greater man himself), thus unthinkingly characterises him.[9] And if indeed he is to be thus regarded as the authentic and pristine type of Australian *greatness*, God help Australia! for she must be otherwise predestined to extreme moral and mental destitution. Now, I grant to Mr. Wentworth a certain measure of rude intellectual power, and even a vast amount of selfish energy; but something of beauty and grace, and truthfulness, in addition, are necessary, to my thinking, to establish a claim to the possession of even second-rate human greatness. The qualities of justice, honesty, and fraternal faith and hope, in holy alliance with genius, or the highest order of talent—these constitute true greatness in man. But will Mr. Wentworth measure up to such a standard? Not by a thousand spiritual

---

[6] See p. 31 n. 7 and p. 33 n. 10. Milton was born in 1849 but would die in January 1851.

[7] See p. 41 n. 5.

[8] 'Wentworth (From an Unpublished Satire by Charles Harpur)' (h713b; *PA*, 18 August 1849, p. 6). CH had sent the poem in MS to Parkes on 26 July 1849 (Letter 18).

[9] The term was bandied about by Wentworth admirers such as Robert Lowe, but not in the newspapers – at least this early – by Parkes. He would incense CH when, elected in 1854 to the NSW Legislative Council in place of Wentworth, he praised the old man as one 'who, whatever his faults might be, was decidedly distinguished by a higher genius than any who had yet trod the walks of political life in this colony' (*SMH*, 3 May 1854, p. 5).

leagues![1] Productiveness of enduring good results is also an essential element and test of real greatness—that is, of greatness worthy of being publicly so called. But will Mr. Wentworth's bear any such test? What "thing of beauty"[2] has he created? What great principle has he built up and fortified for the future? What liberal and *popular* institution has he founded, or suggested, for the exaltation of man? In a word, were he dead to-morrow, what noble, or truthful, or beneficent thing, of all that he has done under the sun, would survive him as a legacy to his country and his kind? Nothing of the kind,—positively nothing! Then would it be seen, unmistakeably, that in all these regards, he was but like the barren fig tree of Scripture—a cumberer of the ground.[3] If, however, it be yet urged in behalf of his *greatness*, that in the Colonial past, he was a stickler for Trial by Jury—what of that? Had he *conceived* or *created* the thing, that indeed would have been something smacking of absolute greatness. As it was, he was but contending, from motives of mere opposition, for an obvious right—obvious to the veriest dullard; and which would have been granted as a matter of course, so soon as the colony forewent that very penal condition[4] into which he,—the same Wentworth,—would now again degrade it! And for what? That he himself, and his class, might have labour for next to nothing. Away, then, for ever with this balderdash about Wentworth's greatness!

I am, Sir,
Your obedient Servant,
CHARLES HARPUR.

24. Charles Harpur to William George Pennington, [1851]

Text: ML C383

My dear Mr Pennington.[5]

I am afraid that you will find anything but a punctual correspondent in my most negligent self; for the epistolary bee is wont to sting one very capriciously. I was always (and doubt I shall be ever) a great defaulter in this respect, as other of my friends in Sydney have perhaps told you. In fact, I do

---

[1] A league was three miles (4.8 km), supposedly the distance a person could walk in one hour.

[2] 'A thing of beauty is a joy for ever: / Its loveliness increases; it will never / Pass into nothingness' – John Keats, *Endymion*, Book I (1818).

[3] 'A certain man had a fig tree planted in his vineyard; and he came and sought fruit thereon, and found none. Then said he unto the dresser of his vineyard...cut it down; why cumbereth it the ground?' (Luke 13.6–9).

[4] See p. 42 n. 2.

[5] William George Pennington (1815?–91), solicitor, associate of Parkes, N. D. Stenhouse and Daniel Deniehy, secretary of and lecturer at Sydney Mechanics' School of Arts, leader-writer for Parkes's *Empire* in its early years and its first legal reporter (Martin, *Parkes*, p. 74). He was later an appointee to the NSW Legislative Council 1858–59.

not know of a more unpardonably remiss correspondent than myself, except Deniehy.[6] This is a bad account that I am constraind to give you of at least one of my habits, the first morning too of our epistolary forgatherment—but, alas! it is an o'er true one.

You must never look, then, for a set series of letters from hand of mine. And I enlarge on the matter (in this my second) in order that all disappointment and possibility of soreness between us, on such an account may be guarded against from the beginning. Besides being thus dissultory as to occasion, you will often find my letters very prosy, and at other times too poetical; that is, too much eked out with short poems, to save appearances as to length, and to compensate as well for the baldness of the prose parts, though ostensibly submitted for the benifit of your critical opinion, (which, however, you will always be generous enough to state truly, and which shall always be dispassionately attended to.)

It is perilously likely also, that there will be great gaps or interregnums in the line of my letters (even though there should not be any such in the succession of yours): for I am constitutionally moody, and when afflicted in this way, I care not for perhaps a month or so at a stretch, to unlock my heart with any other than the Key of Poesy. Be it from pride, or defective sympathy, or what not, when in the above desouled condition of feeling I abhor to address myself to the cross-purpossed intelligence (real or surmised) of man the individual, and would only breathe forth the burthen of my being before the spirit of the race, as abstracted in my thoughts, and generalised for the occasion, into one great intellectual prevalence.

With this much said (somewhat too egotistically perhaps) of the sort of correspondent you will most probably have to bear with in your humble servant, I will proceed (now and for the future) to jot away after my own habitual fashion;—a bad one no doubt, "but mine own", as Touchstone very significantly adds with regard to Aubrey the Shepherdess, after having fully and frankly admitted her sluttishness.[7]

[6] Daniel Henry Deniehy (1828–65), native-born, a precociously talented man of letters, lawyer and radical politician. He was a good friend and early champion of CH, lecturing on his poetry.

[7] 'A poor virgin, sir, an ill-favored thing, sir, but mine own' – Touchstone, of Audrey (not 'Aubrey'), in Shakespeare, *As You Like It*, v.4.60–1; 'having fully…admitted' read 'admitting', one of many revisions in this unsigned draft, retained by CH in ML C343 and the only surviving item in their projected correspondence. The 'egotistically' parenthesis is an addition, and 'your humble servant' replaced 'one'.

25. Charles Harpur to John Byrnes, 6 March 1851[1]

Text: People's Advocate, 15 March 1851, p. 7

TO MR. JOHN BYRNES, OF MUSWELLBROOK.
Per favor of the People's Advocate.

SIR,—

In the PEOPLE'S ADVOCATE of the 1st instant, there appeared a letter of yours, disputing the authorship of the "Exile of Erin"; and as the assertions contained therein are calculated to inflict a shame upon the memory of an author whose poetical character I have hitherto regarded with unmixed veneration, I beg to address to you through the same medium, a few remarks, and to propound a few questions touching the matter of them.

I think it incumbent upon every admirer of the genius of Campbell,[2] to require at your hands some directer proofs than you have yet given, of the truth of the charge therein preferred against his moral honesty, ere they accord to it even the remotest degree of credit: chiefly because he himself is now laid at the mercy of any one who may be sacreligious enough to assail him, by the dumb inertness—the "cold obstruction" of the great leveller— Death.[3] And to this end, I will first merely request that you will favor the literary public with *another* of Reynolds' poems[4]—the *best other one* contained in the manuscript you speak of. All students in poetry, I think, will be disposed in common with myself, to regard the publication of such a poem, as one of the honestest proofs you can adduce in favor of the claim of Reynolds to the paternity of the "Exile." At all events, it will afford such *internal evidence* as will be pretty conclusive, as to whether the writer of the one could *by any chance* have been the *bona fide* author of the other. I, for one, shall be thereby enabled to arrive at a conclusion which shall at least reach thus far: though [e]ven one in favor of the poetical competency of Reynolds, will leave the ultimate fact of his being the author of the song in dispute, still untouched and to be otherwise proven.

But pending the advent of some indisputable specimen of Reynolds's poesy,

---

[1] This letter may be read in conjunction with Byrnes's letter of 22 February 1851, which gives some hints about his background in Ireland (*PA*, 1 March 1851, p. 4), his rejoinder of 22 March 1851 to this letter (*PA*, 5 April, p. 6), CH's response of 7 April 1851, below (*PA*, 19 April, p. 6), and his subsequent letter to *Empire* (undated, not published) – all in *Suppl. Letters*.

[2] Thomas Campbell (1777–1844), Scottish poet much admired in the early 19th century for his sentimental and martial verse.

[3] 'Ay, but to die, and go we know not where, / To lie in cold obstruction, and to rot;...'tis too horrible!': Shakespeare, *Measure for Measure*, III.1.116–26. Cf. also the late 4th-century Roman poet Claudian, *The Rape of Proserpine*, II.302: '*Omnia mors aequat*' (death levels all things).

[4] George Nugent Reynolds (1770?–1802), Irish poet, balladist, dramatist and author of the popular song 'Kathleen O'More'. The controversy over authorship of 'The Exile of Erin' dates from at latest 1830, when a Sligo newspaper published the claims of Reynolds's relatives – see *Memoranda of Irish Matters* (1844; online at Google Books).

let me ask you, sir, and the public, whether it is not *more likely* that *he* (during the visit to his relative, the Duke of Buckingham, which you mention) should have procured a copy of an original poem by Campbell, of a quality so calculated to interest him, as an Irishman; than that the latter should have feloniously possessed himself of the draft of such a poem by Reynolds, in the manner and for the purpose you assert? And whether *afterwards* it is not *altogether more likely* that the said Reynolds should have dared to pass off a production of this kind as his own *amongst his friends in an obscure corner of Ireland;* than that a high-minded and already famous poet, like Campbell, should have ventured to publish to the world in his own name, an effusion obtained in any such miserable manner; especially when the high quarter is taken into consideration, through which you say he became possessed of it, and the interest, moreover, which in such a quarter would inevitably work in vindication of any claim the former might have had to its authorship, upon the strong and moving account, if upon none other, of his aristocratical r[e]lationship?

Thus, upon any intelligible principle of conduct, or drift of motive, all temptation to such a fraud was clearly on the side of Reynolds. The accredited authorship of so beautiful a poem would be a crowning feather in the cap of his literary consequence, adorning the obscurity of his private position, while in Campbell's, it would be but one of a hundred, publicly awarded and universally acknowledged. Then again, detection would be comparatively unlikely and harmless in the one case; while in the other it would be almost inevitable, sooner or later, to the disparagement of every leaf in an otherwise well earned crown of poetical laurels.

As to any argument in favor of Reynolds' claim to authorship of the poem, derivable from its peculiar subject; it may be answered, that the subjects of several other of Campbell's pieces, equally beautiful, have an Irish reference; and that he was, moreover, a profound and most catholic sympathiser with every kind and degree of suffering patriotism, whether in the person of a Pole, a Greek, or an Irishman.[5]

I would observe, in conclusion, that I can have no national prejudice in this matter. But neither have I any of that spuriously patronising sympathy, which at once arrays too many of us on the side of some minor interest at the best, to the envious denial or dismemberment of a manifestly greater one.

I am, sir, your obedient servant,
CHARLES HARPUR.

Jerry's Plains, 6th March.

---

[5] Only a few had an Irish setting: e.g., 'The Harper' (1796) and 'O'Connor's Child; or, "The Flower of Love Lies Bleeding"' (1810). Among his songs in the cause of freedom were 'Lines on the State of Greece', 'Lines on Poland' and 'Stanzas to the Memory of the Spanish Patriots Latest Killed, in Resisting the Regency and the Duke of Angouleme'.

26. Charles Harpur to John Byrnes, 7 April 1851

Text: People's Advocate, 19 April 1851, p. 6

To MR. JOHN BYRN[E]S, OF MUSWELLBROOK.
Per favor of the People's Advocate.

SIR,—

I cannot condescend to reply to the clownish letter [of] yours which appears in the *Advocate* of the 5th instant, at greate[r] length than to observe that the badness of its English is only exceeded by the badness of its manners. And do you pretend to be able to give me, or anyone else, "a sound specimen of the polished manners of a true Irish gentleman?" For shame, you vulgar Jackanapes![1] You cannot even bluster handsomely; having no instinct of elegance—no inventive resource beyond your ineffable impudence.

Your first letter was marvellously ill written, considering pretensiveness; but as I had nothing directly to do with that, I forebore to notice the matter, with a tenderness and consideration you evidently did not merit. Your last, however, places both your intelligence and your behaviour beneath my contempt, and leaves me no option but this, to wash my hands of you.

I am, Sir,
Yours, &c.,

Jerry's Plains, April 7th.   CHARLES HARPUR.

[We must decline any more correspondence on this matter. There is, we think, but little doubt as to the authorship of the Poem in question.[2]]

27. Charles Harpur to Board of National Education, 5 May 1851

Text: NSWSA: NRS-622 [1/369A]

Circular, No. 8.

Anvil Creek[3] 1851 May 5th

Gentlemen,

I have the honor to present to you my application for the situation of Teacher in a National School; and in compliance with the requirement of the Board, that a Certificate shall be produced by me, which has been signed by a Clergyman and some other responsible person who have known me for

---

[1] Person assuming ridiculous airs.

[2] See the editor's note to Byrnes's letter in *PA*, 5 April 1851, p. 6 (in *Suppl. Letters*): he attributes the authorship to Reynolds but does not elucidate.

[3] Anvil Creek joins Black Creek near the present Branxton, between Singleton and Maitland. Black Creek flows into the Hunter River a few kilometres further north.

a period of time which enables them to testify concerning my [so]briety and general moral conduct, I beg to refer you to the Certificate herewith annexed.

> I have the honor to be,
> Gentlemen.
> Your most obedient Servant,
> Chas: Harpur.

222/

> Anvil Creek, 5th May, 1851.

We the undersigned Local Patrons of the National School[4] at Anvil Creek, hereby recommend Mr Charles Harpur as an individual every way well qualified for the Mastership of the same.

We would also mention that Mr Harpur is a married man, and that his wife[5] is also well educated and highly respectable, and therefore more than ordinarily qualified to assist him in discharging the duties of his office.

> Thomas Raisbeck
> Edward Thornton
> Peter Barr
> Patrick Doolan
> Bregan Egan
> Local Patrons.

28. Charles Harpur to My Literary Countrymen, 15 May 1851

Text: People's Advocate, 24 May 1851, p. 4

TO MY LITERARY COUNTRYMEN.

I have been invited from time to time, both privately, by letter, and publicly, through the press, by several of my literary countrymen, to "come forth," and take up that position with regard to the forming Literature of Australia, which they are pleased to think I ought to have long since occupied.

Well, I am *willing* and *ready* to "come forth;" and I now invite, in *my* turn, all such of the friends of Literature, as may peruse this letter, and are disposed to aid me, either by their personal exertions or otherwise, in the

---

[4] Residents of Black Creek were agitating for the establishment of a National School there, meanwhile supporting CH in running a temporary one.

[5] Married candidates were preferred, with wives expected to manage infant pupils and teach the girls needlework. The Harpurs' first child Washington was barely a month old.

publication by subscription of a volume[1] of some three or four hundred pages; to communicate with me on the subject, in any the most convenient mode— by letter or through the press. And then I shall be able to arrive at a decided conclusion as to the probable success or failure of an undertaking of the kind.

I am not so much led into this project by any hope of pecuniary profit, as by a wish to ascertain through the verdict of the public, whether the advancement of our National Literature be or be not my intellectual mission; and I cannot better express what I would say further, in this place, than I have already done in the following concluding passage of the general preface to the work which I have called my "Wild Bee of Australia."[2]

"And with this much premised, I have launched upon the stormy waters of the world, my poetical Argo—not so much in quest of the golden fleece of its material favor, as to test by the verdict of its best heads, the validity of the belief I have hitherto most studiously cherished, and upon the altar of which I have sacrificed nearly all the gains and pleasures, and appearances which most men alone value,—the belief that it is in my destiny, if I *will* it, to do something worthily for the mind and heart of my country, and for the intellectual advantage of man. Finally, I would say to all—Read my Book; but cautiously—thinkingly: for if I know myself at all, I would neither mislead nor be misled. May that only of its contents which is true to the good, and the beautiful, to humanity and nature, to virtue and liberty—may that only survive its perusal. *That* only, at all events, is all that can ultimately survive."

I subscribe myself, gentlemen,
Your friend and countrym[a]n,
CHARLES HARPUR.

Anvil Creek, Maitland Road, 15th May, 1851.

---

[1] 'Wild Bee of Australia'. CH had previously floated with Parkes the idea of subscription for the collection, quoting the same passage from the 'general preface' that he gives here ('…my poetical Argo…') – see Letter 22 and notes.
[2] The first of the collection to appear was 'The Tree of Liberty. (A Song for the Future)/ Morsels from Charles Harpur's "Wild Bee of Australia"' (h644e; *PA*, 1 December 1849, p. 9).

29. Charles Harpur to Bernard McMahon, 13 June 1851

Text: ML *D19

Anvil Creek, 13 June 1851.

My dear Bernard,[3]

I was much gratified by the recpt of yours of the 9th instant. It was such a letter as none but an Irishman could write; full to overflowing of hearty good will: and I write this merely to acknowledge it—being too hurried just now for a lengthy communication.

You ask me to send you a few of my published pieces—but that you would not dream of requesting copies of any of my *unpublished* ones. Tush man! Any thing that the Muse might please to impart to me, I would as freely impart to so good and friendly a fellow as yourself: and here is one of her favors fresh from the mint—and at your service.

Hope On[4]

Gold's a cheat, there's no denying,
Love too hath a faithless wing;
Still 'tis useless, useless sighing—
Rather list to Hope replying:
   "Flowers will come again with Spring!
   And in the desert way we're going
   There's yet *one* stream of bounty flowing—
   Hark! I hear it murmuring."

Fame's a liar, Beauty fading,
Hope itself may plant a sting;
Still forbear, forbear upbraiding—
Rather list to its persuading:
   "Flowers will come again with Spring!

Friendship turns, itself denying,—
Yea, itself! the heart to wring;
Still, even though all faith be dying,
Ever list to Hope replying:
   "Flowers will come again with Spring!
   And in the desert way we're going

[3] Bernard McMahon (1826–63), Irish-born husband-to-be of CH's sister Mary; they would marry at Scots Church, Pitt-street, Sydney, on 30 July 1851. He was a grocer with a shop at 171 George-street, Brickfield Hill. A native of Ballybay, County Monaghan, he had arrived as a bounty emigrant in 1844; the passenger list notes that he was Catholic.

[4] For variants, see h177.

> There's yet *one* stream of bounty flowing—
> Hark! I hear it murmuring.

There is, I believe, a Committee of literary gentlemen forming or formed in Sydney for the purpose of devising means for the publication of my poems: you will add your exertions to it I know; and may learn particulars from Parkes.[1]

Excuse the brevity of this
on the score of haste,
and believe me yours truly
Chas: Harpur.

30. Charles Harpur to George William Rusden, 14 June 1851

Text: Rusden papers, Trinity College, University of Melbourne

Anvil Creek, 14th June, 1851.

My dear Sir,[2]

Since you were here I have recieved a letter from the Board,[3] stating that they see no objection to my appointment, when the proposed School[4] shall have been erected, provided that I shall first attend the Model School[5] at Sydney, *for a month*, and then pass an approved examination by the head master of the same.

If my appointment is to be deferred, and the salary withheld, until the completion of the building—there is an end of the matter, as no master could possibly exist in the meantime upon the mere head money[6]—in all not above five or six shillings aweek. Besides, the when and how the said building is to

---

[1] An unsigned notice about CH's work appeared in *Empire*, 16 June 1851, p. 4, referring to his intention 'at the solicitation of numerous friends, to publish a volume of his poems' by subscription (presumably 'Wild Bee of Australia'). Intending subscribers were invited to contact the paper – but no other reference to a 'Committee' has been found. Parkes was probably the writer: he was now running his recently established *Empire* newspaper and was heavily involved in Sydney politics.

[2] George William Rusden (1819–1903) – CH mistakenly gave 'George K. Rusden' as addressee – was agent for the establishment of National Schools in NSW, 1849–51. He travelled many thousands of kilometres on horseback to set up and inspect schools. He would go on to a distinguished career in government and education in Victoria: see further, Paul Nicholls, *'A Delicious Bundle of Prejudices': The Australian Life of George William Rusden* (North Melbourne: Australian Scholarly Press, 2018).

[3] The Board of National Education in Sydney.

[4] See Letter 27.

[5] The Model National School at Upper Fort-street, Sydney. Teacher candidates spent a month there training for the NSW National School system with headmaster William Wilkins: see p. 192 n. 6.

[6] Payment to the teacher from the parents of each child attending the school, supplementing the teacher's salary.

be erected, is, just now, a problem even more puzzling than any in Euclid; seeing that all the available labor for the purpose is on the "tramp" for the "diggins".[7]

Then with regard to the proviso, as to my attendance for a month at the Model School in Sydney,—I could not comply with it in the present condition of my pocket. Otherwise I am willing and ready to undergo any requisite examination on the spot. On the head of grammatical attainments, I may be pardoned for stating, that I have published compositions in English that have been characterized even by good judges as being "classical"—and I have at this moment by me several English Journals of prime standing, into which some of these have been extracted, with commendation as high as this.[8] And with regard to arithmatic, I have mastered the Science as far at least as the Square and Cube Roots extend—a greater amount of this kind of knowledge than I shall ever have occasion for in the way of tuition—at Black Creek.

As to the mere "details" of the System,[9] I suppose they can be summed up upon a sheet of Foolscap—and such a summary would be amply sufficient for the guidance of any intelligent Teacher. Besides, the less an Educational System is confined (beyond its first principles or elementary frame work) to *mere details* the better; more scope being thereby afforded to the really clever Teacher for improving his pupils according to their specific and individual capacities.

> It is not Methods—it is Men that teach;
> The Men who love to practise what they preach.
> Modes are but lifeless bones, till through the whole
> The *destined* Teacher breathes a living Soul.[10]

You will see by this the forlorn state in which the Educational interests of Black Creek now are, and are likely to continue, unless some very different arrangement shall recieve the countenance of the Board: and by representing the matter to them in the light—the true light in which I have above placed it, you will be doing the district a good service.

I am, my dear Sir,
Your most obedient Servt
Chas: Harpur.

---

[7] Once the discovery of gold by Edward Hargraves at Ophir near Bathurst was announced in May 1851 a rush commenced to fields on the Turon, at Hill End and on Louisa Creek near Mudgee, as well as in the southern districts of NSW. Labour became scarce and expensive.

[8] Three CH poems appeared, without commentary or his notes, in a regular column of prose and verse extracts, 'Stringing Pearls', in *Lloyd's Weekly London Newspaper* in 1848: 'Yes', 14 May; 'The Combat', 21 May; and 'Honest Poverty', 4 June. They were taken, with trivial changes, from November 1847 issues of *Sydney Chronicle*: h245b, h071b and h175a.

[9] See p. 47 n. 4.

[10] CH was probably quoting himself; see 'Educational Mottoes' (h109d).

31. Charles Harpur to George William Rusden, 20 June 1851

Text: Rusden papers, Trinity College, University of Melbourne

Anvil Creek 20 June 1851

My dear Sir,

I recd yours of the 16th inst., containing a cheque for £5., under cover of a letter from my brother;[1] and I cordially thank you for the advice expressed in it, which, in itself, is as judicious as it is friendly. But I have not yet decided as to whether I shall attend the Model School or not. In fact, I am, just now, looking in another direction; in which, if I succeed, any situation in the Teaching line will be no longer an object to me.

Besides, I question whether I could "do the amiable"[2] sufficiently to work myself through the ordeal of your Model School with any *eclat*. I have been, in my time, pretty much snubbed by Fortune[3]—but not by Man; and I am afraid that it is now somewhat too late for me to acquire the knack of official humility:—and so I must even contrive (if I can) to knock myself independently through the world, as heretofore, although, as heretofore, I may sometimes have to go hungry for the stern sake of doing so.

If after all, however, I shall determine (and a few days will decide the matter) upon entering myself at the Model School, I will freely avail myself of your loan, or of a part of it, as I do not know how I could get thither just now without doing so. But in the event of my coming to a contrary resolution, of course I shall have no alternative but to return you the money; esteeming the kindness on your part just the same as though I had applied it to my necessity in the manner intended. And if, in the future, it should ever rest with me to do you a service, or any one belonging to you, I should be the veriest of recreants did I fail in its performance. Not that any calculation of the kind entered into the motive by which you were actuated. Disinterestedness the most noble and generous is evidently impressed upon every feature (if I may so express myself) of your friendly and benevolent act. But still I must be allowed to be very grateful—and in my own way; and whatever resolutions my gratitude may prompt me to register on such an occasion, must also be borne with.

I have a desire to keep your letter, as a token of genuine friendship;—with no other view. However, if it is still your wish that it should be destroyed, of course I must comply with it.

---

[1] Joseph was teaching at a Catholic school in West Maitland, and around this time would leave for the new goldfields at World's End and Louisa Creek. Rusden's loan to a prospective teacher was irregular, and may explain his request that CH destroy the accompanying letter. He seems to have gone out of his way to try to secure CH's appointment.

[2] I.e., engage amicably, pleasantly in the task (19th-century colloquialism).

[3] Cf. CH's public plaint on this score in 1856 in his note to 'Fortunate and Unfortunate' (h140a).

Mrs Harpur desires me to convey to you the unqualified expression of her esteem and gratitude: and it is with no ordinary degree of pride and pleasure that I subscribe myself

Sincerely and gratefully yours,
Chas: Harpur.

P.S. I have seen Baylis, the Secretary, and some of the Local Patrons[4] on the subject of the letter you speak of. They are greatly scandalised at the imputations it casts upon their motives; and suspect a party here as the writer; but as they may be mistaken, I forbear to mention his name. Baylis states that he has only delayed paying in the funds, till he had an answer from the Board to his last letter; a letter I wrote for him, and which you can enquire about—as he suspects that it has not been fairly dealt with at the Post Office here. He states besides that he himself, with some others he did not name, could at once get the building on the way, provided the Board saw that the land was all right— meaning, I suppose, on the Board's ascertaining through their Solicitor that the allotment given by Raisbeck[5] is free from mortgage, and can be properly conveyed, &c. As to the number of children available for scholars, you may safely state to the Board, that the quantity given in is considerably under and not over the mark. C.H.

32. Charles Harpur to Bernard McMahon, 8 September 1851
Text: ML *D19

Anvil Creek, 8 Septr 1851.

My dear Bernard, or rather I should say, My dear Brother in Law.

I am your debtor for two letters. My reason for not answering both of them immediately, was chiefly because of my expecting, ere this, to have been able to reply to them *in propriá personá*.[6] To put myself permanently under the auspices of the National Board, it is necessary that I should enter myself for a month at their model Training School in Sydney—and I have been for some months on the point of doing this—but have been delayed by untoward circumstances. At length, however, I shall be able, in about a fortnight at furthest, to complete the arrangement.

[4] John Bayliss, an early resident of Black Creek (Branxton); he died there in 1898 aged 95. He was secretary and treasurer of the Local Patrons, the committee of local residents charged with managing the affairs of the National School.

[5] Thomas Raisbeck (1811–71), sometime publican of the Bush Inn, Black Creek, poundkeeper and landowner. He had offered a town allotment for the proposed Black Creek school – see Bayliss to Board of National Education, 19 May 1851 (in *Suppl. Letters*).

[6] In person (Latin). CH was uncertain with diacritics and occasionally incorrect: these markings are also unclear (the first possibly a macron, the second possibly a circumflex) but they do occur occasionally with this phrase in the newspapers of the day.

You will believe me, when I say, that I am proud of you as a brother-in-law. I considered you my *brother* in the triunal[1] faith of Honor, Truth and Liberty, before I had even so much as a dream of your ever being otherwise related to me. for such, if you recollect, was the compact between us.[2] But I must defer the thousand and one things I have to say to you on this head—until we meet again face to face.

My little Washington[3] is growing a perfect picture: and if God spares me to watch over his education, he shall be morally as perfect. I will devote him to great and magnanimous principles. He shall believe that *to live* for them is *religion*—and that *to die* for them is something *diviner still*.

Remember me to my dear Sister.[4] You will excuse the brevity of this for the reasons above given: and believe me when I say, it is with no ordinary degree of pride and pleasure that I subscribe myself your brother-in law, and your friend,

Chas: Harpur.

Mrs H. desires me to convey to you her respects and congratulations.

Excuse this scrawlish and ill-written affair. I am hurried—and am not over well besides Farewell till I *see* you.

Yours C.H.

33. Charles Harpur to William Charles Wills, 21 May 1852
Text: NSWSA: NRS-613 [1/387], f.224

Sydney, 21st May, 1852.

Sir,[5]

Feeling still severely indisposed, and attributing the present ill state of my health to the sedentary cares and labor, which the Office of a Schoolmaster has subjected me to in the past, it is my intention, for the future, to forego that line of employment.

Of course you will consider this announcement as equivalent to a resig-

---

[1] In a group of three united things; CH used the noun form elsewhere – see, e.g., 'Cosmoplasticus' (h696c) and 'Collins' (h468a).

[2] Unclear, but presumably a shared political outlook.

[3] The Harpurs' first child, born 31 March 1851; this is the earliest mention of his name in the surviving correspondence. The name reflects CH's republicanism at the time and his admiration for the first American president – see 'The Name of Washington' (1855, h152b).

[4] Mary Chidley McMahon, née Harpur (1817–1913). This was her third marriage; she would survive her husband by 50 years.

[5] William Charles Wills (1807–71), public servant, the Board of National Education's first full-time secretary, later worked for its successor body the Council of Education.

nation of my appointment to the Murrurundi School,[6] and supply it accordingly with another Master.

I will take an early opportunity of delivering to Mr O'Driscoll[7] the letter of introduction which you supplied me with—and there the matter will terminate.

I have the honor to be,

Sir,

Your most obedient Servant,

Chas: Harpur.

34. Charles Harpur to Board of National Education, 5 June 1852

Text: NSWSA: NRS-613 [1/387], f.222

171. George Street, Sydney.[8] 5th June, 1852.

Gentlemen,

I beg to lay before you the following Statement,[9] with reference to the late Presbyterian School at Muswell Brook,[10] of which I was the Master up to end of April in the present year. I beg to do so, because on the occasion of my reporting myself to your Secretary,[11] as the Master of the same, he informed me that all payment for my services would be likely to be withholden from the commencement of the present year, in consequence of the said School having been "dropped": although, even up to that moment, I had recieved no official intimation to that effect from any quarter whatever.—But to proceed to my Statement:

---

[6] CH was master of the temporary school at Black Creek from around May 1851. Reluctant to attend the Model School in Sydney for training, he had missed out on mastership of the newly created National School there, and by October he had left for Muswellbrook for a position at its Presbyterian school, which he occupied until April 1852. He learned only a few weeks after arriving that it was to be handed over to the Board of National Education and would close. He applied for a position at the National School at Murrurundi, in the Liverpool Range (northern boundary of the Hunter region). His appointment was again subject to his attendance for training at the Model School; he travelled to Sydney but instead of attending submitted this resignation.

[7] Daniel O'Driscoll, head teacher at the National Model School, Sydney. He had trained at the Model (Normal) School at Marlborough-street, Dublin, and taught with the Irish Board of Education.

[8] CH's sister Mary and her husband Bernard McMahon ran a grocery business there; CH stayed with them on this visit to Sydney.

[9] See also the unsigned draft of this letter (in *Suppl. Letters*), apparently enclosed to the Board in error by CH.

[10] For this and 'the Murrurundi appointment' (below), see p. 65 n. 6.

[11] William Charles Wills.

Sometime in December of last year, I was asked by the Rev: Mr White,[1] the resident clergiman, whether in the event of its being found expedient to transfer my School to the National Board, I would have any objection to such a transfer being made. I answered that I should have no objection. He then informed me, that should my school be one of those transferred, my salary, as Master, and the rent of the school-house, would be paid, as a matter of course, from the 1st of January 1852, by the National Board; inasmuch as the Legislature had voted a sum of money to enable the said Board to meet the emergency: and that though I should be required to attend their Model School for a month, so soon in the ensuing year as I might recieve notice to that effect—no objection to my continuance in the office would be made on my fulfilling satisfactorily that one condition.

I heard nothing further on the subject up to the end of February in the present year, and consequently sent in my Salary Abstracts for the months of January and February to the Denominational Board.[2] On the receipt of these, the Secretary of that Board wrote to inform me, that as my School was one of those which would be transferred to the National System, he had accordingly handed them over to your Secretary, Mr Wills.

From this time of course I considered my School as so far a National one—and at the end of March wrote to Mr Wills for a supply of abstracts, &c.; requesting at the same time to be informed by him as to the wishes and requirements of the Board in regard to myself and the school. To this communication I received no answer: but, attributing Mr Wills' silence to pressure of business, or perhaps to some delay which might then be lying in the mere way of making the transfer of the School from the one Board to the other, of course I considered myself in duty bound still to keep it on—up to the time of Mr McKean's[3] inspection of it. And even when, at the end of April, I came away to study in your Model School for the Murrurundi appointment, I left it in charge of my wife, until such time as another Master could be supplied to it.

I trust it will appear to the Board from the facts above stated, that to withhold their support from the school for at least the period of the four months which they refer to, would be to inflict upon me, as the Master of it, a very great grievance.

---

[1] The Reverend James Smith White, M.A., LL.B., LL.D. (1822–1902), Presbyterian clergyman based at Singleton. He had married the Harpurs in 1850 and baptised Washington Harpur in 1851, and it was through his intervention with the Denominational School Board that CH was offered the post at the Presbyterian school in Muswellbrook.
[2] See p. 34 n. 3.
[3] Not identified.

In conclusion it may be proper to state, that the amount I conceive due to me is,—salary £11.-13.-4.,—rent £4.-0.-0.,—in all £15.-13.-4.[4]

I have the honor to be, gentlemen,
Your most obedient Servant,
Chas: Harpur.

35. Charles Harpur to Henry Parkes, 8 August 1852

Text: ML MSS 947

Jerry's Plains,[5] 8th August 1852

My dear Parkes,

I wish I had taken your advice, and remained in Sydney a few days longer than I did. It would have been better; because I only arrived here in time to be *too late* for the situation I mentioned[6] to you. A day or so before my arrival, the parson, or rather the "Martext" of our village,[7] taking "occasion by the forelock,"[8] had foisted upon the people a botch-watchmaker[9] for a schoolmaster: the one previously thrust upon them under the same auspices having been a botch-carpenter, and the one before him again a botch-nondescript. Of course I was somewhat disappointed: but I am getting quite used to that sort of thing. My whole worldly career has been be-cornered with obstacles and disappointments of one kind or another: so that *now*, I have but to "grin", and the "bearing it" follows by consequence from the second nature of habit.

It was my intention to have written to you before about several things—my poor book[10] being one of these. But knowing how completely your time and attention must be devoted to keeping the Empire intact—I forbore. As to my

---

[4] CH was claiming for four months (January–April) of his £35 annual salary plus rent he had paid on the school premises at £1 per month.

[5] Home of Mary Harpur's family the Doyles, prominent in the district; CH may have been writing from there.

[6] Reference unclear: CH may have left Sydney hurriedly in the (forlorn) hope of gaining the post of master at the Church of England denominational school at Jerry's Plains.

[7] A blundering preacher, from the vicar Sir Oliver Martext in Shakespeare's *As You Like It*: in this case, Jerry's Plains Church of England minister the Reverend Joseph Cooper. Cf. the Harpurs' neighbour John Smith of Birnam Wood: 'all my Family went to Church at Jerrys plains Mr Cooper Preached from 11 Luke verse 1st & 2nd [the Lord's Prayer] and O, ye Saints & Martyrs what a mess He made of it' – entry for 10 November 1850, in *John Smith of Birnam Wood: Diary 1846–1854*, transcribed by Margaret Hardwick, 1996 (digital version by Stephen Crashaw, 2008, at https://hardwick.site/924d).

[8] Proverbially, seizing the moment or opportunity.

[9] Probably Oliver Saunders (see Returns of the Colony, Return of the Number of Schools, &c., 1852 and 1853). His predecessors at the Jerry's Plains Church of England denominational school were John Elliott (1847–49) and Richard Harrison (1850–51).

[10] CH would have to wait another eight months for the publication of *The Bushrangers; A Play in Five Acts, and Other Poems* (Sydney: W. R. Piddington, 1853; online at SLV).

Book—it seems to be drawing its short length through the Printer's hands as slowly as though it were as long as Pope's snaky alexandrine.[1] I am afraid this delay is in some measure attributable to Deniehy,[2] in whose hands I left the "copy" needful to complete the latter half of the volume; he having a rage for arrangement of parts, and I not being disinclined to gratify him in a matter (to my own thinking) so secondary. Still of course I intended (and so expressed my self to Deniehy) to leave as in courtesy bound to do, the final superintendence of the publication in the hands of our excellent friend Pennington.[3] Deniehy was merely to assist him,—and only in the event of Mr Pennington choosing to avail himself of his assistance.

You will be glad to hear that the National Board have consented to pay me the whole of my demand, £15. odd. On returning the abstracts to Wills their Secretary I requested him, if he could not remit the amount directly to myself on a cheque, to pay it to you on my account,[4] with a request that you would enclose it to me as early as convenient. If he has chosen the latter mode of making the payment, you will greatly oblige me by remitting it at once; as in that case I shall be able to go on with my outfit for the "diggings",[5] it being my intention to try my luck in that direction. I can see no other outlet at present: I must either do so, or be idle.

I hope every thing is going on well with you. Remember me to Mrs Parkes, to Mr Pennington (to whom I must write shortly), and to all other friends,

and believe me, most truly and
gratefully yours,
Chas: Harpur.

P.S. When my book is published, you will please to let Mr Bernard McMahon have 150 volumes, to send to me here. I will tell him to apply for them either to you or Mr Pennington—which?

C.H.

---

[1] A line of verse consisting of twelve syllables, or verse composed of such lines; in English poetry typically an iambic hexameter, used chiefly to vary iambic pentameter. CH's reference is to Alexander Pope's famous illustration, in 'An Essay on Criticism' (1711), of its excessive and unskilful use: 'A needless alexandrine ends the song, / That, like a wounded snake, drags its slow length along.'
[2] Although they corresponded beforehand, Deniehy (see p. 53 n. 6) and CH probably first met around mid-1852 in Sydney. This letter may be the earliest record of personal contact between them.
[3] See p. 52 n. 5.
[4] This the Board did: see Parkes's receipt of 4 September 1852 (in *Suppl. Letters*).
[5] CH's brother Joseph joined the stampede to Louisa Creek and World's End, but there is no evidence that CH followed him.

36. Charles Harpur to Henry Parkes, 10 July 1853

Text: ML MSS 947

Granbelang, near Singleton, July 10 18[53][6]

Dear Parkes,

I send you two poems for the Empire—if you like them. After two or three more batches of original pieces, you must oblige me by publishing as "select poetry"[7] my Glen of the Whiteman's Grave,[8] in its present perfected condition. I wish particularly to have it on record in the Empire, because I have exhausted on the peculiar style of its versification all the metrical skill I am master of, whatever in amount that may absolutely be. My aim throughout the poem has been, not only that the "sound should seem an echo to the sense",[9] but that the whole composition as well—rhymes, metres, and all, should wear the appearance of having fallen together, as it were, by the musical tendencies of nature, as these are gathered and concentrated of the spirit of poesy. And I am curious to see whether any of our sharp nosed critics will smell this out. But they won't—none of them. For even the greatest Prosemen are often singularly awanting in a true insight into the nicer achievements of versification; and even the *ignorance* of considerable critics, with regard to versification in general, has sometimes been matter of unpleasant surprise to me.

Will you publish in some one of your Saturday double sheets[10]—"A lecture on poetry, intended to have been delivered (last season) at the Sydney School of Arts, by Charles Harpur"?[11]

Yours very truly,

---

[6] Granbelang was a large property on the left bank of the Hunter ten km west of Singleton. In April 1853 the Harpurs established themselves there (on lease) to run sheep. The year is illegible due to staining but the letter is postmarked 'JY 13 1853' and 'JY 16 1853'.

[7] Newspapers usually printed verse they copied from books and other journals under the heading 'select poetry', as distinct from 'original poetry', verse not published elsewhere.

[8] Among the most celebrated of CH's poems, originally in *Maitland Mercury*, 1 July 1846, p. 1 (h153a). *Empire* did republish (h153d), but not until 17 March 1857, p. 4.

[9] From Alexander Pope, 'An Essay on Criticism' (1711): ''Tis not enough no harshness gives offence. / The sound must seem an echo to the sense: / Soft is the strain when Zephyr gently blows, / And the smooth stream in smoother numbers flows; / But when loud surges lash the sounding shore, / The hoarse, rough verse should like the torrent roar.'

[10] *Empire* started as a four-pager in December 1850, but soon began issuing two-page supplements and eight-page editions on irregular Saturdays.

[11] *Empire* ran CH's poems and letters around this time, but not the lecture he had been scheduled to deliver on 6 July 1852 at the Mechanics' School of Arts, Sydney, on 'English Poetry, from the Miltonic Era to the time of Wordsworth', part of the School's course of literary lectures for 1852 (see advertisement, *Empire*, 6 July 1852, p. 1; and *SMH* of same date, p. 1). Apparently the lecture did not eventuate; CH had presumably been called away to Jerry's Plains.

P.S. On a slip, I enclose you a little song—not for publication, unless you should think it proper to publish it—but for your own reading: which song wou[ld] be very indicative of vanity perhaps, only that it is put into the mout[h] of my rib,[1] and is moreover, I believe, quite a faithful interpretatio[n] of her feelings upon occasion.

Yours again
C.H.

x By this song you will see that I have another little one—little Charley.[2]

The Song of the Poet Shepherd's Wife.[3]

O weary sometimes seems the day
    As I look forth alone,
And think what might have happened
    In yon dark Bush unknown:
And then my heart is lonely
    As any heart can be,
Till Charley, with his thousand,[4]
    Comes home at eve to me.

Like lines of mist, I see his flock
    Far looming through the trees,
Until its myriad bleatings
    Come thickening in the breeze;
And then my heart is happy
    As any heart can be—
For Charley and his thousand
    Are coming home to me.

My Charley! he hath sung of love
    Till even his native Land
Is hued with rarer colors
    By his so cunning hand!

---

[1] Wife (from the creation of Eve from Adam's rib in Genesis 2.21).

[2] The Harpurs' second child, Charles, was born in the Hunter (possibly at Granbelang) on 15 June 1853. When baptised on 18 August 1853 by Presbyterian minister the Reverend James Smith White he would be given the middle name Chidley, the maiden name of CH's mother, Sarah.

[3] See h530a; not published until 1984. The theme harks back to Robert Greene ('The Shepherd's Wife's Song', 1590) and Robert Burns ('The Shepherd's Wife', c. 1787).

[4] A mob of 1,000 sheep.

And things of light are round him
And spirits eagle-free—
Yet he must tend his thousand
For his little ones and me.

37. Charles Harpur to *Empire*, 26 July 1853

Text: Empire, 6 August 1853, p. 6

OUR UPPER HOUSE OF NOMINEES.
To the Editor of the Empire.[5]

SIR—

In our new Constitution we are to have (you say) an Upper House of Nominees for life[6]—the antipodean ape of a House of Lords—with a Sir Charles Fitz Roy for the nominator of its members. It has been well said, that it requires genius to discover genius. In like manner, it may be truly asserted that it requires a statesman to discover statesmen—that is, fit members for such a House. But then a Sir Charles Fitz-Roy is to be the nominator of these nominees. Now, Sir, such being the case, as it is impossible to hope that it will be composed of members as able and intellectual as might be wished, it is desirable, as the next best thing to these, that it should be as *Lordly* in its look as possible; and to the securement of this end, I have been for several days hunting about in thought for some outward and ocular test, which might be recommended to Sir Charles for his special guidance, in the event of their having to be nominated by him.

First, there is the good old test of drunkenness—"as *drunk* as a *lord*."[7] But this test would be hardly selective enough for a community almost every mother's son of which will occasionally, and but too often, get as drunk as a very lord, or even drunker, if that be possible. It would not be sufficiently *exclusive*, in the ultra-aristocratical sense of the term; albeit some of the very few lords who have as yet rejoiced our shores with the glory of their countenances, might seem to have come hither of set purpose to show us *how far drunk* a *bona fide* lord can really get.

---

[5] Henry Parkes, proprietor and editor of *Empire*, 1850–58.

[6] The 1852 select committee of the Legislative Council charged with developing a constitution for NSW, chaired by William Charles Wentworth, proposed a legislature of two houses, an elected lower one and an upper one of government nominees to be replaced progressively by the representatives of a new colonial peerage. Radicals and liberals – among them Parkes, Piddington, Deniehy, Hawksley and Thomas Mort – reacted by forming a NSW Constitution Committee to publicly fight the proposals, and Parkes's *Empire* carried editorials and correspondence attacking Wentworth's measures. CH may be referring here to a leader, 'The House that Jack Built', in *Empire*, 19 July 1853, p. 2. See also CH's satirical song 'Lord George' (h227a) and the note to 'Petty Pride' (h378b): *PA*, 12 July 1856, p. 2.

[7] Extremely drunk (proverbial).

Then there is property—riches—"as *rich* as a lord." But neither would this good old test answer in a community so plentifully besprinkled as ours with Bill Nashes.[1] Neither could it be recommended on the score of its universality anywhere; for some of the nobles of England are very church mice[2] in several senses (poverty included), and some, too, of the few lords who have as yet honoured us with their presence have contrived not only to show the Australian public how drunk a veritable lord can get, but how marvellously poor he may be at the same time. Neither of these two tests, then, can be sufficiently relied on.

I next bethought me of a hump—"*humped* like a *lord*."[3] Now this test would be one not to be altogether slighted in a Spanish colony about to be blessed with the creation of a race of dons,[4] inasmuch as it would there betoken much filial imitativeness, the aristocracy of Old Spain having so bred *in and in* for ages that it has become deformed to a proverb.[5] It might even have worked appropriately in a French colony before the storm wind of the first Revolution[6] showed how rootless were the crook-backed and bow-shinned aristocrats of Old France, by strewing the highways and byways of half the world with them. But it is questionable whether it would do as a modern test even in England, were it expedient to create there an additional stock of lords after the obtaining pattern; for the noble blood of England has been so adulterated by infusions from the sons and daughters of vulgar millionaires and mere merchant princes, bankers, and brokers (to say nothing of handsome footmen), as to be actually *wholesome*—probably as a ploughman's. Neither would it answer in Australia for a special reason. Our lusters after lordships, even those in whom the taint may be an inherent one,[7] however warped in their principles, are generally in their persons more than commonly upright— probably from their being so well and constantly padded in the belly with the very best of our beef and mutton.

---

[1] William Nash (1803–64), wealthy ex-convict and fraudulent gold dealer. 'Bill Nash' was a byword for ill-gotten wealth, ostentatious display and defiance of the law. See biographical sketch in *Truth* (Sydney), 1 May 1898, p. 6; SLNSW holds a pencil portrait by Charles Rodius at PXB 414.

[2] I.e., impoverished or quiet, like a mouse living in a church.

[3] Not a common expression: CH may have had in mind the (supposedly) crookbacked Richard III, or Robert Cecil, Earl of Salisbury, Secretary of State to Elizabeth I (who called him 'my pygmy') and to James I ('my little beagle').

[4] Spanish lords or gentlemen.

[5] A reference to the physical disabilities – including the so-called 'Habsburg jaw' – of the Spanish Habsburg monarchs, the result of inbreeding, typified in Charles II (1661–1700), last of the line.

[6] The Revolution of 1789–99, as distinct from those of 1830 and 1848. Aristocratic émigrés fled to Britain, the German states and elsewhere, their property confiscated.

[7] Perhaps a sly dig at William Charles Wentworth, proponent of the 'bunyip aristocracy' and CH's political *bête noire*. Wentworth could trace his paternal line to Anglo-Irish aristocracy.

Then there is Byron's test—a delicate hand.[8] I confess that this was long a favourite one even with myself. Not because it happened to be Byron's, but because of certain crochets that chanced to flourish within my own proper cranium, albeit a cracked one—that is, reputedly. I was willing to suppose that Nature might append some such idiosyncratic evidence to high habitudes of refinement. At all events, I knew that, as a racial attribute, it indicated the contrary of mechanical employments. But, alas! I was the other day startled out of all abiding faith even in this test by your Police Report, in which it was stated that the rascal Smith,[9] who bolted from the Bank door with the simple old miner's money, had a hand so delicate in its proportions, so *villanously little*, that no cuffs in the whole armoury of the round-house were small enough to fetter it. Such being the case with regard to myself, of course I cannot recommend this to Sir Charles, though still a pet test with many, as an all-in-all sufficient one.

There is, however, another characteristic test which I think might be relied on. But before I urge it in Australia, I must implore the profoundest attention of the probable nominator of these yet-to-be lordly nominees. And I, too, before I can commit to paper a suggestion so portentous, must even throw myself back in my chair, and indulge in a few whiffs of Raleigh's consolation.[10] But the final test (?) is a much mightier thing, I can tell you, than it looks to be, and is by no means to be sneezed at. In short, it is a *thumping great nose!* a round, robustious, broad-backed, elephantine, Wellingtonian, dodo-like upper mandible![11] Be this your test, Sir Charles. Pack our Nominee Chamber with noses of such amplitude, and consequently of such a roaring sternutational[12] power, that one-and-twenty of them, well provided with *Prince's* mixture,[13] might even discharge (if need were) on the anniversary of a coronation, or what not, a very satisfactory and right royal salute, to the public saving of much excellent gunpowder. Yes, Sir Charles, stick to this nose test.

---

[8] 'Though on more *thorough-bred* or fairer fingers / No lips e'er left their transitory trace' – *Don Juan, Cantos III, IV and V* (London: Thomas Davison, 1821 – online at Internet Archive), Canto V, Stanza 106, to which Byron added the note: 'There is perhaps nothing more distinctive of birth than the hand: it is almost the only sign of blood which aristocracy can generate' (p. 216).

[9] John Smith, sentenced to five years for larceny, escaped from custody on 11 April 1853, the police attesting that he 'had such a fine formation of hand that he could slip the smallest pair of handcuffs' (*Empire*, 22 April 1853, p. 2).

[10] Tobacco, after Sir Walter Raleigh's supposed introduction of the weed to England in 1586.

[11] *Robustious*: strong and hardy, sturdy. *Wellingtonian*: associated with Arthur Wellesley, First Duke of Wellington (1769–1852), victor of Waterloo and twice Prime Minister of Great Britain, but here specifically a reference to his prominent nose (he was 'Old Nosey' in popular ballads). CH was no admirer: see his 'Wellington' (h672). *Dodo*: an extinct flightless bird endemic to Mauritius, bald-headed and large-billed. *Upper mandible*: the upper fixed bone of the jaw.

[12] To do with sneezing.

[13] Coarse snuff flavoured with Attar of Roses, favoured by the Prince Regent (later, George IV).

It will not only give us the shadow, but something of the substance, such as it is, of a genuine House of Lords. For a nose of the size and fashion here meant, when surmounted with a forehead so far recedent as to be incapable of the corrective of deep thinking, is indicative of intense sensualism, selfishness extreme, and a brute obstinacy; and constitutes (thus surmounted) the upper facial type of the great mass of the British aristocracy. And if it be right for us to copy this same aristocracy in its legislative functions, it can hardly be wrong, even for the look of the thing, to copy it also as far as we can in this, the most marked, of its featural idiosyncracies.

I fully anticipate the thanks of Sir Charles for the above suggestion. If, however, he shall not think fit to accord them to me, I shall be able, I dare say, to abide the disappointment.

But seriously, Mr. Editor, what can such a House be but one more cobweb for the besom[1] of future revolution to sweep utterly away—revolution necessitated by it and other such governmental mockeries?

I remain, yours, &c.,
CHARLES HARPUR.

Granbelang, July 26, 1853.

P.S.—Since the above was written, I have learned that our present Viceroy is about to be recalled.[2] But the matter of it will keep, and be, perhaps, just as suitable to his successor.

C. H.

38. Charles Harpur to *Empire*, 28 August 1853

Text: Empire, 16 September 1853, p. 3

To the Editor of the Empire.

Sir—

As constitution making is the order of the day, I beg to submit to you, for insertion in the *Empire*, the following Essay on Government and Governments.[3]

---

[1] A broom of twigs bound together round a handle, capable of being used as an instrument of punishment.

[2] CH, premature in this prediction, had presumably seen recent press speculation based on 'intelligence' from London (e.g., *SMH*, 26 July 1853, p. 2) that Lord Lyttelton was to replace Sir Charles FitzRoy as Governor-General. In fact FitzRoy would not be replaced until January 1855 by Sir William Denison.

[3] It appeared on 16 September 1853, p. 3. CH elaborated in his scathing 'Marvellous Martin' (h281a and its note), in *PA*, 17 December 1853, p. 6. For James Martin, see p. 43 n. 9, and n. 5 opposite.

It was written many years ago, when I was a mere lad; but, notwithstanding that, it may contain some hints not unworthy of consideration at the present political juncture. Of this at least I am sure, that nothing short of some things that are forth-shadowed in it will ever satisfy future Australia. And it will show, moreover, that some of her mere *boys*, even in the past, have had earnest notions about the future government of their country—boys that *thought*, while our Fitzgeralds[4] were branding wool bales or butchering, and our poor, paltry, pedantic Martins pitifully pettifogging.[5]

Presenteeism, and Orders of Merit to console the rejected, will never do,[6] depend upon it. Orders of Merit, forsooth! with which a fullblown Hudson[7] might have *honourable* membership!

I may as well add that, at the time of writing the Essay, I knew little, precisely, of the details of the American form of government.

I am, &c.,
CHARLES HARPUR.

Granbelang, 28th August, 1853.

---

[4] Robert Fitzgerald (1807–65), wealthy pastoralist with extensive holdings, member of the Legislative Council and of the 1851 Select Committee on the New Constitution, under Wentworth's chairmanship, but not the later ones.

[5] A member of Wentworth's constitution-drafting select committee of 1852, James Martin opposed manhood suffrage and advocated an upper house composed of representatives of large landed proprietors. *Pettifogging* is wrangling or quibbling about petty points – from *pettifogger*, an inferior legal practitioner who dealt with petty cases.

[6] A proposal put to the Constitution Committee (see p. 71 n. 6) in August 1853 that aimed to combine nomination and popular election to the NSW upper house as an alternative to hereditary peerage. The Crown would issue a list of 'Crown Presentees' from whom the Council would be elected. The people could elect other candidates, but these 'People's Presentees' would be subject to Crown approval. Those Presentees named in the Crown List but not elected, together with those elected by the people but rejected by the Crown, would be distinguished as 'a particular class in the community' forming 'the germs of such an aristocracy as the world is alone likely in future to tolerate – an aristocracy of merit' – see 'New Constitution', *Empire*, 24 August 1853, p. 1 and 'Abstract of Plans for the Construction of a Legislature for NSW', *SMH*, 6 December 1853, p. 4. The proposer was not named. The Constitution of 1855 had a Crown-nominated upper house.

[7] Joseph Hudson, convicted of robbing the Bathurst mail of its gold consignment in August 1852, had his conviction quashed on a legal technicality. His escape from justice, together with the Attorney-General's decision not to prosecute a second time, aroused public indignation: e.g., *Bathurst Free Press*, 3 September 1853, p. 2.

39. Charles Harpur to *People's Advocate*, [by 18 February 1854]

Text: People's Advocate, 18 February 1854, p. 4

To the Editor of the People's Advocate.

Sir,—

A few slight persons s[e]em inclined to impugn what they are pleased to call the war-spirit evinced in certain late publications of mine.[1] But they mistake me considerably; although I still hold to the opinion that the best consecration of liberty is the blood of the patriot. And I have many good reasons for thus adhering to this opinion. All that is supremely valuable and valued in English liberty has been purchased with the blood of Englishmen. The mountain tree of Switzerland's freedom hath its roots struck deep in the red blood of her bravest children. How much also of all that is glowing in the American's sense of his unequalled freedom, must arise from the noble memory of its having been died for by Americans? These are some of my reasons for holding fast to the opinion in question. To show, however, that I am disposed to love war for its own sake, or as a matter prolific of mere glory, as little as most men, I submit to you for publication the following essay[2] on the subject, wich I find among my papers, and remain

Yours, &c.,
CHARLES HARPUR.

40. Charles Harpur to James Norton, 30 November 1854

Text: ML MSS 947

Granbelang, near Singleton, 30 Novr 1854

Dear Sir,[3]

I have to thank you for your cordial and considerate letter of the 27th inst.,

---

[1] The 'persons' are not identified, but 'certain late publications' must include CH's 'A War Song for the Nineteenth Century' (h670e) in *PA*, 7 January 1854, p. 5, augmented with a new stanza concluding 'But unarmed right aye withers / In wrong's all blasting breath— / Then on, ye Red Republicans, / To Freedom or to Death.' In a note CH renounces his belief in moral force alone, declaring himself 'a physical force revolutionist'.

[2] 'Military Heroes and War', in *PA*, 18 February 1854, pp. 4–5.

[3] James Norton (1795–1862), solicitor, member of parliament, essayist. He was a literary admirer of CH and dedicatee of his sonnet 'To James Norton, Esq.' (h613c). Norton was solicitor for Dr Peter Cunningham's Dalswinton estate (see below and, e.g., *SMH*, 23 April 1861, p. 8).

and for the elegant Essay[4] accompanying it. As far as I can comprehend the drift of your foregone argument on the Resurrection of the Body from the objections of your clerical critics I quite agree with it; while to these objections themselves your answers in the pamphlet before me, numbered from 1 to 17., strike me as being nothing the less conclusive for being very dispassionate.

In your letter you are kind enough to say,—after detailing the circumstances affecting the Estate I enquired of you about,[5]—that if I should still desire to try for it, you would write to Mr Evans of Orange, recommending him to give Mr Ogilvie notice to quit, and make an arrangement with me.[6]

By doing this, Sir, you would greatly oblige me. And the reasons for my making this troublesome request are somewhat urgent—being these. The lease of the place I now hold at Granbelang is nearly out, and I doubt whether I could get it renewed at a reasonable rate. Besides, its grazing capabilities are no longer equal to the requirements of my increased stock, insomuch that I dread remaining another winter upon it—even though I might be able so to arrange the matter. And hence it is that the run of Pagan's land,[7] even for a few months, (should Dr Cunningham's[8] death prevent my occupying it longer) would be a very considerable advantage to me. It would give me time to look about me for a more permanent holding, besides benefitting me in some other minor respects.

With this explanation of the present state of the mainstay of my worldly affairs, I know you will excuse me for the trouble I am giving you.

The following is my latest composition. It was hammered together in head the other day while beating about the Bush for a lot of strayed sheep, and has never until now been put to paper. You will pardon my thus eking out my letter with it. Its text is

[continued next page

[4] James Norton's 'The Resurrection of the Body', in *Essays and Reflections in Australia, by a Layman: Continuation* (Sydney: Daniel Lovett Welch, 1853, online at NLA), argued that the resurrection was essentially spiritual rather than corporeal. In 1854 he issued *Further Observations on the Resurrection of the Body, by a Layman* (Sydney: Daniel Lovett Welch) in answer to 'objections which had been urged by various parties' against the earlier paper. CH evidently read the latter.

[5] The names CH mentions (see following notes) suggest that he was interested in land 60 km west of Granbelang, near modern Denman, where the Goulburn River joins the Hunter, but the letter does not permit identification of the land he wanted.

[6] William Tucker Evans (1811–85) was the brother-in-law and business partner of John Harley Pagan (see next note). He had married Janet Pagan, the niece of Dr Peter Cunningham. William Ogilvie (1782–1859) was a fellow naval officer of Dr Peter Cunningham and an early grantee on the Upper Hunter where he held the neighbouring estate Merton: 'Mr Ogilvie' may be William or a relative.

[7] Probably the land of John Harley Pagan, nephew of Dr Peter Cunningham. He and his brother Peter Cunningham Pagan looked after Dalswinton for the absentee Cunningham, and John had property on the Hunter adjoining his uncle's. Both had died in the 1840s.

[8] Dr Peter Miller Cunningham (1789–1864), naval surgeon and author of *Two Years in New South Wales* (1827), from a distinguished Scottish family (his brother Allan was a poet and biographer of Burns). An early grantee on the Upper Hunter, he and fellow naval officer William Ogilvie had extensive landholdings near modern Denman. He had returned to England by 1830 but retained an abiding interest in the colony.

All is for the Best.[1]

The world is but a boastful weakness—
   Pale with terrors unconfest;
Yet Virtue may not lose *her* treasure,
A God is Power exceeding measure:
   All then—*all* is for the best.

The world is mountained o'er with trouble—
   Cragg'd with danger and unrest;
Yet all things tend to the supernal,
And God is Peace—yea, peace eternal:
   All then—*all* is for the best.

The world is clouded up with error—
   Folly's nourished at its breast;
Yet even wise *men* are forecasting,
And God is Wisdom Everlasting:
   All then—*all* is for the best.

The world is sowed with lies for lucre[2]—
   Falsehoods all its ways infest;
Yet Fraud is overcome by Duty,
And God is Truth, and truth is Beauty:[3]
   All then—*all* is for the best.

Power, Peace, Wisdom, Truth and Beauty,
   These are God—and these attest,
That Evil must be self-consuming,
A bale fire[4] Final Good illuming:
   All then—*all is for the best.*

I remain dear Sir,
with great respect,
Your very obliged servant
Chas: Harpur.

---

[1] For variants, see h583. CH would retitle this poem 'Theodic Optimism'. The refrain echoes Epistle I of Alexander Pope's 'An Essay on Man' (1732): 'And, spite of pride, in erring reason's spite, / One truth is clear, whatever is, is right.'

[2] Mere gain, profit.

[3] Combines the 'God of Truth' (e.g., Deuteronomy 32.4) and John Keats's 'Beauty is truth, truth beauty' ('Ode on a Grecian Urn').

[4] A great consuming fire in the open air.

41. Charles Harpur to Henry Parkes, 4 March 1855

Text: ML MSS 947

Granbelang, near Singleton, 4 March 1855.

Dear Parkes,

Ever since I last wrote to you, many months ago, I have been anxiously d[e]vising some means of permanently settling myself as grazier. On expressing my anxiety on this head, to a relative of mine who has a station on the Namoi,[5] he informed me of a vacated run formerly occupied by a Mr Robertson,[6] lying at the back of his, the fact of its thus lying vacant being known only to himself and certain of his friends—and which fact he, and they at his instance had kept *dark* for several sufficient reasons. One of these was, he said, that he long had a notion of extending his concerns and occupying it himself; but that for my sake he would forego this, and give me all the necessary particulars, in order to my making a tender for it to the Government.[7] I jotted down these particulars and immediately tendered for it—and—fortunate for once in my life, I may even say greatly fortunate—I got it; upon a bonus of £20—a mere trifle. It is not perhaps a first-rate squattage,[8] being somewhat bushy in the back grounds; but it is abundantly watered in all seasons, and by those well acquainted with it, it is declared capable of pasturing 4000 sheep along the sides of the main creek which runs through its centre, with several hundred cattle on the ridges at the back. I consider it therefore worth at least £500. In fact I would not take that sum for it.

Now to stock this squattage—that is, to commence with, I have over 300 head of cattle, about 1000 sheep, and thirteen head of horses. I have means besides to compass all I shall need in the way of supplies &c &c. &c—all except a team to take those supplies thither, and to bring thence my produce. To have to pay carriage for all this at the present rate of carriage would cripple me greatly—would, in short, cost me the price, or more than the price of a team, the very first year, and would still leave me as much in need of a team as ever. Now the cost of a team, namely, a dray (£40) eight bullocks at £5 per head (£40) and gear and fittings complete (£20) would amount to at least a

---

[5] Probably Cyrus Edward Doyle, cousin of Mary Harpur, whose run Thurradulba was on the Namoi River, south of today's Narrabri, 350 km north west of Singleton and across the ranges. It adjoined that of John B. Robertson (next note).

[6] The previous occupant of this run, Garrowramere (later known as Arrarrowme), is claimed to have been John Robertson: see p. 88 n. 2 and Eric Rolls, *A Million Wild Acres: 200 Years of Man and an Australian Forest*, 2nd edn. (McMahons Point, NSW: Hale & Iremonger, 2011), pp. 127, 158.

[7] Individuals could lease squatting runs for up to 14 years on Crown Land beyond the 'settled districts' of the colony by submitting a competitive tender to the Commissioner of Crown Lands. The tenderer could offer an additional yearly premium over the minimum rent set by the government: hence, presumably, the 'bonus of £20'.

[8] Area of land leased from the government for grazing, stock-raising, etc.

hundred pounds: and here is my need. Aid from some capable friend and well wisher is of vital importance to me just now; and as in casting about me in my thoughts, your image was the first to present itself to my hopes, to you will I first apply. Can you, then; will you, lend me £100 or £150 for two years at a reasonable interest, with security (if you would rather) upon the station for its repayment?

If you can thus aid me at this juncture in my fortunes, I think you will. At all events you will see the urgent need there exists for your letting me know at once whether or no. I shall look then to hear from you immediately—and if you can possibly aid me just now,—do.

I enclose you a sort of Naval Ode[1] (a recent composition) for the Empire, if you like it. One epithet in it may remind of Strang's "*able* tea" on an occasion of his wishing to sell you some. "Smell thot" said he, "*able* tea thot!" Still *able*, I think, is the very best epithet I could use in the place where it occurs.[2] Hoping that Mrs Parkes, and all your family are well, and that you too, yourself, are well, bearing your honors meekly and reaping golden opinions from all sorts of people,

I remain
Yours most truly
Chas: Harpur.

P.S. My Mary is well, and my two little boys are thriving bonnily.[3] Washington is allowed on all hands to be a very beautiful little fellow. You will smile at this—but it is a fact nevertheless. You never saw Mrs H, nor she you; yet she thinks she would know you from my descriptions, should she chance to see you—and requests me to tender to you her best respects.

A[4]

---

[1] 'The Anchor' (h009b); it would appear in *Empire*, 13 March 1855, p. 5.

[2] Probably W. J. Strang (see p. 30 n. 5); as Parkes's purchasing agent in China he was evidently wanting to sell tea into Sydney: 'able tea' implying 'able to stimulate', i.e., strong tea. CH distinguishes this use in their standing joke from his own, nevertheless related use of 'able' in 'The Anchor' ('How able is its form!', h009b). 'Able' is used of strong, well built boats in Scottish and northern Irish English.

[3] Washington was now 4 years old, Charley not yet 2.

[4] The significance of this notation in an unidentified hand is unknown, but cf. 'B' at the end of Letter 42.

42. Charles Harpur to Henry Parkes, 15 March 1855

Text: ML MSS 947

Granbelang, near Singleton 15 March 1855

Dear Sir,

I recd your letter in reply to the one in which I requested you to lend me £100 or £150;[5] and I confess it disappointed me a good deal on several accounts—on some, indeed, quite beyond my own present need and interests. But why did I apply to you? I had lately seen your contributions in no less than sums of £50 *flung down*,[6] as it were, at the call of objects afar off and dubious; and I naturally thought that a man to whom such sums seemed but as the loose cash and out turnings of his pockets, on the occasion of his changing his coat or trowsers, was at least in a position to benefit an old friend with the loan of a £100 or so, at a *reasonable interest and on good security*—an old friend, too, that he had assured on several occasions that he "loved him like a brother"—and who, moreover, was at that precise juncture at the very turning point of victory or disaster in a long and cruel battle with the world! But I was not thoroughly aware, it would seem, even up to the time of making that request, how little such an expression as that I have above quoted from one of your own letters,—how *little*, I say, it may mean even in the mouths of the best. You must permit me to say also, that I think it would have been in quite as good taste for you to have gone directly to your refusal, as to have beaten round about to it through such an ostentatious display of your own marvellous prosperity. Yet you must not think from this expression of feeling, that I envy your worldly well doing. On the contrary I rejoice at it.

No doubt, I could raise £100 or more, by the sale of some of my property—but to have to raise it in this way just now would be almost ruinous to me. All my horses, except those I shall need for travel and daily use, are unbroken, and to sell them in this condition would be to sell them for next to nothing. Or to sell any of my sheep, they being a mixed flock and not butchers' meat would be absolutely to give them away while my cattle are 400 miles away,

---

[5] The tone of this letter to an old friend is only partly explained by CH's disappointment at Parkes's declining the loan. In May 1854 Parkes had been elected member for Sydney in the NSW Legislative Council, replacing arch-conservative W. C. Wentworth who had left for London to promote his oligarchical NSW Constitution Bill. His acceptance speech praising Wentworth dismayed the radicals (see p. 51 n. 9). CH fired off his 'Impromtu' (h187a) in *PA*, 13 May 1854, p. 5, blasting Parkes's 'notion of greatness, so bloated and crude' and taking him to task in a footnote: 'The great defect of Mr. Parkes' intellect is its tendency to regard human power and greatness as being identical.'

[6] Parkes had recently '*flung down*' 50 guineas for the Crimean War relief fund, of which he was a key promoter (see his speech, reported in *Empire*, 21 February 1855, p. 2). CH's opposition to the war is manifest in poems such as 'The Battle of Inkermann (The truest version)' (ho31a), *PA*, 19 May 1855, p. 6. Parkes may be the 'Squire Sham' of CH's bitter 'The Great Gun of the Patriotic Fund Brought to a Queer Test' (h163b) in *PA*, 31 March 1855, p. 5.

running on terms at John Doyle's station on the Barwin,[1] and it will take a year or more before I can have them collected upon the station (200 miles distant) upon which I am endeavouring to establish myself permanently.

As to the matter of my book;[2] the following extract from a letter from Mr Pennington, dated 25 Jan 1853, will explain to you the position in which I have conceived myself as hitherto standing with regard to the printing and publishing expenses.

"There is no news of the subscription list, but I can recollect all the parties whom I solicited, and Deniehy will be able to do the like. There is little fear of our fulfilment of our guarantee in this respect; at all events to you let not this be any farther a matter of concern. Mr Parkes has with his wonted consideration done all that was needful to ensure the publication. The rest is a matter between him and your friends and well wishers."

The letter from which I transcribe this was in reply to one of mine in which I had stated that I wished the first proceeds of the sale of the book to be applied to the covering of whatever amount the subscriptions on the whole might run short of the expense, for which I knew you would otherwise be answerable.

In the same letter Mr Pennington requested me to inform him how I wished the books to be distributed amongst the booksellers, and so forth; and I immediately wrote to him detailing my wishes on that head: namely, I wished him to present each of the subscribers with a copy, to send me 100 copies, and to have the rest of the edition distributed amongst the Sydney Booksellers. A copy, I think, was also to be sent to the Editors of each of the Colonial journals.

The 100 copies to be sent to myself I got—but what was done with the rest of the edition I do not know, nor have I been able to learn up to the present time although I have written no less than three letters to Mr Pennington on the subject, to neither of which has he ever thought it worth his precious while to make any reply. But the whole matter must now be enquired into; and it will be incumbent upon all concerned in it, I think, to furnish me forthwith with a clear and straightforward statement

I do not know whether you will be able to read this easily; for my sight is so

[1] Mary Harpur's uncle John Frederick Doyle, with his brother James, held large runs on the Barwon River in the far north-west 650 km from Singleton. The 'terms' probably mean the landholder takes a share of the increase of his cattle or charges so much per head to fatten them.

[2] *Bushrangers* had been published by bookseller W. R. Piddington in April 1853.

much impaired at a short range, that I can hardly see either to read or write.[3]

You might still do me a good office, if you will—and in this way. I think if you were to show my letter to Mr James Norton Senr[4] (as at my request), stating your own inability to serve me, that he would either himself lend me the amount, or procure me the loan of it, upon the terms therein offered.

I remain, dear Sir,
Your very obedt Servant
Chas: Harpur.

P.S. On the other side there is a lyric at your service, if you care to accept of it for the Empire. The name upon which it is written should lift it out of the range of all our petty and private differences. C.H.

B

The Name of Washington.[5]

Ev'n as the one sole star of morning,
    How it shines upon the earth!
Ev'n as a God-lit light adorning
    A great Nation's noble birth!
Or like an altar-flame it rises
    From Freedom's battle truliest won:
        Then send it o'er the wide world—
The Name of Washington.

To breathe it is to brand all trading
    Through dominion for a throne;
To know it is to curse all wading
    Into blood for power alone;

---

[3] CH had had problems with his eyesight before: 'Under his father's tuition the poet became a fair English scholar. But he had to improve the education he had received, as well as he could, by his own reading and study. In this he was indefatigable; and to such an extent that in early manhood his sight was seriously impaired for a time by close application to the only kind of works which his limited means enabled him to obtain – the cheap popular editions of standard authors, in small type': 'Charles Harpur', *ATCJ*, 14 March 1874, p. 13. This impairment may have been blur or a binocular vision problem such as double vision, which can commonly arise with excessive near work and is usually resolved by stopping it – although prolonged spasm in the eye's focusing equipment is a more serious (and uncomfortable) possibility. In 1855 CH, now in his early forties, may simply have needed reading glasses, obtainable locally: oculists (eye surgeons) were advertising in Sydney newspapers by 1831, opticians by 1836, and spectacles were in widespread use by the 1840s.

[4] See Letter 40 and notes.

[5] Parkes declined to print this in *Empire*; it appeared some weeks later in E. J. Hawksley's *PA*, 26 May 1855, p. 6 (h152b).

> While like an altar-flame it rises
>   From Freedom's battle truliest won:
>   Then send it o'er the wide world—
>   The Name of Washington.
>
> No cry is it for frantic Glory
>   Such as sworded hirelings laud;
> No greatness is there in its story
>   Or of conquest or of fraud;
> But like an altar-flame it rises
>   From Freedom's battle truliest won:
>   Then send it o'er the wide world—
>   The Name of Washington.

Charles Harpur.

43. Charles Harpur to *People's Advocate*, [21? April 1855]

Text: ML C380 (cutting)

To the Editor of the People's Advocate.[1]

Sir,—

It would really seem, that whenever a joke, a point, or any other nicety can be thoroughly damaged by a departure from "copy," that just at that instant the compositor's nag is wont to become skittish, and bolt from the course. See, for example, an Epigram of my own, published in a recent number of the Advocate,[2] in which much of the queerness o[f] the joke, and some of the spice of it too, depends on the wilfu[l]l way in which '*Louse and*' is made to rhyme with '*thousand.*' According to custom always, however, just at this point the compositor diverges from his "copy," and by running on the end of one line the "No more" that should form another of itself, he contrives, to the *worst* of his ability, to botch in no small degree the drollery of the effusion. The misarranged lines should stand thus:—

> But to its store
> Dan Cooper flung a *thousand!*[3]

---

[1] The source of this item is an undated cutting in ML C380, p. 89. The letter probably appeared in *PA*, 21 April 1855, an issue missing from the online version via Trove.

[2] 'The Great Gun of the Patriotic Fund Brought to a Queer Test' (h163b; *PA*, 31 March 1855, p. 5). It took a sardonic poke at the donors to the Fund: see further, p. 85 n. 8.

[3] Daniel (later, Sir Daniel) Cooper (1821–1902), merchant, and parliamentarian, politically liberal associate of Parkes and Charles Cowper, one of the wealthiest men in the colony and known for his philanthropy.

And should a beggar fling a *Louse* and[4]
>   No more,
> I wonder which would be, &c.

If the compositor *would* only stick to his "copy" as closely as the cobbler *should* to his "last,"[5] the publishing of one's things in a newspaper would be a much pleasanter matter than it is. But as it is, the annoyances in one scale are such as more than to counterbalance all those gratifications proper to authorship, which can be placed against them in the other. So, at least, does it generally happen in the case of all these newspaper correspondents, who from situation, or what not, cannot themselves correct the press.

Trusting to your insertion of this as a sort of *salvo* to a very general grievance, I remain, Sir, your most patient and long-suffering correspondent.

CHARLES HARPUR.

44. Charles Harpur to *People's Advocate*, [21? April 1855]

Text: ML C380 (cutting)

To the Editor of the People's Advocate.[6]

Sir,—

In reply to a letter containing some slight strictures on the spirit of the present war in Europe,[7] a friend of mine writes me that he is quite an enthusiast with respect to it, and that in attestation of the sincerity of his enthusiasm, he has contributed the annual sum of £10 to the Patriotic Fund.[8] Now in this contribution, he has no doubt, done well—*that is*, if the living presence of his charity *at home*, bears a due proportion to its antipodean effigy[9]—*and not else*. Thus far, however, there is nothing absolutely at issue between us.

---

[4] For this line *PA* had printed 'And should a beggar fling a *Louse* and no more,' thus spoiling the double rhyme.

[5] Proverb, 'Let the cobbler stick to his last,' traceable to Roman author Pliny the Elder. A last is a model of the foot made of wood, etc., on which boots and shoes are shaped.

[6] The source for this item is an undated cutting in ML C380, pp. 89, 91. The letter probably appeared in *PA*, 21 April 1855, missing from the online version via Trove.

[7] The Crimean War (1853–56).

[8] The Royal Patriotic Fund was created in October 1854 when Queen Victoria appealed for public donations to assist the widows and orphans of British servicemen killed in the Crimean War (the state at this time bearing no responsibility for the welfare of dependants). By February 1855 Governor-General Sir William Denison had echoed the appeal (see *NSW Government Gazette*, 3 February 1855, pp. 301–4) and a local fund was started. The response was generous: the Australian colonies would eventually contribute over £60,000. Donation was at once an act of compassion and a public declaration of loyalty to Britain and the Crown. Parkes was a leading promoter: see his speech reported in *Empire*, 21 February 1855, p. 2. Few – among them CH, Daniel Deniehy and John Dunmore Lang – dared publicly question the morality of the war or the rationale for Australia's contribution.

[9] Colonial Australians – even the native-born – called Britain 'home'. CH approves of his friend's charity towards Britain providing it is balanced by his charity locally.

But I should like that he, or any one else, would show me, and many others who think with me—not by clap-trap statements, but by straightforward and rational ones,—in what way this war, undertaken to uphold one despotism against another, is calculated to advance the true liberties of Europe, or benefit her suffering and down trodden nationalities? For myself, I can see nothing in it, either immediately or prospectively, over which a true devotee of Liberty can sincerely and hopefully rejoice—except, indeed, the brilliant evidence it affords that manly valour and contempt of death are undiminished in the race. The whole design of it from the first, has appeared to me, and to many others (in so far, *especially*, as the governing aristocracy of England are concerned) to have been rather to keep things as they are,—to bolster up existing interests,—than to lay any stable foundation for the future liberty and security of Europe. And if there is a reason for believing such to have been its main object from the commencement, what hope for the nations,—for Hungary, Italy, Poland,[1]—what hope, however meagre, can be conjured out of it *now*, under the recent pretensive alliance with Austria?[2]—Austria, forever recking with the blood of patriots![3] Nay, owing to the pernicious influence of this *mis-alliance*, it is exceedingly probable, that the very next thing we hear about from Europe, will be, that it has terminated in a disgraceful and hollow peace;—a peace leaving Nicholas[4] all but as powerful for mischief as before; and making all the blood and treasure which England and France have hitherto expended in its conduct, but so much wash and waste of national means—so much excellent physic thrown to the dogs of war—so much young and noble manhood insidiously kneeded into clay! "O most lame and impotent

---

[1] Failed nationalist and reformist risings occurred across Europe in 1848–49. The Hungarian revolution was crushed by the combined forces of Habsburg Austria and Tsarist Russia. In Italy the Piedmontese and their allies fought in vain to push the Austrians from Lombardy-Venetia, and in Poland the revolts of 1830 and 1846 were followed by the failed Poznań uprising of 1848 against Prussian rule. CH's sonnet 'Kossuth' (h614a; *Empire*, 3 November 1853, Supplement p. 2) celebrated the Hungarian liberator Lajos Kossuth (1802–94), forced into exile in the west.

[2] Although Austria had the help of its ally Tsar Nicholas I in putting down the Hungarian revolution in 1849 it came – like Britain – to view an intact Ottoman Empire as a bulwark against Russian expansion. In August 1854 it joined Britain, France and Prussia in demanding Russia withdraw its troops from the Danubian Principalities. Russia refused, precipitating the British and French invasion of the Crimean peninsula.

[3] A reference to the suppression by Habsburg Austria, under Foreign Minister and Chancellor Klemens von Metternich, of nationalist and liberal political movements in the period 1815–48, and notably of the revolutions of 1848–49.

[4] Nicholas I (1796–1855), Tsar of Russia 1825–55. The quintessentially conservative autocrat, Nicholas's ambition to dominate the Balkans led to a war with Turkey in 1827–29 and finally to defeat in the Crimean War (1854–56). He died 2 March 1855, but news of it did not reach NSW until 19 May (in *Empire*, p. 1).

conclusion!"[5] Heroes of the Alma! heroes of Inkermann![6] in the event of such a peace, how shall your gory dead be kept at rest in those untimely Russian graves!

I am Sir, yours, &c.,
CHARLES HARPUR.

April, 1855.

45. Charles Harpur to *People's Advocate*, [by 2 February 1856]

Text: People's Advocate, 2 February 1856, p. 5

To the Editor of the People's Advocate.

SIR,—

Thank God that we at length have the New Constitution![7] In itself I despise it, as a disgraceful hotchpotch, that shames us by the side of our younger sister, Victoria;[8] and awards us but a second—nay, but a fourth place in a race, in which we should have been first. But I thank God for it, nevertheless, because it will give us rest for at least some years to come, and it may be for good, from the pithless system of political agitation with which we have been deluded for the last two or three years:[9]—a system which never had, nor has, genius for anything beyond the laborious trundling—not away, (that were somewhat!) but backward and forward—of the impedimental lumber and rubbish now lying about the threshold of our national progress, and which should be *stepped over at once, and at a single stride* This is a brief,

---

[5] Desdemona, of Iago, in Shakespeare's *Othello*, II.2.161.

[6] In the Battle of Alma (20 September 1854) the British and French drove the Russian forces from the Heights of Alma before Sevastopol at a cost of 3,600 allied and 5,000 Russian casualties. At Inkerman Ridge, under the walls of the city (5 November 1854), the allies withstood repeated attacks by superior forces, losing 4,400 casualties to the Russians' 12,000.

[7] The *New South Wales Constitution Act* 1855 (UK) established a form of responsible government for NSW: the Legislative Council and a lower house, the Legislative Assembly. The Council's 21 members, nominated by the Governor, were initially appointed for five years and then for life. The Assembly comprised 54 elected members representing 34 electoral districts. Voting was confined to males over 21 who met property or income qualifications. The Governor retained significant powers. The new legislature had wide powers over domestic matters, including the control of revenue and disposal of Crown lands, but London retained the power to disallow colonial legislation. The constitution bore the stamp of the conservative W. C. Wentworth, its chief promoter, but was shorn of the hereditary peerage (Deniehy's 'bunyip aristocracy') he wanted for the upper house.

[8] The colony of Victoria had separated from NSW in 1851. The *Victoria Constitution Act* 1855 (UK) provided for a bicameral system with the upper house elected. Property qualifications for voters were less restrictive than in NSW, and a separate Act in 1856 introduced the secret ballot, two years before NSW.

[9] Despite years of fierce and prolonged protest from liberals and radicals – public demonstrations, petitions and a constant press war – Wentworth took his proposals for a new NSW Constitution to London and the Bill passed through the Imperial Parliament to become law on 16 July 1855.

but a sufficiently comprehensive characterization of the system of agitation to which it refers, and intimates aptly enough, however figuratively, all we ever had, or should have, to expect from its agency—the very "seamark of its utmost sail."[1] Needy men, and political adventurers, have, no doubt, well buttered their bread by it: but having done so, let them now, in the name of all that is downright and earnest, give political place to the apostles—whenever they appear—of something better. At all events, let us be devoutly thankful to Providence, (if Providence has aught just now to do with Australian Politics?) for the rest the New Constitution promises in some measure to give us, from all such worthless agitation; and as a consequence, the time and quietude it will afford to the predestined nationalizers of this people (none, or very few of whom, are yet in its political arena) to think of what better should be done, and to mature their plans for doing it well.

I am,
Yours obediently,
CHARLES HARPUR.

P.S.—I regret to learn from the papers, that Mr. John Robertson of Scone, has been forced from his candidature for a seat in the new Legislature[,] by ill health.[2] This is really a political loss: for if a majority of such as he, and Hardy, and yourself, with some others, could be carried into the House of Representatives,[3] the political salvation of the country might be even wrought out of this New Constitution itself—bad as it is—or rather, it might be then made the occasion of such a consummation. For Robertson is not only clear headed, and progressive in a sufficiently anti-European sense, but he is sound at the core, and a son of the soil. It is not in the nature of things, that men brimful

---

[1] 'Here is my journey's end, here is my butt, / And very sea-mark of my utmost sail.' – Othello, over Desdemona's deathbed, in Shakespeare's *Othello*, v.2.266–7. A sea-mark is a conspicuous object distinguishable at sea that serves to guide or warn sailors.

[2] John (later, Sir John) Robertson (1816–91), land reformer and politician. A friend of CH's, he would be responsible for CH's appointment as Sub-Gold Commissioner in 1859. Robertson did in fact stand as a radical for the electorate of Phillip, Bligh and Brisbane (the upper Hunter) in 1856 and was returned. His platform was 'manhood suffrage, vote by secret ballot, equal electoral districts on population, abolition of state aid to religion, National education, free trade, and free selection of crown lands before survey' (*ADB*).

[3] John Richard Hardy (1807–58), newspaper editor, pastoralist, police magistrate and the first Gold Commissioner of NSW, praised for his 'fairness, rectitude, adaptability and humanity' (*ADB*). He stood twice for parliament, in 1856 and 1858, but was not elected. In 1854 E. J. Hawksley as editor of *PA* ('yourself') – along with Lang, Deniehy and CH – had declared his support for independence of the Australian colonies but he did not stand for parliament.

of Englandism,[4] can ever do us any real national good. It were nearly as well to have a House full of Plunketts[5] as of them. But the days of the political influence of all such men in this land, are assuredly numbered.

C. H.

46. Charles Harpur to *People's Advocate*, 11 February 1856[6]

Text: *People's Advocate*, 23 February 1856, p. 4

To the Editor of the People's Advocate.

SIR.—

It is painful to observe how Irishmen who profess to love their Fatherland, and who pretend to be liberals, and it may be republicans, in this the land of their adoption—to observe how blindly, how pronely such men can be-gull themselves with the shallow claptrap of Mr. Plunkett;[7] a man who began his public career by selling his own country,[8] who has prolonged it as the veriest Government hack, and who would now signalise the close of it by doing something towards damnifying the present and future of Australia. All his antecedents are against him; they are all so many sneers—so many diabolical grins in the sleeve at the foolish hopes of those who can flatter themselves with the notion that he will ever do our country any political good. But passing them by, on what in him do his supporters really found their trust? Out of his official element he is as mere a starveling as could anywhere be met with. Nay,

---

[4] Although Robertson, Hardy and Hawksley were born in England, CH does not seem to extend the charge of 'Englandism' to them. Parkes is neither named as a viable candidate nor exempted from the charge. Cf. Daniel Deniehy's remark to John Dunmore Lang that 'Mr. Parkes has too much not of the English man in but of "Englishmanism" about him', to give sympathy or aid to the Australian republicans (Deniehy to Lang, 6 June 1854, Lang Papers, ML A2227, Vol. 7).

[5] See n. 7, below.

[6] This letter appeared during the election campaign for four Sydney City seats (see next note). For subsequent correspondence, see Joseph J. Harpur to *PA*, 9 March 1856 (in *Suppl. Letters*), and CH's response of 31 March (Letter 47).

[7] John Hubert Plunkett (1802–69), Irish-born lawyer and politician, Solicitor-General of NSW 1832–36 and Attorney-General 1836–56, the first Catholic appointed to high civil office in the colony. An official nominee of the Legislative Council and member of the Executive Council, Plunkett retired in 1856 to seek election to the first Legislative Assembly. His conservative candidacy alarmed the liberals and radicals, as he appealed strongly to Irish Catholic sentiment. He would be defeated in Sydney by the liberal 'bunch' led by Parkes and Charles Cowper, but would then win the country seat of Argyle, only to move to the Legislative Council in early 1857.

[8] In Ireland, Plunkett had worked successfully with Daniel O'Connell in the cause of Catholic emancipation and was credited with the success of O'Connellite candidates in Roscommon at the 1830 general election that put Earl Grey and the Whigs in power. His reward was the Solicitor-Generalship of NSW. On the hustings, Parkes accused him of having 'allowed the temptation of place to have an overwhelming influence upon him' and having 'sold his country' (*SMH*, 6 February 1856, p. 4).

if there were any depth in the man, these Irishmen, these Tipperary Boys,[1] might stand somewhat excused; but he is shallowness itself, even in his craft. For example, at a meeting in Macquarie Ward on the 5th instant[2] he was asked his opinion of vote by ballot,[3] and this was his answer.

"He thought vote by ballot was *desireable in Ireland*, where the thumb screw was often put on electors, and *influence used* to prevent freedom of election. But in this country every man was independent, and in the spirit of independence cared not, and ought to care not, what observations were made as to the way in which he voted. They should therefore be willing to give their votes *like men*."

Now the real English of this is, that it is imprudent in Ireland for Irishmen *to be like men*, it is there quite natural and proper for them to be like beasts and devils; that *here* they should vote openly like men, but that *there* a mere difference of circumstances renders it proper and right for them to vote covertly, if they could, like beaten curs. Or, if you will, that vote by ballot is a political dodge, and that such a dodge in Old Ireland might very properly be part and parcel of a man's political life; but that here Irishmen breathe heroic air, have cast the slough of their paternal snakehood,[4] and may therefore walk upright like so many christians.

Such is the sort of compliment he pays to the intelligence of these Irishmen, these Tipperary Boys, his supporters; for such is positively the real, downright logical sense of what he says. And what a racy morsel it really is! a pure spice of Plunkettonian doctrine! a veritable piece of the speaker's inward man! And whole heaps of Irishmen applauded the sentiment! and Scott Ross,[5] it is likely, called particular attention to it! May St. Patrick enlighten *them*, and may his

---

[1] Fighting Irishmen. The term was adopted by vocal supporters of Plunkett at the hustings in the 1856 election.

[2] Plunkett's speech (actually on 6 February) at the Cricketer's Arms, Pitt-street, was reported in *Empire*, 7 February, p. 4, and *SMH*, 7 February 1856, pp. 4–5.

[3] Voting was by show of hands at a public meeting followed, if need be, by a public poll where each voter's choice was public knowledge. The Australian colonies were early adopters of the secret ballot: Tasmania, Victoria and SA in 1856, NSW in 1858 and Queensland in 1859. Britain introduced it in 1872, and the US states (where it was known as the 'Australian ballot') in the 1880s and 1890s. Hawksley, the editor of *PA*, was a leader of the push for the secret ballot. See CH's squib 'The Ballot', with note (h027a; *PA*, 20 September 1856, p. 5).

[4] CH plays on the popular belief that St Patrick, the 'Apostle of Ireland', banished the snakes from that island.

[5] Robert Scott Ross (1822–1905), businessman, magistrate (owing, some said, to Plunkett's patronage) and – although a Protestant – honorary secretary of the central committee of Plunkett's campaign. Derided by the liberals and radicals, he also stood unsuccessfully for Cumberland Boroughs in the election.

father whip *him* with the energy of a puritan.[6]

But any ma[n], with a clear head upon his shoulders, has only to read Mr. Plunkett's electioneering speeches, as reported in the journals, to find out how enormously unprincipled he is:—an Irish politician of the worst school, one of the needy class of men ever ready to sell their country for the mess[7] of an hireling, and their creed too, upon a pinch. And moreover, it is to be seen from these same speeches, how shallow in reality is the man's mind—pinched and shallow as his brow.

I am, Sir,
Yours obediently,
11th Feb., 1856.   CHARLES HARPUR.

47. Charles Harpur to Joseph Jehoshaphat Harpur, 31 March 1856

Text: People's Advocate, 12 April 1856, p. 5

TO MR. J. J. HARPUR.[8]
Per favour of the People's Advocate.

Dear Sir,—

In a letter of yours which appeared in a late number of the *Advocate*, you state, rather ostentatiously I think, that certain remarks of mine on Mr. Plunkett which were published in a prior issue of the same journal, had given you much pain. Well, what is passed cannot be recalled; and moreover, I am afraid, since you seem to be so transcendantly sensitive, that I shall have to inflict a slight pang or two more upon you, by the tenor of these my remarks in reply. You denounce my Plunkettonion philippic[9] as being excessively bitter. So be it: I will make no apology for it on that account, nor indeed upon any other. * * * * * * * * You twit me also with being unfaithful to the teachings of the illustrious Dr. Channing.[10] But, my dear Sir, I can no more pin myself to the skirt of a Dr. Channing, however much of an oracle with me, than to that of a Dr. Fiddlestick. And as to high flown notions of a super-human purity of motive, and charitableness of feeling, we may easily hear too

---

[6] Ross was a Congregationalist (or Independent), a movement that had its origins in English Protestant dissent of the 16th and 17th centuries. The Reverend John West, editor of the conservative *SMH*, and the paper's owner John Fairfax, were likewise Congregationalist supporters of Plunkett. Lang made much of the association: 'the Tipperary boys and the Independents – What a conjunction!' (*Empire*, 5 February 1856, p. 5).

[7] A serving of food, a meal.

[8] This letter is a rejoinder to CH's older brother Joseph's reply (of 9 March 1856: in *Suppl. Letters*) to CH's letter to *PA* of 11 February 1856 (Letter 46). This rejoinder was written after Plunkett's electoral defeat for a Sydney seat.

[9] Scathing attack, after the speeches made by Demosthenes against Philip II of Macedon.

[10] See p. 27 n. 5.

much of them. They are always somewhat suspected, even in the mouths of the best; and at second hand they are wearisome as well. Certainly I—even I myself, would have no objection to being an angel, were it possible. But as it is, I am *only* a man, and one too, who ventures to hold, that to *love like a God and hate like a Tartar* is no ignoble a rule for so mixed a nature as ours, in this most clannish, contentious, and battle-bearing world.

Then, as to your assertion of the logical correctness of Mr. Plunkett's statement about the Ballot, I deny it, and will disprove it. If logical at all, that statement is only verbally and apparently so. The Ballot is either the best protective clothing of a political right—protective of the weakness, and even the wilfulness, of human nature, and therefore universally fit and cogent; or it is a pure bit of parish expediency, a poor, pitiful, and time-serving dodge. To contend that it is *neither*, would be a mere breaking of words, and clearly at variance with the extreme nature of the question. Thus conservative, then, of political virtue, or thus opprobious to it, it is either *desirable* everywhere, or nowhere. If it is unworthy of practice here, it is a dodge in Ireland. The conclusion is unavoidable. I contend, however, that it is desirable everywhere, as a final institution, answering to and guarding the infirmities of the timid, the socially enthralled, the subservient, and even the wilful keeping them fast and safely to their consciences; and the tergiversation[1] with which I charged Mr. Plunkett had its root in the partial acknowledgment of this. A difference of circumstances, no doubt, may render the want of it more imperative in one country than in another; but this is only as it were the segment of the circle, suggesting the inevitability of the whole figure, the final and comprehensive type of universality. Nor would even the general political heroism of a community be any valid argument against its universal fitness; for the public virtue of such a community, in the matter of the franchise, could not be too well seconded, and nothing could do this so effectively as the Ballot. The brave man, though he records his mere vote under its conditions, can still be as *English* as he would, and proclaim as loudly as he likes, the party he prefers and would have elected. But the facile and the cowardly, and there are such persons in every community, need the protection of its secrecy, and have therefore a moral right to it. All arguments to the contrary are *bosh;* all the heroics about all men, here or elsewhere, voting openly in the spirit of independence, are but so much conscious clap-trap, unsupported by facts, belied by the infirmities of human nature, and therefore essentially illogical. It is wrong in reason then, it is dishonest, it is even shallow, to affirm or admit of the Ballot, that it is desirable *anywhere* and not *everywhere*, except on the Utop[i]an assumption of there being *somewhere* existent, a perfectly fearless, individually independent, infallibly enlightened, and incorruptible community.

---

[1] Desertion of a cause.

So much then for the logical correctness of Mr. Plunkett's statement: and had you pondered the matter a little more, you would have surely have seen it in the light that I do. But whether in that case you would have so seen it or not, you cannot *now*, I think, fail to perceive, that my "bad logic" is better than your own.

To your complaint of my not having taken up Mr. Plunkett on other grounds than those which make the matter of the letter in question, I can only say, that I had not so much time for the work as you seem to have had; and in what I did, intended no more than to have in passing, just one hearty fling at him with my ugliest tomahawk. Besides, it is likely, that I did not then think the subject worth more of my notice.

I remain, dear Sir,
Yours, &c.,
CHARLES HARPUR.

Lowefield,[2] 31st March,

48. Charles Harpur to Henry Parkes, 20 March 1857

Text: ML MSS 947

Jerry[']s Plains, 20th March 1857

My dear Sir,

Some time since I sent you the heading of a Subscription List[3] to print for me: but there is nothing to wonder at, though (as it seems) you should have forgotten to attend to it, under the crush of recent circumstances.

I have read all that concerned you lately[4] in the Empire with a proud sort of pain. I was pained by the disclosures you have had, of necessity, to make; but I was proud at the same time of the lights they let in upon you. Milton has somewhere said, that all those things which, in their apparent nature, seem most to threaten disaster and disgrace to the thoroughly just man, do only in the end prove the greater safety and glory to him: and that this will be the event in your case, I feel satisfied.

---

[2] A property at Jerry's Plains: see p. 102 n. 2. CH moved there to farm sheep some time after March 1855. In other documents connected with CH the name appears as Lowsfield. It occurs nowhere else in newspapers and may have been his own invention.

[3] CH is probably referring to the printed proforma he would enclose in April 1857 in letters to over 50 prominent people. The letters sought help in gathering pledges for the publication of a collection of poems, very probably the projected 'Wild Bee of Australia'. See CH's letters of 2 April 1857 to Donaldson (Letter 49) and to N. D. Stenhouse (in *Suppl. Letters*); and Stenhouse's reply (Letter 53). CH compiled a list of 55 people to be sent such letters, see ML A87-2, pp. 663–4.

[4] Parkes was in desperate financial straits at this time. Facing impending bankruptcy, he had resigned his parliamentary seat in December to devote himself to trying to save his newspaper. He revealed his 'embarrassments' to his readers in a painful confessional statement in *Empire*, 11 March 1857, p. 2. CH must have seen this.

These disclosures have also shown me, that I have myself erred greviously in certain conclusions I had come to against you.[1] But I will make atonement in my heart; and indeed in every other way that I best may.

Under present circumstances then, I shall not trouble you about the List, any further than to request, that you will not let it altogether slip you. And when matters become somewhat smooth again, it will be worth your while perhaps to attend to so slight an affair.

In worldly respects, I am myself doing about as well as usual. But my health is very bad. I have had to do on several occasions latterly, what I never had before—fairly take to my bed. In fact, my constitution would appear to be fast breaking up; and it sometimes strikes me that I am not very long for this side of the clouds.[2]

I remain, my dear Sir,
Yours very truly
Chas: Harpur.

49. Charles Harpur to Stuart Alexander Donaldson, 2 April 1857

Text: ML *D19

Jerry's Plains,[3] 2 April /57

Sir,[4]

I beg to place in your hands the accompanying Subscription List[5] (which explains itself) with a respectful request, that you will do me the important favor of using your influence in promoting the object of it. But should you happen to think that in thus doing I have somewhat overstepped the bounds of a due liberty, my only excuse is, that though I may have no direct claims upon your favor, on any account whatever, I may yet urge those indirect ones, which in educated society are wont to secure to men of acknowledged literary merit, the social good offices (to a reasonable extent) of their intelligent and influential compatriots.

Had I reason to fear the proposed Book would prove a mere ephemeron,[6] and consequently, that the effect of it on the mind and taste of the reading

---

[1] See Letter 42; 'Impromtu' of May 1854 (h187a); and the slighting 'The Great Gun...' of March 1855 (h163b).

[2] Perhaps an early sign of the tuberculosis that would end CH's life in 1868.

[3] CH may have been writing from the township or from his property Lowsfield, around 19 km upriver.

[4] Stuart (later, Sir Stuart) Alexander Donaldson (1812–67), merchant, pastoralist and politician and (briefly) first premier of NSW under responsible government. At this point he was treasurer in the Parker ministry.

[5] See next item.

[6] Something short-lived.

public would be of no abiding benefit, I should no doubt be guilty of some presumption in troubling you with a request like the above, however respectful the mere *manner* of my making it might be. But many of the poems which will be interspersed through the original contents of the volume (should it forthcome) have already been pronounced by competent authorities to be of a high character. Robert Lowe,[7] who is now a member of the Imperial Ministry, and a principal writer in the great *Times* newspaper, has said of some of them, in a letter I have at present by me, that they were in his opinion "very beautiful", and of "extraordinary merit." And another gentleman, equally accomplished in mind, and even farther advanced perhaps in esthetic enquiries, has publicly recorded it as his opinion of others of them, that they have "a spiritual Hesper characteristic of radiant beauty to his feeling unique", and of others again, that he held them to be "equal to any things of the same kind in modern poetry".[8]

My own estimate of the poems thus spoken of, in common with all I have written, may not be nearly so high without being a truer one. Indeed, so little have I been held to them by any active sympathy or likeness of taste amongst my social compeers, and so apt are we to misvalue in ourselves whatever has been much slighted by those most in contact with us, that I think I am quite as likely to under as to over rate their merits. Be this, however, as it may, what I would insinuate is, that I have referred to the authorities above quoted in no vain and confident spirit, but purely by way of a set off, as it were, to any presumption I may happen to be thought chargeable with in the present proceeding. Neither have I used them to commit you, Sir, in any way, to the proposed object of it. For if, from whatever cause, you should be averse to moving in the business, you will only have to re-enclose me the List to get totally rid of it. And though your doing this may very naturally prevent me from thereafter thinking of you as a *friend*, I shall yet hold it altogether unwarrantable to infer from such an act, (in itself) that you are disposed to do me, or even to wish me, any manner of evil.

I have the honor to be,
Sir,
Your very humble Servant,
Chas: Harpur.

[Our govt?] will buy 2 copy to [. . .]—but not Subscribe[9]

---

[7] See p. 26 n. 3. Lowe returned to England in 1850, joined the staff of *The Times* as leader-writer, entered parliament in 1852, and would hold high office (including as Chancellor of the Exchequer and Home Secretary) over the next three decades. He was elevated to the House of Lords in 1880. See further, p. 232 n. 4.

[8] The remarks were made in Daniel Deniehy's review of *The Bushrangers* in *Empire*, 22 April 1853, p. 3. CH was wise to withhold his name: Deniehy had won the southern seat of Argyle in a February by-election, and was no political friend of the self-proclaimed 'liberal conservative' Donaldson. 'Hesper' is the evening star.

[9] The annotations scrawled on CH's letter are difficult to decipher, but are probably Donaldson's. See also next item.

50. Printed subscription list for 'Wild Bee of Australia', [April 1857]

Text: ML A1528

Stuart A. Donaldson Esqr M.P.[1]   No 2.

TO BE PUBLISHED BY SUBSCRIPTION, A VOLUME OF POEMS, BY CHARLES HARPUR.[2]

TERMS:

It is proposed that the Volume shall comprise 300 pages of well-selected matter, and be clearly printed and neatly bound in cloth, at the price of Ten Shillings and Sixpence per copy.

As, however, the Subscription Lists will be placed in none but responsible hands, Subscribers will be required, on putting down their names, to pay at once the amount subscribed for; and if, at the end of four months, the Subscription should be insufficient to warrant publication, the amounts so paid before hand shall be forthwith returned, on application to the holders of the particular Lists on which they severally appear.

NAME AND RESIDENCE.   NO. OF COPIES.   AMOUNT.

1[3]

N.B. About four months hence, every holder of a List will be requested, by note, to return it to the Writer, to enable him to conclude from an inspection of all of them together, as to whether the publication can be proceeded with. If it can, the moneys subscribed will be then collected on account of it; but if not, each List will be re-enclosed to the party whose name it bears, to serve as a guide in refunding them to the proper owners. C.H.

[1] 'M.P.' signifies Member of Parliament, usually (but not invariably) meaning a member of the NSW lower house, the Legislative Assembly (MLA). Donaldson's name (handwritten by CH) was second on the list of those to whom CH sent the printed form: see CH's two lists of subscribers (1857, in *Suppl. Letters*) and his letter to Donaldson of 2 April 1857 (Letter 49), with which this form was probably enclosed.

[2] The form was probably printed by Parkes: see Letter 48. The project fizzled: see Letter 54.

[3] Donaldson seems to have returned the form with a pledge for only one copy. The following paragraph is handwritten on the form.

51. Charles Harpur to Frank Fowler, 9 May 1857[4]

Text: *Month*, 2.3 (March 1858), p. 62

Jerry's Plains, April 30th, 1857.

My Dear Sir,

In a letter I had the other day from my friend *******[5] there occurred the following passage: "You do not know Frank Fowler. He is a very young man—an Englishman of real ability—with the genuine sparkle about him, a vein of imagery of his own, and the only 'chiel'[6] I have seen in New South Wales with a truly brilliant prose style." Well, upon reading this, I at once determined on becoming acquainted with you—if, possibly, I might. But how? I confess I was fairly puzzled as to the *how*—till struck by what seemed to me a lucky thought—lucky as being somewhat likely to conduce to the end I had at heart. I will send him, thought I, one of the Subscription Lists[7]—the only one I have remaining on hand—for my proposed publication; and the doing so will, at least, "break the ice," if it do nothing more. It is true, *my* poetry may not be up to his critical mark—but there may, nevertheless, be enough in it to interest him—a little in *me*, as its author.

May 9th, 1857.

Having scratched down the above, under a sudden impulse, I threw it by—not being very well satisfied with either the manner or matter of it. But I have

---

[4] English journalist, author and lecturer Francis Edmund Town (Frank) Fowler (1833–63) founded *The Month – A Literary and Critical Journal* not long after arriving in Sydney in 1855. It was soon at war with *Empire*; the present letter preceded a multi-stage literary scrap and would be recruited to form part of it: *(1)* *Month* reviewed Henry Parkes's verse collections *Stolen Moments* and *Murmurs of the Stream* adversely: see p. 105 n. 6. *(2)* Angered by Fowler's lack of response to the hand of friendship offered in the present letter, and incensed by the Englishman's stated ambition to 'establish something like a national literature' in his adopted country, CH joined the fray on Parkes's behalf with a new version of 'The "Nevers" of Poesy [Republished, with Additions.]' (h331d), in which Fowler's poetic sense was excoriated in both revised verse and added notes (*Empire*, 9 March 1858, pp. 4–5; for the early prose version of the poem in *PA*, 20 September 1856, p. 5, see h331a). *(3)* Fowler responded in kind in a 'Postscript' to the March 1858 issue of *Month* (2.3, pp. 159–62). It included a printing of the present, friendly letter and countervailing quotation from CH's notes. *(4)* In a long note to 'The Poet' (h459d), CH further mocked Fowler's literary pretensions (in *Empire*, 28 May 1858, p. 2). Finally, *(5)* Fowler's friend and editorial successor at *Month*, Joseph Sheridan Moore, used the present letter as an exhibit, comparing it to the mockery in the note to 'The Poet', as part of a sharp reproof of CH (see Letter 56, in *Empire*, 2 June 1858, p. 5). The first printing of the present letter (in *Month*) is the source of the text here.

[5] If the seven asterisks implied the equivalent number of letters, CH may have meant his friend Daniel Henry Deniehy.

[6] Child; more generally a fellow, chap – popularised by Robert Burns's 'A chield's amang you, taking notes / And, faith, he'll prent it' ('On the Late Captain Grose's Peregrinations thro' Scotland Collecting the Antiquities of that Kingdom,' 1789).

[7] See p. 93 n. 3.

since read your very racy, and in many other respects exquisite "oration,"[1] delivered the other night at the Sydney School of Arts, with its sparkling jets of mimetic verse flying up out of it, as from an over-full fountain of thought and feeling, and the impulse which is indicated above, has been thereby renewed in me: and lo, I obey it, at all risks.

Still, as to the List, if you should not like to move in the business of it—not an over-pleasant one—why, no matter. You can, in that case, re-enclose it to me, or destroy it,—which ever you please.

I remain, my dear Sir,
Your admirer and would-be acquaintance,
CHAS. HARPUR.

52. Charles Harpur to *Empire*, 22 August 1857

Text: Empire, 2 September 1857, p. 5

A POET FLOODED OUT.[2]

THE hand in the following letter, even without the familiar initials at the foot, would be recognised as the author of numerous beautiful poems which have appeared from time to time in the EMPIRE.

DEAR MR. EDITOR—

In writing to you some time since I think I ventured a joke about the seasons on the Hunter having gone mad, and it would really seem as if they had; for there has just been *another* enormous flooding over of the river—the largest, I think, that has ever been witnessed by white men at this, the upper part of it. On Friday last (yesterday) about dusk, I observed, that the stream, after only two days' heavy rain, had risen nearly bank high; a circumstance it is likely I should not have so heedfully noticed had it occurred a few months back. But I have been wary of the Hunter ever since the flood of last June, which, had it have risen but a few feet higher, would have swept away the whole of a flock of sheep I had camping out on the flat in front of my residence. And on the

---

[1] An 'Oration on Literary Portraiture', delivered at the Sydney Mechanics' School of Arts on 4 May 1857, a series of imitations, with criticisms, of the styles of the standard British and American poets of the century – see reports in *Empire*, 5 May 1857, p. 5 and 6 May 1857, pp. 4–5; *SMH*, 7 May 1857, p. 3. Fowler had established a reputation for his 'orations', entertaining lectures on topics political and literary – the war in Crimea, Benjamin Disraeli (from the perspective of the Westminster press gallery), the life and poetry of Edgar Allan Poe. His 'Literary Portraiture' created a minor sensation.

[2] Three major floods occurred in the Hunter Valley in 1857 in June, July and the worst in August. CH was writing from Lowsfield, on the river some 19 km above Jerry's Plains. His letter describes events of the night of 21–22 August 1857. The storms of that week also flooded the Hawkesbury and Nepean Rivers nearer Sydney and, on the night of 20 August, drove the emigrant ship *Dunbar* to its destruction under the cliffs of South Head with the loss of all but one life.

eve of this also I should, in all probability, have had them camped on the same spot—the yard being too mucky to put them into it—but for the so startingly sudden rising of the river. As it was, I had them shifted to higher ground at the back of the house, but still on the flat; for I did not yet think there was any positive danger to be apprehended during the passing night. Nevertheless, I kept a good watch upon the temper of the swollen river, and it was well that I did so; for having set a mark near the bank, I went in about half-an-hour afterwards to look at it, and found that the water had actually advanced more than thirty yards up the slope of the flat in as many minutes; and in no great while afterwards, the darkling gleam of the encroaching flood could be seen from the front door of my house. The danger was plainly becoming imminent, and at about nine o'clock, I and my man Tom[3] had to be thinking of a "flitting" to the heights at the back, and of the best manner of making it. Luckily Mrs. H. with the boys, had left a few days before on a visit to her father's,[4] which was a great relief to me as it happened; for the water had at length reached the house, and the instant removal of my family in such an event would have taken up much of the time that I and Tom could now devote to placing such of the household things as were most liable to damage upon the tables and berths—that is, as high out of the probable reach of the water as we could.

This done, the next thing to be cared for was the safety of the sheep; and so, snatching up as many necessary things, such as food, tea and sugar, &c., as we could conveniently take with us on the nonce,[5] we sallied forth to gather together and move them off at once to the height at the back. But this we found was no easy matter; for the night was exceedingly dark, and sheep are the most stupidly wilful of domestic animals, with a mortal dislike, even in daylight, to be driven in any but some customary direction or way of their own choosing. But they began to move towards the rise at last—all but a sprinkling here and there of elderly ewes, weakened and rendered yet more stupid than they naturally are by the cold and constant rain. These refused to budge, or kept facing about at the barking dogs with that deplorable show of fight which a broken-up sheep is wont to exhibit: so we had to leave them to the mercy of the mantling[6] waters, and hurry away with the rest of the flock. All this time the din of the river was becoming louder and louder; the fallen timber lying in great quantity about the flats was beginning to float, and then go lumbering off, as it became involved with the current, crashing and thumping

---

[3] Not identified.
[4] Mary Harpur had taken Washington (6), Charley (4) and Harold (18 months) to the Doyles's home at Montrose Park, near Jerry's Plains. The Harpurs' fourth child, Ada, was born one week after this letter was sent.
[5] On the occasion (obsolete literary usage).
[6] Spreading, enveloping.

and grinding on, and thus swelling the watery thunder of the time with yet more frightful noises. However, by might of much driving, and a trifle also of objurgation,[1] we at length succeeded in lodging our unhandy charge on the rising ground of the heights, but with the water swirling at our heels.

The next thing to be seen to was to light a camp fire for the night. This I left Tom to do, while I waded back to the house for some necessary traps[2] we had forgotten to snatch up in the haste of our leaving it. And cold work it was, for the water, even on the higher part of the flat over which we had just crossed with the sheep, was now over the tops of my boots, and in the house itself I found the water knee-deep. But as the water did not seem to me to be rising nearly so fast as it did a little before, it struck me that some of the more valuable of my household goods might yet, with Tom's help, be removed to our camp on the rise, and so when I had got back again, loaded to the utmost of my strength, I put the matter to Tom, and he consented to bear a hand in it. To be brief, we then loaded in this way to and fro several times, the streaming light of the fire above serving us bravely for a guide. But on the last occasion, I observed that the water was beginning to run even on the hill side of the house, for it was beginning to bicker[3] as it passed across the gleam of the fire light; and with this warning we desisted from our trips. For there was a creek a little to the right of us, and I knew that if the swell of the river continued to keep backing it up much longer, it would burst over its banks, just under the heights, in such volume as to sweep us both away on the instant, like a couple of ants.

And now, Mr. Editor, as you sit snugly by your safe city hearth, just fancy how your country friend was outing it[4] on such a night. I will describe the *how* as if it were again passing. I am sitting on a wet log, for it is still drizzling drearily, by the side of a most savage looking fire, flaring and crackling and smoking enormously, on the very edge as it were of a coming deluge, and with nothing better to do than to keep watching its broad reflection as it goes glaring through the dark, out over the wild and roaring waters, suggesting rather than revealing their frightful breadth, and half showing in the bickering roadway of its light yonder—far down in the submerged valley, the gnarled and crowding boles of the flooded gums. It is a sight worth seeing—I admit that; but it touches me and others like me too nearly to be at all pleasant. Besides, I have taken the whole of it in, and disposed it finally in my mental chamber of imagery; and now, at last, what lucky expedient may be hit upon to get me best through such a dreary and comfortless night? Tom can only talk about the good quarters the sheep are in under the circumstances, and

[1] Severe scolding.
[2] Colloquial shortening of *trappings* – portable articles, belongings.
[3] Make a rapidly repeated noisy action, as the brawling of a rapid stream over a stony channel.
[4] Living outdoors (*OED*, now rare).

I have had, for the present, more than enough of the sheep. I begin to get perished. I can't help thinking how much snugger one would have been by this time in his comfortable bed, well tucked in and blanketed to the lips. And then this confounded, everlasting drizzle, out of which there is no getting! A downright, pelting, all-in-earnest rain even would be positively preferable, for it would put one on his mettle—his pride of endurance. But how would such a rain agree with the rescued properties lying on a heap there, covered though they be with all our rugs and blankets? I had forgotten *that*. I see, even through my impatience, that patience alone can avail me: the night, nasty as it is, must be gone through with; and so I begin to make the most of the resources nearest me.

Sometimes I take a "blast of the pipe,"[5] and having roasted one side of my body to the very last degree of endurance, I compel the other, by dint of a sudden gyration on my heel, to take *its* turn—of the roasting I mean. Now I whistle "There's a good time coming,"[6] finding the present, I suppose, so little to my liking. Tom is actually asleep, and I break down a sapling on the other side of him, just to give him a bit of a fright. Anon I frame half a wish (and my heart brightens up briskly as I do so) that my sight-loving boys were face to face with a Presence so wonderful as that which is out before me there,— thundering and agonising far away in the dark, or rushing and writhing into nearer view under the red gleams of the fire;—but luckily (and I am right glad of it!) they are in better quarters than these on such a mad-cap night as this is. Then I *croon* a line or so of some old song that has stuck to me for a quarter of a century, with the half conscious design of cheating myself into the notion that I *am* not—*upon the whole*—to say uncomfortable. A little anxious I am, no doubt, about the goods and chattels down in the flooded house yonder, in spite of my philosophy; but that is all. So passes the night.

The view this morning from the heights was at once grand and singular. From Lowe's Range on this side of the river, to Little Bulga on the other,[7] the whole valley between was like a vast but strange and outlandish sort of a lake, with primeval forest shooting out of its gleaming face, and shadowing its depths with a wild and leafy beauty. Just fancy that you are beholding such a scene. Much of the water covering the flats, the back water, is apparently as still as that of a mountain lake; but far away, through the tops of the trees, you

---

[5] A smoke: the phrase occurs in Irish newspapers from at latest 1842, Australian from 1846.

[6] A highly popular song derived from the poem 'Wait a Little Longer' by the Scottish poet and journalist Charles Mackay (1846), almost immediately put to music in England by Mackay's friend Henry Russell and in the US by Stephen Foster.

[7] The precise location of both places is uncertain. Lowe's Range is likely to be the high ground along the western side of Lowsfield. Little Bulga lay east of Lowsfield on the right bank (south side) of the Hunter, towards Cyrus Doyle's Oak Range (see *Maitland Mercury*, 7 May 1874, p. 2). If so, then the 'river' here must be the flooded Doyle's Creek, normally a tributary of the Hunter but now overwhelmed by it.

can trace the mid-current of the river as it goes raging and boiling along in a rough, heaping line or ridge, with the countless sprays tossing and foaming and flashing out of its whole length, like the manes of ten thousand horse (I can liken them to nothing else so truly) charging in column!

Early in the day, finding that the flood was either at a stand-still or rising but very slowly, I again waded into the house, and found that its contents were much less injured than I had feared they would be, the damage falling chiefly on such wearing apparel and sundries as happened to be lying about unthought of on the over night.

It is now about noon, and the waters are subsiding fast, leaving the higher parts of the flats dry, in long strips and indented patches, like so many variously shaped islands. My house itself will be waterless in an hour or so at the farthest, but it will retain a deposit of mud a foot deep at the least. What a job!

I have written this, my dear Mr. Editor, either for your private reading only, or for publication also, at your good pleasure, and remain yours truly.

C.H.

Lowsfield, Upper Hunter, August 22.

P.S.—(August 24th.)—Finding this morning that Doyle's Creek,[1] which hems me in at the back, had run down sufficiently to be fordable, I took a ride to ascertain how my next neighbour Mr. Huxley, senior,[2] who lives about two miles lower down the river, had fared from the flood; and was much grieved to find that his cornshed, stockyard, pigstyes, in short his whole establishment except the side walls of the dwelling-house, had been swept down by it. So rapid was the rise of the water, that Mr. Huxley and his family had only time to carry their household properties to the loft before escaping themselves. Afterwards, however, by means of a ladder, slanted from the hill side under which the house stands, they broke into the roof and got thence some bedding and a few other things; all the rest went with the roof and gables during the

---

[1] A stream flowing north into the Hunter River 14 km west of Jerry's Plains and immediately to CH's east. Doyle's Creek was named after early grantee Cyrus Matthew Doyle, Mary Harpur's uncle. The clan held much land in this area.

[2] Thomas Huxley (1804–80) farmed at Oak Range, Jerry's Plains. CH's description of riding two miles (3.2 km) down the Hunter River to visit Huxley helps to place Lowsfield tentatively as the 724-acre property granted to naval officer Alexander Bell Lowe, subsequently purchased by Cyrus Matthew Doyle, immediately to the west of Doyle's 640-acre block, and better known to locals as 'Lowe's Flat'.

night. With the corn shed also, about 150 bushels of maize[3] (all it contained), were swept away. Verily, some men, more than others, are born to trouble. Mr. Huxley came to reside in this district about a year and a half ago, having been unfortunate as a settler upon the Hawkesbury; and being a striving, hard working man, was rapidly retrieving his circumstances. But now, by the disasters of a single night, he is once again all but ruined! I am greatly afraid that many of the dwellers lower down have fared equally ill.

C. H.

53. Nicol Drysdale Stenhouse to Charles Harpur, 24 September 1857

Text: Stenhouse papers, ML A100

Sydney 21 Elizth St[4] 24 Sepr 1857.

My dear Mr Harpur,

I feel that my delay in writing,[5]—in every view which can be taken of it,— is inexcusable, & that even an attempt to shew that it may accord with true sensibility on my part to the honor, you conferred on me by the dedication of your poems,[6] & to your high claims as a man of genius would to any one,— knowing as little as you do of my unhappy idiosyncrasie[7]—appear merely to aggravate my offence. But, I trust I may find that our mutual friend Mr Deniehy has interposed with some success on my behalf, & that the time, to which I have so long & so ardently looked forward, may not now be far distant when you & I shall meet & when I shall have an opportunity for softening or—to speak boldly—for removing the very unfavourable impression which I must have produced on you by my silence.

I return the list[8] I regret to add with very few names. From the seclusion,

---

[3] Also called 'Indian corn' ('corn' in North America), maize was widely grown in the early days of the colony for cereal, grain or stock feed. It was easier to cultivate than wheat, thriving on roughly cleared ground, less susceptible to pests, more easily harvested and stored – but not much relished as food by the colonists. 150 bushels would weigh *c*. 3.8 tonnes.

[4] Nicol Drysdale Stenhouse (1806–73) was a Sydney lawyer and noted literary patron. The offices of solicitors Messrs Stenhouse and Hardy were at 19 and 21 Elizabeth-street, Sydney.

[5] In reply to CH to Stenhouse, 2 April 1857 (in *Suppl. Letters*).

[6] In 1853 CH had dedicated *Bushrangers* thus: 'To N. D. Stenhouse, Esq., these poems are respectfully inscribed by one, who, though personally unacquainted with him, has learned to appreciate his character and talents.' Apparently, they first met in 1859: see p. 113 n. 5.

[7] Despite his role as literary patron, Stenhouse was a notoriously bad correspondent – see Jordens, p. 2.

[8] Presumably the pro-forma list enclosed with CH to Stenhouse, 2 April 1857 (in *Suppl. Letters*).

10. Nicol Drysdale Stenhouse (by 1873), photographer unknown

in which I live[1]—when my daily toils allow me to return home fretted &
exhausted—& from the very unpoetical temperaments of most of those, to
whom any little influence I have is confined, the result of my efforts in this
matter ought not to have been surprising to myself, but it has mortified &
oppressed me beyond description.—The amount of the sums subscribed I
will remit to you either in bank notes or by cheque as you may direct.—

If you could manage matters so as to afford me the pleasure of a visit from
you for a few weeks, or even days I think that something might be done
material to the success of your proposed volume You & I might confer on
many points connected with it, in a manner much more satisfactory, than (so
far as I am concerned) we ever could in writing, & I should, at the same time
enjoy the privilege I so much desire of shewing you that I fully appreciate
both your *distinctive* & your *general* characteristics as a Poet.

---

[1] By this time Stenhouse had acquired Waterview Cottage in Balmain, a wooden bungalow on
15 acres with spectacular harbour views, a quarter of an hour by ferry from his office in town
(Jordens, pp. 51–2). Here he would build a fine library and offer hospitality to the writers and
intellectuals of colonial Sydney.

I also enclose your excellent preface[2]—as to which I can offer no suggestion except that I think the introductory paragraph might with advantage be omitted.

Do write to me as soon as you can and believe that

> I am My dear Mr Harpur
> Most faithfully yours
> Nicol D. Stenhouse

54. Charles Harpur to Henry Parkes, 22 October 1857

Text: ML MSS 947

Lowsfield, 22nd Oct /57.

My dear Sir,

I find from your printer's estimate, that I shall not be able to bring my book out in so costly a style as the "Murmurs."[3] Unless the Lists which have not yet come in have been more fortunate than those which have, the whole amount subscribed will fall short of the cost of publication—and there would be an end of the project.[4] What then would be the cost of a 300 page vol: in the style altogether (—paper, printing and binding—but with the lines leaded)—of "The Bushrangers"?[5] Or what would be the cost of 300 vols of such a book? for I do not care whether or no I publish a single vol more than the number actually subscribed for.

I have read Fowler's most spiteful and unjust attack upon the 'Murmurs'.[6] So manifestly spiteful and unjust is it, that in the end it will damage no one and nothing but the self constituted critic who has perpetrated it. I have already said as much as this—and more—to Deniehy; intimating at the same

---

[2] CH as early as 1850 had prepared a general preface for the 'Wild Bee', quoting from it in his letter to Parkes, 22 August 1850 (Letter 22), and in his letter-notice 'To My Literary Countrymen', 15 May 1851 (Letter 28). Perhaps he sent a draft to Stenhouse around the time of the April 1857 subscription attempt (see draft letter tentatively dated 1857, recipient not named: at ML A87-2; in *Suppl. Letters*). The present letter is Stenhouse's draft.

[3] In 1853 Parkes had expanded his liberal-radical *Empire* operation to include a job printing works; by 1855 the entire plant was steam powered: the Empire General Steam Printing Office, in Hunter Street. But by 1857 Parkes's hold on *Empire* was tenuous. Struggling against bankruptcy, he had come to an accommodation with his creditors, but would lose the paper in August 1858 (Martin, *Parkes*, pp. 142–6, 154). The 'book' is presumably the projected (but never published) 'Wild Bee of Australia'. Parkes's second collection of verse, *Murmurs of the Stream* had appeared in September (Sydney: James W. Waugh, 1857; online at SLV). It included sonnets dedicated to CH ('To Charles Harpur' and possibly 'To ******* ****** on being disappointed of his society') along with Halloran, Duncan and Lang.

[4] See p. 93 n. 3.

[5] At a page turnover, MS here reads: ' "The Bush-/ Bushrangers" '.

[6] *Month* ran long reviews savaging *Stolen Moments* (1.2, pp. 90–7) and *Murmurs of the Stream* (1.4, pp. 221–31). See also the caustic review of *Murmurs* by Fowler's friend Peter 'Possum (Richard Rowe, 1828–79) in *SMH*, 9 September 1857, p. 3.

time, that either he or I must take up the cudgels[1] against such flagrant critical injustice. Fowler's flanks might be turned without calling for much literary generalship—for he has made objection which could only have been made by one who was calculating upon the densest ignorance in his readers—and this could easily be made apparent to the dullest reader of the 'Month.'—Very few things have annoyed me as much for a long time. The man who could find nothing to sympathise with, nothing to love in such a book, must himself be a miscreant!

I sent you the other day for publication in the Empire some Rhymes,[2] the rough of which I gave you a copy of several years ago. But you have not yet published them: however, as they are really good, I hope you will.

I am, myself, well in health and so is Mrs H and children. I have four now—viz: Washington, Charles, Harold, and Ada.

Remember me to Mrs Parkes and the juvenals,[3] and believe me

Yours truly
Chas: Harpur.

Let me hear from you soon.

P.S. Your Murmurs of the Stream has come to hand, and I have been thumbing it over for the last day or two. Many of the pieces, however, are old acquaintances—but I like them none the less for that; no, but all the more abundantly. The best of them, as poetry, is unquestionably 'Sunrise'; and my other two especial favorites are A Picture of Love, which is beautiful in thought and feeling, and most exquisitely versified; and Yesterday and Tomorrow. Some of the political pieces, too, I like—but not all of them.

Yours truly
C.H.

Charles Harp[...]r[4]

[1] The revised 'The "Nevers" of Poesy' (h331d), with CH's attack on Fowler: for the successive steps of the dispute, see p. 97 n. 4.
[2] *Empire*, 28 October 1857, p. 6, carried a single column of five CH poems: 'Cosmoplasticus' (h696c), 'The Scenic Part of Poetry' (h677b), 'Rhymes to Henry Parkes...' (h611c), 'A Too Common Regret' (h455b) and 'Song' (h232b). All but 'Rhymes...' had previously been published elsewhere.
[3] Youths, juveniles, i.e., children, now five in number.
[4] Annotation in an unknown hand identifying 'C.H.'

55. Daniel Henry Deniehy to *Sydney Morning Herald*, [27] November 1857

Text: SMH, 28 November 1857, p. 4

"HARPUR—HOMER—MILTON."
To the Editor of the Sydney Morning Herald.[5]

SIR,—

My attention has just been called to a series of paragraphs in your issue of this day, headed "Harpur—Homer—Milton."[6] I have neither time nor inclination to retaliate in any shape upon the individual who has been good enough to contribute about a column and a quarter of somewhat vulgar prose to your Journal, for the purpose, perhaps, of showing that I am a lunatic. Allow me, however, to state that every allegation in the article as to what I said of the writings of my friend, Mr. Charles Harpur, at the School of Arts, on Monday evening last,[7] is *grossly untrue.* It appears, however, from the context of the article, that the writer was not present at the lecture, and that the information which has led him into a critical disquisition on the absurdities of the present generation in Australia, was drawn from that very equivocal source for precision—a newspaper report. To those who know me, a charge of having expressed the supreme nonsense put into my mouth by your "Correspondent," would be idle. To those who do not, I think it due to the literary character of one very dear to me, to show that when I undertook to speak in public of the qualities and merits of Mr. Harpur's poems, I did not utter that which would be tolerably fair evidence for a commission *de lunatico inquirendo*[8] that I was out of my senses.

I said nothing—and the assemblage I had the honour to address will perfectly recollect I said nothing—by which I wished arranged the names "Harpur—Homer—Milton," in order of excellence, as the names of the greatest poets the world has yet produced. I did not declare "the writers of namby-pamby, wishy-washy, milk-and-water verses the equals of Homer and Milton." No opinion was expressed in the lecture that Homer and Milton *have* equals. I did not "compare Mr. Harpur to Homer and Milton, and

---

[5] Sydney's pre-eminent daily newspaper, founded 1831. Conservative in outlook, its only real rival was Parkes's liberal *Empire.* The editor at this point was John West, Congregational minister and historian. Given their politics, neither Deniehy nor CH would have expected much kindness from it.

[6] See *SMH,* 27 November 1857, p. 5. Deniehy's letter would appear in the following day's issue, p. 4.

[7] On 23 November 1857 in the hall of the Mechanics' School of Arts in Sydney Daniel Deniehy delivered his long-promised lecture on the poetry of CH. Stenhouse chaired the meeting. The lecture had been announced in *Empire* but the only report of it appeared in *SMH,* 24 November 1857, p. 4 (reprinted in *Freeman's Journal,* 28 November 1857, p. 3).

[8] Also termed 'commission of lunacy', it was an inquiry to determine whether a person was a lunatic or idiot. It took place in open court before a jury and an audience.

pronounce him superior to either." I did not remark that there was in my opinion "nothing superior in the whole range of poetry to 'The Creek of the Four Graves.'"[1]

No reference at all was made in the lecture to Milton, except the very slender one involved in the remark that Mr. Harpur had, in my opinion, chosen as models for poetic study Milton and Wordsworth. I made no reference at all to Homer or his poetry. I *did* allude to a passage in Pope's translations, descriptive of a moonlight scene,[2] for which Homer is not answerable—which is a rhetorical amplification of the Greek text by Pope himself, and which Wordsworth has cited as a signal instance of what is false in poetic description.[3] I said, and, with every respect for the genius of Pope,— those who know a little more about things of the kind than "Correspondent" will agree with me, that the compliment was no extraordinary one,—that Mr. Harpur's moonlight-scene is superior to Pope's. Instead of stating that I knew nothing in the whole range of poetry superior to 'The Creek of the Four Graves,' I merely said there were passages in the poem, to my mind, equal to anything in the whole range of that poetry which describes forest scenery and its influence on human feelings. Perhaps "Correspondent" will believe, without the certificate of every individual of the audience who heard me, that I did not say of "The Creek of the Four Graves," that "this poem was not surpassed even by the productions of the great bard of Greece." Here "Correspondent" seems to quote from the report upon which he has built his observations, and if he does, I have only to regret that your worthy reporter (and the defective character of the hall of the School of Arts as a place for public speaking, and the low tones in which I occasionally spoke, leave him but to a very small extent censurable) did not catch correctly what I said when alluding to Pope's Homer.

D. H. DENIEHY.
Sydney Club,[4] Friday morning.

---

[1] See ho8o.

[2] See Pope's *The Iliad of Homer* (1716), Book VIII, lines 687–708 (edition of 1806 online at Internet Archive).

[3] 'A blind man, in the habit of attending accurately to descriptions casually dropped from the lips of those around him, might easily depict these appearances with more truth...[The lines of] Pope, though he had Homer to guide him, are throughout false and contradictory' – 'Essay, Supplementary to the Preface', in *Poems by William Wordsworth...* (London: Longman, Hurst, Rees, Orme and Brown, 1815), Vol. I, p. 358 (online at Internet Archive).

[4] New club in Castlereagh-street boasting 'no party or clique connections' but favoured by liberal parliamentarians and their supporters, a counterweight to the conservative Australia Club. Deniehy, MLA for Argyle and based in Goulburn, was in Sydney for the parliamentary sitting. He hid himself away in lodgings nearby, emerging for appointments and interviews at the Club (see letter to his wife Adelaide, 18 November 1857, which mentions the forthcoming Harpur lecture: in *Suppl. Letters*). It was renamed the Victoria Club in 1858.

56. Joseph Sheridan Moore to *Empire*, 31 May 1858

Text: Empire, 2 June 1858, p. 5

FRANK FOWLER AND HIS CRITIC-IN-CHIEF.
TO THE EDITOR OF THE EMPIRE.

SIR—

It wasn't my good or bad fortune to see last Thursday's EMPIRE[5] till yesterday; consequently, both Mr. Harpur's model poetry, and Mr. Harpur's indignant criticism of Mr. Frank Fowler, equally escaped my notice. As you have *some* interest in the promotion of Australian literature—of which honest and manly criticism must necessarily be a chief element; and as you have a popular character for giving fair play, or seeing it given,—perhaps I don't ask too much by asking leave and space for a few paragraphs, in reply to Mr. Harpur.

With our laureate's poetry, such as it is, I have, or will have, just now nothing to do. It is a reprint, and seems to have been re-printed for the sake of an annotation; the annotation is *done*—some maliciously say by *order*[6]—for the worthy purpose of vilifying Mr. Fowler as a literary man.

Now, Mr. Fowler has already ably defended himself*—and ably too—from Mr. Harpur's criticisms, sneers, and sarcasms. Lest, however, any portion of the public should remain ignorant of the true nature of the case, I beg to present, parallel, his most recent and most spiteful animadversion, and a letter of his addressed to Mr. Fowler, not many months back. Your readers will please observe that the letter and the annotation in Thursday's EMPIRE, refer to precisely the self-same subject—namely, Mr. Fowler's critical, biographical, and analytical discourse on Coleridge.[7]

* See postscript to the *Month*, for March, Vol. II., p. 159.

---

[5] See CH's 'The Poet' (h459d) in *Empire*, Friday 28 May 1858, p. 2. 'Harpur on Fowler in '58', below, is an extract from CH's long note to this poem; Moore adds '(Coleridge)' for clarity. The note formed part of an ongoing literary scrap: see p. 97 n. 4.

[6] An early version of CH's 'The Poet' had been printed, without footnote, in *Maitland Mercury*, 13 June 1846, p. 1 as 'Rhymes' (h459a). Moore implies that, as owner and editor of *Empire* and a friend of CH, Henry Parkes had ordered the new note in retaliation for Fowler's criticism of his verse in *Month*.

[7] By adding the explanatory '(on Coleridge)' to his transcription of CH's letter to Fowler of 9 May 1857 (the first of the letters quoted here), Moore confused Fowler's two orations. In fact, Fowler's second lecture (Sydney Mechanics School of Arts on 8 June 1857) was entitled 'Samuel Taylor Coleridge: Talker, Poet and Metaphysician' (see *Empire*, 9 June 1857, p. 5; and *SMH*, 12 June 1857, p. 2). Fowler's first lecture, 'Oration on Literary Portraiture', had been given on 4 May 1857: see p. 98 n. 1. CH's letter to Fowler of 9 May 1857 (Letter 51) was a response to that lecture and was subsequently published in *Month* in March 1858, Moore's source here. CH's caustic observations on Fowler (in the second letter, 'Harpur on Fowler in '58') appeared in *Empire*, 28 May 1858, p. 2, three days before Moore's reply.

HARPUR ON FOWLER IN '57.

Jerry's Plains. April 30th 1857

MY DEAR SIR,—

In a letter I had the other day from my friend ******* there occurred the following passage:—"You do not know Frank Fowler. He is a very young man—an Englishman of real ability—with the genuine sparkle about him, a vein of imagery of his own, and the only "chiel" I have seen in New South Wales with a truly brilliant prose style." Well, upon reading this, I at once determined on becoming acquainted with you—if, possibly, I might. But how? I confess I was fairly puzzled as to the *how*—till struck by what seemed to me a lucky thought—lucky as being somewhat likely to conduce to the end I had at heart. I will send him, thought I, one of the subscription lists—the only one I have remaining on hand—for my proposed publication; and the doing so will, at least, "break the ice," if it do nothing more. It is true, *my* poetry may not be up to his critical mark—but there may, nevertheless, be enough in it to interest him—a little in *me*, as its author.

May 9th, 1857.

Having scratched down the above, under a sudden impulse, I threw it by—not being very well satisfied with either the manner or the matter of it. But I have since read your very racy, and in many other respects exquisite "oration," delivered the other night at the Sydney School of Arts (on

HARPUR ON FOWLER IN '58.

What adequate treatment could the verse of such a poet (Coleridge) receive from the musical insight of a pseudo Aristarchus[1] like this?—a creature that was either as tuneless as an ox, or every whit as ignorant of what he was dogmatising about, as Mr. Fowler often is—in reality—of the subjects of *his* criticism. I say this advisedly. And yet this is the man who would assume the most prominent part in the formation of an Australian literature! Nay, possibly, like Bully Bottom in the play, he would assume all the prominent parts; would be Pyramus and Thisbe, and the Lion too.[2] But what one sure promise of supreme literary excellence is there about the character of the man, to justify the assumption? What he has already done amongst us is rather condemnatory of his pretensions than otherwise. For his *poetry*, as he himself almost confesses, is next to nought; and his prose, while it is very questionable in quality, is decidedly vicious in style. It is faulty all over. It wants weight and strength in substance, and coherence and sobriety in method and manner. It is too like a chance-medley of glass

[1] I.e., a literary fraudster: from the fake translation by French mathematician Gilles Personne de Roberval (1644) of a supposedly lost treatise by the ancient Greek philosopher and astronomer Aristarchus of Samos (*fl.* 250 BC).
[2] In 'Pyramus and Thisbe', the mechanicals' play within Shakespeare's *A Midsummer Night's Dream*, Nick Bottom the weaver was not content with the single role of Pyramus (I.2). 'Bully', as used by Bottom's fellow players, was their term of endearment and familiarity.

Coleridge), with its sparkling jets of mimetic verse flying up out of it, as from an over-full fountain of thought and feeling, and the impulse which is indicated above, has been thereby renewed in me: and lo, I obey it at all risks.

Still, as to the list, if you should not like to move in the business of it—not an over-pleasant one—why, no matter. You can in that case, re-enclose it to me, or destroy it—whichever you please.

I remain, my dear Sir, your admirer and would-be acqaintance,

CHAS. HARPUR.

Frank Fowler, Esq.

beads, of all sorts and sizes, slenderly strung together. Or at best, it is but like a deposit of diamond dust—not a display of gems, but a patch of shining granules, petty and valueless for all their glitter. Even when he affects in it to be neat and elegant, as he sometimes does, he only reaches to that smart, small-grained precision which may be proper enough to the theme of a schoolboy, or the paragraph of a report, but which is certainly not much relished by those who love to listen to the "large utterance of *our* elder Gods,"[3] or something akin to it.

[3] The Titaness Thea's words of comfort to the fallen Saturn, in John Keats's epic *Hyperion* (1820), Book I: 'Leaning with parted lips, some words she spake / In solemn tenour and deep organ tone: / Some mourning words, which in our feeble tongue / Would come in these like accents; O how frail / To that large utterance of the early Gods!'

[*Moore resumes:*] I think neither you nor the public requires much more comment on the matter after a perusal of the above.

Much might be said about the cowar[d]liness and meanness of attacking Mr. Fowler during his absence from the colony,[4] but, perhaps, Mr. Harpur shews himself an eclectic philosopher in the matter—or rather that sort of general, who thinks discretion the best sort of valour. He *may* have feared—if patriot poet *can* fear—the Damascus blade[5]—keen as bright, and bright as keen—of my brilliant friend.

I am, Sir, yours, &c., &c.,
J. SHERIDAN MOORE.[6]

[4] Fowler left Sydney in early April 1858 never to return. In England he wrote for and edited newspapers, wrote works of travel and adventure (including his impressions of Australia, *Southern Lights and Shadows,* 1859), and would die of brain fever in London in 1863 at the age of 30.

[5] A sword blade of forged Damascus steel, proverbially strong, resilient and sharp – Moore's riposte to CH's comment on Fowler's habit of recycling his own material: 'He has, in particular, an old Toledo sword blade that he is never tired of flourishing in the eyes of his readers, with the Furioso-bloody-mindedness of a stage-trooper' – note to 'The "Nevers" of Poesy [Republished, with Additions]' (h331d) in *Empire*, 9 March 1858, p. 4.

[6] Joseph Sheridan Moore (1828–91), Irish-born teacher, publicist and man of letters, a future champion of Henry Kendall. He produced *The Month* with Fowler, and on the latter's departure continued the journal for a further eight issues.

57. Charles Harpur to Nicol Drysdale Stenhouse, 2 July 1859

Text: Stenhouse papers, ML A100

Jerry's Plains, 2 July 1859.

My dear Sir,

I have received your letter dated in May last more than a month after its date. The delay in its coming to hand, however, is partly (but not wholly) owing to my only using to send to the Post, which is 12 miles distant, about once a fortnight or so.

With regard to my giving a lecture at the Sydney School of Arts[1]—say on Poetry, I cannot make any positive promise at present. It is quite likely, however, that I shall be able to do so. I am on the point of coming to some arrangements in my affairs[2] here, that will unfasten my social chain for a time, and if I can then come to Sydney for the purpose of giving the said lecture, I will. I will in the meantime prepare it, and then, before the season is over, it is quite likely that, with it in my pocket, I shall be able to pay a flying visit to Sydney. When the coast is clear for my doing so, I will write and let you know, but I cannot yet make any more positive promise than this.

My life here is an extremely wearisome one. For example, every day, from light to dark, hitherto through the whole of this winter, I have been occupied in matters of pure labor. I carry a book about with me, in my pocket, for a fortnight at a stretch, without being able to snatch time enough to glance over even so much as a page of it: and this frets me more perhaps than anything besides. You, my dear Sir, can have no idea of the care required and the labor imposed by sheep, on an indifferent run in a bad season.[3] Off the spot, the bare truth in this respect is well nigh incredible. But I am now about letting mine out on terms,[4] with the view of turning my attention to something else. I have not a sufficient number to be able to work them smoothly, and I can no longer consent to be thus utterly swamped in the care of those I have. Let on terms, they will secure me a slight income, and so far assist me in trying some other line of life.

You assure me you wish to see me,—and certainly I myself shall be drawn

---

[1] CH had been scheduled to lecture at the Sydney Mechanics' School of Arts in 1852 on 'English Poetry, from the Miltonic Era to the time of Wordsworth' (*Empire*, 6 July 1852, p. 1) but this fell through. Daniel Deniehy spoke there on CH's poetry in 1857 (*SMH*, 24 November 1857, p. 4 and see Letter 55). CH would eventually deliver his lecture on 'The Nature and Offices of Poetry' in September 1859, with Deniehy in the chair (*Empire*, 3 October 1859, p. 2; *Southern Cross*, 8 October 1859, pp. 10–12).

[2] This suggests that John Robertson, as Lands Minister in the Cowper government, had by this time offered CH the post of Sub-Gold Commissioner on the southern goldfields, allowing him to let out his stock (see below).

[3] Despite the floods of 1857 the late 1850s were drought years for NSW, including in the Hunter region – see Frances Doyle to Edward Doyle, 2 October 1859 (in *Suppl. Letters*).

[4] Such terms might be half the increase of the flock and a share of the wool shorn, over a given period.

Sydney-ward, not so much by any audiance possible to the School of Arts, as by my desire to see you, and a few other persons, who are I think related to me in mind—that is, spiritually. But no doubt *you* will be disappointed in *me*.[5] I have so long lived solitary, or amongst those with whom I have so few values and feelings in common, that conversation has become somewhat difficult to me from sheer disuse. When our best words all fly over the heads of our companions, we come to give up talking. But the social ice thus induced may break in your presence—nay, I even fore-feel that in some measure it will.

I am, my dear Sir,
very faithfully yours,
Chas: Harpur.

A Poem on a Poem.[6]

Mark yon Runnel how 'tis flowing
Like a sylvan spirit, dreaming
Of the Spring-blooms near it blowing,
And the sunlight o'er it beaming—
Beaming broad, or swiftly showing
With a many checkered gleaming,
Where some denser shade hangs bending
O'er it in green mingled masses—
Lights, and shades, and blossoms glowing,
All for greater beauty blending
In its vision, as it passes.

    Where that shelving rock is spied,
There, with a smooth warbling slide,
It lapses down into a cool
And brimming, not o'erflowing, pool;
Then between its narrowed banks,
Playing mellow gurgling pranks,
It gushes—till a channel'd stone
Gives it a more strenuous tone.

---

[5] This suggests that, despite their correspondence and the dedication of *Bushrangers*, CH and Stenhouse had not yet met. Rawling proposes that the two did not meet until the Harpurs were in Sydney around September, on their way to Braidwood (pp. 180, 236); Jordens appears to agree (pp. 45, 83–4).

[6] First published in *Empire*, 9 March 1852, p. 2 as 'The Verse of Coleridge's "Christabel"' – see h473 for variants. 'Christabel', a visionary narrative poem by English Romantic poet Samuel Taylor Coleridge (1772–1834), was first published in a pamphlet with 'Kubla Khan: or A Vision in a Dream' and 'The Pains of Sleep' (London: John Murray, 1816; 3rd edition, 1816, online at Internet Archive).

Or away it curveth thence
With an even profluence;
(Beaming to the sun afar
Like a mighty scimitar)
Or betwixt thick-reeded beaches
It whispers low mysterious speeches;
Or with an under-swirling spread
Over a wide pebbled bed,
It bubbles with a gentle pleasure,
Ere some new mood change the measure.

Such a Runnel typeth well
The sweet wild Verse of 'Christabel.'[1]
And if, all suddenly, at length
In the fulness of its strength
It sunk, a broken end to make
In some subterranean Lake,
A farther type we might behold
Of this Story—half untold.[2]

But what—with its sweet Verse-flow (snapt
Short as 'twere and half perdu[3])
What might figure to our view
In a picture-light as apt,
The Wonder-World it warbles through?

---

[1] '[T]he metre of the Christabel is not, properly speaking, irregular, though it may seem so from its being founded on a new principle: namely, that of counting in each line the accents, not the syllables. Though the latter may vary from seven to twelve, yet in each line the accents will be found to be only four. Nevertheless this occasional variation in the number of syllables is not introduced wantonly...but in correspondence with some transition in the nature of the imagery or passion' – Coleridge, Preface to *Christabel, &c.* (1816), p. vii. Cf. the metrical form of 'The Kangaroo Hunt' (h209-bc).

[2] Coleridge never completed 'Christabel'. He wrote the first of two parts in 1797, the second in 1800. Three further parts were planned but, 'Since the latter date (that is, 1800), my poetic powers have been, till very lately, in a state of suspended animation' – Preface to *Christabel, &c.* (1816), p. v.

[3] Concealed or hidden from sight (now rare, *OED*).

58. Charles Harpur to Nicol Drysdale Stenhouse, 12 November 1859

Text: Stenhouse papers, ML MSS 27

Araluen,[4] 12 November 1859.

My dear Sir,

I have nothing to write about—positively nothing. This is about as dreary a place as could well be imagined. There is nothing but grim mountains and as grim diggers all around me. In the mountains there is some distinctive character which I may yet turn to account—but in the diggers aforesaid, none—only a sort of gold-madness, varied at short intervals by a very decided rum-madness. So you see I have nothing just now worth writing about; and only take up my pen for the purpose of transcribing a poem for you—just to show that I am thinking about you, being indeed

Yours ever devotedly
Charles Harpur.

"Humanity"[5]

I dreamt I was a Sculptor, and had wrought
Out of a towering adamantine[6] crag
A mighty Figure,—giant-limbed, and faced
As with the front of an Homeric God.
Slightly advanced was one collossal foot,
The other planted on the levelled cone
Of a great tumulus: There aloft it stood
Against the deep of heaven light flecked with clouds
That, reddening from the east on either hand
In swift succession, though extending wide,
Then kindled, with a sudden splendor, all
To shreds of golden fire, as fast the Morn,
Like the glad herald of Almighty Power
Hasting in glory to create anew,

---

[4] Goldfield in the mountains of south-eastern NSW 27 km south of Braidwood, where the Harpur family arrived via Sydney *c.* 14 October 1859. (For their stay in Sydney, see p. 297 n. 5.) Araluen comprised a series of miners' settlements along the valley of Araluen Creek and its tributaries (see Illustration 6, p. xxxv). In August 1859, CH (through the offices of his Hunter Valley friend, Lands Minister John Robertson) had been appointed Sub-Gold Commissioner and, separately, Magistrate there (*NSW Government Gazette*, 19 August 1859, p. 1829). Housed under canvas, he had only just assumed his duties.

[5] Already published in *Empire*, 8 February 1858, p. 4; see h180 for variants.

[6] Unbreakable, impenetrable.

Came burning up, out of eternity.
So, towering heavenward, there aloft it stood
Full in the face of the resplendent Morn,
And I methought was glorying in my work.
One large arm lay upon the roomy breast,
The other held a scroll. The ample head
Whose curving breadth and doming height evinced
August, though bounded, majesty, was raised,
As with a brave air o'er the brightening world
Forthright it looked, with open heedful eyes,
Full and expectant, while the set lips showed
As they *had* smiled or *could*. But on the brows
There pained a weight and weariness of thought,
And the whole visage spake of care, though touched
In its expression with a spirit of faith
Remote and shadowy, and that seemed withal
But half assured itself. Such was my Work:
And all who saw it were constrained methought
To sigh, as they looked up,—"Humanity."

C.H.

Chas. Harpur[1]

59. Charles Harpur to Nicol Drysdale Stenhouse, 20 May 1860

Text: Stenhouse papers, ML A100

Araluen, 20 May 1860.

My dear Sir,

As the expense of my coming hither, with my family, drained me of all my ready cash, I had to go about £60 in debt for the necessary *traps* wherewith to re-commence housekeeping;[2] and besides this, soon after taking up my residence at Araluen, I lost a valuable horse, and had to purchase another one at a pretty high figure. Thus I became indebted in a sum altogether of about £100. Now of this sum I have up to the present time been able to pay off about half—out of my salary, month by month as it fell due; and should be easily able to pay off the whole of it in the same way in about three months more; but the people here to whom I happen to be thus indebted are poor and want

---

[1] Added by an unknown hand, it is upside down at the foot of the last page of MS.
[2] I.e., *trappings*: here, items for setting up house anew.

immediate payment. Hence they *dun* me[3]—a thing I hate like poison: and, under these circumstances, will *you* lend me £50 for three months? If you can, I think you will; but if you cannot, you have only to tell me so frankly; for no one better knows than I do myself from experience, the very truth of poor Burns' lines

> A friend may wish a body well,
> Yet have no cash to spare him.[4]

Believe me, my dear Sir,
Most truly yours
Chas: Harpur.

60. Charles Harpur to Charles Cowper, 2 October 1860

Text: NSWSA: NRS-905 [4/3429], 60/4223

Police Office,[5] Araluen, 2nd October, 1860.

Sir,[6]

I have the honor to inform you, that the Police Office at this place is at present provided with only an incomplete set of the Acts of Council—the set in use (an old one left by Mr Commissioner King at Major's Creek)[7] being short of all the Acts comprised in the 1st and 2nd Volumes of Callaghan;[8]— and to request that you will be pleased to cause the wanting statutes to be supplied for the use of it, at an early date,—as the want of them is calculated to occasion, not only legal informality, but serious error.

The readiest way in which the Books could be forwarded hither would, no

---

[3] Make insistent or repeated demands for repayment.

[4] See p. 46 n. 1.

[5] Besides his duties as Sub-Gold Commissioner and Gold Receiver at Araluen, CH acted as magistrate.

[6] With responsible government in NSW in 1856 the position of Colonial Secretary was no longer occupied by a public servant but by the chief minister in a cabinet government, usually the premier: see the Administrative Arrangements in *NSW Government Gazette*, 4 October 1859, pp. 2171–2. As Colonial Secretary, Charles (later, Sir Charles) Cowper's charge included police and petty sessions. Cowper (1807–75) served as Premier and Colonial Secretary numerous times during 1856–70 and, as such, was leader of the government of the day, as well as its senior official.

[7] William Essington King (1821–1910), Gold Commissioner on various fields 1852–59. Major's Creek is a village and goldfield on the Southern Tablelands 16 km south of Braidwood. Gold was found there in 1851.

[8] *Acts and Ordinances of the Governor & Council of New South Wales, and Acts of Parliament Enacted for, and Applied to, the Colony, with Notes & Index* compiled in 1844 by Sydney barrister and later judge Thomas Callaghan (1815–63), and generally known as 'Callaghan's Acts': see Vols. 1 and 2 (1844) online at HathiTrust. He died in a riding accident at Braidwood in 1863.

doubt, be through the Post.

I have the honor to be,

Sir,

Your most obedient Servant

Chas: Harpur.

Sub Gold Commissioner

60/4223[1]—8th Octr 1860. SubGold Commr Harpur. Applying for Act of Council for the

The Govt Printer for report. B.C.[2] 8th, Oct 60 [P.C.?]

noted 8

The deficiency cannot be supplied as a great number of acts are out of print.

Complaints of this kind are now constantly made; but there can be no remedy, until a reprint of the Statutes shall have been effected. Thos Richards[3] 9 Oct 1860

Retd C.S.O.[4] 11 October

Inform. [Cls?] 12 Oct. Bench 16 Octr 1860[5] √

---

[1] Official correspondence number (year/ item number), then date and summary of content.

[2] Blank Cover, a method of expediting inter-departmental correspondence. A letter received by one department was passed directly to another for a report, obviating the need to write out a copy and a covering letter (hence 'blank cover'). The Colonial Secretary's office, which lay at the heart of the bureaucracy, made much use of this practice. The original letter was registered, then forwarded to the relevant department with its lower right-hand corner turned up for the required report to be written thereon and returned.

[3] Thomas Richards (1831–98), NSW Government Printer 1859–86, responsible for many technical innovations including the introduction to the colony of photo-lithography, stereo-typing and electro-typing.

[4] I.e., letter 'returned to Colonial Secretary's Office'.

[5] This note appears to be Cowper's but its meaning is obscure. The Register of letters received by the Colonial Secretary, 1826–1921 (NSWSA: NRS-922 [5/2502], 4223) records that the letter was 'Answered 16 Octr.' Perhaps Cowper is directing that the Bench – i.e., CH in his capacity as magistrate – be notified of the scarcity of printed statutes.

61. Michael Fitzpatrick to Charles Harpur, 9 September 1861

Text: NSWSA: NRS-7946 [2/1805], 61/3054, f. 170

Department of Lands Sydney 9 September 1861.

Sir

In reply to your letter of the 29th ultimo,[6] respecting your proposed removal to the Western District and the arrear of allowance for Forage and Quarters due to you, I am directed to inform you that it has now been decided that you are to remain in your present position in consequence of the Transfer of Mr Sub Commissioner Scott[7] to the above district, and that the matter of your allowances must await a reply to the reference already made to Mr Commissioner Cloete[8] on that subject.

I have &c
sd. Michl Fitzpatrick

61. 3054 196[9]

---

[6] Michael Fitzpatrick (1816–81), public servant, land agent and politician, served as Under-Secretary for Lands including under John Robertson. CH's letter is unlocated; it presumably responded to being instructed to swap positions with Sub-Commissioner John Murphy at the Hargraves goldfield near Mudgee (Fitzpatrick to Cloete, 30 April 1861; Fitzpatrick to CH, 10 August 1861: both in *Suppl. Letters*). This had been decided upon as a disciplinary measure for both of them. Apparently CH resisted the move, perhaps calling in a favour from his friend Robertson – Fitzpatrick's superior as Lands Minister. He succeeded: perhaps his pre-emptive action in initiating a claim for an unpaid allowance (indicating that he would not go quietly) tipped the balance in his favour. His subsequent request for transfer to the Gulph goldfield at Nerrigundah would be granted, thus avoiding another proposed transfer, this time to Adelong (Fitzpatrick to James Harrop Griffin, 12 December 1861, in *Suppl. Letters*).

[7] James Houghton Langston Scott (*c.* 1825–78) was transferred from the Southern to the Western District on 31 August 1861.

[8] Peter Lawrence Cloete (1829–70) was at this point Commissioner for the Southern Gold District, which stretched from Gundagai eastwards to Moruya on the coast, and included Araluen. For the 'reference', see Fitzpatrick's memo to Cloete, 27 August 1861 (in *Suppl. Letters*).

[9] Official correspondence number. Source for this text is Department of Lands, Copies of letters sent to Gold Commissioners, 1856–66, NSWSA.

62. Henry Halloran to Charles Harpur, 31 December 1861

Text: ML MSS 947

In acknowledgement of
"a Rhyme"[1]
By Charles Harpur

Reap, while it is day, my friend!
    Reap while it is day:
    Tho' no golden gains attend
    The silver shafted lay,—
Reap while it is day!

From the fields of Poesy,
    Bring the sheaves along:—
    Press them close, & firmly tie,—
    Glorious shocks of Song.
      Bring the Sheaves along.

Over hill and over lea
    Let thy footsteps rove;
Reaping in the meadows free,
Sheaves of Truth and Love—
    Let thy footsteps rove.

From the grain the sheaves enfold,
From the golden grain,—
Comes the bread of natives bold,—
The "staff of Life" that is not sold,—
The golden bearded grain.

Then among the stars serene,
May the reaper rest,—
When what "is," shall be "*has been*,"
Shown by his victorious mein,
Shall the Reaper rest.

---

[1] CH's poem had first appeared as 'Rhymes' (h459a) in *Maitland Mercury*, 13 June 1846, p. 1, but in his verse-letter Halloran was probably referring to the later and longer 'A Rhyme', printed, together with 'Coleridge's Christabel', in pamphlet form by *Braidwood Dispatch* in 1861 (h459e and h473-ag), although he had also probably seen the latter in *Empire*, 28 December 1861, p. 8.

My dear Sir

Take the above, hastily scratched off, as a poor acknowledgement of my satisfaction in the perusal of your Rhyme and Christabel.

> Yrs faithfy
> Henry Halloran[2]
> office—no place for rhyme.
> 31 Decr 1861.

63. Henry Kendall to Charles Harpur, 8 January 1862[3]

Text: Kendall papers, ML C199

Kingston, Newtown. January 8th 1862.

Dear Sir

I recieved the two poems that you were kind enough to forward to me, and deemed it my duty to thank you directly. So you must excuse the liberty I am taking in writing to you, and the peculiar hand adopted here. Your brother, Mr Joseph Harpur,[4] will tell you that I am obliged to indite my letters in this fashion, my right arm being lame.

About two months ago Mr Pennington gave me a volume of yours.[5] Since then I have passed many a delightful evening poring over it. Amongst your numerous sincere admirers there are none more sincere than myself; and I rejoice that I have mind enough to appreciate you.

You have a noble soul which never appears to be baffled, though it has so long worked against opposition and unkindness. I grow sick when listening to people talking about "the unfortunate Keats", and the "sorrows of

---

[2] See p. 15 n. 10. Halloran was at this time Secretary and Cashier of the Survey Department as well as Lieutenant of the First Troop of the NSW Volunteer Mounted Rifles.

[3] Thomas Henry (also known as Henry Clarence) Kendall (1839–82) was gaining recognition for his newspaper verse, and October would see his first volume, *Poems and Songs*, published by subscription (Sydney: J. R. Clarke, 1862; online at Internet Archive). His verse had already appeared alongside CH's in the press (e.g., in *Empire*, 26 March 1861, p. 3). This is the first letter between the two and, despite the wide disparity in age, they would remain friends and correspondents until the latter's death. Struggling on the wages of an attorney's clerk, Kendall was supporting his widowed mother Melinda and his three sisters in a rented two-storey terrace house in Kingston, a ward of Newtown, now an inner western suburb but then a scattered village of estates, market gardens, and suburban terraces and cottages. *Sands's Commercial and General Sydney Directory for 1863* gives Kendall's address as Knights Building, Wellington-street (now Chelmsford Street); for a photograph, see Ackland, facing p. 83.

[4] Joseph Harpur wrote leaders for *Empire* supporting the land reforms finally introduced by John Robertson. Encouraged by Parkes, he had stood for and was elected to the Legislative Assembly for the seat of Patrick's Plains in mid-1861.

[5] See p. 52 n. 5. The volume given Kendall was probably *Bushrangers*. Kendall's homage 'To C. H.' ('I would sit at your feet for long days...') had appeared in *Empire*, 13 September 1861, p. 5.

11. Henry Kendall as a young man (c. 1860?), photographer unknown

Chatterton"[1]—remembering your brave life. (Keats and Chatterton were certainly minstrels of a very high order, but they were too selfish, and I can feel no sympathy for them.) Your influence is beginning to be felt, and it is to be regretted that you have been so silent lately. I speak for the rising generation of Australians, who are far more intellectual than their predecessors, and who *must* turn to you, as I have already done, with the love and reverence which is due to their national poet.

I am happy to say that I have secured a kind friend in Mr Joseph Harpur, and would be happier still if I could call his gifted brother by the same name. If you ever visit Sydney it is to be hoped that you will give me an opportunity of seeing you. In the meantime I should like to be a correspondent of yours occasionally.

> Hoping that you will excuse this forwardness I remain
> Yours, Respectfully,
> Henry Kendall.

[1] Two ill-fated English poets: John Keats was killed by tuberculosis in 1821 at the age of 25; for Thomas Chatterton, see p. 126 n. 6.

64. Charles Harpur to Henry Kendall, [*c.* September 1862 – October 1863][2]

Text: Kendall papers, ML MSS 3796/2

Euroma, Gulph Diggings

My dear Kendall,

The enclosed poem[3] is one which has been *many years* under revision, and which has never seen the light. It has never, I think, been even read to any one, or by any one but myself before.

If the Herald folk do not care to publish it on account of its *length*—I wish you to get 200 copies of it printed in a cheap pamphlet form at the Herald or any other office, and then send me 50 copies through the post together with the printer's bill to be forthwith discharged. Or I will send you a cheque for the amount immediately upon your letting me know what it will come to. The remaining 150 copies you can distribute amongst whom you please. But, of course, if the Herald will find room for it in its columns, I would rather that it should be published in that way, the circulation being so much wider.

As soon as I can get time to copy them out fairly, I will send you from time to time for the Herald, 2 papers on versification in general: a paper on Poetry V Music:[4] and a series of "Rhymed Criticisms with Prose Notes"[5]—on the following of our Poets & criticisms &c—viz: Chaucer, Shaksspear, Milton, Dryden, Waller, Pope, Gray, Collins, Burns, Wordsworth, Byron, Shelley,

---

[2] This undated letter is the first addressed from 'Euroma'. While working daily in Nerrigundah, several steep kms away by horseback, CH was 'building and making improvements' to his 100-acre farm, acquired in March 1862: see report 'The Wogonga River' dated 17 October 1862 in *SMH*, 13 November 1862, p. 5. The building of the Euroma homestead was completed by the end of 1862 (Receipt by Nathanel Phillips for building Euroma (Letter 68), and see p. 130 n. 1 for a description of the house and garden). The Harpur family moved to Euroma from Araluen in *c.* April 1863. The approximate dating of the letter is based on a statement by Mary Araluen Baldwin, born 3 October 1861, that she was 1 year 6 months old at the time and that her mother later mentioned her delight at finding 'a garden and orchard' already 'laid out and planted' by her father ('Daughter's Memories'). So CH could have written from Euroma as early as the last several months of 1862 but no later than October 1863, since one of the '2 papers on versification' CH mentions as being revised for publication appeared as 'On Blank Verse' in *SMH*, 2 November 1863, p. 2. This is also the first letter to Kendall in which it is understood that he is acting as de facto literary agent for CH in Sydney, as well as his book-purchaser and source of metropolitan information and gossip. Kendall had good relations with the Fairfaxes, publishers of *SMH*.

[3] The unnamed poem was a publishing problem for newspapers 'on account of its length'. Three long poems are mentioned in correspondence of this period as being in need of publication: 'A Poet's Home' (which appeared as a pamphlet *c.* November 1862: see Letter 69 and notes); 'The Tower of the Dream' (p. 139 n. 10); and 'The Bard of Paradise' (p. 150 n. 6). They had previously appeared in print but in much shorter forms – and so had, in this sense, 'never seen the light'.

[4] Article 'Poetry *Versus* Music' appeared in *Sydney Times*, 28 May 1864, p. 2; it survives in a cutting in ML A87-1, p. 354. For *Sydney Times*, see p. 150 n. 6.

[5] CH's 'Rhymed Criticisms' of British poets (from early 1840s) appeared at various times in *Australasian Chronicle*, *Weekly Register*, *Maitland Mercury*, *PA*, *Empire* and *Sydney Mail*.

Moore, The Critical Reviews of the last Age,[1] Polemical Tractates[2] &c &c

I think I can get leave to come to Sydney shortly for two or three weeks, when we shall meet face to face,[3] and know one another in the right way.

Yours truly
Chas: Harpur.

65. Henry Kendall to Charles Harpur, 25 September 1862

Text: Kendall papers, ML C199

Kingston. Newtown. Sep 25. 1862.

Dear Mr Harpur,

Your welcome letter came to hand on Tuesday, and I hasten at this—my earliest opportunity, to reply to it. I must acknowledge that I was disappointed at not receiving any answer to my last; thinking the silence had proceeded from some fault in the construction of my boyish epistle. But your kind explanation relieved me greatly, and I can well imagine how your time is taken up where you are.

I am very anxious to correspond with you: being assured that, mentally, I shall gain much by your letters. For we cannot leave a cedar grove without carrying away some of the fragrance, and the words of Genius may be fitly associated with the perfume-scattering leaves of those beautiful trees. I feel already deeply indebted to you for the great good and large comfort I have derived from your writings. There is no living author to whom I could turn and say as much. This may be a necessary result of my Australian birth and education. But, strangely fascinated by almost everything you have published, I have always looked upon you as the man who alone could *express* what I had so often dimly thought. While looking round upon external Nature, *some* of us see and feel *that* which we afterwards lose sight of and forget, until we

---

[1] This item survives in manuscript. 'Critical Rhymes on Critical Reviews', intended for CH's 'Wild Bee of Australia' (ML C376, dated by Holt 1851–53), comprises 48 lines of verse dated by CH 1845 and notes dated by him, in part, 1848 (h475a). His targets are the British monthly and quarterly literary reviews of the late 18th and early 19th centuries, and specifically what he considers their misjudgements on the likes of Byron, Shelley, Keats and Hunt on the one hand, and Cottle, Milman and Bowles on the other. A version of 1863 is titled 'Critical Rhymes on some of the English Critical Reviews of the last Age' (h475b, in ML A89). In MS, an end-of-line hyphenation ('Shaks-/ spear') partially explains CH's spelling.

[2] Surviving in two manuscript versions both titled 'Polemical Tracts:' ML A90 of 1863 with footnote (h476a) and ML A93 of 1866 (h476b): 'it was not so much the singular differences existing amongst theologians that provoked my ridicule', CH comments, 'as their singular want of charity as well, and of that philosophic spirit which extends to those who differ from us in opinion'.

[3] No evidence of such a trip in 1863 has emerged. Kendall would recall that they did not meet until 1868 – in 'About Some Men of Letters in Australia' [on CH, Deniehy and Dalley]: *Australian Journal*, 1 October 1869, pp. 84–5.

find it, photographed as it were, in the luminous "limning"[4] of the true poet. I think that there is a fearful gap between thought and language. Perhaps there is no rarer endowment of the poet than the gift of exact expression— the power of subjugating language to thought; so he can conscientiously feel that the whole truth which was in him has been laid before the World in all its unclouded simplicity. How often, burning with the secret power within, do men feel they are incapable of manifesting themselves except through the medium of a dim—a cloudy—ambiguity of words, which either distort the idea they yearn to convey, or else give but its bloodless inanimate outline! I feel sure there is little discrepancy between conception and execution in your poems, and am satisfied your Ideal, with all its delicate lights and shadows, could not, *in any other dress*, be presented to us in its entire integrity. I speak for myself, and, I trust for thousands of my countrymen who have yet to read, to learn and to enjoy.

Very likely I have not read half that which you have published; indeed only by looking over the files of the old "Empire" and the "Australian Home Companion",[5] have I become accquainted with any of it. The "People's Advocate" was before my time, and no copies are now obtainable. In the beginning of the present year however, I secured a copy of the volume containing the "Bushrangers", and a noble poem headed "The Creek of the Four Graves." I *know* that a counterpart of "Egremont" has been with me in a like grand evening Forest, where the fire looked "a wilder creature" than it would have seemed elsewhere, "because of the surrounding savageness"; and where we for a moment appeared to be part of a colossal picture "hung in some vast World." And I am *sure* we have watched the same solitary star which moved "so thoughtfully awake" over that vast Australian gloom. One of your old calumniaters was frightened back to his native mud, after hearing me read the "Creek of the Four Graves".[6] The "Tower of the Dream"[7] is another of my favorites. One of the similes in that poem is the finest I have met with *anywhere*; and the song of the Spirit is so wildly so strangely beautiful that one

[4] Illuminating of manuscripts, painting: hence, depicting or sketching in words.
[5] Both published CH's work extensively, *Empire* (founded and edited by Henry Parkes) from its early days in 1851, and the temperance *Australian Home Companion and Band of Hope Journal* 1858–61 (see p. 152 n. 4). For ' "People's Advocate" ', see p. 45 n. 8.
[6] See ho8of. 'Old Egremont' is the leader of the fateful expedition, the 'kindly sage' who recounts the tale to the author. He reappears in 'The Bush Fire' (ho57c), another poem in *Bushrangers*. The name (a town in Cumbria and a noble family) features in the poetry of Wordsworth.
[7] Not in *Bushrangers*; Kendall probably saw it serialised in *Empire*, 21 February 1857, p. 4 and 10 March 1857, p. 2 (see h642b).

might imagine it to be conceived, as 'Kubla Khan' was, in a Dream.[1] I don't care much for "Yes"—one of Mr Stenhouse's pets—but "Mary", "In Yon Green Wood", and "Cora",[2] are indeed lovely. This, from "Cora" haunts me whenever I turn to the sunset:

> "Bright garments of a Spirit bright,
> That even in the shroud
> *Were like the sunset's golden light*
> *Within a lifeless cloud*!"

"Finish of Style"[3] has all the "bloom of unhandled grapes" about it, and the second of your "Poems of Melancholy"[4] sounds the very depths of feeling. I do not care much for what has been printed of "Genius Lost",[5] although there are so *many* fine passages in it. Perhaps it proceeds from my having no great sympathy for Chatterton.[6] You must forgive me for being so candid. The extracts from "King Saul"[7] have truly a rich, Oriental flush around them, and are as odorous as the cedars of Lebanon. I only regret that you did not publish any more from the same source. In my next, I will mention some others from amongst your poems which have delighted me, and let you know where I have been reading lately. Perhaps you would like to learn what books I am in the habit of looking into, and how far my tastes agree with yours. You could then *certainly* set me right.

---

[1] In 'Of the Fragment of Kubla Khan', Coleridge describes how the poem came to him in an 'anodyne' (i.e., opium)-induced dream, and how his transcription of it was curtailed by 'a person on business from Porlock' – in *Christabel &c.*, 3rd edn., pp. 51–4 (London: John Murray, 1816; online at Internet Archive).

[2] ' "Yes" ' (h245d) and 'To Mary' (h616c) are in *Bushrangers*; 'Yon Green Wood' (h708a) appeared in *Empire* in 1857 and 'Cora' (h077a) in 1856.

[3] Versions of this poem had appeared in *Empire* on three occasions, in 1857 (h132b and h132c on 3 July, p. 5 and 4 December, p. 4) and 1862 (h132d on 31 July 1862, p. 8).

[4] A pair of poems had appeared in *SMH* on 22 September 1862, p. 3: 'The Losses of the Past' (h229b) and 'Obituary Lines' for CH's father (h297d), the poem to which Kendall refers here.

[5] As at 1862 two extracts from this series had been published: 'A Passage from "Genius Lost" ', in *Empire*, 2 June 1862, p. 5 (h151-lb); and 'From Genius Lost, a Psychological Poem, founded on the Text of Wordsworth', in an unidentified newspaper, possibly *Braidwood Dispatch*, c. 1861 (h151-si).

[6] A profound influence on the English Romantics and Pre-Raphaelites, Thomas Chatterton (1752–70) the boy-genius and creator of mock-literary antiquities died from an overdose of arsenic and laudanum at 17. For CH's 'The Sorrows of Chatterton. Genius Lost', 'written in the Author's youth' and 'suggested, as the title indicates, by the fate and character of the "marvellous Boy", Chatterton', see h151-ac.

[7] Verse play surviving only in a passage of 1200 lines in manuscript at ML A87-2, pp. 563–8, in fragments in other manuscripts (the earliest, 1836), and in a few published pieces that Kendall might have seen in back issues, including 'A Song of David, Inciting to Dance' (h526a; *Empire*, 3 January 1853, p. 2), 'The Spirit of Love' (h555b; *Empire*, 5 February 1853, p. 2), 'Joshua' (h207a; *PA*, 1 July 1854, p. 7) and 'Deborah' (h090a; *Empire*, 9 April 1856, p. 3).

I rarely meet with Mr Joseph Harpur now: his parliamentary duties seem to engross nearly the whole of his time. He is one of the purest-minded men I have ever met with. I know Mr Stenhouse: he introduced me to Henry Halloran a few weeks ago.[8] The last-mentioned gentleman magnificently patronises me, and endeavours to impress upon me the "fact" that it is a crime to write when you can't excel. What a pity it is that he don't follow up his theory in his own case, and leave me to take care of myself! I cannot find anything at all approximating to Genius in Halloran's or Evelyn's writings.[9] Parkes had a poetical temperament evidently, and Michael is not so contemptible as interested critics would have him appear to be.[10] Dr Woolley, a *crammed* man—a man who admires Tennyson by rote, and Browning backwards, is another of my would-be patrons.[11] I have cut them all.

Thanking you for your kind letter, and hoping you will reply to this, when you have leisure,

I remain
Yours Respectfully
Henry Kendall.

---

[8] In August 1863 Kendall would accept the post with the Surveyor General's Department offered him by Halloran (see Ackland, p. 84), would work under him there and, from 1866, in the Colonial Secretary's Office. His harsh opinion of Halloran would soften on further acquaintance – see Letter 76; his ode 'To Henry Halloran', *SMH*, 17 September 1864, p. 3; and his article 'Going towards the Sunset', *Freeman's Journal*, 3 May 1879, p. 17.

[9] Alexander John Evelyn (1827?–57), a now-forgotten poet, editor of *Illustrated Sydney News*, much admired in the 1850s; his early death was mourned by the Sydney literary circle (e.g., *Empire*, 23 February 1857, p. 4). For Henry Halloran's elegy 'Evelyn's Grave', see *Empire*, 31 August 1857, p. 5.

[10] James Lionel Michael (1824–68), solicitor and poet, author of the semi-autobiographical 'John Cumberland' and the romance 'Sir Archibald Yelverton', and friend and employer of Kendall. He removed to North Grafton in 1861 to practise there; Kendall joined him as clerk for November 1861 – April 1863 (as dates and places attached to his letters and poems indicate), but with occasional visits to Sydney. Parkes was at this time touring Britain as a government immigration agent and lecturer.

[11] John Woolley (1816–66), Anglican clergyman, scholar and first principal and founding professor of classics at the University of Sydney. Ackland notes that Woolley offered Kendall free education at the University, which he declined, 'reasoning that he could better survive without formal training than his mother and sisters without his salary' (p. 84).

66. Charles Harpur to James Harrop Griffin, 31 October 1862

Text: ML A87-2

Gulph[1] 31 October 1862

Sir[2]

In reply to your letter of the 25th instant, requiring to be informed, whether in my judgement, it is desirable to proclaim this Gold Field, or any portion of it, as a place to which Miner's Rights held by aliens[3] should apply, in accordance with the 5th section of the 25th Victa No 4.: I have the honor to report, that in my opinion, the time has arrived when the Chinese might, with advantage, be unlimitedly admitted upon these Diggings:

First, because at least an entire half of the able-bodied European population, have latterly left them for the Lachlan, Otago, and other more promising fields,[4] and much land in all directions is, in consequence of this exodus, now lying abandoned:

And secondly, because this land, though much worked over, is yet such as might be turned to profitable account by Chinese labor, and by Chinese labor only.

Moreover, there is no longer existing on this Gold Field that feeling of repugnance to the influx of Chinese[5] which did certainly obtain during its more prosperous days. Neither the miners nor the traders of the Gulph (speaking generally) are now at all averse to their incoming, however numerously;

---

[1] The Nerrigundah goldfield, in the mountains of south-eastern NSW 40 km south-west of Moruya, was also known as the Gulf or Gulph (from Gulf Creek, which ran through it to the Tuross River, 4 km to the south). CH, as Sub-Gold Commissioner was transferred there from Araluen in late 1861, though the family would not settle at nearby Eurobodalla until 1863.

[2] The addressee, James Harrop Griffin (1823–91), was appointed as Commissioner in Charge, Southern Gold District, including Araluen and Nerrigundah, on 13 October 1861 (*NSW Government Gazette*, 15 October 1861, p. 2156); his predecessor Peter Cloete was moved to the new South-Western Gold District. Also a magistrate, Griffin braved the mob to read the Riot Act at the Lambing Flat goldfield riot of July 1861.

[3] Aliens living or mining on a goldfield without a Miner's Right could be arrested and fined, but Section 5 of the NSW *Gold Fields Act* of 1861 empowered the Governor to proclaim that a Miner's Right authorised aliens to mine at a particular goldfield. While an alien was defined as 'Any person not being a British subject or a naturalised subject of Her Majesty', the law was aimed at limiting Chinese numbers on the goldfields. Regulations under the Act gave the Gold Commissioner the authority to determine where Chinese miners could live and work (see *Gold Fields Act and Regulations* of 1861), and the *Chinese Immigration Act* of 1861 placed a £10 head tax on every Chinese person entering the colony.

[4] The goldfields around what became the town of Forbes on the Lachlan River in the central west of NSW were opened up in mid-1861 and were still flourishing in late 1862. Around the same time diggers were leaving the dwindling Australian fields for the rich Central Otago fields in New Zealand's South Island.

[5] The 1850s and 1860s saw an influx of gold seekers from south China onto the goldfields of California, Australia and New Zealand. Fear of the Chinese and resentment at their success were rife on the Australian goldfields, leading sometimes to violence, as in the riots on the Buckland River in Victoria (1857) and at Burrangong and Lambing Flat in NSW (1860–61).

because the former, if desirous of shifting, are thereby afforded a chance of selling out to them the partially worked claims they would otherwise have to abandon; and because the latter know they must be benefited in their business by their advent to the extent in which this balances the daily departure of the Europeans.

Under these circumstances, and though the influx of Chinese into these Diggings has of late been rather considerable, I have thought it wisest to set no line between them and the European diggers; but to let them come in and occupy, wherever the ground was already lying abandoned, or wherever the Europeans were willing to sell out to them.

I have &c
(sigd) Chas: Harpur. S.G.C.[6]

67. Charles Harpur to John Robertson, 6 November 1862

Text: ML A87-2

Gulph 6th Novr 1862

Sir,[7]

I have the honor to enclose you the Award of the Umpire and Arbitrators, relative to the passage of Oniel & Party's Head Race through the private lands of Mr Charles Byrnes of this place, in accordance with the Regulations appended to the 12th Clause of the Gold Fields' Act of 1861.[8]

The first annual payment of the rent awarded by them as compensation— viz: £12—has been lodged in my hands by the said Oniel & Party, to be tendered to Mr Byrnes, so soon as the award itself shall have been finally sanctioned by the Executive, as required by the Clause of the Act above referred to.

I have &c
(sigd) Chas: Harpur: S.G.C.

[6] Sub-Gold Commissioner. This and the next letter are fair copies, retained by CH.

[7] The addressee is given as 'The Hon: Minister for Lands', John Robertson: see p. 88 n. 2.

[8] A head race furnishes water for a sluice box where it washes over gold-bearing soil (wash-dirt), the heavy gold particles settling out in riffles (bars or slats) across the base of the box. Where parties disagreed on the compensation to be paid for erecting a water race through private land they each appointed an arbitrator who together appointed an umpire. The award agreed between these three was then delivered to the Commissioner, in this case CH, within seven days. (See 'Water Races on Gold Fields', Rules under the *Gold Fields Act* of 1861, *NSW Government Gazette*, 23 September 1862, pp. 1804–05.) In this case, miner John O'Niel (or O'Neil, O'Neill) and his party, constructing a water-race for their diggings at much expense, were halted at the boundary of Charles Byrnes of Cadgee, the pastoralist who held much of the gold-bearing land along the Gulf Creek. The miners sought redress at ministerial level (see *Empire*, 30 June 1862, p. 8), and some months were lost before CH's doubtless welcome resolution of the problem.

68. Receipt by Nathanel Phillips for building Euroma, 1 January 1863

Text: Manuscripts and correspondence of Australian authors, NLA MS 3605

1st Jan: 1863

Received from Charles Harpur Esqre the sum of One Hundred and seventy seven pounds, being payment in full for building his house at Euroma.[1]

Nathanel Phillips[2]

69. Henry Kendall to Charles Harpur, 13 January 186[3]

Text: ML *D19

North Grafton[3] Clarence River. Jan. 13. 186[3].[4]

My dear Sir,

I have only just received your last, and hasten to reply.

I left Sydney for this red hot locality about two months ago. Did not see Mr Joseph Harpur[5] before I left; indeed I have not met him within the last six

---

[1] CH's granddaughter Dora would remember 'four big rooms with a passage in the middle leading back to a kitchen and offices. On the left as one approached it from the front was the drawing-room, the others being dining-room and two bedrooms.' (Rawling, pp. 254–5 – unsourced, but probably from a personal interview in the late 1950s). Dora's mother Mary Araluen Baldwin recalled: 'He had a comfortable house built and a garden and orchard laid out and planted. As the result of my father's forethought we had a lovely garden and a fine orchard in bearing long before there was another in the district...My mother said she was delighted with it, as she never expected anything so nice in such a short time' ('Daughter's Memories'). See Illustration 7, p. xxxvi.

[2] Possibly the 'N. Phillips' listed at Nerrigundah in 1862 (contributing 5s.) along with CH (£1, the third largest subscription in a total of £90 3s. 6d.) towards the relief of 'Distress in the Manufacturing Districts' of England: *Empire*, 20 October 1862, p. 2.

[3] A settlement on the Clarence River 600 km north of Sydney. Kendall was employed there by James Lionel Michael: see p. 127 n. 10.

[4] MS has '1862', almost certainly a turn-of-year mistake for 1863. Kendall's letter to CH dated 8 January 1862 (Letter 63) was sent from Newtown (Sydney); this one, ostensibly five days later, is signed from North Grafton in northern NSW. In it, Kendall states he left Sydney about two months previously – i.e., early November 1861. A date of 1862 is not impossible if Kendall were making occasional trips by the weekly steamers between Sydney and Grafton. However, Rawling (ML MSS 1326, Box 3) argues for 1863, noting that Kendall tells Miss Hopkins in a letter from Newtown of 2 May 1863 that he had just returned from Grafton where he had been five months. McLaren too (at #2345) opts for 1863. A copy of 'A Poet's Home', mentioned here, which CH had had printed in pamphlet form around November 1862 (see below), might have reached Kendall's Sydney address just too late to catch him there. And Kendall in his letter to CH of 4 July 1863 (Letter 70) returns to two subjects he mentions here – 'A Poet's Home' and CH's brother Joseph.

[5] Contrast Letter 63, which implies Kendall has *recently* 'secured a kind friend in Mr. Joseph Harpur'.

months. So the "Poet's Home"[6] never reached me

I shall not publish or write any more verse; and therefore will [h]ave nothing to do with "*imitation*["] again. I shall at once convey your thanks to Dr Brereton.[7]

Trusting that you are well,
I am, Dear Sir,
Yours Faithfully
Henry Kendall.

Letter to my Father M. BALDWIN.[8]

70. Henry Kendall to Charles Harpur, 4 July 1863

Text: Kendall papers, ML C199

Kingston Newtown. July 4th 1863

Dear Sir,

I am very much obliged to you for the "Poet's Home", and the accompanying Sonnet.[9] With this, I post a letter to Mr Joseph Harpur, with a qualified direction on the envelope. For I have not seen him since last November, and don't know his present residence. I want to see him.

Mr Deniehy has moved to Melbourne, where he is conducting a paper called the "Victorian". I saw an admirable paper on Hazlitt in a late number, and, recognized the "fine Roman hand"[10] of our friend. Poor D— was in

[6] 'A Poet's Home', first published in 1842 as 'The Poet's Wish. A Fragment' (h389a), appeared in pamphlet form dated '1862', printed by Hanson and Bennett, publishers of *Empire* (h389e). Given Kendall's movements, *c.* November 1862 is a probable date for its publication.

[7] John Le Gay Brereton (1827–86), physician, homeopath and author, member of the Sydney literary circle.

[8] This typed annotation is by CH's daughter Mary Araluen Baldwin (1861–1945).

[9] See n. 6 above. The sonnet, presumably in MS, is unidentified: 'The Poet', printed with 'A Poet's Home' in the 1862 pamphlet, is not a sonnet.

[10] I.e., a classically elegant literary style – from Malvolio's 'I think we do know the sweet Roman hand', in Shakespeare's *Twelfth Night; or, What You Will*, III.4.31. The 'paper' was 'The Laconics of an Essayist', *Victorian*, 6 June 1863, p. 151. William Hazlitt (1778–1830), English essayist, drama and literary critic, was hailed as the greatest of his age; he was also a painter, social commentator and philosopher. *Victorian* was launched in July 1862 as a liberal national weekly of events, politics, social science and literature as well as 'all the Catholic intelligence of the Australian colonies': it had a strong Irish-Australian focus. Charles Gavan Duffy invited Deniehy to Melbourne to edit it, which he did – brilliantly – until the paper failed in early April 1864.

great difficulties before he left, and has suffered much physically.[1] "Orion",
who blew his own *horn* so lustily thro' the *Sydney Morning Herald*, is also
connected with the *Victorian*.[2] I can get you a copy of "Orion" if you care to
see it. It has fine things in it.

Henry Halloran lent me your "Preface to a Proposed Volume of Poems" the
other day.[3] Do you intend to go on in the matter? I could be of some service
to you in Sydney—having knowledg[e] of many wealthy men who profess to
admire you exceedingly. But you need not hope for Halloran's sympathy: he'd
see you "blowed[4] first," before a movement was made by him. For Halloran's
idol is Halloran, and his admiration does not extend to anything beyond this
shrine. I am sorry to believe the above and sorry to know that he represents
the majority.

Mr Stenhouse alluded to your "Finish of Style"[5] the last time I saw him.
He agrees with my lofty estimate of it. What a pleasure it is to have that man
for a friend! But he is breaking up fast.[6]

You never write to me, now. The verses you allude to in the "Sonnet"[7] were
disfigured with printers' errors. Some day I shall send you the true copy.

The "Poet's Home" is vastly improved by the additions, and finishing
touches.[8] I have the poem as it appeared in the first volume, and so can

---

[1] Deniehy was constitutionally frail, short, 'slender of limb and delicately made'. Of a
pronounced literary bent and an impressive orator, during his last term in parliament –
which ended in November 1860 – 'he became extremely disillusioned with the moral tone
of politics and politicians' and took to alcohol. For a fresh start, in 1862 he moved his family
to Melbourne where he edited *Victorian*. Desperately poor and ill, he did some good writing;
but he would be devastated by the death of his only surviving son in April 1864; he again
drank heavily. By September he was back in Sydney. 'Colonial society was harsh and generally
unaccommodating to a man of his temperament, insight and sensitivity'; and, in 1865, 'his life
ended in mortification, personal tragedy and failure' (*ADB*).
[2] Richard Henry (Hengist) Horne (1802–84), English-born poet and critic known for his
epic *Orion* (1843), was lured to Victoria by gold in 1852, where he published lyrical dramas,
masques, cantatas and 'no significant poetry but some good prose' (*ADB*). He wrote for
newspapers including *Victorian*. Like CH, Horne worked as a gold commissioner. For his
1854 Australian edition of *Orion*, see Internet Archive.
[3] Not identified, but CH left documents with a similar purpose: 'Poems by Charles Harpur.
General Preface', *Maitland Mercury*, 3 June 1846, p. 1; the manuscript 'Miscellaneous Poems
of Charles Harpur. Preface' (ML C382, pp. 3–6) of 1847; the 'General Preface', quoted in
Letters 22 and 28; and what is presumably a later version of it, mentioned in Letter 53 (and
see p. 105 n. 2). For Halloran, see p. 127 n. 8.
[4] Cursed, confounded, hanged (vulgar imprecation).
[5] Published several times, most recently in *Empire*, 31 July 1862, p. 8 (h132d).
[6] In response in Letter 71, CH would pen his consolatory 'To N. D. Stenhouse Esq.' (h624a).
For Kendall's own 'To N. D. Stenhouse, Esq.', see *SMH*, 15 June 1863, p. 5.
[7] Kendall had recently published two batches of sonnets in *SMH* (15 June 1863, p. 5 and 2 July
1863, p. 5). His sonnet to Stenhouse contains errors of punctuation and in wording: 'passes'
for 'passed' in line 1 and possibly 'far' for 'fair' in line 8.
[8] 'A Poet's Home' had been published as early as 1842, but Kendall is here comparing the
versions in *Bushrangers* of 1853 (h389c) and the 1862 pamphlet (h389e). Besides word changes
throughout, CH had added 16 new stanzas, including the one Kendall quotes next.

appreciate the progress of Art. There is an ethnic luxury of colour and feeling about the last stanzas. The finest lines in the poem are, perhaps, these:

> "Whose memory is like a fervent tune
> Heard *richly prospering in a Summer wind*
> Under the midnight moon.

Now, considering the application, the simile is most sumptuously arrayed in Truth and Beauty. It dazzled me when I looked at it for the first time.

No verse in the "Poet's Home" surpasses the one commencing with

> "Or the slow rising and most summery hum

What a spot for the "Opium Eater".[9]

"The Poet" is one of the best of your short pieces. I have a M.S. copy of it,[10] in your handwriting Mr Joseph Harpur gave it to me.

> Hoping that you are well,
> I am, dear Sir,
> Yours Faithfully
> Henry Kendall.

71. Charles Harpur to Henry Kendall, 14 July 1863

Text: Stenhouse papers, ML A100

Euroma, nr Gulph Diggings. 14 July 1863

Dear Kendall,

I got yours of the other day, and what you say in it about our dear old friend Stenhouse gave me a pinch of grief that I thought I was at this time of day, and weather hardened as I am, incapable of being touched with, by and for almost any thing that could happen: nor could I get any relief from it, until I had poured out the annexed sonnet—which I wish you to show to S. himself if you think sufficiently well of it.

> Yours most truly
> Chas: Harpur.

---

[9] A nickname for essayist Thomas De Quincey (1785–1859). In his autobiographical *Confessions of an English Opium Eater*, a sensation in its day, De Quincey described the effects of his addiction to laudanum (second edition of 1823 online at Internet Archive). De Quincey had a particular interest for the literary friends of N. D. Stenhouse because of the latter's early association with him in Edinburgh (see Jordens, *passim*).

[10] 'The Poet' (h383b) appeared with 'A Poet's Home' in the Hanson and Bennett pamphlet; the 'M.S.' (unidentified) may be related to another MS, h383d, of 1862–63.

To N. D. Stenhouse Esq.[1]

Kendall had written me: "Alas! I fear
    Our dear good Friend is breaking"[2]—meaning you:
And suddenly mine eyes grew dim and blear,
    So that I might not read his missive through,
    Until another time.—Ah, misery! who
Would bear to breathe in this Samaria here,[3]
When haply, with *our* Norton,[4] every frere
    He greatly prized, were gone:—the noble few[5]

'Tis much to have but *met* you—but to say
    "He is in soul my very friend",[6] is what
I would not be content to have decay
    Out of the values of my bardic lot,
    For aught besides my spirit hath begot
Of kindred comfort, through my life's whole way.

                           Charles: Harpur.

72. Henry Kendall to Charles Harpur, [after mid-July 1863]

Text: Kendall papers, ML C198

TO CHARLES HARPUR.[7]

AH! often do I wait and watch,
And look up, straining through the Real
With longing eyes, my friend, to catch
Faint glimpses of your white Ideal.

---

[1] To compare with subsequent versions, see h624.

[2] 'What a pleasure it is to have that man for a friend! But he is breaking up fast' (Kendall, Letter 70).

[3] The historical and biblical name for the hilly central region of ancient Israel, the home of the Samaritans – here, the cultural 'desert' of colonial NSW.

[4] See p. 76 n. 3.

[5] From French *frère* (brother); recalling 'We few, we happy few, we band of brothers', from Shakespeare, *Henry V*, IV.3.60. Stenhouse's old Edinburgh associates Thomas De Quincey and John Wilson ('Christopher North') were dead by 1863. James Norton had died the previous August, Deniehy was in Melbourne, Richard Rowe had returned to England, Frank Fowler had died there, and CH himself was far away on the southern goldfields.

[6] Truly entitled to the name: cf. 'This gentleman, the prince's near ally, / My very friend, hath got his mortal hurt / In my behalf' – Romeo, in Shakespeare's *Romeo and Juliet*, III.1.115–17.

[7] The poem in this letter-fragment first appeared as 'To ——' in *SMH*, 2 May 1863, p. 5; it is not to be confused with Kendall's 'To C.H.' ('I would sit at your feet for long days...') of 1861.

I know she loves to rest her feet
By slumbrous seas and hidden strand,
But mostly hints of her I meet
On moony spots of mountain land.

Too weak to reach her shining place,
I only cross at times a gleam,
As one might pass a fleeting face
Just on the outside of a Dream.

But *you* may climb, her happy Choice!
She *knows* your step, the Maiden true,
And ever when she hears your voice
She turns, and sits and waits for you.

How sweet to rest on breezy crest,
With such a Love, what time the Morn
Looks from his halls of rosy rest
Across green miles of gleaming corn!

How sweet to find a leafy nook,
When bees are out and Day burns mute,
Where you may hear a passioned brook
Play past you, like a mellow flute!

Or, turning from the sunken sun,
On fields of dim delight to lie—
To close your eyes and muse upon
The Twilight's strange divinity!

Or, through the Night's mysterious noon,
While Sound lies husht amongst the trees,
To sit and watch a mirrored Moon
Float over silver-sleeping seas!

Oh! vain regret! Why should I stay
To think and dream of joys unknown?
You walk with her from day to day:
I faint afar off—and alone!

HENRY KENDALL.

If you knew *how sincerely* these lines were written, you would, unhesitatingly, rank me amongst those who are *"in soul your very friends."*[1] Then doubtful letters would not come to me. I am worth the knowing—if only for all this.

The sonnet headed *"Poetry"*[2] is very fine. These are great lines:

> "Mountainous exploits, and the wrecks thick strewn
> By Stormy Passion o'er Life's treacherous sea,
> *Relieved with shores of green delight and boon*
> *And starry dreams, and the serene pale moon*
> *Of Pathos;—&c"*.

I can't resist the temptation to quote something from *"Records of Romantic Passion:"*[3]

> "The themes
> Of some Petrarchian[4] mind *whose story gleams*
> *Within the Past like a moon-silvered Sea.*

> * * * * *

> "The echo's mystery and the streamlet's lore
> Savour of Passion *and transfusive pour*
> *Abroad suggestions to heroic Love."*

To be returned[5]

---

[1] Kendall echoes a line from 'To N. D. Stenhouse Esq.' (h624a), which CH sent Kendall, 14 July 1863 (Letter 71). This dates the present letter. Kendall employed his 'printed' hand, as here, in letters to CH from 1862 to April 1864.

[2] See h385c from *Bushrangers* (1853); the sonnet had been published as 'Poesie' (h385a) in *Colonial Literary Journal*, 20 March 1845, p. 187.

[3] See h452b from *Bushrangers*.

[4] Or 'Petrarchan': of the Italian poet Petrarch (1304–74). The octave of the Petrarchan (or Italian) sonnet rhymes *abbaabba* and its sestet *cdcdcd* or *cdecde*. CH's sonnet does not conform, as he points out in *Bushrangers*, p. 127.

[5] This annotation (at the top of p. 1 of MS) resembles CH's. Perhaps he did return it, for it is preserved at ML in a volume of Kendall's manuscript poems and newspaper cuttings (SAFE/C198), collected by D. S. Mitchell and dated by ML 'ca. 1862–1880s'.

73. Charles Harpur to Mary Chidley McMahon (née Harpur), [after 13 August 1863]

Text: ML MSS 947

My dear Sister Mary,[6]

I have only time to say a few words anent that love letter which you enclosed in your last note to Mrs H. I have little doubt but that you have made up your mind not to marry again, and it is my decided opinion, that it is best you should not. You ought to have had enough of matrimony. You ought almost to have a horror of it. At all events, if ever you should marry again, it should be wisely—even in the worldly sense of the word. As to your thinking of entering into the relation of a wife to any mere adventurer—any poor vagabond who might happen to have acquired the knack of talking somewhat romantically;— why, it would be inexcusable,—it would be sheer madness! Not, my dear sister, that I think there is any likelihood much less any danger of your doing so. Yet understand me. If your hand were sought by a thoroughly estimable and *agreeable* man, having a worldly competency, I do not know that I should dissuade you from marrying him. To do so, would be not only excusable, but it would be due perhaps to your friendless position. But enough of this.

From the cheerful tone of your letters, I suppose you are in good health— the main thin[g] after all in this life. I, too, enjoy excellent health upon the whole;[7] and I do not think I am a whit older in *constitution* than I was ten years ago. And if I am not getting rich, I at least owe no man anything that I cannot pay; if I have not much to spend in luxury, I am at least gradually placing myself out of the shot of that *need* which is so inimical to the full characteristic growth and nobility of manhood.

All my little men[8] are well, as I suppose their dear mother has told you in hers—

I remain, my dear Sister
your affectionate brother
Chas: Harpur.

[6] CH's sister Mary Chidley McMahon (née Harpur, 1817–1913) had survived three husbands: Walter Palmer (disappeared 1844), John Clarke Ward (d. 1846) and Bernard McMahon (d. 13 August 1863). James Hackett would be her fourth, though no record of a marriage has been located. Probably known to CH, he was a goldfields mining engineer, including at Araluen in 1862. A notebook of CH's (ML C384) includes a list, apparently in his own hand, of 'Payments made by Hackett' during that year. The present letter bears no date or addressee details; it may have been enclosed in Mary Harpur's reply to the letter and enclosed 'love letter' Mary McMahon had sent her (none of the three has been located).

[7] A regular salary and a farm of his own (the Harpurs moved to the property Euroma on the Tuross River, Eurobodalla, in *c.* April 1863: see p. 123 n. 2) seem to have done wonders for CH's health and outlook. But only five more years remained to him.

[8] The children now numbered five: Washington, Charley, Harold, Ada and the youngest, Mary Araluen, born at Araluen in 1861. CH was presumably using 'little men' broadly.

74. Henry Kendall to Charles Harpur, 16 August 1863

Text: Kendall papers, ML C199

Kingston. Newtown Aug. 16th 1863.

My dear Charles Harpur,

In my last I promised a fuller reference to the *Sonnets* you were kind enough to send me.[1]

"Poetry"[2] is familiar, through the published volume; "The First Great Australian Poet"[3] is *rocky*. "True and False Glory",[4] although good, was written at a time, I think, when your "singing robes"[5] were not on. "Charity"[6] brims over with tenderness. These are lovely lines:—

> "On thy maternal bosom many a time
> I lay my head, and dream that yet thy reign
> In its faith-widen'd influence every clime
> Shall sweeten; and, as o'er some torrid plain
> Fresh airs breathe vigor, quicken Man to attain
> Capacity for Love's millennial prime."

"The Tear"[7] is the most musical of the Seven. It is full of *tearful* Pathos. I like it even better than "Love's Star"[8] notwithstanding the investiture of more

---

[1] CH had sent Kendall what were probably two leaves (four pages) of manuscript copies of seven poems, (the first leaf is extant: ML MSS 9536/1/1). Their texts are much closer to those in ML C376, pp. 344ff. of 1861 than to those in ML A90, pp. 241ff. (copied and revised from C376 and dated 3 September 1863). Copying and revising the sequence for A90 from C376 may have led CH to send copies of favourite ones to Kendall. The source of the 'seventh sonnet' (see below) was probably A90. The other poems Kendall quotes derive from printed sources, especially *Bushrangers* and *Thoughts*.

[2] See versions h385e (from ML C376) and h385f (A90). In 'Old Manuscripts', Kendall quotes it at length, from manuscripts in his possession.

[3] See versions ho19d (from ML C376) and ho19e (A90). Kendall's *'rocky'* responds to CH's: 'Quarrying from Nature's everlasting frame / The sculptured beauty of his lofty Rhyme!' (ho19d).

[4] See versions h154d (from ML C376) and h154e (A90). Kendall printed the poem in 'Old Manuscripts' – see above.

[5] '[A] poet, soaring in the high region of his fancies, with his garland and singing robes about him...' – Milton, *The Reason of Church-Government Urg'd against Prelaty* (1641).

[6] Only partly preserved in ML MSS 9536/1/1 (see n. 1 above): cf. versions ho65d (in ML C376) and ho65e (A90). Kendall printed the poem in 'Old Manuscripts'.

[7] Probably from the lost second leaf of ML MSS 9536/1/1: cf. h423b (in ML C376; no counterpart in A90). First published in *SMH*, 7 November 1866, p. 3 as eighth of ten 'Sonnets: With Prefatory Remarks on the Sonnet: By Charles Harpur' (h423d).

[8] Probably from the lost second leaf of ML MSS 9536/1/1. It appears in ML C376 as 'Emblems' (h110b), but CH is more likely to have copied from *Bushrangers* (h110c) or ML A90 (h110e). Daniel Deniehy quoted with approval the same lines (from h110c) in his 1857 newspaper article, observing: 'Vesper has almost in every age divided bardic homages with the moon. But notwithstanding the long accumulation of compliments, my gifted friend Harpur has found something new to say, and as beautiful, to my mind, as ever was said' (*Empire*, 19 May 1857, p. 2).

than one beautiful thought in the latter. It, Love's Star, was evidently born of this:

> "The Star of Evening is a gracious feature
> *Instinct as 'twere with all the Love that eyes*
> *Have looked through at the skies.*"

In the seventh sonnet,[9] and in your last letter to me you express a keen discontent with regard to your present lot. I can well understand how a Poet must suffer the hair of whose head is turning grey in the chilling blasts of Neglect. But this Neglect is only ephemeral—and the author of the "*Tower of the Dream*" is no butterfly. He ought to be all-sufficient for the troubled Present, who has such a goodly heritage in the clear Future.

If any one asked me to point out Harpur's most characteristic poem I should turn to the "Tower of the Dream".[10] And if any one asked me to point out Harpur's *best* poem, I should again turn to the "Tower of the Dream." Yet I speak, very likely, out of a limited knowledge of your writings. I don't forget the "Creek of the Four Graves"[11] when my belief is stated that the "Tower of the Dream" is the greatest of Australian Poems; and one of the finest of its kind in the English language. The Dream-Song[12] is instinct with Dream-Music.

"Freedom in Faith"[13] has the roll of an unknown Sea in it. "Records of Romantic Passion"[14] should be read in a mountain-glen, at night, with a glimpse of "moonsilvered Sea" far, far away. These are your greatest Sonnets.

I hate praising a man to his face, as Stenhouse, Woolley,[15] &c would tell you. But in talking to a Poet who is wholly without the sympathy which he *must* look for, I do not unrighteously bridle my tongue.

Yours very truly
Henry Kendall

---

[9] Probably from the lost second leaf of ML MSS 9536/1/1. The sonnet was 'To Henry Kendall', first recorded in manuscript dated '1863' (ML A90, see h607a). CH speaks there of Kendall's 'votive lines so sweetly bland / (Yet bravely worshipful)', presumably with Kendall's tribute 'To C. H.' in mind (*Empire*, 13 September 1861, p. 5). Kendall printed the sonnet in 'Old Manuscripts'.

[10] Unless he had a manuscript copy of this long poem Kendall was probably referring to h642b (in *Empire*, 21 February 1857, p. 4 and 10 March 1857, p. 2). Kendall would ultimately arrange publication in *Australian Journal* on 25 November and 2 December 1865 (h642f) and would see the complete, pamphlet version (h642g) through the printers.

[11] Already among CH's best known (and subsequently most anthologised) poems, published in Duncan's *Weekly Register* in 1845 (h080a: 9 August, p. 67, 16 August, p. 78, 23 August, p. 90) and in *Bushrangers* in 1853 (h080f).

[12] The 'mystic song' of the Lady of Light comprising the last four stanzas of Part I of 'The Tower of the Dream' (h642b).

[13] Published in *Thoughts* in 1845 as 'Intellectual Majesty' (h199a) and in *Bushrangers* as 'Freedom in Faith' in 1853 (h199b).

[14] Published in *Thoughts* as 'The Poetry of Love' (h452a) and in *Bushrangers* as 'Records of Romantic Passion' (h452b).

[15] See p. 127 n. 11.

75. Henry Kendall to Charles Harpur, 19 August 1863

Text: Kendall papers, ML C199

Kingston. Newtown. Aug. 19th 1863.

My dear Mr Harpur,

I have just got your's dated August _. On Monday I posted a letter[1] in *anticipation* of something from you.

I am much obliged to you for the four Sonnets. The one addressed to that fine fellow Andrew Marvel,[2] is my favorite. "A Worldling"[3] is very effective. "My Faith in Poetry"[4] could only have been written by one fully conscious of his *Life* in Poetry. And of the rare felicity in that Life above a Life. "The Poverty of Genius"[5] is, perhaps, the wisest of the lot. With regard to the *rhyme* and *construction* of your Sonnets I will here say a few words:

The rhyme-arrangement I like exceedingly. Through its agency each line dies off like a sea-wave. I have often wondered about the origin of this form so distinct from the Italian.[6]

---

[1] CH's 'August' letter (Kendall left an underlined blank for the day of the month, presumably intending to fill it in later) must have enclosed the 'four Sonnets' (below), presumably in MS; it is not extant. Kendall's letter would be his dated 16 August (Letter 74), posted Monday 17 August.

[2] Andrew Marvell, English metaphysical poet, satirist and parliamentarian (1621–78). CH addresses him reverently in the sonnet as 'Spirit, that lookest from the starry fold /Of Truth's white flock, next to thy Milton there'. Marvell served as assistant to his older friend John Milton, as Latin Secretary under Cromwell, and, after the Restoration, used his influence to protect Milton from execution for his anti-monarchist writings and activities. Well versed in Milton's writings, CH may have read Marvell's 'On Mr. Milton's Paradise Lost', which often appeared as a preface to Milton's epic from the second edition of 1674 onwards including in at least 12 editions in the 18th century and in an 1829 edition (London: Septimus Prowett), with plates by John Martin, that was advertised for over 20 years from the 1840s in Australian newspapers. Several of CH's poems show the influence of Marvell, and 'A Basket of Summer Fruit' (h030a, in *PA*, 18 March 1854, p. 5) lifts images directly from 'Bermudas'. CH probably copied 'Andrew Marvel' for Kendall from ML C376 (h010d) or A90 (h010e); it had first appeared in *Colonial Literary Journal* in 1845 (h010a) with the conventional 'Marvell' spelling, but CH favoured 'Marvel' in all subsequent versions.

[3] Published in *Thoughts* in 1845 as 'Worldly Success' (h701a); CH probably copied this version for Kendall from ML A90 (h701b).

[4] Not published in CH's lifetime or in *Poems* (1883); probably copied for Kendall from ML A90 (h311a).

[5] Published in *Colonial Literary Journal* in 1845 (h681a) and in *Thoughts* that year (h681b) as 'The Poverty of Greatness'; probably copied for Kendall from ML A90 (h681e), although the 1861 version in C376 (when the title changed to '…Genius') is a possible source.

[6] CH claimed to have invented the form of the sonnets he presented in *Thoughts* (1845), which he prefaced: 'In this Series of Sonnets the arrangement of the rhymes is somewhat peculiar. In departing from the Italian model in this respect, I am conscious of not being induced thereto by a desire merely to innovate. But carefully trying the Form I have here chosen, not to say invented, by my own ear, I venture to believe that it fits the English Sonnet—or rather, the sonnet in English—more agreeably than the adopted one above referred to.' He would make a similar point, at greater length, in his 'Prefatory Remarks on the Sonnet' (see h385j) in *SMH*, 7 November 1866, p. 3.

You *construct* many of your Sonnets with an utter disregard for superficial harmony. They are about as uneven as a rain-rutted mountain-crag. Yet there is, for me, a wild beauty in this ruggedness.

I don't remember having met with, anywhere, a Sonnet which has impressed me more than your's headed, "Freedom in Faith".[7] What a grand *under-tone* rolls through it! Wordsworth has written nothing finer.[8]

Tennyson is over-rated and under-rated.[9] One of the best lyrics in the language is "Locksley Hall"[10]—one of the vilest poems in the same tongue is "Maud."[11] The "Two Voices"[12] will be more generally admitted as Tennyson's completest and most direct work *yet*. With him Art rules Thought like an *autocrat*. His most ardent admirers must admit that the "mechanism" of his Poetry delights him more than doth the Poetry itself. The trouble evidently expended over the excruciatingly elaborate "Idylls of the King"[13] will bear witness so far. "In Memoriam"[14] is one of the noblest things, of its kind, that has been given to us this century. But I can't help suspecting that Tennyson will be chiefly remembered through *passages*—not through *poems in their completeness*. I have only read him through *once*, and have not looked at

---

[7] Published in *Thoughts* as 'Intellectual Majesty' (h199a) and in *Bushrangers* as 'Freedom in Faith' (h199b), but CH probably copied this version for Kendall from ML C376 (h199d) or ML A90 (h199e).

[8] See p. 10 n. 1.

[9] Alfred Tennyson, later first Baron Tennyson (1809–92) and Poet Laureate of Great Britain and Ireland. Kendall was aware of CH's 'estimate' of Tennyson (see below), perhaps from the lost August letter, perhaps having seen the report of his 1859 Braidwood lecture: 'From what I have seen of Tennyson's Poetry, I should be inclined to class it under that of Genius; esteeming it, however, either too microscopic (so to speak), or, on the other hand, too indefinite; that is to say, his pictures are too much made up of minute details, without breadth and continuity of outline; or they are of a consistence so thin and subtle as to present us with no substantial body and no definite outline at all' ('Mr. Harpur's Lecture on Poetry, at Braidwood', *Southern Cross*, 5 November 1859, p. 4 and p. 5). In an 1863 newspaper article CH would object to the 'general feebleness in the flow' of Tennyson's blank verse ('On Blank Verse', *SMH*, 2 November 1863, p. 2), and he extended the charge in correspondence (see Letter 109).

[10] Written 1835, published 1842 in Tennyson's early collection *Poems* (London: Edward Moxon: vol. II, pp. 92–111 – online at Internet Archive), it is a dramatic interior monologue of 97 rhyming couplets. It moves from the narrator's bitter lament for lost love to a rumination on social and material progress.

[11] Dramatic narrative in lyrics that vary in scansion, length and style, said to be Tennyson's most experimental poem: *Maud, and Other Poems* (London: Edward Moxon, 1855), pp. 1–100 – online at Internet Archive.

[12] 'The Two Voices' appeared in *Poems* (1842; online at Internet Archive), vol. II, pp. 116–47. A poetic dialogue, titled in manuscript 'Thoughts of a Suicide', it was written 1833–34 after the premature death in 1833 of Tennyson's dear friend Arthur Henry Hallam.

[13] Tennyson's *magnum opus*, a cycle of twelve narrative poems in blank verse, published 1857–85. A retelling of the legend of King Arthur, it is also a commentary on the state of society in mid-Victorian Britain. By 1863 only the first four poems – 'Enid,' 'Vivien', Elaine' and 'Guinevere' – had appeared (London: Edward Moxon, 1859; for the 1862 edition see Internet Archive). Kendall would change his mind about the 'Idylls' within a few weeks – see Letter 77.

[14] 'In Memoriam A. H. H.', a requiem for Hallam (see above) and first published anonymously (London: Edward Moxon, 1850 – online at Internet Archive). Modern opinion tends to back Kendall's judgement here.

him since 1861. Nevertheless he has made a deep impression I confess. Your estimate of the poet *jars* against mine not a little; but you ought to be the best judge.

I am not acquainted with "Young Night Thoughts".[1] To tell the truth, my reading has been very limited: the rough life I have led hitherto has kept me from many good things. I have a mother and three sisters to look after, and the struggle for their comfort absorbs most of my time.

I see Mr. Halloran every day. I am employed at the Survey Offices. H.H. is a queer fellow. Every morning he calls me in, and treats me with an emphatic recital of his latest. I could no more do the like with my verses than fly. I even hate to make the faintest allusion to Poetry while abroad. I am my own critic, my own audience; and live completely within myself. So the epithet "Silent" has been generally applied to me. I only mention this as a kind of defence against your charge of "super-social" tendencies.[2]

Hoping that you, and all dear to you are well,

I am,
Yours Sincerely
Henry Kendall.

76. Henry Kendall to Charles Harpur, 2 September 1863

Text: Kendall papers, ML C199

Kingston. Newtown. Sept 2nd 1863.

My dear Mr Harpur,

I have your short note with the three *sonnets* appended.[3] I like the one

[*continued next page*

---

[1] Kendall had misread CH's letter: the poem is by Edward Young (1683–1765), *The Complaint: or, Night-Thoughts on Life, Death, & Immortality*, a dramatic monologue in blank verse, published 1742–45 and highly popular in its day. Over nine nights the poet muses on the loss of those dear to him and on human frailty. The edition of 1797 was famously illustrated by William Blake (London: R. Edwards, 1797; online at Internet Archive).

[2] Presumably that Kendall was a creature far more sociable than CH himself: Kendall had a responsible job, knew many people, apparently mixed easily with them and had felt no compunction in writing to CH out of the blue.

[3] We do not have CH's note, nor do we know which three sonnets CH sent with it; but their copying for Kendall was likely another by-product of CH's revision of a long sonnet-sequence for ML A90, his source being mainly the counterpart sequence in C376 of 1861.

headed "Emerson at the Best."[4] "The wrongs of Poland" is a noble outburst.[5] I think it is one of the very best of your late publications. Bennett of the *Empire*[6] was telling me yesterday that he had a long poem of yours in hand.[7] I shall be very glad to meet with it in type. Whenever you want a Sydney paper, of any date, for reference, let me know, and I will get it for you—if possible.

With reference to what you say in your last, I am only a nominal Spiritualist.[8] I am not at all satisfied yet.

Promising to write a longer letter next time, I am,

My dear Mr Harpur,
yours Faithfully
Henry Kendall

Excuse haste.

The more I see of Mr Halloran the more I like the man.[9] There is a wealth of good-nature underneath the superficial crust of indifference that I have already spoken of.

My conclusions have been too hasty.

H.K.

[4] Published in *PA*, 21 June 1856, p. 5 as 'Emerson' (h111b), retitled 'Emerson at the Best' in ML A90 (h111d). A second, satirical poem (h112a) also at first entitled 'Emerson' and critical of the American for his affected mysticism and internal inconsistency was retitled 'Emerson at the Worst' in ML A90 (h112b); it may have been one of the three sonnets. See also the note to h112a in 'Songs, Epigrams, Notes, and Opinions, &c., No. 12.', *PA*, 20 September 1856, p. 5. CH would write a series of articles on Emerson for *Sydney Times*, 23 and 30 April, and 7 May, 1864.

[5] CH's reaction to the 1863 Polish insurrection against Russian occupation known as the January Uprising. This sonnet appeared in *SMH*, 27 August 1863, p. 8, and see h705a for an 1863 text in ML A90. All subsequent versions have a qualifying footnote: while CH still wholly approves of 'the spirit of this Sonnet, as it applies generally to the sacredness of the rights and pieties of nations and of races…my later readings have much altered my sentiments as to the national worth of the Poles, & their so called wrongs as a distinct People' (see, e.g., h705b).

[6] Samuel Bennett (1815–78), journalist, newspaper proprietor and historian. With printer William Hanson he acquired *Empire* from Henry Parkes in 1859; CH's poetry continued to appear until mid-1862. In 1867, CH would fall out with Bennett over his offer, ignored, to become a regular contributor – see his scarifying but undelivered letter to Bennett of September 1867 (Letter 126).

[7] *Empire* published nothing by CH between July 1862 and July 1867, most of his material going instead (through Kendall) to *SMH*. The 'long poem' under consideration may have been 'Bard of Paradise'. Its length probably led CH once again to consider pamphlet publication, which was ever on his mind: see p. 131 n. 6, Letter 83 and p. 150 n. 6.

[8] One who believes that the spirits of the dead can hold communication with the living. Modern Spiritualism developed in USA in the 1840s and spread through Britain, Europe, Australia and South America. Notable Sydney Spiritualists included John Bowie Wilson (member for the Southern Goldfields and, from late 1863, Minister for Lands), judge William Charles Windeyer and Mary Woolley, wife of the first principal of the University of Sydney. Articles in *Empire* of 1862–63 by Frederick Sinclair (proprietor of *Illawarra Express* and *Australian Spiritualist*) possibly piqued Kendall's interest – see, e.g., 'Spiritualism in Australia', *Empire*, 6 January 1863, p. 3, and also p. 151 n. 13.

[9] See p. 127 n. 8.

77. Henry Kendall to Charles Harpur, 26 October 1863

Text: Kendall papers, ML C199

Sydney. Oct 26th 1863.

My dear Mr Harpur,

I have your admirable critical paper on "Blank Verse".[1] As cordially as yourself do I set my face against the pretenders, who are only notorious for their pretensions. But these men are somehow *necessary* in their way: they do all the needful brooming in dirty corners. Literature could not thrive without them. With regard to the "lectures" before the "societies" you refer to,[2] I must say I am more amused than edified after the knowledge of them. What intelligent thinker could do otherwise than laugh at them. If I had time and aptitude to night, I should analyse for you *some* of the precious scribblers who have been dubbed "poets" by a recent "lecturer".

I shall get your paper published in the "*Herald*": it, the Herald, is the best medium for publicity. Your prose is a treat: it is so refreshingly original. With the criticisms on the "blank verse" styles of Milton, Akenside, Thomson, and Cowper,[3] I most faithfully concur. The passage from "*Alastor*"[4] is glorious. I don't know much of Young's blank verse, and cannot judge sufficiently from your quotation.[5] You may not have read the "Idylls of the King"—in which,

---

[1] I.e., in MS: it appeared – thanks to Kendall (see below) – as 'On Blank Verse', *SMH*, 2 November 1863, p. 2.

[2] A lecture on the 'Poets and Poetry of Australia' was delivered on 23 September 1863 by Joseph Sheridan Moore (see p. 111 n. 6) to an association of the employees of mail-order draper Francis Giles at Denison House in George-street, Sydney: see *SMH*, 26 September 1863, p. 6; and also *Empire*, 25 September 1863, p. 5, which quoted Moore as saying: 'Messrs. Kendall and Wilson were the only two [poets] who looked upon Australian scenery with purely Australian eyes, and sent forth their thoughts in an Australian garb.' Moore's letter of correction (in *Suppl. Letters*) appeared in *SMH*, 29 September 1863, p. 5. He denied that he had placed Kendall and minor poet Frederick Sydney Wilson (1839–1901) ' "in the van" of Australian lyric writers to the exclusion of Charles Harpur. While denying that Harpur possesses a musical ear, and asserting that he embodies a grim philosophy of human progress in his poetic utterances, I admitted that he possessed the creative faculty...in a higher degree than any of his contemporaries.' Kendall does not name Moore here but he was the likely, as the most recent, source of offence.

[3] British poets: John Milton, Mark Akenside (1721–70), James Thomson (1700–48) and William Cowper (1731–1800). CH's article demonstrates the importance and role of modulation in blank verse, the 'cadences...of well-constructed numbers, when unshackled with rhyme'. He quotes passages from each of these poets with qualified approval, reserving his greatest attention – and praise – for Milton.

[4] *Alastor; or, The Spirit of Solitude* by English Romantic poet Percy Bysshe Shelley, 1792–1822 (London: Baldwin, Cradock and Joy; and Carpenter and Son, 1816; online at Internet Archive). CH quotes with approval a passage selected 'almost at random'. He had a set of Shelley's works: see p. 5 n. 7.

[5] See p. 142 n. 1. In his essay, CH argues that Young's blank verse, while precisely balanced, is 'well-nigh intolerable to a judicious ear. It wants all the compensations of rhyme, while lacking, at the same time, all that variously interflowing melody of cadence which should be primarily distinctive of unrhymed numbers'.

I think, some of the most melodious blank verse in the English language is to be found. Milton's verse is like Beethoven's music, Shelley's like Mozart's, and Tennyson's like Handel's. The first *rolls*, the second *gushes*, and the third *flows*.

I am very ill to night, and have been vexe[d] to death with many troubles[6]— so don't look for a fluent letter this time. After your paper appears, I will write at length [to] you; and not make so many blots, scratches, &c.

The blank verse of the "Creek of the Four Graves" is not thoroug[h]ly understood by Deniehy; or I am confoundedly mistaken.[7] I should like to be able to read it to *you*; for I feel sure you would agree with my rende[r]ing of it. The form is quite new.

More next time.

I am
Yours very Sincerely
Henry Kendall.

78. Henry Kendall to Charles Harpur, 3 November 1863

Text: Kendall papers, ML C199

Survey Offices.[8] Sydney Tuesday Evening. November 3rd 1863.

My dear Mr Harpur,

I have posted you a copy of the *Herald* of yesterday (Nov. 2nd) in which your paper on "Blank Verse"[9] appears. I can't answer for the correctness of the typography: it may be all right. Mr Stenhouse was greatly taken up with the article: he asked to tell you how much he was delighted by it. Any thing you may wish to see in print, I will gladly insert in the *Herald* for you. In a letter addressed to you, and posted last week, I have told you of my preference for the one daily journal.[10] The *Empire*, with all its professions, is the worst foe

[6] Besides his illness Kendall was saddled with constant debt and a dipsomaniac mother (Ackland, pp. 119–24, 151, 277).

[7] See Letter 55. Kendall was perhaps linking Deniehy (whom he may have heard read CH's verse) to CH's 'On Blank Verse': 'And what is more rare than a good reader of continuously varied blank verse? or, indeed, of any kind of verse whereof the melody is achieved through other than the most obvious and ordinary cadences?'

[8] See Letter 75: in August 1863 Kendall had obtained the post of Extra Clerk with the Surveyor General's Department offered him by Chief Clerk Henry Halloran. The offices were in Bridge-street, Sydney; they were replaced in the 1870s by the present Lands Department building.

[9] See Letter 77.

[10] Kendall would increasingly act as CH's unpaid metropolitan literary agent, placing his writing with Sydney papers and keeping an eye out for publishing opportunities. An intimate of Charles Fairfax, one of the proprietors of *SMH*, Kendall's influence with that paper outlasted Fairfax's early death in a riding accident in December 1863 (see Rawling, pp. 259, 267–9; Ackland, pp. 106–7). The 'letter' is Letter 77.

Australian Literature has.[1] I have known this fact long enough: so have Messrs Stenhouse, Deneihy, and Joseph Harpur. Yet, if it is worst, it is contemptible. The *Herald* is *comparatively* liberal; and far more influential.

Excuse haste and the paper. Like a good fellow, let me know when you have received this; the newspaper; and my note of last week. I *want* to hear from you.

In a galloping hurry for the Mail,

I am,
My dear Mr Harpur,
Yours Sincerely,
Henry Kendall.

Address your letters to Kingston, Newtown, as usual.

79. Charles Harpur to Henry Kendall, 9 November 1863
Text: Kendall papers, ML C199

Euroma, Gulph Diggings, 9th Nov 1863

My dear Kendall,

Your two last[2] came duly to hand.

As you say, I have no doubt but that the Herald *is* the best medium for literary publication—and any thing that I may wish to see in print, I will from time to time send through you for insertion in that journal—viz: some further papers on Versification (in general); some other prose pieces; and now and then a poem or two.[3] These poems (you may explain this to the Herald folk) will not *always* be original, but they will be *better*—that is, they will be as *finished* as I can make them.

I am glad that our old friend Stenhouse was pleased with the paper on Blank Verse. His approval of a thing of the kind is of more value in my estimation, than that of all the rest of our literary judges bunched together. But I think he knows this. Next to his in value would be Dan Deniehy's; and next to Deniehy's, in some things, *yours*.

---

[1] '[T]he most damnable rag on the face of God's earth...How I hate that paper! How I detest the lot that are on it: from the mealy mouthed shopman upward to Hanson and that fiddle-faced imposter Bennett. Why are they and men like Fairfax allowed to trample on the head of Genius?' – Kendall to Joseph Sheridan Moore, 9 September 1864, quoted in Ackland, p. 115. See p. 143 n. 7.

[2] Letters 77 and 78.

[3] Apart from the paper on blank verse, the only item by CH in *SMH* by the end of 1863 was the poem 'Cora' (h077d; 8 December 1863, p. 3); an earlier version (h077a) had appeared in *Empire*, 26 April 1856, p. 5. However, Kendall would contrive to place a good deal of his friend's verse with the paper through the 1860s.

I live a very solitary life here—utterly solitary, except so far as I am mixed up very unpleasantly with the petty fretting disputes &c of that most contentious class of men—our diggers. They sometimes make me almost a man-dispiser—so grasping are they—so unfraternal & dishonest. And it almost always so happens that when I would devote an hour to all serene & beautiful things, their calls upon me as a Commissioner, are most frequent & exacting.

Whenever I enclose you any "copy", you may take it for granted that I wish to see it in print.

Yours most truly
Chas: Harpur.

80. Charles Harpur to John Bowie Wilson, 17 November 1863
Text: Rawling papers, ML MSS 1326, Box 3[4]

Nerrigundah, 17th Novr / 63.

Dear Sir,

As late as the 14th instant, I received a copy of a telegram through the post here, from the Returning Officer at Adelong,[5] requesting me to appoint a Deputy Returning Officer, & prepare &c for a poll at this place: & seeing that not moment was to be lost, if we were to have a poll at all, I at once appointed a Deputy &c,[6] improvised a ballot box, & caused manuscript voting papers to be written on. By these several contrivances a poll was secured at all

[4] Source of this letter and annotation is a handwritten transcription by Harpur biographer J. Normington Rawling, made probably in the 1950s, of an official memorandum in a file then held by ML, since transferred to NSWSA but not found.

[5] The official who conducts or presides at an election and reports the result – here, at Adelong, a village in southern NSW between Gundagai and Tumbarumba, which mushroomed with the discovery of gold in 1853. The NSW Electoral Act of 1858 (s. 5) introduced three special goldfields electorates (South, West and North) that covered declared goldfields within specified general electorates. Rolls were not kept; voters established their right to vote by presenting a mining licence or goldfield business licence. The Returning Officer for Gold Fields South was David Wilson, prominent Adelong mining engineer. Polling places were declared at 14 centres including Adelong, Araluen, Major's Creek, Burrangong (Young), Kiandra, Tumberumba (Tumbarumba) and Nerrygundah (Nerrigundah) (notice, *SMH*, 11 November 1863, p. 8). John Bowie Wilson and F. A. Cooper (see p. 148 nn. 1 and 2) opened their electoral campaigns contentiously at a nomination meeting at Adelong on 5 November (see *SMH*, 13 November 1863, p. 8).

[6] George Porter (see *Empire*, 23 November 1863, p. 5).

events, & closed with 50 votes for Wilson[1] & 1 for Cooper,[2]—the townsfolk of Nerrigundah alone being able to appear at it, on account of the shortness of time & suddenness of the occurrence.

This account of the proceeding will show that I, at all events, have done whatever I could to remedy any neglect there may have been elsewhere (& there seems to have been some) in regard to Nerrigundah as a polling place in the present election for the Southern Gold Fields

The result of the poll was at once sent to the Master of the Telegraph Office at Braidwood, to be announced to the Returning Officer at Adelong.

I am, dear Sir,
Your most obedient Servant,
Chas: Harpur.

P.S. The squabble amongst the Chinese at this place[3] has been magnified most ridiculously. C. H.

Letter to Col. Secy. 63/6434
[sent by W. to Chief Secy] [ref. to 63/6991 q. v.]

81. Henry Kendall to Charles Harpur, 24 November 1863

Text: Kendall papers, ML C199

Kingston. Newtown. Nov: 24th 1863.

My dear Mr Harpur,

Your poem "Cora" will appear in one of the "Heralds" of this week.[4] When

---

[1] John Bowie Wilson (1820–83), free-thinker, spiritualist and phrenologist, and MLA for Gold Fields South. A former (and unsuccessful) digger at Araluen, he won the seat three times between 1859 and 1863. He would replace CH's brother Joseph as member for Patrick's Plains in 1864. As Secretary for Lands, he saw through Parliament the amending Act (29 Vic. No. 20) that would effectually retrench the Gold Commissioners including CH in 1866. Wilson had been elected for the seat in July 1859 and December 1860, but when James Martin's administration replaced Charles Cowper's in October 1863 Martin and his ministers had by custom to stand for re-election. Wilson (as incoming Secretary for Lands) won comfortably, polling from other centres reflecting that of Nerrigundah (*Goulburn Herald*, 18 November 1863, p. 2), which town neither candidate visited – see election report from there (*Empire*, 23 November 1863, p. 5); it ends: 'Our local gold commissioner [i.e., CH] is very popular'.
[2] Frederick Augustus Cooper (1834–1908), barrister, who in a long career practised in NSW, Queensland, New Zealand and Victoria. He was MLA for Braidwood, 1859–60, and a controversial Sub-Gold Commissioner at Kiandra and Araluen, 1860–63.
[3] In mid-November 1863 newspapers were reporting 'a serious row' between Chinese miners at Big Flat, Nerrigundah, over water rights, with one man dead and others seriously wounded, and police reinforcements standing by at Moruya (*Goulburn Herald*, 14 November 1863, p. 2). For an account of the fight, characterised as 'a war between Canton and Hongkong', see *Empire*, 23 November 1863, p. 5. It is probably to this contemptuously facetious report that CH refers.
[4] See p. 146 n. 3.

they publish it, I will send you the paper, and a long letter with it.

"Cora" is a lovely thing. I would like to have a M.S. copy of your "*Finish of Style*".[5] Can you send it? I am very much troubled about the illness of my brother[6] just now: he has been for some time hanging between life and death. Mr Joseph Harpur[7] met me to-day, and asked me to mention him. He looks well.

I have much to write about, but can't go on now. This last great sorrow seems to shut out everything.

Yours Sincerely
Henry Kendall.

82. Charles Harpur's reference for Ah Min, January 1864

Text: ML *D19

Gulph, January 1864[8]

I know the within named applicant, Ah Min,[9] and believe him to be in everyway well qualified for the office he solicits.[10] He bears a good general character, and is much trusted and looked up to by many of the Chinese inhabitants. He speaks English fluently, and is besides (as I have been informed by several of the most respectable of the Chinese residents) more than commonly well acquainted with the various and much-differing dialects of his Countrymen[11]—a qualification quite indispensible in a Chinese Interpreter. Adding to all this, the absolute necessity there is for having

---

[5] CH's advice to 'young authors' about the desirability of careful revision (h132a), first in *PA*, 4 October 1856, p. 5, with another three published versions, 1856–62. For a manuscript version of 1863, see h132e (in ML A89).

[6] Kendall's twin brother Basil Edward Kendall (1839–74), a minor poet in his own right (see, e.g., his 'Kembla' in *Empire*, 13 August 1861, p. 8) and a cause of much heartache to Henry, impersonating him and forging his name to bills – see Henry's public 'Caution' in *SMH*, 5 August 1864, p. 1. A heavy drinker and fragile in health, Edward had returned to Sydney perilously ill with an aneurism in late 1863 but would be nursed back to health by the end of 1865: see Ackland, pp. 40, 104, 106, 125, 133.

[7] Joseph was currently member for Patrick's Plains in the Legislative Assembly of NSW.

[8] A later pencilled annotation, '(now Nerrangundah)', was added to the address line in a hand similar to CH's, though the name was being used for the goldfield as early as 1861.

[9] A common name, anglicised in a variety of ways: probably he was the Ah Mun appointed Chinese Interpreter at the Gulph goldfield on 2 June 1864 (see *NSW Government Gazette*, 3 June 1864, p. 1315) and the Ah Man listed as Chinese interpreter at Nerrigundah in Bailliere's *Official Post Office Directory of NSW*, 1866 and 1867, and in court reports (e.g., in *Empire*, 17 November 1871, p. 3).

[10] With increasing Chinese immigration in the 1850s interpreters were needed for the courts. Chinese interpreters for the goldfields were appointed by the Governor on the advice of the Executive Council.

[11] The majority of Chinese arriving in NSW in the goldrush era came from the Pearl River Delta of southern China and spoke Cantonese (Yue) but with many local dialect variations, some mutually unintelligible. See Michael Williams, *Chinese Settlement in New South Wales: A Thematic History* (Parramatta: NSW Heritage Office, 1999).

some such authorised person at the Gulph, which is evidently destined ere long to become mainly or wholly a Chinese Diggings[1] (not only to act in our Police Court, but also in all Mining cases when required), I would strongly recommend the appointment of the worthy man Ah Min to the office of Chinese Interpreter or of some other equally eligible person

CH

83. Henry Kendall to Charles Harpur, 4 February 1864
Text: Kendall papers, ML C199

Survey Offices. February 4th 1864.

My dear Mr Harpur,

Your genial letter of the 29th ultimo[2] reached me to day. I am much obliged to you for your enquiries about my brother's health. He *is* better; but very shaky yet.

You underrate the newspaper people: they do "admire poetry" sometimes. For instance a political squib[3] with happy local hits! Or even an eloquent stave or two about Dick Green and the English Cricketers.[4] The present droll political debate is occupying all the spare columns of the *Herald*,[5] and, until it is over, the "Bard of Paradise"[6] will not appear in print. Seeing that they have promised to publish the poem, I think it the better plan to leave it with them a while yet. For in the *Herald* it would have more publicity than it could possibly have in the pamphlet form. And, after all, why should we care a jot

---

[1] See CH's advice on the Chinese diggers (Letter 66).

[2] Not extant: evidently in reply to Kendall's of 24 November 1863 (Letter 81).

[3] Short satire or lampoon. Kendall was not above producing his own, e.g., 'The Song of Ninian Melville' (1880).

[4] Richard Augustus Willoughby 'Dick' Green (1836–1921), Australian champion sculler, arrived back on the steamer *Great Britain* in December 1863, having lost a race on the Thames to his English rival under controversial circumstances. Also aboard were the All England Eleven cricket side on their 1864 tour of the colonies.

[5] The Martin government, inheriting a serious public deficit, hoped (despite its uncertain majority) to rectify it through the radical – and divisive – step of imposing temporary tariffs on imports. The free-trade *SMH* saw the spectre of full-blown protectionism, and reported at length on the parliament's sometimes farcical proceedings.

[6] CH's panegyric on Milton and 'Paradise Lost', previously published in 1836 and 1841. Kendall finally placed the 1864 version of 'Bard of Paradise' (h029d) in *Sydney Times*, 14 and 21 May 1864, a protectionist weekly edited – according to G. B. Barton in his *Literature in New South Wales* (1866: online at Internet Archive, p. 65) – by CH's brother Joseph. The paper, which described itself as 'a journal for the promotion of Australian literature and the advocacy of encouragement to native industry', republished 'The "Nevers" of Poesy' in its first issue and would contain something of CH's in all subsequent numbers. John Shaw in his booklet *J. G. O'Connor: A Short Biography* (Newcastle, NSW: Davies & Cannington, 1910, p. 5) claims that O'Connor founded the *Times* along with W. B. Dalley, William Macleay, J. J. Harpur and CH – a claim appearing in several other sources. The SLNSW Catalogue gives O'Connor and Francis Mason as its publishers.

for apathy and delay if we *gain* our end? If you have no objection, I shall wait another month before taking further steps.

Tomorrow evening I'll price those volumes for you,[7] and send you the list by next week's post. Of course, you have read some of Stuart Mill's book[8] before? If you haven't you will find, in him, a shrewd thinker of the McCulloch[9] brotherhood.

About the worst thing he has done is the "Essay on Poetry."[10] *His* Poet is the accomplished *mechanic*. He looks to the "metre-making"—not to the "metre-making argument" that Emerson insists upon.[11] All this is the result of the absence of Imagination in the critic. But Mill has thought deeply and thought well; and I admire him especially for the broad Utilitarianism[12] he preaches.

Howitt's "Supernatural" Work is an entertaining book, yet a mad one.[13] It was a false report that led us to believe Emerson a Spiritualist.[14] There is

---

[7] On an Assistant Gold Commissioner's annual salary of £350, CH could now afford a library. Kendall acted as his purchasing agent, placing orders with Sydney booksellers.

[8] Possibly *On Liberty* (1859) or the more recent *Utilitarianism* (1863) by British philosopher and political economist John Stuart Mill (1806–73).

[9] John Ramsay McCulloch (1789–1864), Scottish economist, statistician, author and editor, exponent of the classical 'Ricardian School' of economics.

[10] Mill's 'What Is Poetry?' and 'Two Kinds of Poetry' (in *Monthly Repository*, 1833) were republished as 'Thoughts on Poetry and its Varieties' in *Dissertations and Discussions: Political, Philosophical and Historical* (London: John W. Parker, 1859; online at Internet Archive).

[11] See Ralph Waldo Emerson's essay 'The Poet', in his *Essays: Second Series* (Boston: James Munroe, 1844), p. 10; online at Internet Archive). Poetry is not solely a product of talent, industry or metrical skill: 'For it is not metres, but a metre-making argument, that makes a poem, – a thought so passionate and alive, that, like the spirit of a plant or an animal, it has an architecture of its own, and adorns nature with a new thing. The thought and the form are equal in order of time, but in the order of genesis the thought is prior to the form.' The first sentence of this passage is marked in CH's copy (p. 12) of Emerson's *Eight Essays* (London: W. Tweedie, n.d.: held by ML at shelf-mark DSM/814.36/E, this copy available online). The British Library dates the Tweedie edition '[1852]': the accession date stamp is '24 AU 52' (p. 208 of its copy).

[12] An ethical theory: the best action is the one that maximises *utility* – that which produces the greatest well-being of the greatest number of people. English philosopher Jeremy Bentham (1748–1832), founder of utilitarianism, described utility as the sum of all pleasure that results from an action, minus the suffering of anyone involved in the action. Mill's *Utilitarianism* (London: Parker, Son, and Bourn, 1863; online at Internet Archive), an exposition and defence, did much to popularise utilitarian ethics.

[13] *The History of the Supernatural in All Ages and Nations, and in All Churches, Christian and Pagan, Demonstrating a Universal Faith*, by William Howitt (1792–1879), English poet and writer on nature, history and society (London: Longman, Green, Longman, Roberts, & Green, 1863; online at Internet Archive). Lapsed Quakers, Howitt and his wife Mary were leading campaigners for Spiritualism in the 1850s and 1860s. (Howitt visited Australia in 1852, spending two years on the goldfields).

[14] Kendall was half attracted to Spiritualism: see Letter 76.

nothing sufficiently transcendental in "Spiritualism" for him.[1]

Will you oblige me by sending a copy of your "Finish of Style"[2] some day. I did not like your amended "Cora" so well at first as I do now. But it is altered for the best, and very much for the best. Still I can't get over "aureate", and miss the natural epithet "golden", so lovely in its place.[3] It may be my fault. I have found a poem headed "The Dying Sorrow of the Widow's Boy" (in an old Australian Home Companion[4]) the last verses of which are full of wisdom and beauty. Dr Brereton[5] admires the "Kangaroo Hunt:[6]—it is *too lush* for me. But the "Murder of the Lamb"[7] was written in your best mood.

No more till next week. Hoping you are well,

I am,
Yours very Faithfully
Henry Kendall.

---

[1] Transcendentalism was an American literary, political and philosophical movement of the early 19th century; Emerson (1803–82) was its chief exponent. 'Against Locke's claim that there is nothing in the mind not first put there through the senses', it emphasised 'the role of the mind itself in actively shaping experience'. It thus went beyond Kant 'in insisting that the mind can apprehend absolute spiritual truths directly without having to go through the detour of the senses, without the dictates of past authorities and institutions, and without the plodding labor of ratiocination' – Martin Bickman, 'An Overview of American Transcendentalism', American Transcendentalism Web.

[2] See p. 149 n. 5.

[3] Kendall was comparing version h077d (in *SMH*, 8 December 1863, p. 3) with h077a (*Empire*, 26 April 1856, p. 5): for details, see the CHCA collation of the two.

[4] *Australian Home Companion and Band of Hope Journal*, vol. 4 (29 January 1859), p. 43 (see h684c). A fortnightly temperance paper run by philanthropist H. B. Lee, it carried several of CH's poems during 1858–61, and was also the earliest outlet for Kendall's verse from 1859. The poem had previously been published in 1843 and 1845 in *Maitland Mercury*, and in *Weekly Register* in 1845.

[5] See p. 131 n. 7.

[6] 'The Kangaroo Hunt; or, A Morning in the Mountains' (h209-bc etc.), published in *Australian Home Companion* in seven parts, 30 June – 3 November 1860, with CH's extensive footnotes (first part: vol. 5, p. 297).

[7] 'The Murder of the Lamb: A Legend of the Sheep-Fold' (h305b), published in *Australian Home Companion* in three parts, 7 April – 2 June 1860 (first part: vol. 5, p. 148).

84. Charles Harpur to Henry Kendall, 21 March 1864

Text: Kendall papers, NLA MS 9368

Euroma, via *Bodalla*,[8] 21st March 1864[9]

D[ea]r Kendall,

I have written by to day's post to Maddock,[10] telling him how to send the case of books.

I do not recollect ever having said that our good old friend Stenhouse was the best of our Colonial critics.[11] But if I did say so, it was not saying very much in his behalf. That he was a very nice-nosed flower-finder in certain poetical fields, I could not but perceive: but I never thought him to be the possessor of enough of any kind of genius himself to be the *discoverer* of it in others. And I also saw that he never cared to patronise any writer, until he became *pronounced* in some high critical quarter—and that then, and not till then, his *furore* in his favor came to a flood-tide. Thus you see, my dear Hal,[12] that my measure of him has always been pretty much what yours is now. In certain tracks, first indicated it may be by deeper spirits, his judgments are correct enough, and sometimes even admirable. But he is a good man rather than a great one—a feeler of the Sublime and Beautiful, after they have been *shown* to him, not in his own light a perceiver of them in the sense that a poet is, or even a great critic.

Yours most truly
Chas: Harpur.

I enclose a sort of Burnsonian Song for the Herald,[13] if the spirit of it is not too much in advance of that Journal.

---

[8] Bodalla was the village attached to Thomas Mort's Bodalla Estate, nine km from Euroma towards the coast. It had a post office.

[9] This letter would be published by 'Bookfellow' (A. G. Stephens), Red Page, *Bulletin*, 30 September 1899, and in 'The Bookworm's Corner', *Freeman's Journal*, 5 May 1910, p. 33. *Bulletin* received the item from well-known Sydney collector Thomas Handcock Lennard, who added 'The original is in my possession.' Now at NLA.

[10] Initially manager of the Sydney branch of Melbourne publisher and bookseller George Robertson at 383 George-street, William Maddock (1835–1917) bought the business in 1862, added a circulating library and was soon the largest bookseller in Sydney. He was also a publisher, including of Kendall's *Songs from the Mountains* (1880). For a typical range of titles for sale and loan, see *SMH*, 8 August 1863, p. 9.

[11] CH was apparently responding to a comment in a letter from Kendall that we lack. Cf. CH's judgement in Letter 79.

[12] See p. 36 n. 1.

[13] I.e., song in the style of Scottish bard Robert Burns, for Kendall to place with *SMH* – perhaps 'A Man Shall Be a Man Yet' (h278b), which appeared not in *SMH* but in *Sydney Times* on 30 April 1864.

85. Henry Kendall to Charles Harpur, [*c.* 15 May 1864]

Text: Kendall papers, ML C199

In haste.[1]

There is a power in the "Bard of Paradise"[2] that you have never exceeded. You are one of those that must, perforce, be listened to. The description of the chaotic regions, in the 4th division of the "Bard," is terrible. Eve is a lovely glimpse of light thereafter.

There can be nothing *wilder* than the passage beginning with

> "the ghostly uproars ever heard beside" &c &c.

to the end of that part.

H. K.

To Chas Harpur.[3]

86. Nerrigundah Bench Book, 8–11 October 1864

Text: NSWSA: NRS-3230 [1/3367], pp. 185–6

8th October 1864

Nerrigundah New S Wales[4] to wit.
Regina v Louis Des Coudres[5]

[*continued next page*]

[1] Kendall's note is dated provisionally on the assumption that it was his response to reading 'The Bard of Paradise' in *Sydney Times* on 14 and 21 May 1864 (see ho29d), the earliest known version with the line he quotes: 'the [properly, 'And'] ghostly uproars ever heard beside'. Kendall had earlier tried to place 'The Bard' with *SMH* (see Letter 83) and possibly, before that, with *Empire* (see p. 143 n. 7).

[2] CH's tribute to John Milton, first published as 'Milton' in *Australian*, 30 December 1836, p. 3 (ho29a) and subsequently in *Sydney Herald*, 12 February 1841, p. 4 (ho29b) and *Sydney Times*, 14 and 21 May 1864 (ho29d).

[3] Added later in another hand.

[4] Source of this selection is the Bench Book [Nerrigundah Court of Petty Sessions], 1862–70, NSWSA. Bench Books recorded minutes of proceedings of the Bench of Magistrates (on which CH sat, as a Justice of the Peace), including summaries of evidence. The hand is that of Adolphus Norblad or Nordblad (1810? –72), Clerk of Petty Sessions at Nerrigundah: cf. his letter to CH, 18 July 1862 (in *Suppl. Letters*).

[5] The Crown (literally, the Queen) versus Louis Des Coudres – a prosecution by the police. Little is known of Des Coudres (*c.* 1831–81); he was reported to be at the Turon diggings in 1855.

Furious Riding[6]
plea Guilty

Fined 40/. & Costs 2/6.

Chas: Harpur. J.P.

11th October. 1864

Regina v. Jonas.[7]
Obscene & Threatning language.
plea Guilty
discharged.

Chas: Harpur. J.P.

Nicholas Leon v Thomas Heydon[8]
assault.

postponed to 18th Inst.

Heydon v Nichola[s] Leon
larceny.
plea not Guilty

Thomas Haydon being duly Sworn Saith I keep a dairy and reside at Nerri-gundah. I have known the defendant for 19 months he was a lodger with me and has not paid me to the present time. I missed the articles before the Court for about Six Months the Candle[stick?] for Six Months and the Pillow for 8 or 9 Weeks. I recognize the articles before the Court. I took out a Search war-rant this day The defendant has a Case of assault against me I never doubted the mans honesty until now.

---

[6] Riding a horse dangerously (commonly, in impromptu races along the main street). Section 40 of the NSW *Towns Police Act* of 1838 (2 Vic. No. 2), which was extended to Nerrigundah in 1863, provided 'That any person who shall ride or drive through any street...so negligently carelessly or furiously that the safety of any other person shall be actually endangered shall on conviction forfeit and pay a sum not exceeding ten pounds nor less than two pounds.' CH imposed the minimum penalty.

[7] Nothing known.

[8] Nicholas Leon from the Gulph was described as 'a Greek' in an early news report from Moruya (*Armidale Express*, 5 September 1863, p. 3); in 1866 he had a hut at Fern Flat, Nerrigundah (*NSW Police Gazette*, 30 May 1866, p. 195). Thomas Heydon (or Haydon, Hayden, Heyden), an Englishman, kept a small farm on the Nerrigundah diggings (*Empire*, 21 December 1863, p. 5.) The two men had some history: Haydon would name Leon years later in divorce proceedings (e.g., *ATCJ*, 24 June 1876, p. 9.)

x. ed¹   I have missed the pillow for 8 or 9 weeks and the Candlestick Six Months. I never doubted the mans honesty. I did not know the defendant had the things in his possession

Bench²   I knew he had the Candlestick but did not think it worth my while to Speak of it.

Sworn before us this 11th Oct. 1864

W Stewart Caswell PM.³ T. Heyden
Case dismissed.

W Stewart Caswell PM.
Chas: Harpur. J.P.

87. Charles Harpur to William John Clements, [1865]

Text: ML A87-2

Dear Clements,⁴

Oblige me by printing this⁵ as correctly as may be, with your present means: and henceforth send me two copies of the Examiner⁶ weekly. I want an extra paper to send to a literary friend in Sydney.⁷ The subscription for the additional number I will pay you on my next visit to Moruya,⁸ or whenever I next see you.

Yours truly
Chas: Harpur.

---

¹ In response to cross-examination (by or on behalf of the defendant).

² In response to a question from the magistrates.

³ William Stewart Caswell (1828–1909), police magistrate based at Moruya; his other offices included Clerk of Petty Sessions, Registrar of the District Court and Registrar of Births, Deaths and Marriages. He attended the funerals of Charley Harpur in 1867 and CH in 1868.

⁴ William John Clements (1821?–77), proprietor of *Moruya Examiner*. A compositor by trade, he had arrived in Sydney in 1853 to join the Government Printing Office.

⁵ This letter (evidently a draft or copy made by CH) follows the final stanza of 'A Vision of an Angel' (h664f) in ML A87-2, p. 444 itself dated 'Euroma, 1865'; and a newspaper cutting of the next version (h664g) preserved in ML A92 has been tentatively identified by Holt (p. 156) as from *Moruya Examiner*. Kendall's reference to that 'Moruya "rag" ' in Letter 95 supports this linking.

⁶ *Moruya Examiner, Miners' Advocate and the Eden District Advertiser*, established in September 1864 by Clements and two others, ceased publication in mid-1868 but was re-launched by Clements in 1870, continuing into the 1960s (see Rod Kirkpatrick, 'Scissors and Paste: Recreating the History of Newspapers in Ten Country Towns,' *BSANZ Bulletin*, 22.4 (1998), p. 242). While few complete issues of the paper of 1864–68 have survived, and none carrying CH's verse, over 30 of his poems have been sourced to *Examiner* via cuttings (see Holt, *passim*).

⁷ Probably Kendall, who in his letter of 29 April 1865 (Letter 89) would thank CH for newspapers with CH items that he had received.

⁸ Coastal town and port on the Moruya River, 300 km south of Sydney and 34 km north of Euroma.

88. Charles Harpur to *Sydney Morning Herald*, 23 January 1865

Text: SMH, 22 February 1865, p. 5

To the Editor of the Herald.

SIR,—As you have heretofore exhibited from time to time in your columns certain specimen translations (from the pens of Tennyson and others) of the famous Night Scene in the 8th Book of the Iliad,[9] perhaps you will also give insertion to the ensuing attempts to transfuse into English verse as much as may be of the singular beauty which characterises that truly Homeric draft, as it stands in the original Greek.[10]

> I am, Sir, yours, &c,
> CHARLES HARPUR.
> Euroma, 23rd January.

89. Henry Kendall to Charles Harpur, 29 April 1865

Text: Kendall papers, ML C199

Surveyor General's Office. April 29th 1865.

My dear Mr Harpur,

Many domestic troubles have hindered me from writing back to you before

---

[9] This letter appears above CH's three translations (in dactylic hexameters, in blank verse and in 'heroic rhyme') of the Night Scene in the 8th Book of the Iliad (h127-ad, h127-ba and h127-ca) in *SMH*, 22 February 1865, p. 5. A fourth translation, rendered 'very literally', did not appear there: it dates no earlier than 1866 (ML A87-1, see h127-da) and was first published in *Poems* (1883). CH had produced a translation in hexameters of 'A Night Scene from Homer' as early as 1855 (ML B78, h127-aa); and a later version (h127-ab) appeared in *Empire*, 5 March 1858, p. 5. He must have seen the review in *SMH*, 8 November 1864, p. 3 (copied from the London *Athenæum*, 13 August 1864) of Tennyson's *Enoch Arden, Etc.* (London: Edward Moxon & Co., 1864 – see Internet Archive). That volume included some 'Experiments' in classical meters, among them a 'Specimen of a Translation of the Iliad in Blank Verse' (pp. 177–8), the 'night scene' depicting the night watch of the Trojans outside the walls of Troy after the day's fighting. The review compared translation extracts from Tennyson, Pope (unfavourably) and Chapman; it elicited a response from 'H. M.' (possibly Herman Merivale), who had completed nearly 14 books of the *Iliad* in English heroic rhyme, and 'could have accomplished much more had I contented myself with blank verse, as Mr. Tennyson has done' – see *SMH*, 11 November 1864, p. 2. For CH's other translations (from Homer and German), see p. 216 n. 4.

[10] Scholarly opinion differs on whether CH had sufficient Greek to undertake translation (e.g., Rawling, pp. 230–1) or whether he relied on earlier translations (e.g., Jordens pp. 94–5, who points to Cowper's Homer in the library of Nicol Stenhouse). CH's discussion of Greek translation in his introductory note to 'Similes from Homer' (h501c; ML A87-2, p. 527) does not answer the question. See also C. W. Salier, 'Charles Harpur's Translations from the *Iliad*', *Southerly*, 7.4 (December 1946), p. 223 and 'The "Little Learning" of Charles Harpur', *Australian Quarterly*, 19.1 (March 1947), p. 5; and Marcel Aurousseau, 'Charles Harpur and his Biographer', *Meanjin*, 22.1 (March 1963), pp. 75–8. CH's translation in hexameters would be satirised mercilessly in *Sydney Punch* in 'The Night Scene (From Harpur)' (4 March 1865, p. 323).

this date. I have received at different times the newspapers[1] for which I thank
you. I do not like your new readings of your older poems at all times, but the
latest draft of the blank verse fragment "To a Comet"[2] is *capital*. I like the
epithet "gipsy" in the recent version of the "*Master Mariner's Song*",[3] but in
other respects you cannot well overcome my prejudice in favour of the lyric as
it stands for us, in the published volume. There is at all times a charm about the
rough rock that we cannot discover in the polished masonwork. Nevertheless
I know you are right in the main; for the true poet is a sleepless artist. Yet you
must forgive me for my overfear lest the "freshness of the morning prime"[4]
should be sullied in the least where it is so pure and so abundant.

Let "*The Tower of the Dream*"[5] stand for us as we know it. Never doubt its
immortality; but, for the sake of hereafter delights, keep a jealous watch over
its present integrity. I believe it is the highest result of your genius. It is even
a Wonder Dream more wondrous than "*Kubla Khan*".[6]

When I read a poem once and remember it (through that one reading only)
my faith in its beauty is thereafter established for ever. I cannot forget "*Dora,
the gentle and the good*".[7] The "wordless "*Eva Gray*"[8] is to me a continual
face alight with the shining patience of perpetual pain. Have you not heard
in your forest walks, a wild broken wind, which after a day of shattered life,
had fallen down to its softer evening passages? Have you not heard then a
recurring sound forever like the sound of a fitful Æolian Harp?[9] You *have*

---

[1] See, e.g., CH's request to Clements (Letter 87) for extra copies of *Moruya Examiner* for 'a
literary friend in Sydney'.

[2] First published as 'Lines Suggested by the Appearance of a Comet', *Maitland Mercury*,
2 December 1846, p. 1 (h595a), then in *The Bushrangers* in 1853 as 'To the Comet of 1843'
(h595b); but 'the latest draft' suggests a manuscript copy (now lost). The poem appeared
under the title Kendall gives it here in a newspaper – probably *Braidwood Dispatch* – of 1860–
63 (see cutting as amended by CH, ML C384; h595d).

[3] Kendall was evidently reading a recent manuscript version. In both the 'published volume'
The Bushrangers (1853, h369d) and *SMH*, 29 September 1864, p. 5 (h369h), the last line of the
second stanza reads: 'And her spouse is the wind'. The manuscript (ML A95) of 1865 reads:
'Her wild spouse the gipsy Wind' (h369i).

[4] 'Or sleep she on the mossy bed, / Under the blossom-breathing lime, / That sheds sweet
freshness over head— / The freshness of the morning prime' – from 'Edwy: A Poem, in
Three Parts' by Ann Radcliffe (1764–1823), English author and pioneer of the Gothic novel
(in *Gaston de Blondeville...with Some Poetical Pieces* (London: Henry Colburn, 1826), Vol. IV,
p. 260, via Internet Archive).

[5] Kendall would arrange publication in *Australian Journal*, November–December 1865
(h642f): see correspondence 30 September – 20 December 1865.

[6] See p. 113 n. 6.

[7] From 'Yon Green Wood' (h708a), which Kendall may have seen in *Empire*, 28 March 1857,
p. 5. In 'Old Manuscripts', he quotes the first three stanzas (under the title 'Dora') from a
manuscript in his possession: stanza 2, line 3 has 'my bosom's burning secret' for 'my bosom's
beating secret' in all lifetime versions, possibly his or a typesetter's error.

[8] 'Eva Gray', from *Bushrangers*, 1853 (h120a).

[9] Stringed musical instrument played by the action of the wind, named after Aeolus, keeper of
the winds and king of the island of Aeolia near Sicily.

and therefore, "*Gramachree*", full of the "red" sunset and perplexed with a perplexing sorrow was written.[10] Its beauty makes the heart ache.

Excuse haste and paper. Just now I am scribbling this in face of an antithesis.[11] The fellows in this office, with the exception of our old friend, Halloran, are a hopeless set.[12] I have managed to get hold of the 1845 collection of *Sonnets* headed "*Thoughts*".[13] They are all familiar to me, and I have heretofore spoken to you of them. As I grow older my faith in your genius takes a deeper growth, even though I sometimes carp, like a critic.

When an opportunity occurs, I will write to you concerning another matter. They print your contributions after a vile fashion in the "*Moruya Messenger*".[14] Why will you not send them to the "*Sydney Mail*"?[15]

I have seven shillings of yours in hand. You[r] brother objected to take them, and suggested that I should wait till you came to Sydney. I am waiting a long time.

Believe me,
Yours, Faithfully,
Henry Kendall

[10] Irish 'gradh mo chroidhe': 'love of my heart', familiar to CH's readers from popular airs such as 'Gramachree Molly'. His 1849 draft of 'Under the Wild Fig Tree' (ML C376; h238a), at first entitled 'Love in the Past', shows that he added 'Gra Machree' and 'Gramachree' as part of an echoing refrain between some lines. He developed the addition in a version (h238b) that appeared in *SMH*, 8 May 1863, p. 8, perhaps with Kendall's assistance. Deniehy as editor published it in *Victorian* in September 1863 (h238c), his headnote praising it as 'the finest lyric, to our mind, that has yet been produced in Australia…[with] the passion interpenetrating it of the music of Ireland'. The Gramachree phrasing was further developed, yearningly, in 1865 (h238f; first mentioned in Letter 99 – see p. 174 n. 3).

[11] Kendall may mean a scornful opposition to his sentiment towards poetry.

[12] Kendall would immortalise his fellow workers – as 'Goths' – in the bitingly witty 'Government Clerks in Gotham', *Freeman's Journal*, 5 January 1878, pp. 13–14.

[13] CH's first volume, *Thoughts. A Series of Sonnets*.

[14] *Moruya Messenger, Miners' Advocate and Southern Coast District Advertiser*, launched by Edward Wainwright of the *Braidwood Observer* in October 1862 to cater for the Moruya hinterland and the then new Nerrigundah goldfield. Reportedly defunct by May 1864, references to a paper of this name (perhaps a successor) nevertheless appear in other newspapers as late as 1869. No copies have survived.

[15] Established July 1860 by John Fairfax and Sons as a threepenny 8-page weekly precis of *SMH* for country readers, it was soon also popular with city readers that could not afford a daily newspaper. It grew into a substantial illustrated weekly, lasting until 1938: Gavin Souter, *Company of Heralds: A Century and a Half of Australian Publishing by John Fairfax Limited and its Predecessors 1831–1981* (Carlton, Vic.: Melbourne University Press, 1981), pp. 52–3, 112–13. In the 1860s *Sydney Mail* ran little colonial verse. It took only one CH poem: see p. 185 n. 7.

90. Charles Harpur to Henry Kendall, 10 May 1865

Text: Kendall papers, ML C199

Euroma, 10 May 1865

My dear Kendall,

I got your letter of the other day,[1] and was greatly gratified to hear *again* from you. Of course I did not think for a long time past that you had absolutely *cut* me: but I wondered at your long silence. Yet being myself, as a correspondent, a man of a thousand sins—was not my mouth shut against any thing like reproach, just as effectually as if it were sewed up with pack thread. But I will mend one of these days.

I send you a paper containing a re-print of an old poem of mine with some re-touches and additions. It is, or was once, a great favorite with Halloran, to whom I have also sent a copy of the paper, accompanied by a note.[2]

You advise me to send these things of mine to the Mail. Well, try if the Mail people will extract this Lament—as an earnest-token that such pieces from my pen would be acceptable to them; and thereupon I will, from time to time, treat them to a draught of my best. They need not say whence they get it, but give it as if furnished directly to themselves.

You express some fear lest I should re-touch my poems too much: but do not be in the least alarmed on that head. I try all the alterations I make *as by fire*,[3] before I venture upon them, and, if face to face, I could give you such reasons for any or all of them, as I am sure would quite satisfy you.

Yours very truly
Chas: Harpur.

P.S. Give the 7/0 you mention[4] to some little boy to buy lollipops with—or what else he likes.

---

[1] Letter 89.

[2] Poem not identified, but possibly 'Coleridge's Christabel' or 'A Rhyme', with which Halloran had conveyed his 'satisfaction' (Letter 62; see h473-ag and h459e). The fact that CH was sending newspapers to Sydney suggests they were country papers, perhaps *Moruya Examiner*. If so, they have not survived: see p. 156 n. 6.

[3] *Try*: separate metal from the ore or dross by melting; refine or purify by fire. Kendall's concern was well founded: CH was an inveterate reviser, especially in his last years, as he prepared manuscripts for his hoped-for English edition.

[4] See Letter 89. Rawling speculates that this was change from a book purchase with Maddock (p. 269).

91. Henry Kendall to Charles Harpur, 26 August [1865]

Text: Kendall papers, ML C199

Surveyor General's Office Sydney. Aug 26th

My dear Harpur

I have handed your poem to the people of the "Illustrated News"[5] for publication. It will appear in the next number of that journal and the proprietors desire me to let you know that they will be willing, after its appearance in their paper, to strike you off 200 copies of the poem and publish it for you in the pamphlet form. For this additional publication of "The Tower of the Dream" they would require £4. As many of my friends who have read the poem in M.S. are anxious to have a copy of their own in print, I would advise you to get the thing done in the fashion proposed. I will attend to the proofs and see to the punctuation. By the way I am at issue with you in the matter of your late mannerisms in orthography Why not spell "hony" hon*e*y? Certain peculiarities of this kind somewhat mar the effect of your finer poems.[6] Very likely you have the best of reasons for these new methods of writing words, but I cannot well see why the Poet should be a mere lexicographer.[7] He is a maker and adapter of languages but hardly an arranger of letters. After all the best objection to your novelties is the objection of the everyday reader. To him you would convey a *consecutive* pleasure through your poem, and yet you force him to break over a mere word in the middle of a noble passage of dreams. Why should the "Tower of the Dream" in the least degree suggest a dispute over orthography? For the sak[e] of the otherwise marvellous effect of the poem, I think familiar words ou[ght] to be spelled in a familiar way.

Halloran desires me to express for him his belief—his high belief in

---

[5] The 8-page monthly *Illustrated Sydney News*, established by printers Clarson, Shallard & Co. in 1864 (and distinct from its short-lived predecessor of 1853–54), aimed to provide 'concise verbal narratives, supplemented by pictorial illustration' (woodcuts) on the lines of the *Illustrated London News*. It published local poets (F. S. Wilson was a favourite) but never CH. Kendall would withdraw 'The Tower of the Dream' ('your poem') due to 'delay' (Letter 93), lodging it first with *Empire* and then with the Melbourne-based *Australian Journal* (Letter 95).

[6] Spelling was becoming more regularised in the course of the 19th century, in part because of the immense expansion of the publishing industry with its own requirements for regularity, especially for bookwork. Kendall seems to have been more attuned to the shift than the older poet who occasionally used what seem now (and seemed to Kendall) eccentric spellings. Some were simply 18th-century spellings, e.g., *-or* rather than *-our* endings. Nevertheless, CH sometimes simply misspelt, both names (e.g., Sapho, Shilock) and common words (e.g., phamphlet, perhapse, cronicle, arithmatic). He acknowledged that 'Shilock' was an error (Letter 118 and ho89c). 'Hony' appears to have been an aberration, as the surviving manuscripts and printed versions all have 'honey'. The MS that Kendall was quoting is lost, presumably discarded in the production process in Melbourne.

[7] Echoes Dr Samuel Johnson's famous definition of *lexicographer*: 'A writer of dictionaries; a harmless drudge, that busies himself in tracing the original, and detailing the signification of words' (*A Dictionary of the English Language*, 1755).

the pieces "The Tower of the Dream" and the "Bard of Paradise".[1] The movem[ent] in both he says is fine. In the "Bard" the blank verse sounds like thunder. I did not hand the poem to Mr Stenhouse for he is *moony*[2] in these days. I will let him hav[e] "The Tower of the Dream" in print.

Excuse my hurry for the post. I have not been very well lately, and therefore have been obliged to put off the writing of this letter. I liked your sonnet on the "criticlings",[3] but did not choose to glorify them by sending it to the papers. They, the mildly malicious scribblers complained of, have a characteristic vehicle for their "jargonings" in a *provincial* Punch.[4] I hear no more of Jean Ingelow[5] now a days. Tennyson's last volume[6] was, comparatively, a very poor affair. Not so *that* by Robert Browning.[7] It is a book of steel and gold. I hope you have heard of the new poet, Algernon Charles Swinburne:[8] a writer as luxuriant as Keats and as lyrical as Shelley. Will you ever publish a volume again? You ought to be able to spare the cash.[9] I could get an edition of 500

---

[1] Halloran might have seen this in *Sydney Times*, 14 and 21 May 1864 (h029d).

[2] Dreamily distracted.

[3] Holt (p. 192) dates the manuscript series in ML A95 that includes 'To the Criticlings of Doggreldom' to 1866 (h605a), but at the time of this letter there must already have been a copy in existence. CH must have retained a copy, revising it for *Moruya Examiner* (where it appeared in August 1866: h605b), perhaps when he was fair-copying and separately revising the original for the long series in A95 (p. 60) entitled by him 'Poems: By Charles Harpur' (p. 1). A second copying of the poem in 1867 (h605c in A95, p. 134), follows version h605a in some readings and h605b in others: CH had retained a copy of the printing in a clippings scrapbook (ML C381). 'Criticling' is an 18th-century variant spelling of 'critickin', a small or petty critic.

[4] Several attempts were made to establish a Sydney *Punch* along the lines of the famous London comic and satirical weekly and its Melbourne offspring. Sydney versions came and went in 1856, 1857, 1860 and 1862 before printer Edgar Ray, co-founder of Melbourne *Punch*, launched his Sydney weekly in May 1864. This would flourish, under various proprietors, for more than two decades. Kendall, initially a target (along with his fellow poets) for Mr Punch's barbs, was a regular contributor by 1867 and would write the obituary for CH (see *Sydney Punch*, 4 July 1868, p. 7).

[5] Jean Ingelow, English poet and writer (1820–97), her *Poems* (1863) was a sudden popular success, as were the verses set to music. By the mid-1860s she had turned to novels and children's stories.

[6] *Enoch Arden, Etc.* (London: Edward Moxon & Co., 1864; online at Internet Archive); for Tennyson, see p. 141 nn. 9–14.

[7] *Dramatis Personæ* (London: Chapman and Hall, 1864; online at Internet Archive), a collection of dramatic monologues by English poet Robert Browning (1812–89).

[8] Algernon Charles Swinburne, English poet and critic (1837–1909). His verse drama *Atalanta in Calydon: A Tragedy* (London: Edward Moxon, 1865; online at HathiTrust) had not long appeared. Kendall had read from it in his recent poetry lecture at the Windsor School of Arts (see *Empire*, 27 July 1865, p. 5) and would advise Mary Harpur to send a copy of CH's *Poems* (1883) to Swinburne for review, calling him 'the most liberal-minded of living English poets' (22 March 1882: in *Suppl. Letters*).

[9] CH had two 'volumes' to his credit, *Thoughts* (16 pages containing 23 poems) and *Bushrangers* (127 pages containing 43 poems, seven of which form part of the play). The first was printed, W. A. Duncan maintained, at his expense ('The Late Charles Harpur', *ATCJ*, 28 March 1874, p. 14), and there is no record of a public subscription campaign. Kendall was consistent in advising against subscription: see Letters 97 (1865) and 153 (1881).

copies out for £50. Some portions of the "Saul"[10] which I have seen have a lyrical quality second to nothing in the language. But whilst you remain in forced seclusion, your best friends are obliged to be timid in according to you your proper place in letters.

Nothing more to say. Awaiting your answer.

I am, My dear Harpur
Faithfully Yours
Henry Kendall.

92. Charles Harpur to Charles Cowper, 31 August 1865

Text: NSWSA: NRS-905 [4/555], 65/4021

Gulph, 31st Aug 1865.

Sir,

I have the honor to inform you that a few days since, at the Nerrigundah Police Court, I sentenced a man of the name of William Guest, a publican of Nerrigundah, to a month's imprisonment in Braidwood Gaol,[11] for insulting language, under the 6th Section of the Vagrant Act[12]—he having been twice before convicted of similar offences under the same Act, and fined in the first instance £2, and in the second in the extreme penalty of £5. My main object, however, in so punishing him, rather than by again fining him, or by calling upon him to find surities for good behaviour,[13] was to detach him from drink, as by the evidence of the sergeant in charge it appeared, that he had been in a state of constant drunkenness for a month previously, and was certainly not in his right mind in consequence, nor fit to be at large. Still, in since looking over the Vagrant Act, I have my doubts as to whether the sentence was strictly legal; and if in your opinion it *was not*, I most respectfully request that you will be pleased to cause the same to be remitted by telegram.

I have the honor to be,
Sir,
Your most obedient Servant
Chas: Harpur. J.P.

---

[10] Verse play published only in fragments: see p. 126 n. 7.

[11] Small gaol operating 1862–1909; its ruins are still visible at the northern end of Wallace Street, Braidwood.

[12] The NSW *Vagrancy Act* of 1851 (15 Vic. No. 4) provided that any person convicted of using threatening, abusive or insulting words or behaviour in a public place 'with intent to provoke a breach of the peace or whereby a breach of the peace may be occasioned' could be fined up to £5 *or*, in default of immediate payment, gaoled for up to three months.

[13] A surety is money deposited or pledged by or on behalf of a person, and liable to be forfeited in the event of failure to fulfil certain conditions. Typical sureties for such offences in NSW in the 1860s might be £10 found by the offender and £5 found by two others.

65/4021[1] — 4 September 1865 Charles Harper J.P. Respecting legality of sentence passed by him upon a publican named William Guest.

The Attorney General.
B.C. 4th Septr The Secretary to the Crown Law Offices Wm Owen noted 4 Sepr '65 for the Cln: Secretary.

BC

I am of opinion that the Justice Exceeded his Authority, & the error ought to be rectified as soon as possible JHP [struck through] 5 Septr 1865

His Excellency. Wm. Owen. for the Colonial Secretary. 5 Sep / 65

Give authority for the remission of the sentence accordingly JY

5th Sep. 1865.
[As Chp.?]

[Stamped 'SHERIFF'S OFFICE N.S.W.'] 65/2425 6 Sept Noted 6/9/5 Bench Sheriff 6th Septr 1865

65/4021. The necessary authority for the liberation of the prisoner has been sent by telegram, and by post. P[rincipa]l. Under Secretary B.C. 6 Septr 1865. H.M

Retd C.S.O 7 Sept

---

[1] For this numbering system, the Colonial Secretary's responsibilities and 'B.C.' (below), see p. 118 n. 1, p. 117 n. 6 and p. 118 n. 2. The following notations track CH's request for advice through the NSW bureaucracy. Charles Cowper, Colonial Secretary, refers CH's enquiry to his Attorney-General, John Hubert Plunkett ('JHP'), who in turn advises NSW Governor Sir John Young (1807–76) that CH has exceeded his authority. Young ('JY') then directs that the sentence imposed by CH be remitted. The Sheriff, Harold Maclean ('HM'), then sends to Braidwood the authority to release the prisoner. CH had publicly attacked Plunkett nine years before (Letter 46) but may not have been aware of his very recent appointment as Attorney-General.

93. Henry Kendall to Charles Harpur, 30 September 1865
Text: Kendall papers, ML C199

Surveyor General's Office Sydney, Sept 30th /65.

My dear C.H.

I have been awaiting your reply. Any coming? I have withdrawn your poem from the "News" in consequence of their delay. If you like, I will give it to the "Empire".[2] It is too long for the "Herald". Do write like a good fellow and tell me what to do.

I have been very much out of sorts lately. Thanks for the poems The "Spirit of Love"[3] and "Absence by the Sea Shore".[4] The latter is memorable.

Yours truly in haste
Henry Kendall.

I am suffering from a severe attack of neuralgia—

94. Henry Kendall to Charles Harpur, 22 October [1865]
Text: ML C199

Surveyor General's Office Sydney. Oct 22nd [1865]

My dear old fellow,

Your poem "The Tower of the Dream" will appear in the Empire during this coming week. I am very sorry to hear of your illness—hope you are all right at the present date. Of course you must expect to suffer being possessed of that "great sad gift the poet's twofold life".[5] Poets are as it were, *cursed* with a peculiar temperament which renders them wholly vulnerable to that perpetual fiend *Melancholy*. Let it be even as it is. It is better to be a racehorse than a rock. No man can realize the world till he sees the Sea. And in a like manner, I say, no man can comprehend life who is not set face to face with the boundless joys and sufferings of the "pardlike spirit"[6] you speak of. The poet is the only Master of Life.

---

[2] Kendall did give 'The Tower of the Dream' ('your poem') to *Empire*: see p. 161 n. 5 and Letter 94.

[3] Song from CH's unpublished verse play 'King Saul': in *Empire*, 5 February 1853, p. 2 and *Sydney Mail* twice posthumously; for a manuscript version of 1865 (ML A95), see h555e.

[4] First published as 'Song' in 1844; for a manuscript version of 1865 (ML A95), see h004f.

[5] Echoes the verse novel *Aurora Leigh* (1856) by Elizabeth Barrett Browning (1809–61): 'O sorrowful great gift / Conferred on poets, of a twofold life', describing the poet's dual humanity and divinity. The idea would recur in Kendall's own verse – e.g., 'The Late Mr. A. L. Gordon: In Memoriam' (1870) and 'Basil Moss' (1872).

[6] I.e., the plight of the Romantic type of the poet: see Introduction, pp. xl–xlii.

I repeat what I have often said to you: Never fear for your ultimate recognition by your fellows. It will come as surely as tomorrow's sun. Much that you prize now may be thrown away as worthless but more will only die with the English language.

I saw J:J:H.[1] the other day looking very well. Old Mr Stenhouse is getting along in the familiar way, dividing his time between Wordsworth and his parchmen[ts]. Your nephew[2] is turning out to be one of the most intelligent and useful men in this office.

> Believe me to be
> Yours Faithfully
> Henry Kendall.

95. Henry Kendall to Charles Harpur, 28 November 1865

Text: Kendall papers, ML C199

Surveyor General's Office Sydney: Nov: 28th 1865

My dear Harpur,

I have received the Moruya "rag" with that fine fragment of yours—the "Vision of An Angel".[3] I think I can recognise the "Vision" (not the "rag") as an old friend and favorite of mine. The "Tower"[4] is at last published but not in the "Empire". Somehow the people of that paper did not like the "Tower": it was too massive for them. They backed out of the printing of it by urging that their precious *daub* was a "commercial and *not* a literary journal". They are "willing to take short pieces" however. The journal in which I have printed the "Tower" is a Melbourne affair of no very high literary character, but it is pretty widely circulated throughout all the colonies. At all events it was the very best vehicle I could get for my purpose It (the poem) is not well printed, but in the copies which I have distributed I have made with the pen, the necessary corrections. As the paper was printed in Melbourne I could not get a proof.

Poor Deniehy is dead. Stenhouse and Horne have been "botanizing" over

---

[1] In 1958 in his unpublished thesis, 'A Critical Edition of the Letters of Henry Kendall', Donovan Clarke proposed 'Probably Jakes J. Hinchy', who 'was to contribute to Moore's *Sydney University Magazine* in 1878' (2 vols., University of Sydney, II.176). In 1993 Ackland proposed '[Holdsworth?]': *Henry Kendall: Poetry, Prose and Selected Correspondence*, ed. Michael Ackland (St Lucia: University of Queensland Press), p. 216. But CH's brother Joseph Jehoshaphat Harpur is clearly intended: Kendall considered him a friend and mentions him elsewhere in letters to CH (e.g., Letters 63, 65, 78 and 81).

[2] Henry Stephen Harpur (1835?–80) was appointed Extra Clerk in the Surveyor General's Office in October 1863, and by 1865 was Supernumerary Clerk (Returns of the Colony and Public Service Lists, 1863–91).

[3] See p. 156 n. 5.

[4] 'The Tower of the Dream' (h642f): see p. 167 n. 7.

his grave,[5] but more of this next time. I have been bothered with many troubles of late, and *therefore* it is that I am a bad correspondent. In another letter I shall say much that I have no room for here. Your poem "The Tower of the Dream" shines, like a bit of Shelley at his best, in print. It is beyond all doubt your most characteristic work. There are splendid things in the "Vision of an Angel"—such for instance as "the illimitable dark of Sleep"—"shadowing his snowy beauty"—"ample folding wings"—"luminous waves"—and *"his words came raying each word like a star"*.[6] These are instances of the quintessential language of Poetry.

They, the Melbourne firm, are printing "The Tower" in a pamphlet form.[7] Two hundred copies are to be struck off, for which they will require in payment some sum between £3 and £4. Of course I will take good care of the correctness of the copy this time for I will *demand* proofs.

Hoping you are all well at Euroma,

I am
Truly Yours—
Henry Kendall

I have just received your note.[8] Your indignation is very natural. Write soon.

I have sent you the *Australian Journal*.[9]

96. Henry Kendall to Charles Harpur, 2 December 1865

Text: Kendall papers, ML C199

Survey Office—December 2nd 1865—

My dear Harpur—

I have posted to you six "Australian Journals":[10] three bearing date 25 November and three, 2nd December. I want you to acknowledge the receipt of them if you get the parcel safely to hand.

---

[5] For Deniehy, see p. 53 n. 6; for his last years, p. 132 n. 1; and for more details from Kendall, Letter 97. Horne (see p. 132 n. 2) was close to Deniehy during his years in Melbourne. Kendall is alluding to Horne's obituary in *Herald* (Melbourne), 27 October 1865, p. 3 (copied in *Freeman's Journal*) and Stenhouse's in *Empire*, 22 November 1865, p. 8. Cf. William Wordsworth's 'A Poet's Epitaph': 'Physician art thou? One, all eyes, / Philosopher! a fingering slave, / One that would peep and botanize / Upon his mother's grave?'
[6] In the clipping from *Moruya Examiner* (ML A92, p. 163) there is a comma after 'raying' and the passage is not in italics.
[7] Clarson, Shallard, & Co., at 72 Little Collins-street East, Melbourne, printers of *Australian Journal: A Weekly Record of Amusing and Instructive Literature, Science, and the Arts* serialised CH's long 'The Tower of the Dream' on 25 November and 2 December 1865 (h642f) and then printed it as a 24-page pamphlet (h642g). The firm also had a Sydney office at 140 Pitt-street. See further, p. 161 n. 5 and Letter 96.
[8] Not found.
[9] See note 7 above.
[10] See related correspondence: Letters 91, 93, 95, 98 and 99.

The "Tower" is very much admired. In my next I will send you a printed copy with my particular "marginalia" against noted passages. I do not know whether I am competent to judge upon the work, but perhaps I am one of the best you can get out here.[1] At all events I am an honest admirer. I have written a Satire upon some mock "men of Letters"[2] which you will like I think. It is to be published in a pamphlet form. If I *haven't* walke[d] into Barton, Martin, Dalley[3] &c "it's a caution" as the natives say[4]—I am,

Yours Ever
Henry Kendall

97. Henry Kendall to Charles Harpur, 12 December 1865

Text: Kendall papers, ML C199

Survey Offices. Dec. 12th 1865.

My dear Harpur,

If you can, will you send the "Ghost of the Cattle Flat" down to me. I have never met with the poem,[5] but I expect much from the title. If it is not too long, I will get it into one of the dailies. With reference to the pamphlet, and to the proof sheets of the "Tower" I will exercise every care in order to secure a correct result. Herewith I forward the journals with some hasty

---

[1] I.e., 'in the Australian colonies' as opposed to 'at home' for Great Britain.

[2] *The Bronze Trumpet* (Sydney: All Booksellers and Newsmen, 1866), dedicated 'To the shams, Political, Clerical and Critical of Sydney and (in particular) the Puny Punsters of *Punch*' – online via NLA. For identifications by Kendall scholar T. T. Reed, see McLaren, pp. 9–10.

[3] Made a vigorous attack upon: *(1)* George Burnett Barton (1836–1901), lawyer, journalist and historian, reader in English Literature at the University of Sydney. He edited and wrote for *Sydney Punch*, wrote *Literature in New South Wales* (the first history of Australian literature, 1866) and edited the anthology *The Poets and Prose Writers of New South Wales* ('1866' but issued January 1867). For CH's opinion of him, see Letter 127. *(2)* James Martin (see p. 43 n. 9), who had written for and edited newspapers in the 1830s and 1840s. CH was no admirer – see, e.g., 'Marvellous Martin' (h280b). *(3)* Native-born politician, lawyer, man of letters and wit, and generous patron of young artists and writers, William Bede Dalley (1831–88). He wrote articles and reviews for *Freeman's Journal* (of which he was editor and part-proprietor), *Sydney Punch* and *SMH*.

[4] Anything that staggers, or excites alarm or astonishment; an extraordinary thing or person (slang: *OED* notes its U.S. origin; it had evidently travelled, since 'natives' here means locally born white settlers).

[5] Kendall could have encountered it as 'Ned Connor. A Tale of the Bush' (h554a) in *Maitland Mercury*, August 1846, p. 1 and then in *Bushrangers* (h554b), of which he had a copy. This was G. B. Barton's source for a long extract (h554g), described as a 'ballad of bush life', in *The Poets and Prose Writers of New South Wales*. An augmented 'The Spectre of the Cattle Flat' (h554f) of 1867–68 appears in manuscript in ML A97 but not in the Sydney papers. The story of the murder of an Aboriginal guide by a settler who is then haunted by him and frightened to death was substantially true, according to CH's footnote in A97. Neither Connor nor the incidents have been identified, though a probate notice for 'Edward Connor, late of Jerry's Plains...laborer, deceased' (*NSW Government Gazette*, 13 November 1846, p. 1434) appeared at the time CH was living there, soon after the poem's first appearance.

THE TOWER OF THE DREAM.
BY CHARLES HARPUR.

PART I.

How wonderful are dreams! Yet, are they but
(As some suppose) the thin disjoining shades
Of facts or feelings long foregone or late,
As recomposed and put in ghostly act,
And strange procession, wildly mixed, and yet
So life-like, though thus composite and wild,
By mimic Fancy; when, alone awake,
And thence unhindered in her mystic craft,
She tracks again the drifts of wearied Thought,
Itself sunk sleepward? Wonderful no less
Are they though this be true; and wondrous more
Is she who in the dark, and stript of sense,
Can claim such sovereignty—the Queen of Art!
For what a cunning painter is she then,
Who hurriedly embodying from the waste
Of things memorial littering life's dim floor,
The forms and features, manifold and quaint,
That crowd the timeless vistas of a Dream.
Fails never in a stroke; and breathes as well
(With powers that laugh at Sculpture,—or make good
The fabled influence of Pygmalion's weird
Devotion to his own creative craft)
A spirit of motion into all her work—
The test of Deity;—inspiring too
Her phantom creatures with more eloquent tones
Than ever broke in subtle light-like waves
Upon the province of a waking ear.

But are they more? Sure glimpses oft, though vague,
Derived from some unnavigable sea
Of mystic being, on whose lonely shore
The normal terminates; and where the pent,
Impatient Soul, from its sleep-shrouded crib,
Is sometimes wont to slip, and roam at large,
Like Crusoe, staring forth; or musing, stand
As did the intelligence of Newton once
On the bare beach of time, while the great deep
Of Truth, by Science yet uncharted, loomed
In shoreless width,—illimitably out,
Under the incommunicable sky?

No answer cometh, and as vain is all
Conjecture: they are dreams! but wonderful,
However we may rank them in our lore.
And worthy of some fond record are those states
Of our interior being, though aberrant,
That with so capable a wand can bring
Back to the faded heart, the rosy flush
And sweetness of a long fled love, or touch
The eyes of an old enmity with tears
Of a yet older friendship; or restore
A world-lost mate, or reunite in joy
The living and the dead! And this can Dreams:
With more as wonderful;—can, when so wills
Their wands weird wielder, whatsoe'er it be,
Lift up the fallen—fallen however low!
Rejuvenate the worn, enrich the poor,
The past imparadise, and enchant the present;
Build in the future higher than the hope
Of Power, when boldest, ever dared to soar;
Annul, as with the sanction of the Infinite,
The prison bars of place, the dens of time,—
Giving the rigid and cold clanking chain
Which Force, that grey iniquity, hath clenched
About its captive, to relent,—yea, stretch
Forth into Fairy Land; or melt like wax
In that fierce life whose spirit lightens wide
Round Freedom, seated on his mountain throne!
Or witching Memory, where she darkling lies,
Can so accomplish her that she can make
All brute bulk ocular—the great Earth itself
Diaphanous, like a mighty globe of glass
Hung in the dim Inane, and thence reveal
Some yearned-for hearth at the antipodes,
With all its loves; or spread at once her wings
O'er all the eras of a wandering life,
As from the orient to the ends of heaven
The silvery fans of light, evolving, show
All things beneath them in one world-wide act
Instant and universal.—Wonderful!

But not thus always are our dreams benign:
Oft are they miscreations—gloomier worlds,

Crowded tempestuously with Wrongs and Fears,
More ghastly than the Actual ever knew;
And rent with racking noises—such as might,
If audible ever to a soul awake,
Go thundering only through the wastes of Hell.

So wonderful are Dreams: and I have known
Many most wild and strange. And once, long since,
As in the death-like mystery of Sleep
My body lay impalled, my soul arose
And journeyed outward in a dream of wonder,
In the mid hour of a dark night, methought
I roamed the margin of a waveless lake,
That, in the knotted forehead of the land
Deep sunken, like a huge Cyclopean eye,
Lidless and void of speculation, stared
Glassily up,—forever sleepless,—up
At the wide vault of heaven; and that I had
Also a vague and mystic consciousness
That over against me, on the farther shore,
Which yet I might not see, there stood a Tower
Such as we read of in some old romance.

The darkness darkened, until overhead
Solidly black the starless heaven domed,
And earth was one wide blot:—when, as I looked,
A light swung blazing from the tower (as yet
Prophesied only in imagination,)
And brought at once its rounded structure forth
Out of the mighty gloom, wherein, till then
So shut, it seemed as one in substance with it.
And when this light had steadied, hanging there
Suspended as by magic, I might see
In the wide lake, whose whole disc now first shown,
Glimmered enormous,—the far falling stream
Of its wild radiance, columnar and vast,
Reach quivering—down, like a great shaft of fire,
Through the lit fluid, that, so lightened, seemed
A vague abysm infinitely deep.

Long at that wild light was I gazing held
In speechless wonder—till I thence could feel
A strange and thrillingly attractive power
In gradual operation; and ere long
My bodily weight seemed witched away, and up
I mounted, poised within the passive air;
Then glode ascendingly sheer o'er the lake,
Which far below, as tow'r's the wondrous light
The attraction drew me, I beheld illumined
Even to its sullen depths with shifting beams,
That tangled tower-ward into one broad path
Of multifarious splendour—one red blaze
Yet various, interwithing, wild and quick,
As every molecule of the watery mass
Had an organic life, and played a part
Restlessly proper to its wayward self,
Though tending all into one glow of bright
Disunion in bright union—one red blaze.

Still poised within the soft air, on I slid:
Nor knew I why—but my amaze wore off
As thus I glode over the lake, and still
Approached the tower, and that so wondrous light!
And soon, instead, a many-branching warmth
Like the sweet inklings of new love, began
Began to tingle in my blood, and so divine
The nearness of some yet unseen Content,
Still nearing, or some yet inaudible Joy,
So great, so reconciling, that it seemed
It was a golden destiny whose spell
Had lifted me aloft, and tower-ward on
Thus richly attracted:—and with this so sweet
Conception—lo, how beautiful a change!

PART II.

WITHIN a circular balcony, whose roof
Was fluted silver, ledging at the eaves
Outward, and resting upon shafts of jet,
Whose polished pencils, in a curving row
Descending to an ivory balu-trade
Glistened in contrast with a covert gleam;
And which, high up the tower, emporched a huge
And brazen door—behold a Lady, all
Of light immaculate! Yea, face and form
All of a Hesper radiancy composed,
And lovelier than lustrous, stood alone.
Yet, as it seemed, expectant; for as still

12a. Henry Kendall's marginalia on first instalment of 'The Tower of the Dream',
Australian Journal, *25 November 1865*

She witched me tow'rds her, she kept beckoning still
With tiny hand more splendid than a star:
Reckoning, and smiling—not as mortals smile,
With visible throes, to the mere face confined,
But with her whole bright influence all at once
In gracious act—as the immortals smile,
God-happy; or as smiles the morning, when
Its subtle line in rosy glory part
Full many a pearly cloud, and breathe the while
A golden prevalence of power ab oad,
That takes them all into i s own delight—
Transfiguring all ! And with a voice intense
And intimately tender as the first
Fine feeling of a love-born bliss— and oh !
More silvery in its sweetness to the soul's
Oracular ear than seemeth to the eye
The wild b he radiance of the maiden moon,
When from some cape's dark beak her rising mass
Looks o'er the ocean—even with such a voice,
So keen, so silvery, did she ask me then,
" Where hast thou stayed so long ? O tell me where ! "

With thrilling ears and heart, I heard—but felt
Pass from me forth a cry of sudden fear,
As swoonin through the wildness of my joy,
Methought I drifted :—whither ! All was now
One wide cold blank—the Lady and the Tower—
The gleaming lake, with all around it—one
Wide, dreary blank,—the drearier for that still
A dizzy, clinging, ghostly consciousness
Kept flickering from mine inmost pulse of life,
Like a far meteor in some dismal marsh :
How long I dreamt not—but the thrilling warmth
That like the new birth of a passionate bliss,
Erewhile had searched me to the quick, again
Shuddered within me, —more and more,—until
Mine eyes had opened under two that made
All else like darkness , and upon my cheek
A breath that seemed the final spirit of health
And floral sweetness, harbingered once more
The fond enquiry of that silver voice
Which once to have heard was never to forget—
" Where hast thou stayed so long ? O tell me where ! "

And when she thus in her so wondrous way
Had spoken, there came, warbled as it seemed
In mystical respondence to her voice,
Still music, such as Eolus gives forth,
But purer, deeper ;—warbled as from some
Unsearchable recess of soul supreme—
Some depth of the Eternal ! echoing thence
Through the sweet meanings of its spirit speech,
The fond enquiry that awoke me now :
" Where hast thou stayed so long ? O tell me where ! "

I answered not, but followed, in mute love
The beamy glances of her eyes with mine,
As in that balcony which up the Tower
Euporched the brazen door, methought I now
Close at her side reclined upon a couch
Of purple, blazoned all with stars of gold,
Tremblingly rayed with spiculated gems,
And argent moons,—and bearing cus ions, rough
(Save where they met the flexure of the arm)
With sheaves of flowers in glowing tissue wrought.
Th s sat we, looking forth ; nor did I marvel,
As her's now led my vision, to remark
How the broad lake, with its green shelving shores,
Swarming with honey-yielding flowers, or hung
With vines in masses, bunched with fruit ; and thence
The prospect all—hills, skies, and winding vales,
And bloomy forests of unspeakable beauty,
Wore basking in the blessedness of a day
So goldenly serene, that never yet
The perfect power of life-essential light
Might so enrobe, since Paradise was lost,
The common world inhabited by man.

I saw all this surpassing beauty—but
I saw it thus through her superior life,
As orbing mine in love—yea, saw it through
Her mystic moon like sphere of being, that seemed
(Transpicuously) the inexhaustible source
Of holiest motives, and truth breathing thoughts—
Breathing abroad like odours from a flower ;
And orient idealities ; and more
Of rosy passion, and affectionate joy,

And earnest tenderness, than many souls
Of Earth's most fervent and ecstatic daughters
United might possess ;—all interflowing
Through the fine issues of a love at once
Wilful and nice, but sanctioned none the less
By its so brilliant purity. Nor might
The glassy lake below more quickly give
Nimble impressions of the coming wind s
Invisible footsteps, dimpling swift along,
Than instant tokens of communion sweet
With outward beauty's subtle spirit, passed
Forth from her eyes, and thence in lambent waves
Suffused and lightened o'er the splendid whole
Of her bright visage, or about her head
In spheres ran raying like a glory of bliss !

But as upon the wonder of her beauty
My soul now feasted, even till it seemed
Instinct with kindred lustre,—lo, her eyes
Suddenly saddened ; then abstractedly
Outfixing them as on some far wild thought
That darkened up, like a portentous cloud,
Over the morning of our peace, she flung
Her silver voice into a mystic song
Of many measures, which, as forth they went,
Slid all into a sweet abundant flood
Of metric melody ! And with this, as still
She poured it out, invisible singers mixed
A choral burden that prolonged the strain's
Rich concords, till the echoes of the hills
Came challengingly forth, and backward then
Subsiding, like a refluent wave, afar,
Blent all into one mystery of sound—
One manifold cadence—dying down. The Song
(Which strangely seemed through all its mystic drift
Addressed to the so stubborn fact, that I
Was sleeping, and its utterer but a Dream)
Is traced upon the tablet of my soul
In shining lines that intonate them elves—
Not sounding to the ear, but to the thought,
Out of the vague vast of the wonderful !
And might, when hardened into mortal speech,
And narrowed from its wide and various sweep
Into such flows as make our waking rhymes
Most wildly musical, be written thus :—

THE SONG.

Wide apart—wide apart,
    In old Time's dim heart,
One terrible fiend doth his stern watch keep
    Over the mystery
    Lovely and deep,
    Locked up in thy history,
        Beautiful Sleep !

Could we disarm him—
    Could we but charm him.
The soul of the sleeper might happily leap
Through the darkness so dreadful—so deathly and deep
    That shroudeth the triple divinity
    Composing thy mystical trinity :
        Liberty, Gratitude,
        B undless Beatitude :
        Beautiful Spirit of Sleep !

Beautiful Spirit of sleep !
    Could we contound him
        Who darkens thy throne—
    Could we surround him
        With spells like thy own ;
        For the divinity
        Then of thy trinity.
Oh, what a blesseder reign were begun !
    For then were it evermore one
With all that soul, freed from the body's strait scheme,
Inherits of secr-light and mystical dream.

And to sleep were to die,
    In o life in the infinite,
Holy and high,
    Spotless and bright,
And so peacefully deep :
And thence unto Liberty, thence unto Gratitude,
With the third in thy Trinity—Boundless Beatitude :
Beautiful Spirit of Sleep !

[To be concluded in our next.]

12b. Henry Kendall's marginalia on first instalment of 'The Tower of the Dream',
Australian Journal, *25 November 1865*

marginalia[1] thereto: hasty through the hurry for the post. Mr Halloran says that poems published by subscription are generally unsuccessful, and I am inclined to agree with him. I cannot bear the sight of fine poems begging for publication. There is a certain degradation in it. If you could spare £40 for an independent volume, you would not lose much in the long run. Think over it.

I have little to tell you of poor Deniehy. After his return from Melbourne, he lived through a few hard months in Sydney—drinking all the while— and then, for the sake of a last brave attempt at reformation, he went up to Bathurst to get out of the way of temptation. There he remained sober for about six weeks but at the end of that time he went into the cursed drink with more infatuation than before. The result you know.[2]

I need not tell you his letters were admirable. Some of his last, addressed to his wife, are steeped, as it were, to the very lips in the bitterness of sorrow and remorse. I may mention here the fact that Mrs Deniehy was left almost destitute. However about £60 have been gathered for her, and, as she is very clever with the needle, I think she will be able to weather it out for the rest of her patient uncomplaining life.[3]

I am
Yours very truly
Henry Kendall.

---

[1] See Letter 96; facsimiles appear on pp. 169–70, with 'H. Kendall. writing & criticism.' in Mary Harpur's hand. The following glosses relate to his handwritten comments: *(1)* 'I like the old line better': it read 'Through the darkness so dreadful and deep' in ML C376 (h642a) of 1851–53 and in *Empire* (h642b), 21 February 1857, p. 4, and 10 March 1857, p. 2. *(2)* 'You know…this "dream song."': Kendall repeatedly made known his love for both song and encompassing poem in letters to CH, e.g., Letters 65, 74, 89, 95 and 132. *(3)* 'the wild cadences of "Kubla Khan" and the spell in "Christabel"': see p. 113 n. 6 and 'His Christabel' (h473-ai).

[2] Deniehy had gone to Bathurst, a large town on the Central Tablelands about 200 kms northwest of Sydney, to practise law. After falling and striking his head in the street, Deniehy died in hospital on 23 October 1865, from 'loss of blood and fits induced by habits of intemperance' (*ADB*). See also Letters 98 (including CH's affectionate 'To My Young Co[u]ntryman D. H. D.') and 99. For Horne's and Stenhouse's obituaries, see Letter 95. Kendall's elegy 'Daniel Henry Deniehy' appeared in *Empire*, 7 November 1865, p. 8. A statue of Deniehy (with other literary figures) graces the Lands Department Building (1876) in Bridge Street, Sydney.

[3] Adelaide Elizabeth Deniehy, née Hoalls (1830?–1908). N. D. Stenhouse was prominent in raising a public subscription to help her. She supported herself and her three young daughters by teaching at Woollahra, and raised some funds by auctioning Deniehy's library of 5,000 volumes. In 1877 she married noted metallurgist and bacteriologist John McGarvie Smith.

98. Charles Harpur to Henry Kendall, 17 December 1865

Text: Autograph collection, SLV MS 13020

Euroma, via Bodalla. 17 Dec: 1865.

My dear Kendall,

I have recd the Journals containing your Marginalia,[1] which I like. I like them, I say, because, I think, that if the Poem were not my own, and I had my critical stylus[2] in hand, the passages marked, and the lines underscored, would be mainly those which, in that case, I should myself have so marked & underscored. But this, of course, I offer you, in the way of a literary compliment, for only so much as it may be worth. Not much perhaps. (You will see that I have begun at the wrong side of my paper.)

In the second stanza of the first song drop (in the pamphlet) "so deathly", as you suggest. Let the line run

Through the darkness so dreadful/deathly and deep[3]

I leave you to your choice between the words *dreadful* and *deathly*.

Punctuate the following lines in the 5th par: of Part I thus:

, my soul arose
And journeyed outward in a dream of wonder.
—In the midhour of a dark night, methought
I roamed the margin &c

And in the next par: of the same Part, correct the punctuation of the following lines in this manner:

And brought at once its rounded structure forth
Out of the mighty gloom, wherein, till then,
So shut it seemed, as one in substance with it &c

that is to say, as *if it had*, till then, *been* one in substance with it.

I am infinitely sad at what you tell about the last days of poor Deniehy![4] Ah me! when I think of the time when I addressed the following song to him, how forlornly disappointed do I feel!

---

[1] See p. 171 n. 1. The first paragraph here follows very closely the reply CH drafted at the foot of Kendall's letter.

[2] Instrument with one end sharp-pointed for incising letters on a wax tablet and the other flat and broad for smoothing the tablet and erasing what is written (metaphorical here).

[3] Either Kendall was reluctant to meddle (the line remained as 'Through the darkness so dreadful—so deathly and deep') or the Melbourne printers pressed on without waiting for the corrections as soon as they had time to turn to the job immediately after Christmas: see Letter 99.

[4] See Letter 97.

To my young Co[u]ntryman D. H. D.[5]

Little Dan Deniehy!
Brilliant Dan Deniehy!
Dear is the light of thy spirit to me!
    Dear as a streaming ray
    Out from a gleaming bay
Is to some weather-worn bark from the sea.

    Little Dan Deniehy,
    Where'er true men there be,
Glow in their midst may some spirit like thine;
    Making all stories high,—
    Lifted to Glory's sky,—
Dear to their souls as thy soul is to mine.

    Little Dan Deniehy,
    Well do I ken you see,
How your life's promise keeps bright'ning apace;
    As an adorning cloud
    Robing the morning proud,
Reddens to fire in the Sun's mighty face!

I think I will publish in the way you suggest:[6] of which more anon,

Yours truly
Chas: Harpur.

(1)[7]

---

[5] This is the first known version (ho48a), although the letter, and the poem's tone and subject ('your life's promise keeps bright'ning'), suggest an earlier manuscript, now lost, which this copies or revises. The poem was first published in 1984 from ML A96 – an 1867 copy with slight development (ho48c) of A87-2 of 1866 (ho48b), both entitled 'A Blighted Promise'. The poem is not to be confused with the better known 1851 sonnet 'To My Young Countryman, D. H. D.' (h622a). The attribution to CH of the tag 'brilliant little Dan Deniehy' (which presumably derives from this poem) probably dates from E. A. Martin's *The Life and Speeches of Daniel Henry Deniehy* (Sydney: McNeil and Coffee, 1884; online at Internet Archive), p. 22.

[6] See Kendall's advice (Letter 97) that CH publish via an 'independent' (self-funded) volume rather than by trying to raise subscriptions.

[7] The significance of this numbering (in red ink in an unidentified hand at the top of p. 1 of MS) is unknown.

99. Henry Kendall to Charles Harpur, 20 December 1865

Text: Kendall papers, ML C199

Survey Offices. December 20th 1865.

My dear Harpur,

I have received your note with the songlike little poem on Mr Deniehy. I like the latter: it was evidently written at a time when the subject was in the morning of his life. There is a gladness too in the poem which indicates how warmly and with what a "believing Kindness"[1] you must have loved one another.

You have great foundation fo[r] your sorrow as regards poor Deniehy. In him you lost one of your sincerest admirers, one of your bravest defenders

You have not sent me the "Ghost of the Cattle Flat"? I will attend to the "Tower" and alter punctuation &c. as you desire.[2] But the pamphlet will not be out till after Christmas: the printers being busily engaged on the inevitable jobwork of the holiday advertisements.

I must have your lovely lyrics on "Love in the Past" printed at once. It is not often that I admire your additions to your earlier poems, but in the case of "Under the Wild Figtree"[3] the new "refrain like" verse runs like the undertone of a wild melancholy wind through the whole song. It makes *that* perfect which I thought was complete long ago.

As "Gramachree" stands now I do not at present know of a Song out of the old Celtic ballad literature that can bear comparison with it. Perhaps I should make an exception for a remarkable "willow song" by the author of "The Roman".[4]

I have in a former letter spoken to you of "Under the Wild Figtree", and there you will find recorded the particular *impression* which the lyric left upon me.

---

[1] Quoting CH's 'To an Old Friend' (h603a), first published in *SMH*, 27 May 1863, p. 5. CH himself quotes the phrase in Letter 102 to his friend of old, Parkes.

[2] For 'Ghost', see p. 168 n. 5. Kendall had been correcting proofs of 'The Tower': see Letter 98.

[3] Kendall had commented on this poem before: see p. 159 n. 10. CH evidently sent Kendall a manuscript of this new 1865 version as part of a newly copied series entitled 'Love in the Past' (ML A95 of 1865, pp. 102–6): I. 'What now in the world might move' (h303d), previously entitled 'Morning Love'; II. 'Many and many a day has flown' (h238f) – originally, 'Under the Wild Fig-tree'; III. 'I wandered east, I wandered west'(h239e) – originally, 'The Girl I Left Behind Me' (see n. 5, opposite); IV. 'Heaven's whole round was bright as now' (h660c) – originally entitled 'Vanished Away'. This series received another copying with revisions in 1867 in ML A88, pp. 103–7 – the series referred to in Letter 129. 'Gramachree' was Kendall's shorthand title for 'Many and many a day has flown'.

[4] Song from Scene II of *Balder: Part the First. By the Author of "The Roman"* (London: Smith, Elder, 1854; online at Internet Archive), pp. 7–9. The author was English poet and critic Sydney Thompson Dobell (1824–74), who wrote as 'Sydney Yendys'. For his *The Roman: A Dramatic Poem* (London: Bentley, 1850), see Internet Archive.

As for the "Maiden I left behind me"[5] the last verse is *sui generis*. The whole of the piece is eloquent with passionate yearning and with infinite regret.

The first and last portions of "Love in the Past" are in your best style, but they fall by comparison with the second and third songs.

Yours Ever
Henry Kendall

Excuse haste—

100. Charles Harpur to Henry Parkes, [after 22 January 1866]

Text: ML MSS 947

Euroma, via Bodalla.

My dear Parkes,[6]

Some time in the last half of 1857, I published in your *Empire*, a series of papers on *The Beautiful*.[7] The numbers of the Journal containing the *first* and *last* of these papers came to hand; but that number which contained the *second* paper, from some cause or other, went astray, so that I never saw it in print, and now find that I have no copy of it. Will you therefore be kind enough (if you cannot otherwise furnish me with it—as most likely you cannot) to get some one to copy it from your bound-up volume of the Journal for that period (some time in the last half of 1857) and enclose it to me, as I want it for a very particular reason? To the person so transcribing it, I shall of course be glad to make any reasonable payment for the job. I hope I am not asking too much of you—full of high official care and important work as you must now be.

---

[5] Initially untitled, this appeared in *Empire*, 25 May 1857, p. 5 as 'The Girl I Left Behind Me' (h239b). In ML A90 of 1863 (h239d), CH struck out 'girl' in both title and first stanza (but not elsewhere) and substituted 'maiden'. In 1865 and later manuscripts it is untitled but 'Maiden' is used in the refrain-like last line of each stanza. *'sui generis'*: of its own kind (Latin).

[6] Good friends in the 1840s and early 1850s, CH and Parkes became estranged as Parkes increasingly involved himself in liberal parliamentary politics. This letter probably dates not long after 22 January 1866 when Parkes was made Colonial Secretary in the ministry of James Martin.

[7] Parkes established *Empire* in 1850. Hopelessly in debt by 1858, he was forced to sell – to Samuel Bennett and William Hanson in 1859. Poems and notes by CH series-titled 'The Beautiful' appeared 1856–57: 'I. Beauty' and 'The Spirit of Beauty (A Prophecy)', and II. 'The Terrors of Beauty' and 'Animal Human Beauty' (respectively, ho35d, ho35-ac, ho36e and ho36-ab; *Empire*, 12 September 1856, p. 5); III. 'A Lady by Moonlight', IV. 'A Youth of the Utopian Era' and V. 'To Helen' (ho37b, ho38b and ho39c; *Empire*, 13 October 1856, p. 5); and Third Paper – VI. 'Love the Exalter of Nature', VII. 'To a Girl', VIII. 'There is no curve of sea or sky...' and IX. 'Dawn in the Forest' (ho40a, ho41d, ho42a and ho43d; *Empire*, 17 September 1857, p. 6).

I sent a Sonnet to Martin[1]—but with no name, and for a reason I had merely dated 1866. I think—but others may think differently—that it was a right good one: bold, and inspirited with a lofty political advice.

Yours very truly,
Chas: Harpur.

101. Charles Harpur to Henry Parkes, 3 February 1866

Text: ML MSS 947

Euroma, via Bodalla. 3rd February 1866.

My dear Parkes,

I congratulate you on your having at length mounted to the "top of the tree",[2] though, I opine, you will find that that same top of the political tree is just now no bed of roses whereupon to "repose your wearied virtue".[3] Still you have, no doubt, right manfully "served up" to the position—and it is greatly better I suppose that a *man* should at any time be worn out with work (of which you will have no stint), than that he should be eaten away by the rust of any sort of idleness.[4] Perhaps even *to die in harness*, if on a right road, would be a wise man's choice: and wisdom I think you have.

As for myself, poor unprovided-for devil that I happen always to be, I am in no small terror just now of that diabolical Spectre to all officialdom yclept *Reduction*:[5] albeit I believe that my particular berth is one as little deserving of abolition as any in the country—due regard being had to the efficiency of the Government service. It is so, in fact, on the six several grounds following:

---

[1] Probably 'To the Hon: James Martin'; the version at ML A87-2 (h628a) is unsigned and dated '1866'. Martin was at this time the newly commissioned Premier of NSW.

[2] Parkes had served in the Legislative Council and Assembly since 1854 in opposition, but in early 1866 he and his faction allied themselves with James Martin to form government. Parkes was commissioned Colonial Secretary on 22 January 1866; Martin was Premier and Attorney-General. While the goldfields were technically the responsibility of the Secretary for Lands (John Bowie Wilson), Parkes had great influence. CH had reason to be wary of Wilson: see p. 148 n. 1, and Peter Cloete to John Black, 16 January 1860 (in *Suppl. Letters*).

[3] '...have ye chos'n this place / After the toil of Battle to repose / Your wearied virtue, for the ease you find / To slumber here, as in the Vales of Heaven?' – John Milton, *Paradise Lost*, Book I, lines 318–21.

[4] Proverbial, in, e.g., Ben Jonson, *Every Man in His Humour* (1598), II.2.76–7: 'Not caring how the temper of your spirits / Is eaten away with the rust of idleness'.

[5] '*Reduction*': the (previous) Cowper government's intention, in the face of a serious budget deficit and following an 1865 board of inquiry, was to retrench goldfields magistrates and Assistant Commissioners; this was public knowledge by January 1866. There was to be one police magistrate at Moruya and Nerrigundah acting also as Gold Commissioner, and one Clerk of Petty Sessions there acting as Sub-Commissioner. The new administration under James Martin would continue the policy. See 'Retrenchment in the Public Expenditure', *SMH*, 18 January 1866, p. 5. 'yclept' means called, named, styled (Old English, but still current in the 19th century as an ironic affectation).

1st There is no other magistrate resident within a distance on all hands of 35 miles. 2nd The nearest other Gold Field—viz. Araluen—is 70 miles distant by the only practicable road. 3rd Moruya, the head-quarters of the Police Magistrate (as proposed in the reduction-scheme of the late ministry) is 35 miles distant from even Nerrigundah the trading township of the Gulph Diggings. 4th These same Gulph Diggings, with Nerrigundah for centre, are a congeries[6] of separate Fields, lying some of them 15 miles apart, and extending upward and laterally over 40 miles of country: 5th All mining disputes require to be settled at once, or as they arise, much more than any other kind of legal disputes do—all work having to be suspended pending their settlement; and they require also to be *dealt with upon the spot.* 6th The right settlement of them requires also that the adjudicating magistrate should have considerable experience in the deciding and adjusting of such disputes, which are often, not only greatly, but *peculiarly* complicated.

From what is above said, it will be obvious, I think, that no Police Magistrate, stationed at Moruya, could be the Commissioner of such a scattered Gold Field as well, except in *name* only—and to the wholesale neglect of its mining interests.

Moreover, my dear Parkes, having now the power, and the opportunity, you will, I doubt not, be duly influenced by the spirit of the wise man's saying: "How can he get wisdom who holdeth the plough, and whose talk is of bullocks? But *they*"—the men of mind and study—"*will maintain the state of the world*"[7]—will keep it from becoming a dungheap. While in proof of my being the right man in the right place, need I say more than this: I have now had sole charge of the Gulph Gold Fields for a period of four years, during which time I have had to decide *some hundreds* of mining disputes—perhaps a thousand altogether;—and yet not one of these judgments of mine has ever been appealed from? What other Commissioner in the service can point to his official work as being thus characterised? Not one other of them all.

Remember Mrs Harpur and myself to Mrs Parkes and all the young folk,

and believe me yours
very truly
Chas: Harpur.

---

[6] Collection of things merely massed or heaped together.
[7] CH misremembers Ecclesiasticus 38. The distinction is between the learned and those of humbler callings; but it is the farmer, the smith and the potter who will 'maintain the state of the world' (38.33–4).

102. Charles Harpur to Henry Parkes, 17 February 1866

Text: ML MSS 947

Euroma, via Bodalla, 17th Feb: 1866.

My dear Parkes,

You say in your kind note to me,[1] that you have long thought that for some cause or other you had forfeited my friendship. Now to show that no evil of this sort has been rankling in me, need I mention more than this? It is not above a month or two since I set myself to the task of perfecting the Sonnet that I had formerly addressed to you in the "long ago" and in the first warmth of a "believing kindness"[2]—and ended it in making the first one run as follows:

To Henry Parkes.[3]

[Before having seen him, but after
the passage between us of several
letters, and many *friendly* tokens.]

Dear Henry, though thy face I have not seen,
  Nor heard thy voice,—assured that one doth glow
  With truth, and that the other hath a flow
Like a broad stream,—there dwelleth none between
The waters of Port Jackson and this scene
  Where now I muse, that I so far would go
  To talk with, and more intimately know,
In these so golden Autumn eves serene.
And when we yet shall meet, say shall not we
  Be as old friends at once, and sit and pour
Our souls together? which, so mixed, shall be
  A flowing draught of thought-thick bardic lore,
  Such as Keats reeled with when he looked out o'er
The Ocean of old Homer's minstrelsy.

But perhaps you care nothing about this sort of things now.

I will only add, that if ever I do presume again to trespass upon your time through the medium of a letter, I shall say nothing about *Retrenchment*[4]✳— the devil take it! nor indeed about any Governmental matters and things whatever. I know a good deal now about official etiquette and—I was going to

---

[1] Presumably Parkes's response to Letter 101.
[2] See p. 174 n. 1.
[3] CH wrote this sonnet at Jerry's Plains in 1844 (see h610a), sending it with Letter 3 to Parkes. His revision of 1863 (h610c; in ML A90) is fairly close to this version (h610d).
[4] See p. 176 n. 5.

13. 'Sir Henry Parkes, c. 1866', photographer J. T. Gorus

say something else—and, whether wisely or foolishly, have no small contempt for much of both.

I remain,
My dear Parkes
Yours very truly
Chas: Harpur.

✳ Though "The great Emathian conqueror bid spare the house of Pindarus, when temple and tower went to the ground."[5] And though the great Burk has said, "Whoever protect a man of genius *confers a favor upon the State*."[6]

[5] 'Lift not thy spear against the Muses' Bowre, / The great Emathian Conqueror bid spare / The house of Pindarus, when Temple and Towre / Went to the ground' – John Milton, 'Sonnet VIII' (1642). 'The Emathian' (i.e., Macedonian) was Alexander the Great. In Plutarch's *Life of Alexander* the conqueror, in levelling the city of Thebes, spares the house of the poet Pindar.
[6] Edmund Burke (1729–97), Irish-born statesman, political theorist and philosopher, now widely regarded as the philosophical founder of modern conservatism. CH's view of Burke had mellowed: in 'Marvellous Martin' (1853), he was 'that prince of sophists' (h281a). Quotation not identified.

103. Henry Kendall to Henry Parkes, 19 February 1866

Text: Kendall papers, ML MSS 957

Enmore Road Newtown[1] Feb: 19th 1866.

My dear Mr Parkes,

Somehow I cannot help thinking you were on the occasions of my last visits not as you *have* been with me. I am very sorry that this impression is forced upon me, for after all, it may be a false one. Although I have made a certain application to you as my official chief,[2] I do not wish to be ranked amongst those who may be inclined to take advantage of your friendly feelings. I have never been a parasite, and I am not inclined to be one now. So let me rank myself amongst your true friends—not amongst your interested followers. *I do not want a situation.* I hope you will give me credit in this matter. For many months past I have kept away from you in order to avoid suspicion. I repeat again let me be your friend without regard to profit.

Charles Harpur desired me to forward you a pamphlet containing one of his best poems,[3] and accordingly I sent it to you. I have had a letter from one of the chief contributors to "*Fraser's* Magazine" He—the Fraser gentleman—is about to write an exhaustive paper on the "Genesis of Australian Literature",[4] and he wants me to assist him in getting up the material. This is very encouraging to me.

Mr Halloran and others some time ago urged upon me the "desirableness" of my being in the Assembly[5]—I somehow think I could be useful there. Do you think it would be wise to risk it at the first possible moment? I certainly cannot afford to go in now. You may laugh at me, but this thing is a dream of mine. Although I am poetically given I have by no means neglected political social and statistical literature.

Believe me,
My dear Mr Parkes,
Yours Faithfully,
Henry Kendall.

[1] In 1866 Kendall and his three sisters moved from St Peters (now Marrickville) where they had moved in 1864. They were now living in Randall Terrace, Enmore Road, Newtown.

[2] Kendall was a Clerk in the Surveyor General's Office from 1863 until 6 February 1866, when he was appointed to the Colonial Secretary's Office under Parkes; his salary increased from £150 to £200.

[3] *The Tower of the Dream* (Sydney & Melbourne: Clarson, Shallard, & Co., Printers, 1865) – see h642g.

[4] *Fraser's Magazine for Town and Country* was a general and literary journal published in London, 1830–82. No article on Australian literature appears around the time of this letter.

[5] Parkes replied, advising Kendall against running for the Legislative Assembly: 'I could not honestly advise you to think seriously of this for the present. You can well afford to wait for a few years' (Ackland, p. 208, citing ML 3775/9–11).

104. Charles Harpur to Henry Kendall, 10 June 1866

Text: Autograph collection, SLV MS 13020

Euroma, 10th June, 1866.

My dear Kendall,

If you knew how lonely I am here, I think you would write to me somewhat oftener than you do. There is not a single soul within thirty miles of me, that I care even to talk with—or *to*. How is dear old Stenhouse? What sort of a chap is Dr Brereton?[6] How much taller does Halloran stand in his stockings since he became the Secretary's secretary?[7] You see, you could tell me lots of things: and thereby provoke me, perhaps, to tell *you* lots of things in return. Still, if you really have not time, I am content to take the will for the deed.

I do not continue to send you the "rag" you wot of[8]—having become tired of publishing my "things" in it, even with the view that I think I told you I had in doing so.[9]—I should like, had I the means, to publish (as you once suggested) a vol: for the English critics:[10] for I know well enough, that I have long left all my Australian critics—many a year ago—standing hopelessly behind me, and mostly, too, upon the lowermost ledges of Parnassus.[11] But this, in one sense, is my misfortune. I have not the means, however, to publish on my "own hook", as a gold-digger would phrase it.[12]

I never see anything of yours now. Why is this?

The period of my official life is running short—ending with the present

---

[6] John Le Gay Brereton (1827–86). The enquiry suggests they had not yet met, but Brereton would treat CH in the final year of his life.

[7] Chief Clerk above Kendall at the Surveyor General's Office, Halloran was appointed Under-Secretary to the Colonial Secretary in February 1866 soon after his friend Henry Parkes took office. Kendall would also be transferred there in 1866, enabling *Punch* to make fun of 'The Three Jolly Poets': e.g., 'An Hour in the Colonial Secretary's Office', *Sydney Punch*, 26 January 1867, p. 75.

[8] *Moruya Examiner*: Kendall had dubbed it 'the Moruya "rag"' (Letter 95); *wot*: know (archaic).

[9] Nowhere in the surviving correspondence does CH explain his policy in placing his verse with small regional newspapers such as *Moruya Examiner* or *Braidwood Dispatch*, whose circulation was limited and whose contributions were unpaid. These more or less guaranteed printings nevertheless offered conveniently clean copy for Kendall to place in Sydney papers and for CH to revise.

[10] In December 1865 (Letter 97) Kendall had tried to persuade CH to fund his own (colonial) publication rather than relying on subscription – but CH now faced redundancy. This letter provides the first hint that he was looking to English publication, which meant finding a London publisher willing to speculate on a colonial unknown; in the attempt, CH would enlist his wealthy neighbour T. S. Mort (see Letter 133).

[11] Mount Parnassus in Greece, regarded as the source of literary, especially poetic, inspiration; and hence the world of literature and poetry.

[12] At my own risk (colloquial: *OED* cites American sources as earliest; anglicised by Thackeray in *Pendennis*, 1850).

month.[1] Whether the set now in power,[2] will prolong it in any way, remains to be seen.

If you should see Maddock the Bookseller,[3] be good enough to mention, as from me, that I will settle with him in a short time.

Yours very truly
Chas: Harpur.

105. Charles Harpur to Henry Parkes, 28 June 1866

Text: ML MSS 947

Euroma, via Bodalla, 28th June /66

My dear Sir,

I am in receipt of your favor of the 21st instant;[4] and at another time, I intend to write to you an answer to it in full—in which, I doubt not, I shall be well able to show you that the ex parte statements[5] of volunteer informers and self-constituted spies are in no wise to be depended upon, but rather that the reports of such characters—always base & detestible—are to be ever taken with much salt; that the "freaks"[6] you speak of as being all known in Sydney, were either sheer lies, or mere minor matters of morals & manners that have been most egregiously distorted into enormities, or invidiously magnified out of all life-likeness: and with which infact the Government had properly nothing to do.

But in the present note I intend to touch upon nothing but the Superannuation Fund. You [tell?] me[7] that I have no claim upon that Fund. Why, when a common Constable is turned adrift, he is allowed a month's pay for every year of service.[8] And such was the rule, I believe, throughout the

---

[1] CH's position as Assistant Gold Commissioner at Nerrigundah would be abolished on 30 June 1866.

[2] The second Martin ministry of 1866–68, in which Parkes served as Colonial Secretary.

[3] See p. 153 n. 10.

[4] Parkes's letter of 21 June must have been very different from the 'kind note' CH received in February. It was private rather than official, according to CH (see Letter 109); but this angry response (along with the draft of his letter to Parkes, Letter 106) suggests its contents: CH's attempts to retain his post in the public-service retrenchments of 1866, and accusations as to his conduct. From this point his relations with Parkes deteriorated, never to be mended.

[5] Statements made with respect to, or in the interest of, one side only.

[6] *OED* defines *freak* as 'A sudden causeless change or turn of the mind; a capricious humour, notion, whim, or vagary' or 'A capricious prank or trick, caper'.

[7] MS reads 'You / me'.

[8] The *Superannuation Act* of 1864 (27 Vic. No. 11) established a Superannuation Fund for the NSW public service. Though he had contributed to the Fund, CH at 53 did not qualify for a pension, so he could only hope for a compensation payment at the pleasure of the government: see p. 192 n. 2. Superannuation provisions under the *Police Regulation Act* of 1862 (25 Vic. No. 16) were similar to those for the public service, except that any police officer of up to ten years' service declared unfit could receive up to one month's pay for each year's service.

whole Civil Service, previous to the passing of the Superannuation Act, which was to make all Officialdom more easy in mind as to the future, and which to that end has exacted from me monthly ever since it came into operation the sum of £1–3/4.[9] For what, as it turns out? To provide a comfortable retiring allowance for a few favored old fogies[10] some twenty years hence— and who, all of them, will, until then, have been comfortably lapped—not in superannuation lavender, but in what is nearly as good—big and constant pay: not a mere pittance which at a dear outpost was barely a living! This surely is not just. And I think Mr Martin (being a logical lawyer) will at once see that it is not.

I remain, dear Sir,
Yours very truly
Chas: Harpur.

P.S. As this is the last letter but *one*, which it is likely I shall ever write to you, perhaps you will do me the favor of answering it. C.H.

106. Charles Harpur to Henry Parkes, [after 28 June 1866][11]

Text: ML C376

As to my efficiency in the general discharge of my official duties, both as a magistrate & a Gold Com: I refer you,—not to my enemies, not to *sub umbra*[12] informers,—but to those gentlemen with whom I have acted, for seven years; and if the[ir] report of me, in this respect, be not to the effect, that I was to their thinking somewhat remarkable first, for getting at the tangles of a knotty case, and secondly, for the firm and impartial decision of it; *then* I will "shut up". But you really seem to think that no magisterial fitness can exist apart from a parsonical white cravat, or unless shelled over with a quaker-demeanour.[13] For my part, however, I have found those sort of things accompanied mostly by mere pretence and inability—nay, the integuments[14] very often of the rankest imposture. You say all my freaks are known in Sydney. Yes, more freaks I doubt not are charged against me at head quarters than I suspect ever indulged in

---

[9] Annual deductions were set by the Superannuation Fund Commissioners at 4 per cent of salary. On a salary of £350 CH was contributing £1 3s. 4d. every month.

[10] The Fund was designed to cater for long-serving officers retiring at 60 years of age.

[11] This partial draft letter (in ML C376, pp. 485–6) is probably in response to Parkes's of 21 June 1866 mentioned in CH's letter to him of 28 June (Letter 105). It is not known whether CH sent a final version.

[12] Shadowy, literally 'beneath the shade'.

[13] *Shelled over*: encased. A reference to the plainness of dress and speech associated with Quakers (members of the Religious Society of Friends). The 'white cravat' is the neckcloth of a 19th-century Protestant (notably, Anglican) clergyman.

[14] Coverings, garments.

even in my dreams. But it is evident, at all events, that your Government is cognisant of more than as it seems to me any manly Government should condecend to be; that is, of matters touching the minor morals & manners of its officials which could only have been acquired through the medium of spies and detectives,—characters always as questionable as they are detestable;—a sort of information, in short, which is essentially as abject as were that which should be a cronicle of the daily enormities of an official's bread-and meat appetites, or the fact of his going to the water-closet[1] more than seven times per week. A Cabinet thus kept posted up in the minor moralities and personal proclivities of its outpost officials, would be very Godlike, I suppose, if it were not very snobbish.[2]

107. Charles Harpur to [John Bowie Wilson?], [after 1 July 1866]

Text: ML A87-2

But as the Government partly owe me this money (Mr Griffin[3] not having paid it) I have thought it best to submit my claim finally to you, nothing doubting but that you will see me righted

I respectfully refer you to Mr Griffin's note (annexed) in which he admits that there were arrears due me; as also to my Bank account wherein it is plainly shown that Mr Griffin paid nothing over to me for the first six months of 1864 though he continued to be the paymaster of all such allowances up to that time.[4]

I have the honor to place before you the following documents, from which it will plainly appear that the late Commissioner Griffin failed to pay me certain Allowances in lieu of Forage & quarters. The statement of the case is surely as follows

Finding sometime in the beg[inning] of 1865 from my bank account that Mr Griffin had not paid over any thing to my account on the score of Forage & Quarters Allowance for the first six months of 1864 and that I could get no satisfaction whatever from himself in the matter, as he would not even answer my letters, I sent in my Abstracts for those two quarters to the Treasury

---

[1] Toilet.

[2] From *snob* in the now-obsolete sense of someone with little or no breeding or taste. Cf. Thackeray, *The Book of Snobs* (1848): 'O you pride of all Snobland! O you crawling, truckling... lacqueys and parasites!' CH offers his own definition in the note to his satirical song 'Petty Pride' (h378b) in *PA*, 12 July 1856, p. 2.

[3] CH's (former) superior: see p. 128 n. 2. In addition to his salary of £350 CH was entitled to allowances of £50 p.a. for forage for a horse and £40 p.a. for accommodation, paid quarterly. Arrears were due to him, and he used the verso of an old letter (from Adolphus Norblad, 18 July 1862) to draft a formal complaint, probably to Lands Minister John Bowie Wilson in Sydney (see Rawling, pp. 278–9). CH's reference to 'late Commissioner Griffin' indicates that the draft post-dates 1 July 1866, when, in a general reorganisation of goldfields administration, Griffin was replaced in the Southern Gold District by George O'Malley Clarke.

[4] A draft 'Abstract', in CH's hand, 'of Bank Entries' of 'Allowances' paid is in A87-2, p. 773.

direct,[5] with an explanatory memo attached. But these Abstracts remaining undischarged at the Treasury, I subsequently sent in another set (those annexed) which were at length returned to me with the letter and memo which is [here] affixed to them: and thus repulsed at the Treasury, I thought it was of little use for me to try further for the payment of the money. But as the Government justly owe it to me, Mr Griffin not having paid it I have finally determined to submit my case to you &c

I should mention further perhaps, that Mr Griffin always sent me the Abstracts for these Allowances, for signature in quarterly and half yearly sets, sometimes partly and sometimes wholly in advance; and hence no doubt the reason of their having been paid to *his* account at the Treasury

108. Charles Harpur to Henry Kendall, [after 5 July 1866]

Text: Kendall papers, ML MSS 3796/2

Euroma via, Bodalla,[6]

D[ea]r Kendall,

I wish the enclosed[7] to be published in the Herald. Read it first, and then be good enough to send it, as at my request, through old Mr Fairfax,[8] who I think has a soft place in his heart towards me.—I know that the Poem is good in its kind: and after a few more contributions in this way, I intend to ask Mr Fairfax for some regular engagements on the Herald: as under my present altered circumstances[9] it is absolutely necessary that I should get something to do in this way. I know I could serve Mr Fairfax in a literary way with some—perhaps, with greater, effect, than even those most disposed to think highly of my intellectual powers, are prepared to expect. And if *you* happen to be acquainted with the old gentleman, perhaps you could put in a feeler in my regard—and let me know the result. You must forgive me for troubling you to the extent I do; but I know of no one else that I think would feel so much interest either in me or my doings. With ever so small a pittance earned in the above way, I would not condescend to be the flunkey[10] of any

---

[5] In 1864 a system of direct payments from Treasury was adopted. Gold Commissioners and other public officers in the country areas were required to send their monthly salary abstracts, properly receipted, direct to Treasury for payment on the first of the following month. See notice re Public Accounts, *NSW Government Gazette* Supplement, 21 June 1864, pp. 1441–2.

[6] Letter undated: it must postdate 5 July 1866, when the *SMH* published 'The Forging of the Armour of Achilles' (see below).

[7] Possibly 'Poem on Shakspere', which it is known CH sent to Kendall for *SMH* in July (see Letter 110). The Fairfax weekly *Sydney Mail* of 11 August 1866 would print 'Shakspere' (h462f), the only Harpur poem it would carry during his lifetime.

[8] John Fairfax (1804–77), proprietor of *SMH*. Kendall was a close friend of co-proprietor Charles Fairfax: see p. 145 n. 10.

[9] As at 1 July 1866 CH was no longer on the government payroll.

[10] A footman or lackey.

Government upon earth—much less such a snob one,[1] as ours in Australia must for a long time inevitably be.

If the thing is published send me the paper containing it, as usual. By the bye, though, I got *three* copies of the Herald containing the Forging of the Armour &c[2]—all addressed in your hand.

Believe me yours most truly
Chas: Harpur.

109. Charles Harpur to Henry Kendall, 7 July 1866

Text: Autograph collection, SLV MS 13020

Euroma, via Bodalla 7th July, 1866.

My dear Kendall,

"Telegonus" came duly to hand. I like it upon the whole. There are, to my thinking, some very happy lines in it. But you could have made the verse better, with better models, for your skill in versification is generally somewhat remarkable.[3] "Telegonus", however, wants variety of pause and cadence. You say yourself that it is not Tennysonian; but it might easily be better. Tennyson's blank verse is always chargeable with a similar defect—a want of *numerosity*;[4] not, mind you, a slip-slop or piggled interflow of parts, but a nicely varied cadential one. But, generally, in Tennyson's verses of all kinds,—when not *sweet*, as in lyrical pieces,—there is a feebleness, or I might say, *feminineness* of movement and flow. I cannot call to mind a really thundrous line that he has written—such as either of the following:

> "Hurled heàdlong, flàming from the ethereal sky,
>   With hideous ruin and combustion, dòwn
>   To bottomless perdition."[5]

[continued next page

---

[1] See p. 184 n. 2.

[2] 'The Forging of the Armour of Achilles. (From the XVIIIth Book of the Iliad.)' (h138a), in *SMH*, 5 July 1866, p. 2.

[3] Kendall, 'The Voyage of Telegonus' (*SMH*, 11 June 1866, p. 2) would be included in his *Leaves from Australian Forests* (1869). Telegonus, son of Odysseus by Circe, having been sent to Ithaca to find his father, fails to recognise him in combat and slays him. Like Tennyson's 'Ulysses', the poem employs blank verse in iambic pentameter.

[4] Rhythmical or metrical quality deriving from the numbers of metrical feet or stresses (obsolete, *OED*). For CH's earlier judgements on Tennyson, see p. 141 n. 9; *piggled* means overworked, jumbled.

[5] From John Milton, *Paradise Lost*, Book I, lines 45–7.

Study Milton & Wordsworth for a blank verse style, and combine the master-movements of the two.[6] Wordsworth will teach you how to loosen & modernise Milton's, so as to make it more eloquent, and Milton will show you how to put thunder into Wordsworth's. I recd a *private* letter from Parkes[7] that shows I think that I have little to expect from the present Cabinet.[8] The fellow presumes to lecture me upon some "freaks", as he calls them— matters of minor morals & manners with which no Government have aught to do; and with which no manly Government would condecend to become acquainted—through spies or volunteer informers, characters always base and detestable—but no more base & detestable than those who employ and listen to them. This fellow Parkes![9] who has himself done things that would have hanged an honester and less subtle man! This fellow, I say, who has not even two qualifications for the high office he now fills, unless the profoundest hypocrisy be one, and preeminency in failure another!

The Secretary's secretary's note[10] to you made me "laugh consumedly" as Scrub says in the Play.[11] What a prig it is.[12] And only that the note is a private one *to you*, I would make it the theme of some lines that should render him a laughing-stock for life. He is not worth talking about.

[6] Both poets were profound influences on CH: see p. 10 n. 1, p. 48 n. 2, and p. 144 n. 3. Both were subjects for his verse – e.g., his 'Rhymed Criticisms' of Milton (h463-aa, h463-ba) and Wordsworth (h472a), and 'Wordsworth's Poetry' (h695a).

[7] Not extant but see draft reply, Letter 106.

[8] See p. 176 n. 5 and p. 182 n. 8.

[9] CH's judgement of Parkes oscillated: cf. his affectionate letter of 17 February 1866 (Letter 102). CH had since lost his job, and his old comrade had been unwilling or unable to help him. That this former radical, Parkes, should serve under James Martin, a symbol of reaction for the radicals of the 1850s, must have seemed to CH 'an act of base betrayal' (Rawling, p. 289). Similarly, a version of 'The Scamper of Life' from earlier in the 1860s (h491f in ML A87-2) lambasts Parkes as 'a bladder of the most / Specific humbug—mind & heart!' Sandwiched between two fragments intended for the same poem of 1866 (h491g) in ML A95 is more invective, clearly concerning Parkes: 'But what of the Public Schools Act?—is that not somewhat of a political achievement? Why, yes. But that measure was originated by Charles Cowper—and not by *him*: nay, even *that*, his now pet bantling and political boast, would no doubt have been opposed by him, tooth and nail, had Cowper the father of it been also its initiator. For the man is a humbug pure and simple, from the top to the bottom—from his Tartar snout to his negro shanks!' For Parkes and his Public Schools Bill of 1866, see Martin, *Parkes*, pp. 223–30.

[10] Halloran's note is lost.

[11] 'Ay, he and the Count's Footman were Gabbering French like two intreaguing Ducks in a Mill-Pond, and I believe they talk'd of me, for they laugh'd consumedly' – the servant Scrub, in George Farquhar's comedy *The Beaux Stratagem*, III.1 (1707; online at Internet Archive).

[12] '[W]hat a prig it is! How it struts, and perks, and prates! – It is truly an "impudent varlet"' – 'Christopher North' (John Wilson), likening Leigh Hunt to a magpie in his review of Hunt's *Lord Byron and Some of his Contemporaries*, in *Blackwood's Edinburgh Magazine*, XXIII.136 (March 1828), p. 407. *Varlet*: a menial or groom, by extension a rogue. In *Volpone, or, the Fox*, Ben Jonson has Corbaccio call Mosca 'impudent varlet' (V.8).

Do you ever see my brother Joe?[1] For some reason, he will not let *me* know anything of his present whereabouts or doings. Do you then, like a good fellow, tell me whatever you may know about him.

Don't forget to send me the Herald containing the "Forging of the armour of Achilles"—if they publish it.[2] It is my intention to try and get a literary engagement with Fairfax:[3] for I must supplement my present means in some such way. I have, it is true, a snug well-furnished house over my head, with a good farm for its size; but I am otherwise poor, and have a large and helpless family.[4] Hence I must now see what my pen will do for me.

Yours very truly
Chas: Harpur.

110. Charles Harpur to Henry Kendall, 10 August 1866

Text: Kendall papers, ML C199

Euroma, via Bodalla. 10th Aug, 1866.

My dear Kendall,

I wrote to you about half a dozen posts ago, enclosing a Poem on Shakspere, for publication in the Herald;[5] and as I have not since heard from you, I am in some doubt as to whether my letter has reached you. If, however, it has reached you, and the commission I therein lay upon you is in anywise an ungrateful one, you need not mind it. In that case, I will treat with Fairfax for myself, at once (on hearing from you) and directly.

I do not know whether you, or other of my Sydney friends, have by this time found out that I have nothing to expect from the present Cabinet,—but I myself am satisfied that I have not: not even the retiring allowance of a month's pay for every year of service which is commonly given to a common Constable upon his being turned adrift.[6] Well, so be it. I will write——I have already written—a thing that shall make Parkes, my old heartless friend, who has heretofore told me over and over again that he "loved me like a brother"—

---

[1] CH's older brother Joseph. On 30 June 1866 he had buried their mother Sarah at Penrith, having conveyed her, dying, in a dray from Forbes: see CHCA, Biographical entry for 29 June 1866. CH's query suggests he did not yet know.

[2] The poem with CH's headnote (h138a) had been published in *SMH*, 5 July 1866, p. 2.

[3] John Fairfax and Sons, publishers of *SMH*, Sydney's pre-eminent daily, as well as its weekly *Sydney Mail*. Thanks to Kendall, *SMH* was the main Sydney outlet for CH's work in the mid-to-late 1860s.

[4] This was the first week of CH's life post-retrenchment, celebrated in a couplet: 'This day I've lost my office, and again am a free man, / With the wide world for mine oister, which I'll open if I can' (h586a). The dependent family was now Mary Harpur and children Washington (15), Charley (13), Harold (10), Ada (8) and Mary Araluen (4).

[5] 'Shakspere' (h462f); it appeared in *Sydney Mail*, 11 August 1866, p. 11.

[6] See p. 176 n. 5 and p. 182 n. 8.

that shall make him, I say, shiver in his grave.[7] And that other ineffable hound, Wilson,[8]—a fellow whose *spiritual* belief it is, that God is nothing but a blazing fireball in the centre of the universe,—him too, will I visit in a manner that shall surprise him. Nor shall H.H.[9] go scot free.

But come what may, I can, I doubt not, keep myself above actual want— and manage to live upon my little farm, apart with the Muse, and not without dignity. And to this end, I am turning to work like an old lion,—getting my crops in &c &c, pruning my fruit trees, grape vines &c &c:[10] and if you could manage to run up thus far about January next,[11] I should be able to set before you twenty kinds of prime fruit. Come.

Yours truly
Chas: Harpur.

111. Charles Harpur: epitaph, [1867]

Text: Stenhouse papers, ML A100[12]

Here lies Charles Harpur, who at fifty years of age[13] came to the conclusion, that he was living in a sham age, under a sham Government, and amongst sham friends, and that any world whatever must therefore be a better world than theirs. And having come to this conclusion, he did his dying and now lies here with one of his sons,[14] in the hope of their meeting in some place better fitted to make them happy, and to keep them so, than this from which they have departed. And even if all that now remains of them is what remains below,—it is still well: inasmuch as in that case, they are safe from all malignity, whether proceeding from God or Devil, that would any farther afflict them.

---

[7] The 'thing' is not identified, unless CH means 'The Scamper of Life' in a new, 1866 version (h491h, in ML A93): Parkes, as 'Hansard Halloran's / Most mighty Chief' is trenchantly satirised as 'a huge wind bag of pretense / Yet self deceiving blind of heart!' – tougher than in h491f of the early 1860s (in A87-2).

[8] John Bowie Wilson: see p. 148 n. 1.

[9] Henry Halloran.

[10] To the original 100 acres of Euroma the Harpurs had added conditional purchases adjoining or nearby in the names of Washington in 1864 (40 acres) and Charley in 1865 (150 acres, forfeited in 1869): see further, p. 225 n. 9. Besides the orchard, the Harpurs grew corn, potatoes and hay, and almost certainly ran dairy cattle.

[11] Kendall would never visit Euroma: see Letter 158. After a correspondence of six years, CH and Kendall finally met in January–February 1868: see Kendall's article on CH, Deniehy and Dalley: 'About Some Men of Letters in Australia', *Australian Journal*, 1 October 1869, pp. 84–5.

[12] Presumably CH sent this curious document to Stenhouse: see Rawling, pp. 297, 321 n. 11; and Jordens, pp. 92–3, 168 n. 40.

[13] CH consistently understated his age by four years. He turned 54 in 1867.

[14] CH's son Charley, 13 years old: for his death, see Letter 116.

112. Charles Harpur to [*Sydney Morning Herald*, early 1867][1]

Text: ML A87-1

The Editor may publish the foregoing with or without my name—just as he pleases.

If my critical papers are not worth being printed according to copy[2]—that is, in a scholarly and respectable manner,—they are clearly considered as scarcely worth having: and I have my answer. Not only am I made to write nonsense by the most stupid errors of the press, such as "a *suffering* (for sufficing) and final *repose* &c"[3] but all the *niceties* of the criticisms depending on italicised lines & passages, scanned metres and so forth, are quite set at naught—separate passages all run and blurred together—&c &c &c!

If therefore there is not henceforth some improvement in the above respects as regards my contributions, I shall take it for granted that (as the old proverb has it) *unfeed* or *p[r]offered* service *stinks*.[4] In other words, I shall have my answer.

C.H.

---

[1] The date and recipient given to this draft letter are inferential: see n. 3.

[2] CH had long complained of newspaper compositors: e.g., Letters 3, 43 and 160.

[3] This line appears in CH's essay 'The Poet's Moon' (serialised in *Sydney Times*, 4, 11 and 18 June 1864); a clipping is in A87-1, p. 350, marked with CH's handwritten correction 'sufficing'. (An undated MS version of the essay that also contains the line is in A87-2, p. 657; Holt dates it to 1855–58. An earlier version, lacking the line, appeared in *PA*, 4 February 1854, p. 5.) The last issue of *Sydney Times* appeared on 25 June 1864 (SLNSW catalogue). CH collected his clippings as 'Pieces in Verse & Prose, contributed to the Sydney Times by Charles Harpur'; he affixed them to folded blue leaves of paper allowing room for corrections (A87-1, p. 333). His handwritten correction, one of many, proves only a post-mid-1864 date for this round of revision and therefore for the letter – in which CH quotes an old proverb that Chaucer also quotes (see n. 4). Chaucer would have been on his mind in November 1866: his essay 'Chaucer's Poetry' was so dated when published in *SMH* on 26 December 1866, p. 2. (For an earlier version of the essay, see *PA*, 13 May 1854, p. 6.) A fair copy that became a working manuscript (C381, pp. 7–25) bears handwritten revisions that *SMH* incorporates. On p. 25, CH drafted – as an afterthought, on the angle – a 'Memo': 'The printer is particularly requested to adhere strictly to copy in the annexed article,—especially as regards all the italicised paused and accentuated passages,—as much of its critical nicety will depend upon his doing so.' Letter 112 expresses CH's frustration at the outcome: *SMH* has many deviations from his italics and stress marks. The letter is evidently linked to his campaign to ensure correct typesetting of his work, mentioned in Letter 115 of 29 January 1867. A provisional date of early 1867 is therefore preferred and the recipient taken to be *SMH*.

[4] CH has misspelt *proffered* – i.e., offered as a gift. The proverb was old when Chaucer wrote his *Canterbury Tales* in the late 14th century: ''Ful sooth it is that swich profred servyse / Stynketh, as witnessen thise olde wyse' – 'The Canon's Yeoman's Tale', lines 513–14.

113. Charles Harpur to Henry Kendall, 19 January 1867

Text: Kendall papers, ML C199

Euroma, 19th Jan/67

My dear Kendall,

How happens it that you have not written to me at all since your official promotion? Of which, however, I wish you joy.

The things I send you for publication in the Herald, are evidently inserted therein as it were with a grudge, or unwillingly. It would almost seem as if Fairfax were ashamed to have them for nothing, and yet had not the heart to pay anything for them. If therefore, when you receive this, my last paper (on Chaucer) is not printed, will you be good enough to get it back: and let me know that you have done so?[5]

So far as to all publication in the papers, it is my intention to "shut up",[6] for the next five or six years: when I hope to be able to put forth at my own expense a volume of three or four hundred pages, trusting thereafter to time for the sale of the edition.[7]

If there is any subject on which you have anything particular to say to me, write in reply to this, and at length—as it is likely that this is nearly the last letter I shall write to you or to anybody else (except on matters of pure business) for several years to come: for I intend to withdraw myself entirely from the outward world for a long time: and during which time I shall attend solely, first to my farm, & secondly, to a subject which I have chosen for an *Epic*.[8] I am engaged just now in founding a poem of considrable extent upon a Rabbinical tradition—the Widow of Hebron:[9] and which is turning out quite to my satisfaction; magnificent as an oriental palace and terrible as a thunder-storm.

[5] See p. 190 n. 3.

[6] CH would not keep to this resolve: his next contribution appeared in *SMH* in March. He 'wanted the recognition afforded by featuring in the local press, yet railed against its consequences: reliance on editors for whom he had little respect, and the temptation to create lesser works for a popular general readership...Harpur's misfortune was his virtual dependence on this mode of publication' – Ackland, p. 107.

[7] Kendall had suggested this approach in late 1865 (Letter 97); CH was attracted to the idea of a volume 'for the English critics', but pleaded poverty (Letter 104).

[8] See Letter 115.

[9] I.e., 'The Witch of Hebron', a seven-part blank-verse romance. In an early draft (ML A90 of 1867), CH amended the title from 'The Widow of Hebron' to 'The Witch of Hebron. A Rabbinical Legend' (h689-ab). The poem when completed was offered to *Empire* (Rawling, p. 300), while a later version (h689-ac) intended for *Colonial Monthly* was in type when withdrawn (see ML A87-2, p. 433, of 1867; and p. 215 n. 8). The work did not see publication until *Poems* of 1883 (h689-af). CH's source was the story of the Widow of Hebron as recounted to Rabbi Joseph, son of Jehoshaphat, from the series 'Traditions of the Rabbins' by Irish writer George Croly (1780–1860) in *Blackwood's Edinburgh Magazine*, 23.207 (April 1833), pp. 628–50 [pp. 630–40; online at Google Books]; the piece was at one time mis-attributed to Thomas De Quincey.

The only two things—a couple of Satires—full of scorn and wildfire, that I shall publish before shutting up, and which shall shortly appear, it would not be prudent for you to know anything about[1]—that is of course prior to their publication.

I see the Government have given us poor devils—the sacked Gold Commissioners, a trifle of compensation for their loss of office.[2] But if the number is so great as I think it is, amongst whom this sum of £1629 is to be apportioned, it is a trifling compensation truly! Well, "Fate & Jenkins"[3] are just now uppermost, and one must only "*grin*."

Yours very truly
Chas: Harpur.

114. Charles Harpur to William Wilkins, 23 January 1867

Text: NSWSA: NRS–2621 [1/741, Vol. 7], ff. 34–34a

Eurobodalla[4] 23rd Janry 1867

Appointment of Mr Blyth[5] as Teacher

Sir,[6]

I have the honor to inform you that the Board of Local Patrons[7] of the

---

[1] Presumably 'A Scamper of Life' (h491h, 1866) was one. Its satire of government jobbers would compromise Kendall if he knew of it in advance.

[2] In December 1866, the Legislative Assembly voted £1629 'compensation for gold commissioners for loss of office' in the additional Estimates for 1867 (*SMH*, 13 December 1866, p. 4): it was restricted to those under 60, few of whom would have been eligible for a superannuation pension (see p. 182 n. 8).

[3] '...forced, conglomerated, crowded onwards, irresistibly impelled by fate and Jenkins [the swineherd]' – Leigh Hunt (attrib.), 'On the Graces and Anxieties of Pig-Driving', in *Companion*, XII (26 March 1828), p. 159 (online at Internet Archive).

[4] Formerly only the locale of CH's and neighbouring farms including early settler William Coman's Eurobodalla (or Urobodalla), the name now applies to a much wider district, the Eurobodalla Shire.

[5] Henry Blyth, teacher at the National School at Nerrigundah and Public School at Eurobodalla. He would be a witness at the burial of CH's son Charley on 4 March 1867, and of CH in 1868.

[6] CH's addressee here ('The Secretary / Council of Education Office') was William Wilkins (1827–92), teacher, educationist and public servant, author and pamphleteer. He was principal of the Model School in Sydney, inspector and superintendent of NSW National Schools, secretary of the Board of National Education and its successor the Council of Education, and 'the one educational theorist in the colony to whom Parkes deferred' (Martin, *Parkes*, p. 224). With the educational reforms of 1880 (which introduced compulsory education and withdrew state aid to denominational schools), Wilkins would head the Department of Public Instruction.

[7] See p. 35 n. 5. CH was secretary of the Patrons Board at Eurobodalla.

School at this place, hitherto under the National Board of Education,[8] has offered the management of the School to Mr Blyth, late of the Nerrigundah National School, and that the School was re-opened on 21st inst. under his management with 23 in attendance, with every prospect of a speedy increase. The re-opening of the School has been delayed in consequence of our acceptance of an application made to us some weeks ago; but after waiting a reasonable time and hearing no further news of the applicant, we considered that the interests of the School should no longer be jeopardized by keeping the re-opening thereof in abeyance.

It is with regret that I have to inform you, that with the exception of one family, all the Catholics are keeping back;[9] the children thus withdrawn were all upon the roll of the National School, up to the Christmas vacation last past; and have been now taken away by their parents, with the avowed design of breaking up the Public School at this place, and getting up instead thereof, a private one amongst themselves. And they have been partly moved to this, they say, by the advice of their priest, the Revd Mr Birch of Moruya,[10] who has told them that if they could so contrive matters and secure an attendance of about twenty pupils at this private school, he should be able, under the 13th clause of the "Public Schools Act," to get them eventually some assistance from the Government.[11] But I doubt not that as soon as they see the uselessness of setting up an opposition School, where a public school is already in existence, they will patronize the public one.

I have the honor to remain
Sir
Your most obedient servant
Chas: Harpur.
Hon: Sec:

---

[8] Reforms under the *Public Schools Act* of 1866 (30 Vic. No. 22), which became law on 22 December 1866, abolished the two boards responsible for National and Denominational (Church) schools, replacing them with a single Council of Education which would fund, administer and staff all schools, supervise the training of teachers, set curriculum and standards, prescribe texts and inspect schools. National Schools became 'Public' Schools.

[9] The Catholic clergy strongly opposed elements of the Public Schools Bill in 1866, and opposition continued after passage of the Act, particularly over Council inspectors and the prescription of textbooks – see Martin, *Parkes*, pp. 225–30.

[10] The Reverend Patrick Birch (1828–1914), Irish-born Catholic pastor at Moruya, 1859–70. He built churches and schools at several locations in NSW including St Mary's, Moruya, and St Patrick's, Eurobodalla.

[11] Section 13 of the *Public Schools Act* of 1866 provided that in remote and thinly populated districts where no public school existed, the Council of Education could grant assistance to a private school even though its enrolments were fewer than the 25 minimum otherwise stipulated.

115. Charles Harpur to Henry Kendall, 29 January 1867

Text: Kendall papers, ML C199

Euroma, 29 Jan /67.

My dear Kendall,

I have got your last note.[1] The local post office knows nothing of the papers you refer to: so if you can get a back number from Fairfax, you will oblige me by sending it: as I wish to see how far the printer has followed 'copy'—whether faithfully or not.[2]

The Rabbinical Legend, the Witch of Hebron,[3] is still turning out well. I have it about half done. It will be a piece of considerable extent—and of an epical character—but it is not *the* Epic, that I meant,[4] and which I intend before a great while to settle down to: of which more at some future time.

I will take your advice as to continuing my contributions to the Herald for at least some time to come; and enclose with this the only thing that I happen just now to have perfectly copied. I will send the second part soon enough for it to appear in an issue or two after the first.[5] I find that I have copied both parts—and so enclose both.

It is seriously my intention of 'shutting up' in the manner I mentioned to you,[6] before a great while:—but I will still keep a door open to *you*—and to you *only*.

Yours truly
Chas: Harpur.

Of the Satires[7] anon:

---

[1] Not extant, but it must have post-dated CH's letter of 19 January to him (Letter 113) complaining he does not write. Before correction, MS continued: 'The local post offices ['pr'*deleted*] know'.

[2] See Letter 112 and notes. The present letter suggests he routinely retained a copy in manuscript against which to check, since the submitted manuscripts would likely have been discarded by the newspaper once typeset.

[3] See p. 191 n. 9.

[4] This confirms that the prospective 'Epic' mentioned in Letter 113 was *not* the 'Witch of Hebron'.

[5] Probably 'A Storm in the Mountains', much revised and augmented since *Empire* printed it in 1856 (h571a). Parts I and II (h571d) appeared together in *SMH*, 14 March 1867, p. 2.

[6] I.e., in Letter 113.

[7] Ibid.

116. Charles Harpur to Henry Kendall, 10 April 1867

Text: Kendall papers, NLA MS 9368

Euroma, 10th April /67

My dear Kendall,

I got your last, dated 30th March[8] last. I duly recd the Herald & the enclosed slip containing the "Storm".[9]

The 3rd of the "Autumnal Leaves"[10] would, as you say, stand very well for poor Dan Deniehy. In fact, I had a case very like his in my mind's eye, when I wrote it.

I don't think I told you before, that I had buried my poor boy on the top of Mount Euroma,[11] within the boundaries of my own land: so that at Euroma "we are *seven*" still.[12]

I am about having a head-stone placed at the grave;[13] and I wish you to tell me how you like the Inscription which I give upon the last page, and which this headstone is to bear.

I am very lonely; and actually feel many years older than I did five weeks ago. Poor Mrs Harpur is also terribly cut up; and Washington[14] has grown pale and thin, and has become strangely solemnised in his whole bearing,—even to the tones of his voice. His brother's untimely death at his side will no doubt hang over him like a cloud for ever. Ah! in the shape of woe, what cannot one fatal moment bring to us poor sons of time!

---

[8] This has not survived.

[9] See p. 194 n. 5.

[10] A series of six poems of loss, hope and resignation (in *SMH*, 7 May 1867, p. 5.) The first (h020a) was new; the rest had appeared elsewhere under different titles or none. The third (h022e) had originally been published in *PA*, 28 May 1851, p. 4 as 'An Epitaph' (h022a).

[11] CH's son Charley had been killed by the accidental discharge of his own gun while hunting with his brother Washington near Euroma on 2 March 1867. After an inquest (reported in *Empire*, 12 March 1867, p. 5, quoting *Moruya Examiner*), Charley was buried on 4 March on the hill overlooking the Harpur homestead. 'Mount Euroma' would also be known locally as 'Harpur's Hill'. In due course, both CH and Mary Harpur would join Charley there.

[12] CH's footnote to 'The Night Bird' (h334b; *PA*, 6 May 1854, p. 6) describes the family of CH's own childhood in Windsor: ' "We *were* Seven"—and our family in its earlier years was pre-eminently a happy one. In fact, I have never since seen a greater degree of domestic peace and unity than was presented by my Father's household for many prosperous years.' In William Wordsworth's poem 'We Are Seven', the little maiden insists 'Seven boys and girls are we' though 'Two of us in the church-yard lie': from *Lyrical Ballads, with A Few Other Poems* (London: J. & A. Arch, 1798; online at Internet Archive).

[13] If CH placed the stone he describes here, it is lost. The cast-iron memorial tablet over Charley reads 'Sacred to the Memory of Charles C. Harpur Died March 2nd 1867'.

[14] Washington Harpur (1851–1938), the eldest son. His younger sister Mary Araluen recalled that the shock almost unbalanced his mind for a time, adding 'From this time, my father was a changed man. Instead of being kindly and loving, he became stern and silent, and as children do not understand grief we grew to be rather in awe of him' ('Daughter's Memories').

The late flood[1] has nearly ruined me for the present—having destroyed upon me about £300 worth of corn, potatoes, hay, and other produce, together with fencing: one whole sideline[2] will have to be nearly renewed. I am afraid also, that I have had a couple of horses swept away: for they are no where to be seen since—Charley's mare—the one he rode on his death-day—being one of them. But for all these things there is no help.

Yours ever
Chas Harpur

Sacred
to the Memory
of
Charles Chidley Harpur,
who departed this life on the
2nd March 1867,
Aged 13 years.

Human Affection would for ever have held him
Imprisoned with herself amid the Appearances of Earth:
But Divine Love had higher claims upon his Spirit,
And called him early to the Realities of Heaven.

The Lord gave, and the Lord hath taken away: Blessed be the name of the Lord.[3]

117. Henry Kendall to Charles Harpur, 30 April 1867

Text: Kendall papers, ML C199

Colonial Secretary's Office. Sydney 30th April 1867.

My dear Harpur,

It has been raining here for the last month, and there is no appearance of its clearing up. I am afraid to make a guess as to your condition at Euroma.[4] It is to be hoped however that you have escaped the worst of the weather.

I believe your poems are in type,[5] and I know they will appear in the course

---

[1] A series of severe floods on the Tuross River in the autumn and winter of 1867 – as elsewhere along the east coast of Australia – drowned several people, did great damage to crops, and swept away fences and topsoil, including part of the road along the river at Euroma. For flood reports, sourced from *Moruya Examiner*, see *Empire*, 2 April 1867, p. 3 and *SMH*, 2 April 1867, p. 5; and *Empire*, 1 July 1867, p. 8, from *Moruya Messenger*.

[2] I.e., a fence along a side boundary line.

[3] Thus Job, upon learning that his flocks and servants had been taken and his sons and daughters killed. 'In all this Job sinned not, nor charged God foolishly' – Job 1.21–2.

[4] See n. 1, above.

[5] 'Autumnal Leaves': see p. 195 n. 10.

of a day or so. There has been the usual delay about them, but, from what has been said to me, I am under the impression that the thing was unavoidable.

"The Death of Shilock"[6] is with me yet. Why "Sh*i*lock"? I do not think it would be wise to print the piece notwithstanding its excellence. You are evidently in doubt yourself, and therefore I have the less fear in stating my impression. At all events your reply will decide.

The epitaph for your son Charles[7] is very much to the purpose. It has that best quality, simplicity about it.

The more I look at your Autumnal Leaves (for I have taken a draft of them) the more I like them. The 3rd, and the last, go to the heart.[8] I must wind up here. My pen is of the vilest description, and my sisters are teasing me[9] by knocking about with the dinner plates.

Yours Ever
Henry Kendall.

118. Charles Harpur to Henry Kendall, 4 May 1867

Text: Kendall papers, ML C199

Euroma, via Bodalla, 4th May /67

My dear Kendall,

Yours of the 30th ulto has just come to hand. Truly my papers hang fire at the Herald office[10] in a strange way. That such things should have to beg their way into print in so hard a fashion is a fact I think which is peculiarly antipodean.—I am sorry that your mother is so unwell.—With this, I send you an Essay on 'Milton's Poetry'[11] for publication through the usual channel: for if sent in any other way it would certainly never see the light through the columns of the *Herald*. You can hold over till afterwards the Death of Shylock:[12]—(Sh*i*lock is an error which you will be good enough to correct.)

---

[6] CH's new scene for Shakespeare's *The Merchant of Venice* (IV.1): the soliloquy and suicide of Shylock following the court's decision that he forfeit half his property, convert to Christianity and bequeath his estate to his daughter Jessica. Unpublished until 1984, the poem exists in three manuscript forms of 1866–67 (ML A93, A87-1 and A87-2 – see h089). For the 'Shilock' spelling, see Letter 91 ('orthography').

[7] See Letter 116.

[8] For the third, see p. 195 n. 10. The last poem (h025c) had appeared in *PA*, 6 May 1854, p. 6 as 'Elegiac Verses'.

[9] Kendall and his three sisters (Christina Jane, Edith Emily and Mary Josephine) were still living in Randall Terrace: see p. 180 n. 1.

[10] 'Autumnal Leaves' would appear in *SMH*, 7 May 1867, p. 5, the last of CH's verse the newspaper would publish before his death.

[11] 'Milton's Poetry', in *SMH*, 5 June 1867, p. 2.

[12] See Letter 117. The piece did not appear in a journal and may never have been offered.

Yes: you can show my letter to Parkes[1]—and tell him farther by authority of this; that he would do me a good turn just now, by expediting the payment of whatever the Govt mean to allow me as compensation for the loss of my late office:[2] for I have lost nearly all that would have kept me above the immediate want of it. Luckily I do not owe £10 in the world—but then I have next to nothing to repair my losses and recommence with.

Can you tell me whether the "Belmain Reporter",[3] a paper which my brother Joseph had something to do with, is still in existence or not. The first number was sent to me, but I have received no *second*: though it should have reached a good many numbers now, if still alive.

Do you think I have friends enough in Sydney, to warrant my venturing upon a publication?—that is, of course, "by Subscription"; for it would never pay to venture upon otherwise than so.

Yours ever
Chas: Harpur

119. Henry Kendall to Charles Harpur, 8 May 1867

Text: Kendall papers, ML C199

Colonial Secretary's Office May 8th 1867.

My dear Harpur

I send the "Herald", containing the "Autumnal Leaves", by today's post. I wrote to you the other morning[4] and in the letter referred to, I said something of your fragment on Shylock—not "Shilock". Have you received the note in question? Will you kindly acknowledge the receipt of the Herald?

I have received your note of the 30th ultimo[5] which reached me about 5 minutes ago. I will take the liberty to shew it to Mr Halloran who has apparently a warm regard for you. He spoke very highly of the "Autumnal Leaves".

If you should like to have another copy of the "Herald" let me know. I will

---

[1] Probably Letter 116, about Charley's burial and the flood on the Tuross that has 'nearly ruined me'.

[2] See p. 192 n. 2.

[3] *Balmain Reporter*, short-lived suburban newspaper (one of Sydney's earliest) established by Catholic politician-journalist J. G. O'Connor, edited by CH's brother Joseph, and only published 2 February – May 1867 (*Balmain Association News Sheet*, 25.191, May 1990, p. 2); and see Letter 120, reporting the paper was 'dead'.

[4] See Kendall's Letter 117 and CH's reply, Letter 118.

[5] This has not survived.

do my best with Halloran and Parkes in the matter you speak of.[6] You *know* how I feel for you.

Yours Ever
Henry Kendall

I have written this against time.[7]

120. Henry Kendall to Charles Harpur, 18 May 1867

Text: Kendall papers, ML C199

Colonial Secretary's Office Sydney, 18th May 1867.

My dear Harpur,

Yours containing the admirable "Essay on Milton"[8] in hand. The "Herald" containing the "Autumnal Leaves" was posted to you nine or ten days ago.[9] Will you drop me a line or two acknowledging the receipt of that journal. The paper on Milton has been forwarded to Mr Fairfax for publication— Never bother your head about the trash in the Sydney Mail. The writer, "A Fogie",[10] is a miserably bitter poetling of the name of Hutchinson. For the last three years he has scarcely let a week pass without a wretched attack upon me in "Punch".[11] His chronic virulence only amuses the reader. Dont think of him. Your reputation with the right people is impregnable, and it must be imperishable.

I shewed your letter, through Halloran, to Parkes; and your case is now before the Executive. I saw the address from the diggers and your private note

---

[6] Presumably an issue raised in CH's 'note' to Kendall of 30 April. It may have involved a request to Parkes as Colonial Secretary either to rethink CH's dismissal as Assistant Gold Commissioner or to expedite compensation for his retrenchment.

[7] Against a (presumably postal) deadline.

[8] See p. 197 n. 11.

[9] See Letter 119.

[10] *Sydney Mail*, 6 April 1867, p. 3 carried an article by 'A Fogie' entitled 'Thoughts in Tatters. No. 3.—A Bilious Attack', a sarcastic 'kick' at the pretensions of colonial poets – CH (with quotes from 'A Storm in the Mountains'), Kendall, Joseph Sheridan Moore, Halloran and the anonymous author of the doggerel couplets gracing the advertisements of butcher Philip McCarroll. 'A Fogie' was Frank Hutchinson (1836?–1916), journalist and poet.

[11] The satirical journal *Sydney Punch* (see p. 162 n. 4). Hutchinson was a regular (anonymous) contributor in the early years, as were William Bede Dalley, Daniel Deniehy, George Barton, Charles de Boos, Henry Halloran and Kendall himself. There was scant solidarity or mutual respect among *Punch* contributors, and colonial poets and poetry were a favourite target: 'proximity bred jealousy and spite between literary hacks, and the magazine's policy of authorial independence, whereby writers were responsible for their work from its inception through to page proofs, allowed malicious passions ample scope' (Ackland, p. 110).

to Parkes a few days ago.[1]

The stamps on your enclosure were sufficient. The "Balmain Reporter" is dead.[2] About your idea of publishing a volume,[3] more anon.

Yours Ever
Henry Kendall.

121. Charles Harpur to Henry Kendall, 26 May 1867

Text: Kendall papers, ML 3796/2

Sunday 26th May /67

My dear Kendall,

The "Herald" containing the Autumnal Leaves has come safely to hand.

The piece I now enclose you[4] to be sent in the same way for publication in the Herald, is one that I was obliged to write, *or else go mad.* It was actually, as it purports to have been, *poured out over the grave of my poor Boy.* And after the paper on Milton has appeared, you can either give them it *first,* or the Death of Shylock[5]—at your own discretion. Excuse the shortness and haste of this—as I expect company to day—Caswell the Police Magistrate[6] of Moruya and some of his friends. I expect them every moment.

I got your last note, and thank you for what you have done in the matter you wot of.

Write to me at once, if you at all can; for I am very lonely.

Yours ever
Chas: Harpur.

---

[1] The 'private note' may be the one mentioned in Letter 119, and see p. 199 n. 6. For 'your letter', see p. 198 n. 1. The diggers' 'address' arose from a meeting of businessmen and miners at Nerrigundah on 12 February 1866. They adopted a petition calling on the Colonial Secretary to retain CH as Gold Commissioner there, and to effect the required savings by making him police magistrate and by dismissing the Chinese interpreter at Nerrigundah and the Clerk of Petty Sessions at Moruya (report in *Empire,* 22 February 1866, p. 8).

[2] See Letter 118.

[3] Although the recent floods had been a severe financial setback, the prospect of receiving some financial redress from government could have led to the revival of this hope.

[4] CH began 'Obituary Lines' for his son Charley on 22 May 1867 (h298a, in ML A87-2), revising it several times. It did not appear in *SMH*: see p. 201 n. 12.

[5] CH would ask Kendall for its return, unpublished, in Letter 127.

[6] See Letter 86 and p. 156 n. 3.

122. Henry Kendall to Charles Harpur, 2 June 1867

Text: Kendall papers, ML C199

Enmore Sunday 2nd June 1867

My dear Harpur

Yours of the 26th ultimo in hand. The poem on Charley[7] is strikingly beautiful, and I shall send it to Mr Fairfax immediately after the appearance of the paper on Milton. Tell me when you hear the results of the "Executive" proceedings in your case.[8] Halloran cannot be pumped. I saw Maddock[9] the other day, and he told me that he did not intend to trouble you for the balance of his account until you were well able to meet him. He said he was satisfied with the tone of your letters. Of course I was *dark* as to your prospects. Did I tell you that Halloran and Stenhouse were greatly taken by the beauty of the "Autumnal Leaves"? I have seen and spoken to Dr Woolley's successor— Dr Badham.[10] He reminds me of the parched up grammarian in Browning's poem.[11] I think however that I shall like him on the whole. Can I publish some of your papers and poems in the Empire?[12] There would be less delay in that quarter.

You must not give way to your sorrow as indicated by your last poem I wish I could see you face to face in order to impart to you in some measure the equivalent sympathy intellectual and otherwise, which you have not known since the death of poor Deniehy. I never, or very rarely, see Mr Parkes now. Mr Halloran has lost his eldest son—a young man in his 25th year. The father is terribly cut up.[13] It pains me to hear of your losses. May I show your note[14] to

---

[7] See p. 200 n. 4.

[8] See Letter 118. The Executive Council advised the Governor on matters of state. At this point it comprised the Governor Sir John Young and Cabinet Ministers including the Premier and Attorney-General James Martin, Chief Secretary (or Colonial Secretary) Henry Parkes, Colonial Treasurer Geoffrey Eagar and Secretary for Lands John Bowie Wilson.

[9] See p. 153 n. 10.

[10] See p. 127 n. 11. Woolley was drowned returning to Australia from England in January 1866. His successor was English classical scholar Charles Badham (1813–84).

[11] The departed scholar of 'A Grammarian's Funeral' by Robert Browning – in *Men and Women*, vol. II (London: Chapman and Hall, 1855; 1910 reprint online at Internet Archive).

[12] The daily rival to *SMH*, since 1859 owned and run by Samuel Bennett and printer William Hanson. Kendall's query suggests a change of heart about 'the worst foe Australian Literature has' (Letter 78; and see CH's reply, Letter 79). 'Obituary Lines' appeared in *Empire*, 26 July 1867, p. 5, but the accommodation with Bennett (if any) was brief.

[13] Halloran's son Henry Walter Halloran, manager of the Oriental Bank, Grenfell, died there on 22 April 1867 suffering 'affection of the lungs'. The father's grief is palpable in his later 'Wandering Thoughts', *SMH*, 4 February 1876, p. 3.

[14] Not identified – this may be the letter of 26 May 1867 (Letter 121) enclosing the elegy for Charley.

Parkes? My mother's health[1] has hindered me from answering you before this date; and *now* I am writing against time.

They work me like a [n——][†] here.

Yours Ever
Henry Kendall.

When the poems appear, I will forward the paper as usual. I told Halloran of your losses. He expressed his regret, but nothing more. Possibly he was bitten too deeply by his own sorrow to be able to think beyond it.

H. K.

123. Charles Harpur to Nicol Drysdale Stenhouse, 17 July 1867

Text: Stenhouse papers, ML A101

Euroma, Bodalla July 17th 1867

My dear Mr. Stenhouse,

I am too sick[2] to be able to write myself: but I have got Mrs. Harpur to hold the pen for me. I enclose you a document which is the second to a similar effect that I have rec. during the last two years from two different attorneys.

The man Parker[3] who makes the claims came into this district about two years ago to practice as an attorney. Having a slight job[4] I employed him to do it, paying by agreement two guineas for it which was to include the registration

---

[†] MS spells out the word (see CHCA); the present publisher required the substitution, *eds.*

[1] In 1879 Kendall confided to Halloran that for the last 30 years his mother Melinda Kendall (1815–93) had been 'a confirmed dipsomaniac'. 'Knowing what dipsomania is I will not send her money. There is no hope for her outside restraint'; and 'During the weary time I was in Government service I had to keep her quiet by bribing her with brandy every night…she is too insane to be responsible for her actions' (Ackland, pp. 151, 277, citing ML 3775/9–11); for a contrary view, see Adrian Mitchell, *Where Shadows Have Fallen: The Unhappy Descent of Henry Kendall* (Mile End, SA: Wakefield Press, 2020). Melinda would outlive her son. A teacher and a newspaper poet, she would acknowledge her demons: 'I've tried to drown in lethean drain / This ruthless voice; but all in vain; / It comes with ten-fold force again, / And brings remorse to swell the strain—/ A wasted life! A wasted life!' ('A Wasted Life', *Illawarra Mercury*, 8 April 1884, p. 4).

[2] During July–September 1867 CH was 'almost entirely confined to my bed, by low fever and the emaciation consequent upon it…brought upon me by much grief and many losses' – his job, Charley's death and the floods of 1867 (Letter 126). In fact, he was in the late stages of tuberculosis.

[3] Edward Parker (1812–73), English-born solicitor, admitted to the bar in Sydney in 1849. By 1854 he had 'ceased to practice' but was calling himself a solicitor at Bathurst in 1859 and at Cooma and Bombala in the 1860s.

[4] On 8 December 1864 CH transferred his 100 acre conditional purchase – i.e., the home farm Euroma – to his eldest son Washington. The name 'Edwd. Parker Attorney' appears against this transaction in the Register of Conditional Purchases 1862–1883, Crown Land Agent, Moruya (NSWSA: NRS 9024, Lands Department, Reel 2131). The land would be transferred back to CH on 18 June 1867.

and all other expences. This document contained about a hundred words, with a list of perhapse two hundred more. Nor did he ever complete this in a proper manner, as subsequent events proved, for it was found to be improperly registered and consequently not legal tight. The man never did any other work for me of any kind, nor made any claim upon me until he had to fly from the district having victimized almost every second person in it. Then, from Sydney, he made this trumped up claim for work done &c. &c. through an attorney named Milford.[5] However of this I was inclined to take no notice. Nay, not being short of means I was curious to see whether a man could be robbed in a land of law and in the name of law. But the thing apparently was let drop; for I heard no more about it. But now two years afterwards when this Parker is I believe undergoing imprisonment[6] for making away with a clients money this claim is renewed through another law attorney. In the event of their consummating this legal robbery now the difference to me would be this, that so meansless am I and down smitten by losses of all kind that they would have in satisfaction of their claim to sell from under me the very bed upon which I am at this moment lying sick, Under these circumstances my dear Mr Stenhouse I wish you to call upon the Chief Justice[7] and state my case to him, asking him how a man is to be protected from legal dodges made as it were in the dar[k] through his Court; and why if any just claim had existed against [me] it would not have been compulsory on the claimant to sue me for it through the proper Court—the Court of my district;[8] and not get it by [default by the smuggling?] it through the Supreme Court; for surely the Chief Just[ice] must have some just power over the practices of his Court.

Trusting you
will attend to this case for me
I remain my dear [...]
Yours truly
Chas Harpur

P.S. All this man did for me is on record in the Supreme Court; and must be open to inspection. Forgive me for troubling you my dear Sir, with my troubles.

---

[5] Probably Henry Milford, solicitor, of 267 George-street.

[6] Parker was gaoled in Sydney for three months for theft of clothing and silverware in 1867; he died at Darlinghurst lockup on 7 December 1873: see *Empire*, 6 December 1867, p. 5; *SMH*, 14 December 1867, p. 5.

[7] Sir Alfred Stephen, C.B. (1802–94). CH had sent Stephen a copy of 'The Tower of the Dream' (h642g) in 1865 marked 'with the Author's respects' (ML C378).

[8] Claims for sums of £200 or less would normally be dealt with in a District Court operating under the *District Courts Act* of 1858. The next sitting of the Court nearest to CH was gazetted for Braidwood on 15 November 1867. The remainder of the sentence is obscured by conservator's tape in MS and is only partly legible.

124. Charles Harpur to Nicol Drysdale Stenhouse, 12 August 1867

Text: Stenhouse papers, ML A100

Euroma, via Bodalla 12 Aug /67

My dear Sir,

I recd your letter enclosing Parker's[1] discharge. What 'oracle' you worked upon that beast of prey, of course I do not know; but it seems to have been a very effective one, and has done me a very great service.

I have some expectations from the Government. They are, I believe, after all, going to give me as compensation for the loss of my office as Gold Commissioner, what common constables are entitled to on their discharge as supernumerary—that is, one month's pay for ever[y] year of service—or about £140 in all: and so soon as this money is paid over to me, I will send you by cheque the four guineas you advanced to Parker with much gratitude.

I was sorry to learn from your letter that your health had not been good latterly, and that you still had bad eyes. For myself, I am still very ill, though now able to write; nor do I think that I shall ever be right well again. But I do not much mind this now. In the words of Browning[2] I have had "enough for one", and begin to look grave-ward with a grim satisfaction.

I remain, yours very truly,
Chas: Harpur.

P. S. Mrs Harpur is just now in Sydney, and will, I think, call upon you.

C.H.

125. Charles Harpur to Henry Kendall, 14 August 1867

Text: Kendall papers, ML C199

Euroma, 14 Augt / 67

My dear Kendall,

If you have by this time recovered as I hope you have, I wish you to perform a service for me, the last of the kind which I shall ever impose upon you. I

---

[1] Evidently, Stenhouse promptly paid Parker: see Letter 123.
[2] Robert Browning's 'Old Pictures in Florence': 'There remaineth a rest for the people of God: / And I have had troubles enough, for one.'

have lately sent several things for publication in the Empire;[3] and which, as they have been taken no notice of whatever, seem to be rejected by the great Light of said Journal. For what reason I cannot make out; as they are all of my very best. But what I want you now to do for me—the last job of the kind I will ever ask you to do—is to call on Mr Sam Bennett,[4] and get from him (if they are rejected) the several M.S. And in doing this, you will only do what I premised with him you would do on my behalf in that event. This job done for me—I shall have done for some years with the whole of you Sydneyites in all matters literary. Some years hence the time may be riper; when those fellows like Fairfax and our friend Sam, who now stand as kings in the high places of the Press, shall probably have "done their dying" and gone to Hell—fellows that are not only not *gentlemen*, but not *human*.

Mrs Harpur is at present in Sydney. She is at her sister's—Mrs T. Parnell,[5] Gainsboro Villas, Paddington, nr Sydney: and I doubt not she would for my sake, be very glad to see you, if you could find time to call upon her. I am here at home with my boys—with those that remain to me, I mean.[6] I am still very bad—and do not think I shall ever again be very much better. Still, I am content. All this would be as nothing to me, if I but found the men and things about less of brutes and less brutal. Still, never mind. I shall live long enough. So long as I have any essential thing to do I can not die. No man can.

Let me [hear] from you at once in reply to this—if only to let me know that you are well again. Let me know exactly the result of your call upon Bennett on my account: as I mean then to write a final note to Master Sam,[7] that perhaps will astonish him.

Do not fail to call upon Mrs Harpur (for my sake, if not on any other account), if you can. I am sure you will thereby give her a pleasure,—call therefore.

My Witch of Hebron[8] is finished—was finished before I fell sick—all but copying the 7th or last part. This poem I offered to publish part by part in the Empire as soon as I found myself well enough to copy it fairly: and in making the offer to our Sam I told him that the Poem in the very nature of

---

[3] CH had written to Bennett *c*. June–July 1867 offering to become a regular contributor (see Letter 126). *Empire* printed 'Obituary Lines', 26 July 1867, p. 5, but nothing more during CH's lifetime. He offered and perhaps sent parts of 'The Witch of Hebron' (see later in this letter).

[4] See p. 143 n. 6.

[5] Mary Harpur's sister Isabella Sophia Parnell, née Doyle (1829–87), wife of grazier Thomas Liverpool Parnell. Gainsboro (or Gainsborough) Villas were a pair of houses on the corner of John-street and Old South Head-road (now Oxford Street) Paddington, opposite Moore Park.

[6] Washington (16) and Harold (11); Charley had been killed in a shooting accident six months before. The girls, Ada (10) and Mary Araluen (6) may have been with their mother in Sydney.

[7] Letter 126.

[8] See p. 191 n. 9.

its subject was highly sensational—and therefore very suitable to the present race of newspaper readers as I understand them. But Sam's ear seems to have been as deaf as that of the adder to the voice of the literary charmer.[1]

Write at once—if you are able—and believe me yours ever truly

Chas: Harpur.

P. S. My damned liver has pulled me up all at once.

Benedicta Look for dates[2]

Maranoa

Monday Tuesday Moment[3]

126. Charles Harpur to Samuel Bennett, September 1867[4]

Text: ML A87-2

Euroma, via Bodalla September, 1867.

Sir,

More than two month ago, I wrote to you, offering to become a constant contributor to your paper[5] upon what I myself considered terms merely nominal—viz: that for these contributions you should give me a "gratis" number of the Journal, and just such other payment as in your liberality you might be able to afford me. These were my whole terms. Subsequently, I wrote another note to you saying that supposing, whether you could accede to my whole terms or not, you would at least send me the "gratis" number

---

[1] Snake traditionally believed to be deaf: 'The wicked are...like the deaf adder that stoppeth her ear; / Which will not hearken to the voice of charmers, charming never so wisely' (Psalm 58.3–5).

[2] Annotation at top of the first page of MS, in an unknown hand. It may be connected with the serialised novel 'Benedicta' by 'Alethea', identified as Clarinda Sarah ('Menie') Parkes (1839–1915), daughter of Sir Henry. 'Benedicta' ran in 20 instalments in *Sydney Mail*, 8 June – 19 October 1867.

[3] Annotations in unknown hands, perhaps the jottings and scribblings of young Kendalls.

[4] Rawling (pp. 302–4) argues that this letter was sent to Kendall to be handed to Bennett, but that Kendall managed to persuade CH not to take this step (see Letter 151), returning the letter to him (see Letter 130). It has been preserved, with the unstamped envelope, in ML C376, pp. 382–9. Mary Harpur would tell Parkes (Letter 151) that this was the only letter by CH she possessed. A draft of the present letter survives in ML A87-2; its leaves were separated when it was bound. The first two pages appear at pp. 716 and 715 and the remainder at pp. 769–70 (in *Suppl. Letters*). CH's earlier letters to Bennett have not survived, though he told Kendall (Letter 125) that he had offered 'The Witch of Hebron' to *Empire* to be published in parts.

[5] Bennett had recently established *Evening News*, but CH more likely meant the established *Empire*.

of the Journal in payment for my matter—or at *the least* those numbers of it which might from time to time contain any contributions of mine—that supposing this I had continued my communications. And in this last note I took occasion to inform you that the reason I had been unable to copy some parts of a particular poem which I had promised to send you, was, that for the last three months I had been almost entirely confined to my bed, by low fever and the emaciation consequent upon it—and that this low fever itself had been brought upon me by much grief and many losses.[6] Now this circumstance alone, one would think, was of a kind to awaken some little sympathy in the breast of any man. But let all that pass:—to quote Burns:

> "I ask no kindness at thy hands,
> Since thou hast none to give:"[7]

—a fact, I think, which in this affair you have made very manifest.

It is now, I say, more than two months since I first wrote to you—and even if this first note had by any chance gone astray, my second was so far a restatement of its contents as to demand some notice from you as to the matter of both. Had you indeed, sent me the "gratis" number of your paper which I had bargained for, or even a number of it containing some contribution of mine, no other reply would have been absolutely due to me as a matter of common courtesy, or required as a matter of business. But failing to do either of these things, some form of notice from you, declining my offer, I had a *social right* to look for: nor could I have believed up to this time, that any person whatever who passed for a civilised man—to say nothing about a *gentleman*—could have acted as you have done under the circumstances.

Nay, tell me, whether upon any concievable ground of probability, a clown—a well-meaning clown—would have treated some fellow clown who had offered to deal with him for a *lot of turnips*, with a discourtesy so flagrant as that which you have shown to me?—to *me*, I say, who in character, in intellect, and even in reputation, am greatly *your* superior!

I will only remark farther that in one regard at least I am almost disposed to thank you for your unexampled barbarity, since one sure result from it will be this, that I shall ever henceforth be most feelingly reminded by it of the Scriptural injunction: "Cast not your pearls before swine, lest they turn and rend you."[8]

---

[6] See p. 195 n. 11 and p. 196 n. 1.

[7] The final lines of one of the epigrams against the Earl of Galloway by Robert Burns: 'I ask no kindness at thy hand, / For thou hast none to give.' ('To the same, On the Author Being Threatened with his Resentment').

[8] Matthew 7.6. The King James version reads: 'Give not that which is holy unto the dogs, neither cast ye your pearls before swine, lest they trample them under their feet, and turn again and rend you.'

This letter I have written coolly and deliberately, though it may appear otherwise and though I always remember the great Roman warning *Nescit vox missa reverti*.[1]

Since the above was written, I have received from Mr Kendall a note in which he says that on returning my M.S.S.[2] to him you were pleased to say, that they were not declined from any want of appreciation on your part, but simply because they were unsuitable for publication in a mere newspaper. Now in this (though merely evasive) there is somewhat in the way of amends, but not to my thinking enough. But in one respect you are quite right. To publish such poetry as mine, or like it, in any such paper as the *Empire*, or even the *Herald*, is in some sort to profane it: papers that seem to delight— that seem to find their mission in the publication of the veriest trash. For example, in the last number of your Journal now lying before me, I find a thing given as original poetry[3] in which *sunbeams* are spoken of as "creeping."

> "And sunbeams now and then would *creep*
> The leaves between."

Of course you did not nor could not perceive that no *Poet* could ever write thus—that his insight and the mere logic of his instincts would prevent the possibility of such a thing;—because, I say, such men as you are utterly unfit for the positions they occupy; because, so far as true literature—the literature of *power*—is concerned, you are but as blocks and impediments in the way of all advancement; and should in fact be wholly and always engaged in doing nothing higher than in devising bill-heads and setting up advertisements[4]

I am, Sir
Your &c.
Chas: Harpur.

127. Charles Harpur to Henry Kendall, 8 September 1867

Text: Kendall papers, NLA MS 9368

Euroma via Bodalla, 8 Sept /67

My dear Kendall,

I was sorry to learn from your sister's note that you were still too unwell to write. But it is not my intention to trouble you any more with my literary

---

[1] Loosely, 'A word once spoken can never be recalled', from Horace, *Ars Poetica*, 390.
[2] These probably included 'The Witch of Hebron'.
[3] Poem not identified. It does not appear in *Empire* and may have been in Bennett's new venture the *Evening News*, a daily first issued on 29 July 1867; however there are no extant copies from around this time.
[4] *Bill-head*: paper ruled for a tradesman's bills, having the name, etc. printed at the top. *Setting up*: i.e., in type, for the newspaper.

affairs; and as I do not wish to have any thing farther to do with Sydney Journals of any kind—magazines or newspapers—will you be so good therefore as to return to me by post the M.S.S. you got from Bennett together with the M.S. of the Death of Shylock:[5]—to which end I enclose you 1/- in postage stamps and remain

Yours truly
Chas: Harpur.

P.S. In my determination to have nothing farther to do with any of the Sydney Journals or Journalists[6] I am decided. For example, the flagrant discourtesy of that fellow Bennett alone, will everlastingly and most feelingly remind me of the Scriptural injunction Cast not your pearls before swine, lest they turn and rend you.[7] I have written a letter to Master Bennett which will be the least pleasant one he ever recieved in his life, and which, if he endeavour, after the manner of such cattle, to make a garbled use of it, I will print for distribution amongst my literary *friends*, A letter that must move him—even *him*: albeit I know that a good long packing needle stuck home into the fellow's breech[8] would communicate with his tender feelings much more effectually.—I have read Barton's book,[9] and what think you were my feelings on performing said feat? "What *man*, having a dinner independently of literature, would subject himself by writing, to even the chance of having his claims manipulated by a donkey like this! I'll have done with it: until at least, I have the means, which I shall have before long, of coming forth on my own account in a fair volume of

[5] The 'M.S.S.' probably included 'The Witch of Hebron': see p. 205 n. 3. On 30 April 1867 Kendall had written to CH: ' "The Death of Shilock" [ho89] is with me yet...I do not think it would be wise to print the piece'. See p. 197 n. 12.
[6] CH had renounced newspaper publication before (e.g., Letter 113); but this time, except for one contribution to *Colonial Monthly* (Melbourne) in January 1868, he would keep to his resolve.
[7] See p. 207 n. 8.
[8] *Packing-* or *pack-needle*: a large strong needle used to sew up packs made of tough material. *Breech*: buttocks.
[9] *Either* (1) Barton's anthology *The Poets and Prose Writers of New South Wales* ('1866' but issued January 1867), which included 'The Creek of the Four Graves' and 'Ned Connor' but faulted CH for 'the want of harmony in his verse, and the want of taste displayed in his selection of language' (online at Internet Archive, p. 38) and added: 'Nevertheless he may justly claim the honour of having laid the foundation stone of our national poetry' (p. 48); *or* (2) *Literature in New South Wales* (1866), the first history of Australian literature (online at Internet Archive): 'Mr. Harpur has some true poetry in him. He has written two or three pieces which deserve to live, and will live' (p. 99). Both volumes were commissioned by the NSW Government for the Paris Exhibition of 1867. For Kendall's spirited defence of CH against Barton's strictures, see 'Notes upon Men and Books, No. 2. – G. B. Barton, Charles Harpur, G. R. Morton, and Walt Whitman', in *Freeman's Journal*, 9 December 1871, p. 9. For Barton, see p. 168 n. 3.

some 300 pages—backed if need be by another book[1] of say 100 ditto, which I shall call my slaughter-house for donkeys, and plan of extinguishment for all false lights—all shams."

Yours
C.H.

I have got in the Press here a satire that will astonish some of your big wigs down there. It is by Timon of Tadmor[2]

128. Charles Harpur to Nicol Drysdale Stenhouse, 26 September 1867

Text: Stenhouse papers, ML A100

Euroma, via Bodalla, 26 Sept 1867.

My dear Sir,

I enclose you with many thanks, the four guineas you were so good as to pay for me towards staving off the claim of that man-scandal Parker.[3]

I was glad to learn the other day through Kendall that your health had latterly improved somewhat. My own is better,[4] though yet far from good. But I have much to occupy me, in the way of redeeming past losses,[5] and though I am still unable to do much work myself, I can nevertheless keep up a constant supervision over my "helps."[6]

Believe me,
My dear Sir
Ever & gratefully yours
Chas: Harpur.

---

[1] This is the first indication that CH was considering publishing a separate volume, evidently of satirical verse and prose.

[2] CH himself. Timon was the legendary misanthrope of ancient Athens; the Biblical 'Tadmor in the Wilderness' is the city in the Syrian Desert called Palmyra by the Greeks and Romans. The 'satire' is unidentified, possibly an updated 'Scamper of Life' (e.g., h491h of 1866) in a local newspaper, probably the *Moruya Examiner* or *Moruya Messenger* and taking aim at prominent Sydney identities, political, literary or both.

[3] See p. 202 nn. 3–4 and (re the four guineas) p. 204 n. 1.

[4] See p. 202 n. 2.

[5] The damage to the farm wrought by the floods of autumn and winter 1867.

[6] Farm workers. Mary Araluen Baldwin, née Harpur, remembered farm manager Mr Glover and children's nurse Bella accompanying the family from Araluen in 1863 and being present at CH's deathbed five years later ('Daughter's Memories'). She would tell scholar Cecil Salier that the farm 'was worked by native boys and managed by a Mr Glover, Harpur himself riding each day to and from his office at The Gulph' (C. W. Salier, 'The Life and Writings of Charles Harpur', *RAHS Journal and Proceedings*, 32.2 (1946), pp. 96–7; online via NLA).

129. Charles Harpur to Henry Kendall, 1 October 1867

Text: Kendall papers, ML MSS 3796/2

Euroma. 1 Oct 1867

My dear Kendall (Copy)

I am in rect of your last, with regard to Bennett.[7] I still feel that he richly deserves a knouting. To treat *me*, forsooth, as he is in the habit no doubt of treating one of his half starved and abject penny-a-liners![8] Dr Johnson on a somewhat like occasion—as you will recollect—knocked down,—floored instanter—with a folio that happened to be handy, the brazenfaced publisher, and bookseller, Cave—the same Cave, I think that Pope has [con]demned to fame in the Dunciad,[9] And in a matter like this between Bennet & myself the feeling of every literary man should be, to my thinking: *Lay the knout on well, and cut the fellow to the bone*

Still, in consideration of what you offered on his behalf, I am willing to pass him over, you are at liberty therefore to confiscate my letter: and there by ensure the silence you desire

On farther lookings into the Empire and other Sydney Journals, I see that there really is what Bennett distinctively calls a ["]Newspaper Poetry"[10]: a showy, dancing sort of verse, having in its subject a sort of progress-bent, and which regarded as composition, is neither good nor bad, One reads it and says, Well, this is not *bad*, and yet if looked closer at there is nothing in it—not one truly poetic stroke, And this will be Newspaper poetry so long as Newspaper Editors are the mere Kitchen Gardeners of Literature. Nor is there any wonder in the fact that such poetry should gravitate as it were towards mere creat[ur]es, like this Benne[tt] or that creatures of such a calibre

---

[7] Kendall's letter is lost, but it seems to have persuaded CH against sending to Samuel Bennett, *Empire* proprietor, his savage letter of September 1867 (Letter 126). Until early 1867 Kendall had been courting Bennett's daughter Rose and appears to have become Bennett's close friend: see his elegy 'By the Cliffs of the Sea. In Memory of Samuel Bennett' (*Freeman's Journal*, 1 February 1879, p. 13). *knouting*: severe flogging (a knout is a heavy multi-thonged whip).

[8] Journalists paid a penny a line; by extension, writers of low-quality material.

[9] Dr Samuel Johnson (1709–84) – English poet, playwright, essayist, moralist, literary critic, biographer, editor and lexicographer – knocked down *not* Edward Cave (1691–1754), founder of *Gentleman's Magazine* in 1731 and publisher of Johnson's periodical *The Rambler* (1750–52) and others of his works, *but* bookseller Thomas Osborne: 'It has been confidently related, with many embellishments, that Johnson one day knocked Osborne down in his shop, with a folio, and put his foot upon his neck. The simple truth I had from Johnson himself. "Sir, he was impertinent to me, and I beat him. But it was not in his shop: it was in my own chamber."' – James Boswell, *Life of Samuel Johnson, LL.D.* (London: Charles Dilly, 1791; online at Internet Archive), Vol. 1, p. 81. *Instanter*: emphatic substitute for *instantly*. In *The Dunciad*, a mock-heroic narrative satire published 1728–43, English poet Alexander Pope (1688–1744) condemned not Cave but another London publisher and bookseller, the unscrupulous and piratical Edmund Curll (1675?–1747), a sworn enemy of Pope.

[10] See postscript ('Since the above was written…') to Letter 126.

should gravitate towards it, Is there not something—co-natural between them—like the chemical affinity that draws like to like? As to the postage stamps:[1] I am a simple minded fellow, and sent them merely because it seemed to me proper that I should not put *you* to any expense in a business that was purely *mine*

I see you have been lecturing on love[2] Well, it is a subject I should once have liked to have lectured upon myself: but—my beard is grey, or nearly so. As to the poems in your hands: of course I do not know which of them you have sent to the Magazine:[3] but the rest you can be good enough to enclose me per post—if you cannot do better by them; that is get them well published: What of "Love in the past" containing, as one of its members, Gramachree?[4] Urge them to send me the magazine as soon as printed; I am greatly in need of a little intelectual excitement in this solitude of mine, In the November number, I intend to have two articles (if they suit), the first part of my dwarf epic, The Witch of Hebron[5] (to be continued part by part monthly) and a piece of critical prose which I call the Poet's Morning.[6] Are you going to grace its pages with anything; or are you Evclyn?—Mamba is a poor affair, to my thinking, not worth criticism. Mere rhyme in short[7]

Yours ever
Chas Harpur.

[1] CH had enclosed with Letter 127 one shilling's worth of postage stamps for return of manuscripts that Kendall was to retrieve from Bennett.

[2] Kendall had delivered his lecture 'Love' at the Sydney Mechanics' School of Arts on 17 September 1867. At that event – around six months after his break-up with Samuel Bennett's daughter Rose – Kendall met his future wife Charlotte Rutter: see Ackland, p. 92. Kendall had lectured before on this subject: 'About Love', *Clarence and Richmond Examiner*, 17 January 1865, p. 4.

[3] *Colonial Monthly*, a newly established Melbourne journal issued by Clarson, Massina & Co. in Melbourne and Gibbs, Shallard & Co. in Sydney, edited for a time by journalist and novelist Marcus Clarke. The sole CH item to appear there (1 January 1868, p. 330) was 'Love Dreaming of Death' (h234d dated 1867). See Letters 131 and 136.

[4] See Letters 89, 99 and p. 174 n. 3.

[5] See p. 191 n. 9.

[6] CH's essay on morning in the work of eight English poets from Herrick to Shelley, with extensive quotations, first appeared as 'Literary Papers. No. 2. Morning' in *PA*, 8 April 1854, pp. 6–7. A revised version, 'The Poet's Morning', survives in manuscript (ML A87-2, pp. 505–16) dated Euroma 1867, perhaps prepared with *Colonial Monthly* in mind.

[7] *Māmba ('The Bright-Eyed'): An Aboriginal Reminiscence*, a long poem supposedly based upon Aboriginal story (Melbourne: H. T. Dwight, 1867 – online via NLA). Its author was George Gordon McCrae (1833–1927), poet and man of letters. *Māmba* was reviewed by 'H.G.T.' in the first issue of *Colonial Monthly*, 1 September 1867, p. 29. 'Evelyn' was the pseudonym of George Northwood Oakley (1847?–99), Melbourne journalist and poet, and friend of Kendall's (not the 1850s Sydney poet Alexander John Evelyn). The Melbourne 'Evelyn' reviewed *Māmba* for *Australian Journal* and wrote a 'Book World' review-column for early numbers of *Colonial Monthly*. SLV holds a Kendall letter of 30 June 1868 telling Oakley of CH's death (in *Suppl. Letters*).

130. Henry Kendall to Charles Harpur, 3 October 1867

Text: Kendall papers, ML C199

Colonial Secretary's Office. Sydney, 3rd October 67.

My dear Harpur,

Yours of the 1st in hand. As I am pushed for time, I will have to hurry through this reply. With reference to the "Colonial Monthly", the proprietors have been asked to make no delay in sending you the numbers as they appear. *I am not "Evelyn"*. "Mamba" is wretched stuff. I have not written a line for the journal as yet: indeed I am obliged to supplement my means by sticking to political prose[8]—a thing scarcely suitable for the "Monthly". I send, by this post, Bennett's letter and the "Death of Shylock."[9] The other poems I reserve for publication. Bennett has sinned against his own interest in objecting to print your noble contributions. I am certain that I have by me three or four of your pieces which will rank through all time amongst our highest poetic possessions. Your estimate of newspaper verses is about the truth.

I lent the M.S. of "Love in the Past" to Halloran who subsequently mislaid it. "Gramachree" is one of most beautiful lyrics in the English language. How poor Deniehy used to light up about it.[10] The last version is eminently the best

Yours Ever
Henry Kendall.

131. Charles Harpur to Henry Kendall, 15 October 1867

Text: Autograph collection, SLV MS 13020

Euroma, via Bodalla, 15th Oct /67

My dear Kendall,

I thought the first number of the Colonial Monthly flimsy enough; but the second is even contemptible: the poetic contents absolutely *infamous*.[11] I have come to the conclusion therefore that it would be best for me not to mix up with any such affair. A thing so written for in the main, would weigh down into the mire even the songs of the Gods. I wish you therefore, to be so good as to withdraw or withhold my contributions from it. Do this for me, and upon

---

[8] Probably Kendall's contributions to *Sydney Punch*. His poems and prose would appear in *Colonial Monthly* from November 1867.

[9] I.e., Letter 126 and the unpublished MS (see Letter 127).

[10] 'Gramachree' was Kendall's shorthand title for the second poem in the series CH entitled 'Love in the Past': see p. 174 n. 3. For Deniehy, see p. 159 n. 10.

[11] For *Colonial Monthly*, see p. 212 n. 3. Its first issue (1 September 1867) contained 'The Phantom' by W. Carleton Jun.; the second (1 October): 'Two Roses; A River-Side Idyl' by G. G. McC. (George Gordon McCrae), 'Two Evas in One Life' by Theresa Tasmania (Lucy Anna Edgar), and 'The Soul Test. From the German of Freiligrath', translation unattributed.

my honor, it is the last trouble of the kind I will ever give you.

My broken resolve[1] of some months ago was altogether the best and wisest I could have come to: namely, to have nothing more to do with Sydney Journals of any kind—or with publication of any kind, until I could come forth with a volume on my own account. And to this old resolve I now recur for good.

As the copies in your possession of certain of my poems, are the most perfect perhaps of any, it would be as well that you should send me them. The Personal Sonnets[2] I wish back especially: because it is my intention to finally preserve of them, only such as happen to be poetic both in *subject* and treatment. I will in future lend no hand in the celebration of men whom I find to be faithless and selfish—mere human beeves.[3] At all events, in my final publication, the only interest I shall regard is the *essential poetry* of the piece under consideration. Those that would have their end in associating or mixing me up with the present race of Australians, could only have a damaging effect in some way—even the best of my contemporaries being such a —— lot: fellows that make one "hang his head, to call himself a *man*"[4]

Yours ever truly
Chas: Harpur.

When you next see Mr Stenhouse, will you ask him whether he got a letter of mine, containing a cheque on Bank of N.S.W?[5]

(9) N.S.W?

Soapy Sonnettaken[6]

132. Henry Kendall to Charles Harpur, 16 October 1867
Text: Kendall papers, ML C199

Colonial Secretary's Office. Sydney 16th Oct. 1867.

My dear Harpur,

Excuse the paper and the haste for the post. I have just received your

[1] See Letters 113 and 127.
[2] In an 1867 manuscript (ML A87-2, pp. 465–72), CH collected 'A String of Personal Sonnets', 14 sonnets inspired by or addressing individual people: Henry Parkes (I, h610f), Daniel Deniehy (II, h622g), John Dunmore Lang (III, h632e and IV, h606e), the Reverend John Saunders (V, h633f), James Norton (VI, h613f), Louis Kossuth (IX, h614h), John Heki (X, h203g), N. D. Stenhouse (XI, h624d), Henry Kendall (XII, h607c) and James Martin (XIII, h628a), and three unnamed: An Old Friend (VII, h603d), A Lady (VIII, h600b) and '——' (XIV, h422f). Though the series is dated 'Euroma 1867' the poems were written 1845–66.
[3] Oxen, cattle.
[4] 'And what man seeing this, / And having human feelings, does not blush / And hang his head, to think himself a man?' – William Cowper, against slavery, in *The Task, Book II:* 'The Time-Piece' (1785). The long dash stands in, perhaps, for 'blasted'.
[5] Referring to CH's recompensing Stenhouse for settling the Parker affair: see Letter 128.
[6] Annotations in an unknown hand.

note containing a letter from a Maitland gentleman,[7] and intimating your wishes with respect to the "Monthly." I quite agree with your estimate of the magazine in question, but as the first part of the "Witch of Hebron" is in type, I cannot very well withdraw it.[8] I have, however, secured the other M. S. S. which I return herewith.

You overrate newspaper people by expecting them to see the great beauty and the genuine power of your writings. The public to which your poems will appeal is not in existence yet, but its advent is inevitable. Long ago Deniehy said you were very foolish in throwing out your best efforts before the world through the medium of advertising rags. Take my advice and bring out a volume the moment you have the cash to spare. In England, at all events, the publication suggested would cause not a little commotion. If a striking originality wedded to the music of waters and the strength of thunder is only necessary to constitute the first great Australian Poet, certainly the author of "The Tower"[9] and the "Witch of Hebron" may lay claim to the crown.

I am not at all well this week, else I should write more at length. Take my advice and expect nothing from the newspaper lot in Sydney. If you knew them so well as I do, you would be actually *disappointed* at any recognition on their part.

Yours Ever,
Henry Kendall.

133. Charles Harpur to Thomas Sutcliffe Mort, November 1867[10]

Text: ML A87-1

Dear Sir

I believe that you are on the point of paying a visit to England for the purpose of advancing in a very important way certain material interests of the Colony.[11] Now no person can be more quick to perceive than myself, or more ready to admit, the laudableness of all this. But the Colony has other

---

[7] Unidentified; the 'note' (preceding Letter 131) has not survived.

[8] See p. 191 n. 9. 'Witch' did not appear: Kendall must have managed to withdraw it.

[9] 'The Tower of the Dream'.

[10] This is the draft of a letter to CH's neighbour, businessman Thomas Sutcliffe Mort (1816–78). Mort, one of the richest men in the colony, drew his wealth largely from wool-broking and pastoral finance, but also from his Sydney dry dock and engineering enterprises. His estate at Bodalla on the Tuross River, bordering CH's land, was designed as an integrated dairy estate and settlement of tenant farmers – 'a challenge to his concept of the productive purposes of capital' (*ADB*). See further, Mort's reply to CH (Letter 134); CH's draft letter to London publisher Moxon & Co. (Letter 135); and John Le Gay Brereton to CH (Letter 139).

[11] Mort, an early experimenter in refrigerated transport, was at this time preparing a trial shipment to England of meat frozen at the NSW Ice Company's plant at Darlinghurst, and considering a visit (see *SMH*, 18 September 1867, p. 5 and 29 February 1868, p. 6). The trip never came off.

important—perhaps more important—interests, which are but too much neglected on all hands—namely her moral and intellectual interests.—But it is no doubt needless to remind *you* of this; and would be quite as well for *me*, perhaps, to quit all "beating about the bush", and come at once to the matter I have in hand.

I wish to try a publication in England,[1] and to this end would so far trespass upon your goodness, as to make you the bearer to England of certain packets of M.S.S. to be offered to some London publisher on the usual terms.[2] In making my selection, I have been careful to choose those of my writings which are the most informed with the genius loci[3] of the land of their nativity; and the conveyance of them by a hand like yours, would be an ample warrant, that these productions are bona fide, what they profess to be—the productions namely, of a self-educated bush-born Australian, albeit that there may be amongst them many specimens of translation,[4] and from several tongues. One main reason with me for wishing to try a publication in England, is the belief that I shall never live to accomplish such an undertaking in my own country, except at such an outlay of money *on the nail* as would be ruinous to one in my circumstances; for my health is utterly shattered—to such an extent indeed, as precludes all hope of any thing like length of days.

---

[1] CH had long been considering publishing a volume at his own financial risk. In 1866, he began to see it as 'for the English critics' (Letter 104). Now it would be publication in England rather than locally (cf. Letter 132). In a draft preface 'To the English Reader' (ML A87-1, p. 17), in which CH dedicates the contents to 'the People of England', he explains that he is 'a self-taught man...never out of his native country, and has passed the greater part of his mature life in what may be called the *backwoods* of it'.

[2] In Victorian England, publishing could be 'on commission' (where the author paid the publisher for production and took all income); on 'half profits' (where the publisher met all costs of production and split with the author whatever profits accrued after costs were covered); or on outright sale (where the author took a lump sum in exchange for copyright in the work). After the 1860s the royalty system (where the publisher paid the author an agreed percentage of the cover price of each copy sold) became increasingly common, but it was slower to develop in Australia because of the higher financial risk for local publishers faced with a smaller literary book-buying readership. CH's draft letter of early 1868 to publishers Moxon & Co. (Letter 135) indicates that he hoped for a 'half profits' contract.

[3] Spirit of the place.

[4] On CH's capacity to translate, see p. 157 nn. 9–10. CH's translations from Greek were: 'Homer's Iliad, Book 1' (1851, h174); 'The Famous Night Scene in the VIII Iliad' (1855, h127); 'A Battle Piece from Homer' (1855, h575); 'The Forging of the Armour of Achilles' (1866, h138); and 'Similes from Homer' (1867, h501 etc.). For his German-inspired pieces CH appears to have relied on the work of others: 'The Cloud. (Imitated from the German)' (1851, ho67a), from the children's tale 'Die Wolke' by Richard Reinick in a prose translation by Miss Margaret Taylor, sister of London printer and publisher Edward John Taylor, which CH may have found in the anthology *The Playmate: A Pleasant Companion for Spare Hours* (London: Joseph Cundall, 1847, pp. 191–2) and which he appends to ho67; 'Thekla's Song' being 'from the German of [Friedrich] Schiller' (1851, h582), much translated, including famously by Coleridge in 1800 and anonymously in *Empire*, 23 May 1851, p. 3 (as 'The Maiden's Moan'), four months before CH's appeared; and 'The Infinite in Space' (1866, h196, from De Quincey's 1846 'homage' to Jean Paul Richter's 'Traum über das All').

I will do myself the honor of making an early call at Comerang,[5] and of unfolding myself more fully to you as to the matter of this note.

> I remain, dear Sir
> Your very humble servant
> Chas Harpur

134. Thomas Sutcliffe Mort to Charles Harpur, 25 November 1867

Text: ML C376

> Comerang Novr 25th 1867.

My dear Sir,

You do me no more than justice when you express an assurance that I should not be unwilling to take charge of your manuscript poems for publication in England in the event of my paying that Country a visit. At present my plans are somewhat hazy, and I cannot say for a certainty that I shall fulfil my present intentions, but in the event of my doing so, you may rest satisfied of my willingness to do all in my power to promote your wishes, and thereby give to the *old* world some of those poems, which you have scattered amongst the people of the *new*.

With my kind regards to you & yours,

> Believe me to be
> very faithfully
> Thos Mort

135. Charles Harpur to Moxon & Co., 1868

Text: ML A95

Copy of a Letter to Messrs Moxon & Co.[6] Publishers, London.

> Euroma, Australia, 1868.

Gentlemen,

Mr T. S. Mort, an eminent Australian merchant,—a gentleman indeed, who would be a true Merchant Prince as the citizen of any country,—has, on the occasion of his having to pay a visit to Europe, very kindly consented to become the bearer of the Manuscripts of certain poems of mine, for the

---

[5] Mort's country house and home farm of his Bodalla Estate near Euroma. For a near-contemporary description, see 'A Tour to the South: No. 11 – Moruya to Bega', *ATCJ*, 28 October 1871, pp. 10–11.

[6] Firm founded by Edward Moxon (1801–58) in 1830. Dubbed 'publisher of poets', its list included Charles Lamb (Moxon's friend and father-in-law), Shelley, Wordsworth, Browning, Tennyson and Swinburne. By 1868 the firm, managed for the family by James Bertrand Payne, was in trouble, heading for a sensational legal dispute and eventual collapse.

purpose of offering them on my behalf to some London publisher;—and to your Firm preferably, or in the first instance. Now, as these poems have all, or most of them, passed muster with the best heads in Australia, I can hardly believe that a publication of them in England will be a dead failure. But of this of course you must yourselves be the properest and best judges. If, however, you decide upon their acceptance and publication, and if the undertaking shall happen to be a success, I shall expect, as their *producer*, to become a sharer in the profits of it, according to the trade-rule in such case established.[1] But in any business-matter of this nature, Mr Mort has also consented, and is authorised, to act and arrange for me; and all that I bargain for farther of my own head is, that if my poems are published at all, they shall be published in their integrity. I do not mean by this that they shall be given in the exact order in which I have myself arranged them; but that they shall if published at all be printed *verbatim*, or exactly as written:[2] except, of course, where it is evident that some mere slip of the pen or clerical error has occurred.

> I am, Gentlemen,
> Your very obedient servant,
> (signed) Chas: Harpur.

P.S. The Manuscripts are numbered seriatum[3] from 1 to

136. Charles Harpur to Gibbs, Shallard & Co., January 1868

Text: ML C376

Euroma, via Bodalla January 1868

Gentlemen,[4]

I send you the accompanying Paper for the Colonial Monthly[5]—but in doing so, I bargain, that in the event of its not being accepted, the Manuscript

---

[1] See p. 216 n. 2.

[2] A perennial concern for CH; it contrasts with the freedom with which some of CH's works would be reshaped in *Poems* (1883). Revised from '…arranged them, or in whole; but that, whether published in whole or in part only, they shall each of them be printed *verbatim*, exactly…'.

[3] Correctly, *seriatim*: one after another; in serial order. CH does not provide the final number.

[4] 'Messrs Gibbs, Shallard & Co', the addressee, was a leading Sydney printing firm that began as a branch of Melbourne partners Joseph Burton-Gibbs, Joseph Shallard, Alfred Henry Massina and William Clarson. Around 1866 the partnership was dissolved, the Sydney firm trading as Gibbs, Shallard. It specialised in quality lithographic printing, including of *Sydney Punch* and *Illustrated Sydney News*. *Colonial Monthly* was published simultaneously by Gibbs, Shallard in Sydney and Clarson, Massina, and Co. in Melbourne. It was printed by the Melbourne firm, but the contributions and advertisements came from both cities.

[5] 'Paper' not identified. CH had asked Kendall to withdraw all his contributions to *Monthly* (Letter 131): there had been a change in strategy. One poem appeared: see p. 212 n. 3.

shall be returned or returnable, either to myself or to some other person applying for it on my behalf: for I would not do the mere copying of it—to say nothing of the brain-work—for the £1. payment,[6] *if that were all I had in view.*

> I remain,
> Gentlemen
> Yours very obediently
> Chas: Harpur.

137. Henry Blyth to William Wilkins, 31 January 1868

Text: NSWSA: NRS-2621 [1/775, Vol. 41], f. 305

Eurobodella[7] 31st Janry 1868

Sir[8]

I have the honor in handing you salary abstract[9] for Janry, to hand you also, under seperate cover, a petition to the Council of Education; respectfully requesting them to grant me the difference, or such part of it as they may deem fit, between my salary and that portion of it received during 1867; as the reduced salary is inadequate to maintain a respectable position. I earnestly entreat your powerful advocacy in laying the petition before the Council.

In spite of the secession of the Roman Catholic Body, the school has reopened with 18, and I am using my utmost endeavors to persuade the different families supporting it, to engage married couples *with children* as farm servants. I have already succeeded in one instance, that of Mr Manusu one of our Local Board;[10] and hope shortly to announce that two others have followed his example.

Mr Harpur our Chairman is at present in Sydney for the benefit of his

---

[6] This is the sole piece of evidence so far found of a per-item anticipated payment by a magazine or newspaper for a literary contribution by CH. In Letter 126 CH refers to his having offered his services as a paid *Empire* contributor, but the offer was not taken up.

[7] Variant spelling of Eurobodalla.

[8] CH's addressee here ('The Secretary / Council of Education / Sydney') was William Wilkins: see p. 192 n. 6.

[9] The teacher's monthly abstract of salary, signed by the local Public School Board ('provided they are of opinion that his duties have been regularly and punctually performed') and forwarded to the Council of Education for payment (see Regulations under the *Public Schools Act* of 1866, *NSW Government Gazette*, 1 March 1867, p. 593).

[10] Michael Manusu (1826–1902), one of the earliest Greek immigrants to NSW. He owned the farm just south of the Harpurs where he ran the Grecian Inn, strategically placed not far from where the Nerrigundah road met the main road from Bodalla to Bega (an inland route via Cobargo: see Map 4). See further, biographical note at syndesmos.net. Each Public School Board consisted of three members approved by the Council of Education and was charged with maintaining, inspecting and reporting on the school under its care.

health,[1] and intends to do himself the honor of calling on you.

I have the honor to remain
Sir
Your most obedient Servant
H Blyth[2]

1142. Enclosing petition for payment of part of his reduced salary

Council

S25. 13.2.68 40. 17.2.68

JM 24.2.68.

No 68.1112[3]

138. Charles Harpur to Joseph Jehoshaphat Harpur, 23 February 1868

Text: ML A87-2

23 February 1868.

Sir,[4]

When I was in a position to lend you money, I used to get a letter from you very frequently, and mostly a long one. But since I have not been in such a position, I have never received anything of the sort from you, long or short: not even upon the occasion of the disastrous death of one of my little boys.[5]

But I learn that you are now in a situation,[6] while I, as you know, am out of

---

[1] Earliest evidence that CH travelled to Sydney intending to consult doctors: John Le Gay Brereton (see Letter 139) and, possibly, George Fortescue (1838–1885), a surgeon with a flourishing practice in Sydney from the early 1860s. Two letters from Fortescue to Mary Harpur survive (29 November 1877, 8 May 1881: both in *Suppl. Letters*); and, at her request, he subscribed to *Poems* (see Letter 154). *Evening News*, 5 April 1882, p. 3, refers to 'many conversations' (presumably in Sydney in early 1868) that CH had with the then newly admitted barrister Simon Belinfante about 'the want of sympathy and ordinary humanity exhibited towards Deniehy in his fall'. Belinfante was also a medical practitioner, at Wynyard Square, East Sydney, so may have provided a third medical opinion for CH. See further, M. Z. Forbes, 'Simon Belinfante in Australia 1863–1874', *Australian Jewish Historical Society Journal*, 11 (July 1991), Part 2, 273–98.

[2] See p. 192 n. 5.

[3] Annotations by Council of Education officers.

[4] In this retained copy CH accords his older brother Joseph a coldly formal salutation. His address is given only as 'Kiama', then a small town on the south coast of NSW 217 km north of CH at Euroma.

[5] I.e., Charley: see p. 195 n. 11.

[6] Joseph had struggled since losing his parliamentary seat in 1864, doing hack work for Henry Parkes for little if any pay and battling with alcohol (Rawling, pp. 305–6). He was editor of the short-lived Sydney suburban *Balmain Reporter*, then gained a position with the weekly *Kiama Pilot, Shoalhaven Gazette and Impartial Reporter*, established by printers Robert Barr and W. C. Logan in May 1867 in opposition to the *Kiama Independent*. The paper lasted until December 1871. Parkes, member for Kiama at this time, may have had a hand in Joseph's appointment.

one. I am also out of health: am suffering, in short, from a disease that must be mortal within a limited period.[7] Yet if I were to die to-morrow, there is not in my house enough cash to procure for me a coffin and a shroud. They would have to be got on *tick*.[8]

Now, under these circumstances, I write to inform you, that unless you repay me, in whole or in part, the money which I have from time to time advance[d] to you, I will at once put the matter into the hands of a solicitor for recovery, and cause you to [be] sued for the whole amount at the next District Court to be held at Moruya.[9]

I am Sir,
Your very obedient servant
Chas: Harpur.

139. John Le Gay Brereton to Charles Harpur, 11 March 1868

Text: ML C376

Turkish Bath.[10] *Bligh Street. Sydney* Mar 11 *1868*.

Dear Mr Harpur,

I was away from home on a holiday of three weeks when your welcome letter & portrait[11] arrived. I am sorry you do not give a better report of yourself. If you think I can do anything for you after a trial which satisfies you of the other treatments, I hope you will not fail to [regard?] & use me as a brother. I have not yet seen Mort, but will not forget my promise, both for your own sake & that of Colonial literature.[12] I would enclose my portrait in return, but have not one in my possession. At a future time I will remember you. It will give me

---

[7] CH would die (from tuberculosis) in a little over three months.

[8] On credit.

[9] The next session of the court at Moruya was scheduled for 13 April 1868; cf. p. 203 n. 8.

[10] Brereton (see p. 131 n. 7) was involved in the establishment of Turkish baths in England and set up the first one in Sydney, where he held consultations. He also lectured and wrote on the Turkish bath 'as a means of sanitary and social reform' (1869 pamphlet, *The Turkish Bath: A Lecture*, online at SLV).

[11] CH's letter is lost. He was in Sydney in January 'for the benefit of his health' (Letter 137); CH and Brereton may have met then. See also Letter 141. For the small portrait (of *carte de visite* size), probably made in multiple copies at Albert Lomer's studio in Sydney on the same trip, see Introduction, n. 20.

[12] When CH had approached Mort about publication in England, Mort had warned him that his plans to visit England were 'hazy' (Letter 134). CH apparently asked Brereton to follow up with Mort in Sydney. Brereton had known Mort in England before immigrating in 1859. They travelled to Australia on the same ship, the *Dover Castle*, and Mort would claim the credit for bringing Brereton to Sydney.

great pleasure at any time to hear from you. There ought to be no strangeness between us.

With kind regards
to Mrs Harpur.
Your sincere friend,
J Le Gay Brereton

140. Thomas Harris to William Wilkins, 24 March 1868

Text: NSWSA: NRS-2621 [1/775, Vol. 41]

Memorandum for the Secretary.[1]
Eurobodalla: Situation of Public School:[2]

Sydney, 24th March, 1868.

On the 19th September last, I was at Eurobodalla. At the request of Mr W. Coman,[3] whom I met at Nerrigundah on the previous day, I called at a school situated about a quarter of a mile from the Public School but upon the Western side of the Tuross river. This school was opened in February 1867, by direction of the Rev. P. Birch of Moruya.[4] It is conducted by a Mr McGrath in a building which was left by a Mr Millar upon his forfeited selection.[5] There were 23 children present, but I was informed by Mr Manusa,[6] a respectable resident, that they had been specially collected for the occasion, and that, as a rule, there were not more than 9 or 10 in regular attendance. At the public school, there were 19 pupils present. This school was formerly held in a building upon the Western side of the river, but as this was a hut totally unfit for the purpose, it was removed to the Eastern side to a building the use of which was granted by C. Harpur Esq. J. P. This gentleman who resides close to the crossing-place of the river informed me that he regarded the objection on account of the river simply as a pretext for obtaining a grant for a separate Denominational School.[7] He assured me that, except in

---

[1] I.e., William Wilkins (see p. 192 n. 6), 'the Secretary' of the Council of Education (see p. 193 n. 8).

[2] See Letter 114. The Eurobodalla Public School was at this time situated on Harpur land.

[3] Early settler in the Moruya district, William Coman (1812–95), took up Eurobodalla station in 1854. He was Irish-born, 'honourable, generous and hospitable' and 'a staunch, uncompromising Catholic' according to *Freeman's Journal*, 9 March 1895, p. 15.

[4] See p. 193 n. 10.

[5] Possibly Thomas McGrath, a local teacher. Nerrigundah storekeeper James Millar sold provisions to diggers along the Tuross River and its tributaries. The Harpurs let him a store on their property for a year in 1865: see Memorandum of Agreement signed by CH and Millar (in *Suppl. Letters*). A conditional purchase of Crown land could be forfeited for failure to meet conditions including payments or improvements to and residence on the land.

[6] See p. 219 n. 10.

[7] Under Section 13 of the *Public Schools Act* of 1866: see p. 193 n. 11.

times of heavy rain when it would be impossible for children to attend any school, the river presents no real difficulty. He has placed a small punt at the crossing for the use, when required, of the children attending the school. I have visited the locality upon three occasions at different seasons of the Year, and never found the water much above my horse's fetlocks. The residents upon the Eastern side of the river do not object to the removal of the Public School to the opposite side, if a suitable building be provided. Indeed they are disappointed that the site with the buildings upon Millar's forfeited selection was not granted for the public school in accordance with their application to the Hon. the Minister for Lands, instead of to the Roman Catholic Church in answer, as they affirm, to a subsequent application.

In my opinion, one school is quite sufficient to meet the wants of the locality. The maintenance of two would not only be a waste of public money, but a sure means of rendering both inefficient.

T Harris,
Inspector,
Goulburn District.[8]

2/68

141. Mary Le Gay Brereton to Charles Harpur, 7 May 1868
Text: ML C376

Turkish Bath.[9] *Bligh Street. Sydney* May 7th *1868*

Dear Sir,

Dr Brereton has just received yours of the 1st inst[10] and desired me to write a few lines for him as he is so much hurried by stress of business as to be unable to spare even the five minutes necessary to do it himself and yet would not have you think that he is forgetful or careless of your sadly isolated position. He bid me say that your report of your state of health is very encouraging, showing more improvement than he had hoped for in the time; he has sent another prescription to Bell[11] who will forward the medicines; but for the future the Dr intends enclosing the medicines to you himself whenever practicable.

For myself, I have not the pleasure of knowing you personally but I am

---

[8] Thomas Harris, former principal of the Fort Street Model School, teacher training master and school inspector under the former National Schools Board. Based at Goulburn, his district as inspector extended from Mittagong to Yass, Adaminaby in the Snowy Mountains and Eden on the far south coast.

[9] See p. 221 n. 10.

[10] CH's letter of 1 May 1868 has not survived.

[11] John Bell, homeopathic pharmacist of George-street, opposite Bridge-street, Sydney.

interested in all that concerns the establishment of an Australian literature and I trust that it is not yet to lose one of its most efficient contributors; your desire to live for a noble purpose will surely strengthen your hold upon life. Your muse is to you what the more ordinary interests and ties of affection are to others; one without an object in life must needs part with it the more easily. Mr Kendall has lately been increasing *his* interests by taking a wife[1] so you must not be surprised at his silence. He will probably have the more to say when he does write.—We have not seen him since his marriage so perhaps his bride is a little exigeante[2] or he is so entranced in his new happiness as to be unable to give his mind to friendship at present.

The Dr says he has not forgotten the business with Mr Mort[3] concerning your poems but he has not had a favorable opportunity of introducing it at present. He will however continue to bear it in mind and you are not to suppose that he forgets or regards it as unimportant.

Believe me, dear Sir,
Yours very truly
Mary Le Gay Brereton.[4]

142. John Le Gay Brereton to Charles Harpur, 30 May 1868

Text: ML A1528

Turkish Bath. Bligh Street. Sydney May 30 *1868*

Dear Harpur

Yours just at hand—medicine will arrive by the mail. Try the inhalation of Sulphur fumes,[5] gently at first & increase if you bear it. It is easily applied by burning a little Sulphur in the room you are sitting in in an iron spoon, or on a bit of iron, made hot over a flame. The sulphur will burn & emit the fumes into the room. If you bear it it is quite safe & will promote expectoration & ease your breathing. The *medicine* must not be exposed in the same air, as it

---

[1] Kendall married Charlotte Rutter on 7 March 1868 at St John's Bishopthorpe, Glebe. Kendall was seriously in debt and 'depressed and withdrawn' (Ackland, pp. 148–9). In April, the body of his friend and mentor James Lionel Michael had been found in the Clarence River, the cause of his death – foul play, accident or suicide – uncertain.

[2] French for *exigent*: demanding, exacting.

[3] See p. 221 n. 12.

[4] Mary Le Gay Brereton (1839–1923), née Tongue, wife of Dr John Le Gay Brereton. The Breretons were members of the Swedenborgian New Jerusalem Church in Sydney, and Mary was the translator from French of missionary Bishop Francois Louis Bugnion's New Church *Catechism* (Sydney, 1874).

[5] Use of sulphur dioxide fumigation for the relief and cure of phthisis (tuberculosis) was advocated by Scottish physician James Dewar – his pamphlet *On the Application of Sulphurous Acid Gas to the Prevention, Limitation and Cure of Contagious Diseases* (Edinburgh: Edmonston and Douglas, 1866; online at Internet Archive). But CH was beyond help: he died on 10 June 1868 (see Biographical entry in CHCA).

will spoil it. With affectionate regards, in which Mrs Brereton unites,

Very faithy Yours
J Le Gay Brereton

143. Mary Harpur to Nicol Drysdale Stenhouse, 27 September 1868[6]

Text: Stenhouse papers, ML A101

Euroma Bodalla Sept 27th/1868

Dear Mr Stenhouse

Although I have not heard from you, I feel assured your kind heart sincerely mourned for the sad fate of your literery friend C. Harpur; The particulars of whose death you are doubtless acquainted with: Within a short period of that sad event we had hopes he might survive for months, He poor sufferer hoped to the last, He thought it hard, hard to die ere he knew his intelectual labours would meet with that success he so sanguinely believed they justly merited. Sad 'tho it seems it was the will of God to call him along before half his intelectal labors was finished. My heart aches to see his fine poems on the shelf as silent and neglected as their poor author in his *humble nameless* grave on the hill.

As my dear husband died intestate,[7] I am now in great trouble about the piece of land in which he lies at rest beside my darling boy.[8] Through some informality the Gov. have declared this additional selection of 40 acres forfieted, and refuse to refund me the money until a copy of the will or letters of administration are sent to the Lands Office.[9] I have had no means to obtain Letters of Administration, Will you my dear Sir kindly assist me in this painful dilemma giving me a little time to repay you for any expence you may be put to in granting me this favour.

---

[6] This is the first letter after CH's death.

[7] Without having made a will. Letters of administration (see below) authorise a person to administer the estate of someone who dies without a will. Administration of CH's goods, chattels, credits and effects would be granted to Mary on 13 October 1874, the goods valued at a modest £50.

[8] See p. 195 n. 11.

[9] Under section 21 of the *Crown Lands Alienation Act* of 1861 conditional purchasers or their legal alienees could make an 'additional selection', purchasing Crown land adjoining the original selection provided the combined area did not exceed 320 acres. The long, narrow 40-acre (16-hectare) block bordering Euroma on the south had been forfeited by an earlier selector, Bryan Rooney. Washington Harpur selected it in 1864 only to have the purchase later disallowed on a technicality. Mary Harpur would overcome the problem: the property appears as C.P. 69.2745, marked 'Mary Harpur', on a parish map (NSWLRS Parish and Historical Maps – Parish of Eurobodalla, Sheet 1, Edition 2, 1896: see Map 4). The Crown Lands Office, Spring- and Gresham-streets, Sydney, was responsible for administration of conditional purchases.

I wish to get the money from Gov. to make fresh application for the land,[1] worthless in itself, and only prized by me as the buriel place of those [nier?] and dear to me, Tis a dry barren hill just above my cottage, I am so anxious; and had no idea letters of Admin. had to be shewn before I could get even the small deposit for 40 acres returned to me; Feeling sure you may if possible help me

I am dear Mr Sten[house]
Yours truly
Mary Harpur

Bodalla (Post Town) Recd Sep 29/68 and verbally by Rev. P. FitzGerald 29 Oct/68[2]

144. John Robertson to Mary Harpur, 9 November 1868

Text: ML C376

Sydney. 9th Novr 1868

My dear Mrs Harpur

I am just finishing up all the papers that came to my address during my late visit to the Gulf of Carpentaria,[3] and have come upon a note of yours with its enclosure, & slip from the Herald.[4] It is I assure you very gratifying to me to receive from you so kind a letter. I had observed the paragraph at the time of its publication, but only looked upon it as a part of Parkes' [cretinous?] plan

[1] In July 1869 Mary acquired the site, putting down a £10 deposit on the price of £40. She would meet interest payments over the next 26 years, but may never have paid off the principal. Land boundaries and ownership would change over the years, but the grave site would be protected from alienation as part of a State Travelling Stock and Camping Reserve in 1929; and then, in 1968, would be declared a reserve for the purposes of public recreation and preservation of graves.

[2] The Reverend Patrick FitzGerald (1824?–1902), Presbyterian Minister at Moruya 1863–71 and Windsor 1872–96; he had officiated at the funerals of both Charley Harpur and CH. Annotations in Stenhouse's hand.

[3] With entrepreneurs John Graham MacDonald and Robert Towns, Robertson had taken up and stocked large pastoral stations in the Gulf country of northern Queensland. He and MacDonald toured to inspect their company's holdings June–September 1868. An old friend of CH, Robertson was at this time Premier of NSW. As Lands Minister, he had been responsible for the *Crown Lands Alienation Act* of 1861, which opened Crown lands to selection by small settlers (including the Harpurs).

[4] Generally sympathetic, 'The Late Mr. Charles Harpur' (in *SMH*, 7 July 1868, p. 5) had claimed that CH's friends Henry Parkes and W. A. Duncan had 'assisted the poet, who seems to have been of a wayward and restless nature, in many of his later undertakings; and it was mainly due to their influence that he obtained a situation under Government in the capacity of Gold Commissioner'.

to cry him up, and others down.[5] However that may be it is quite certain that neither Mr Parkes nor Mr Duncan ever spoke to me about doing anything for Charles. You will remember that I went many miles out of my way to call upon you and him, on one of my visits to the Hunter, and that it was while at your house,[6] I offered poor Charles the appointment which *I* and neither *Parkes* or *Duncan*, gave him. I was then Minister for Lands, and in that capacity alone had the power.

I shall be glad to learn from you of any issue if I can be of service to you, or to you[r] any of your family:[7] and you may rely upon my doing anything that may be in my power.

I don't quite understand the merits of the case about the £45.[8] If there is a case have it put in official form and sent on to me.

I do not of quite say that it shall be complied with: but I do say it shall be carefully considered and dealt with justly at the very least.

Mrs Robertson[9] desires her best and kindest compliments

I am my dear Mrs
Harper
Yours &c
John Robertson

145. Subscription List for an Edition of Charles Harpur's Poetry, 1 February 1871

Text: ML MSS 947

THE LATE CHARLES HARPUR, ESQ.

IT is proposed to publish, by Subscription, for the benefit of his Widow and Children, the Poems of the late CHARLES HARPUR, ESQ.,[10] a native of the

---

[5] Henry Parkes, until recently Colonial Secretary in the Martin government, had resigned from the ministry in September 1868 after quarrelling with treasurer Geoffrey Eagar who had (as Parkes saw it) engineered the dismissal of W. A. Duncan as Collector of Customs. Martin's government soon collapsed, Duncan returned to his position and Robertson was commissioned by the Governor to form an administration.

[6] This was in 1859, when the Harpurs were farming at Lowsfield on the Hunter River near Jerry's Plains and Robertson was Member of the Legislative Assembly for Upper Hunter and Secretary for Lands and Public Works.

[7] Robertson failed to delete 'you[r]' – and similarly 'of' in 'I do not of quite say' (below).

[8] Mary Harpur's note to Robertson is lost; it may have concerned the land adjoining Euroma: see p. 225 n. 9 and p. 226 n. 1.

[9] Margaret Emma 'Madge' (later, Lady) Robertson, née Davies (1823–89). Harpur family legend had it that CH stayed with Robertson on his visits to Sydney (the Robertsons at this time lived at 'Clovelly', Watsons Bay), so it is possible that the women knew each other.

[10] This initiative received mentions in the newspapers – e.g., *Armidale Express*, 8 April 1871, p. 6; and *Argus* (Melbourne), 5 April 1871, p. 5 (citing the *Sydney Mercantile Advertiser* and reprinting the prospectus). At home with Mary Harpur were Harold (15), Ada (13) and Mary Araluen (9); by this time Washington (19) was established in northern NSW.

Colony, and for several years before his death Gold Commissioner at Nerri-gundah and the Gulf Diggings[1] of New South Wales.

Many of Mr. Harpur's minor poems were published from time to time in various colonial journals during his lifetime; but it was his earnest desire, some time before his death, to have them published in a collected form and in a separate volume, either in the Colony or in England. With this view, that eminent patron of colonial talent and enterprise, T. S. Mort, Esq., when contemplating a visit to England himself in the year 1868, had arranged to carry home with him Mr. Harpur's manuscripts and to negotiate for their publication in London. But as Mr. Mort subsequently gave up the idea of going to England on that occasion, and as Mr. Harpur died shortly thereafter, the literary friends of the deceased deem it preferable, especially considering the benevolent object they have in view, to publish the volume in the Colony. This will be done accordingly in the exact form and style in which the manuscripts were left by Mr. Harpur for the press. The Poems will form an octavo volume of about 300 pages,[2] and will be sold at half a guinea, payable in advance.

Mr. Harpur's Muse, as will be evident from the Poems, was somewhat of an erratic character, and perhaps, from his solitary life in the Australian bush, disposed to mysticism: but his poetical talent, as has been acknowledged again and again by many intelligent persons, was unquestionably of a high order. It will therefore be a graceful act, as well as one of duty to the colony and to posterity, thus to enshrine in the mausoleum of a separate volume the literary remains of one of the gifted sons of the soil who flourished in those years of the nonage[3] of Australia, in which the vision of her future greatness was revealed only to a few solitary ones like the poet himself.

JOHN DUNMORE LANG, D.D.[4]
N. D. STENHOUSE, M.A.[5]

Sydney, 1st February, 1871.

---

[1] 'Gold Commissioner' is used loosely: CH rose to become an Assistant Gold Commissioner, answerable to the Southern Gold District Commissioner, J. H. Griffin. Nerrigundah and the Gulf were identical; for 'Nerrigundah' read 'Araluen'.

[2] Octavo is a book format: a full sheet of paper printed both sides folded three times to form eight leaves or sixteen pages – each leaf representing one eighth of the size of the original sheet. The traditional British crown sheet is 15 x 20 inches (380 x 508 mm); crown octavo (then commonly used for literary works) has a page size of 7½ x 5 inches (190 x 127 mm) – approximately the size and bulk of *Poems* (1883).

[3] Early stage, immaturity.

[4] See p. 49 n. 5. Lang took his Doctor of Divinity from the University of Glasgow in 1825.

[5] See p. 103 n. 4. Stenhouse took his MA from the University of Edinburgh in 1825.

SUBSCRIPTION LIST.

	£ s. d.
R. B. Armstrong	1. 0 0
J Gardner	1. 0. 0
Thos. Roberts	<u>1. 0. 0</u>
	£3. 0. 0

146. Subscription list for an edition of Charles Harpur's poetry, 28 March 1871

Text: ML MSS 947

Harpurs Poems[6]

Date 1871	Subn Lists sent to	Retd 1871	Amount		
	T S Mort	23rd March	2	2	.
March 28	Hon John Robertson				
	John Lucas				
	Wm Laidley				
	Dr Brereton				
	Marshall Burdekin				
	Sheridan Moore				
	N D Stenhouse				
	Dr Muller				
	Rev P Fitzgerald				
	John McArthur & Co				
	Henry Parkes				
	John Fairfax				
	Henry Halloran				

[6] In an unknown hand, this list gives those to whom a subscription form was sent in March 1871 (see Letter 145). Most names here are of figures prominent in the political, social or literary life of NSW, and most (if not all) known to CH: for the most prominent, see Index. *Also*: John Lucas (1818–1902): politician and pamphleteer; William Laidley (1828–97): merchant and politician; Marshall Burdekin (1837–86): barrister and politician; Dr Charles Muller (1815–75): surgeon; John McArthur (1828–1904): South Coast merchant and shipowner.

147. Joseph Jehoshaphat Harpur to Mary Harpur, 9 June 1871

Text: ML C376

Botany Road, Waterloo[1] near Sydney, June 9th 1871.

Dear Mrs Harpur,

I have deferred replying to your kind letter of the 1st instant[2] with the expectation of being enabled to communicate to you the result of an interview I proposed having with Dr Lang and Mr Stenhouse. Unforeseen circumstances have hindered me from calling on these gentlemen, however, and will prevent my doing so till next week. And as that would be too long to postpone the acknowledgement of a letter which has given me so much pleasure and satisfaction, and which does you, my dear Sister, so much honour, I feel constrained to write to you at once, though I have not much of a definite nature, with reference to the publication of poor dear Charles's poems, to say.

But before I write a word upon that head permit me to assure you that your testimony, warm from the heart, and breathing the true spirit of an affectionate wife, to the honorable motives and conduct, the pure morals and the generous, affectionate and forgiving dispositions by which *Charles Harpur* was distinguished through life, has made my heart full of happiness and of love and respect for you. His faults as you know, were faults of temper. I suffered from them as well as you did,[3] though not so much, I confess, as you did. But such faults, or *failings* rather, are all forgiven and forgotten now. May God Bless you for having assured me of that! I think of proposing to Dr Lang and Mr Stenhouse the formation of a Committee, to be composed of our leading literary and political men for the purpose, of devising means, that is, procuring subscriptions for the publication of the poems. I am already in communication with several warm friends and admirers of poor Charles, as to the best means of forwarding the publication. One of them—a Mr Portus, of Morpeth,—a gentleman whose *specialty* is a knowledge of the name, the residence and belongings of every man of any eminence in the country,[4] has

---

[1] Inner southern suburb of Sydney, then an area of mills, tanneries, terrace houses and workers' cottages, wetlands and sandy scrub. Botany Road ran down its western side south to the shores of Botany Bay.

[2] Not extant.

[3] CH died estranged from his brother (see Letter 138). This relieved response on Joseph's part to Mary's peace offering could lead to little practical help for her mission to publish CH. Both were poor.

[4] Morpeth lay at the head of navigation of the Hunter River, 47 km above Newcastle; John Portus had established a flour mill there in 1839. His son James Alexander Portus (1827–86) was a friend of and political organiser for Henry Parkes and was said to have been 'unusually well informed on public events of his time' (obituary, *Newcastle Morning Herald*, 8 October 1886, p. 4).

this very day favoured me with a list of gentlemen to be written to in reference to the getting them printed. I enclose the list to you just to show you that we are not idle—but you must return it to me at your earliest convenience under the same enclosure (say) as your next letter.

I will write you again as soon as I have seen Dr Lang and Mr Stenhouse

Give my love to the dear children, especially to Harold,[5] and accept yourself Dear Mrs Harpur, the assurance of my high respect for you, and

Sincere affection
Joseph J. Harpur.

148. Mary Harpur to Henry Parkes, 26 August 1872

Text: ML A887

Euroma Bodalla Aug 26th –72

Dear Sir[6]

I have taken the liberty of enclosing to you a letter for the Min. for Lands[7] trusting you will give my son your influence which I know is great. I feel assured from a letter I read yesterday of yours to poor Mr Harpur and which I found amongst his papers that you had a kind feeling for your old friend and brother poet, Had you known all his sufferings, you would indeed have deeply sympathized with him, How he yearned to live to know whether he had mistaken his mission or not and how deeply he felt the falling away of some of his old friendships

He only gave up composition when he could no longer hold a pen All his writings are on the shelf where he left them, seemingly forgotten and the Poet lies beside his darling son on the wild lonely hill without a stone to mark the spot.[8] I have planted many flowers, but the kangaroos and opossoms[9] destroy all, so that I feel disheartened.

You who have suffered some reverses of fortune can conceive the hard battle I have had with the world;—left as I was penniless, on a poor, flooded farm,

---

[5] Joseph's solicitude for Harold (now 15) is noteworthy given the young man's later struggles with mental illness.

[6] Henry Parkes formed his first government in May 1872 after the resounding electoral defeat of James Martin.

[7] James Squire Farnell (1825–88), a loyal political ally of Parkes. It is not clear what assistance Mary was seeking from Farnell. Harold Harpur made numerous conditional purchases of Crown land around Bodalla and Nerrigundah during 1873–85 but failed to meet conditions and they were forfeited or transferred to others.

[8] See p. 195 n. 11. Cast-iron memorial tablets mark the graves; they were probably placed in the 1880s or 1890s.

[9] Common term in colonial Australia for the possum, the tree-dwelling Australian marsupial distinct from the opossum of the southern USA.

amongst strangers, and a low neighbourhood.[1] In the midst of all difficulties I have done my duty by giving my children the best education I could: and by instilling into their minds good principles Harold[2] for whom I ask your aid is a fine youth in his 17 year—truthful, careful, and industrious, I deeply regret being unable to educate him as he deserves to be from his high character.

It is the will of God and I submit. Trusting I have not trespassed on your valuable time

I am dear Sir
Yours respectfully
Mary Harpur

149. William Augustine Duncan to *Australian Town and Country Journal*, [by 28 March 1874]

Text: Australian Town and Country Journal, 28 March 1874, p. 14

The Late Charles Harpur.

(To the Editor)

Sir—

I read with considerable pleasure your account of the late Charles Harpur,[3] and I subscribe to the writer's appreciation of Harpur as a poet. I cannot help, however, expressing my surprise that a writer who knows so much about Harpur should know nothing at all about the way in which he became known as a poet, and came to be appreciated by Robert Lowe and the other literary men mentioned by his biographer. Certainly, neither Mr. Lowe,[4] nor Mr. Deniehy, nor Mr. Stenhouse, had anything to do with bringing Mr. Harpur into notice as a poet; that was solely the work of the present writer. The whole of Harpur's early poems were printed in the papers then edited by

---

[1] The Harpur farm had suffered badly in the floods of May 1870 and April–May 1871. Mary's complaint to Colonial Secretary Charles Cowper, 25 July 1870 (in *Suppl. Letters*) shows that her relations with neighbour Michael Manusu ('a *characterless Greek*') and others, were strained.

[2] Harold Harpur (1856–1940), the Harpurs' third son, never married but farmed at Eurobodalla, helping out at Euroma. For his later life, see p. 303 n. 11.

[3] A half-page retrospective on CH, illustrated with a newly engraved portrait made from the photograph of 1868 (see half-title page and Introduction, n. 23), in *ATCJ*, 14 March 1874, p. 413.

[4] See p. 26 n. 3. Lowe's association with CH is unclear. He had complimented the poet on his sonnets of 1845: see Letter 49. In 1847 CH gave Lowe's name as a referee for his literary attainments (Letter 12). An unsourced item in *Bulletin*, 23 October 1897, p. 13 – possibly originating with John Charles Lucas Fitzpatrick: see p. 303 n. 13 – claimed that CH 'was urged by Robert Lowe about 50 years ago to pack up his literary accomplishments and share his (Lowe's) luck in England. Lowe's liking for Harpur's verse was not a passing weakness; all through his life he insisted on placing the Hawkesbury native among the immortals.' Rawling (p. 135) attributes the England invitation (where Lowe lived from 1850) to CH's daughter Mary Araluen Baldwin, but cites no documentary source.

me, and were published at a time when no other paper in the colony would have admitted them, or indeed anything else of a purely literary character.[5] They were scoffed at by small critics, but I stoutly maintained their poetical merit against all comers; and I proved my sincerity by printing at my own cost 500 copies of his collected poems[6] and presenting the edition to the author as a gift. This is the small volume which his biographer says he "published during that period," and which brought him the recognition of Mr. Lowe, Mr. Stenhouse, and the other literary men of that day.

An incident occurred immediately after the publication of his collected poems, which always amuses me when I think of it, and which may also amuse your readers. Mr. Harpur, of course, sent me a warm letter of thanks for my present, but not content with this he also sent a poem for publication in my paper, which I inserted but with a slight alteration, toning down some praise of myself which I thought it hardly modest for me to print.[7] A day or two after it appeared, Mr. Harpur walked into the office of the paper in a state of great excitement, and asked how I had dared to alter his poem? I stated the reason, when he burst forth as follows:—"You! a thirteenth rate writer to dare to alter a line of mine. Sir, there is not a poem you ever printed for me that will not be read and admired a thousand years after you are dead and damned!"

I need hardly add that this exhibition of the *genus irritabile*[8] gave me no offence, and did not alter my friendship for Harpur, but I really believe he never quite forgave me for tampering with his poem.

A year or two after this I went to Queensland,[9] and gentlemen who came to know him through me in the way mentioned took an interest in him, and the praise his biographer gives them I believe to be well merited; but again it is strange that he should know nothing about how Harpur came to be known to these gentlemen, or as a poet to anyone.

[5] An exaggeration: CH's poems had been published in papers including *Currency Lad*, *Australian*, *Sydney Times*, *Monitor* and *Sydney Herald* before their first appearance in *Australasian Chronicle*, edited by Duncan, in 1842.

[6] *Thoughts. A Series of Sonnets* (Sydney: W. A. Duncan, 1845), 16 pages.

[7] 'To W. A. Duncan Esq.' (h638a). CH sent the sonnet to Parkes in his letter of 16 August 1844 (Letter 4); as requested, Parkes forwarded it (Letter 5) to Duncan for *Weekly Register*. He initially declined to publish it, but when he did so on 21 June 1845, p. 290, as 'Sonnet. To ——' (h638b), his name was removed from both title and text.

[8] The irritable or over-sensitive race or class (of poets) – after Horace, *Epistles* II.ii.102. If the tirade in CH's 1856 poem 'To W. A. Duncan, Esq.' and its note (h639a; *PA*, 8 March 1856, p. 2) is a guide, Duncan was right that CH could hold a grudge – though his ire was prompted by Duncan's recent defence of nomineeism in his pamphlet *A Plea for the New South Wales Constitution* (online via NLA).

[9] For Duncan, see p. 8 n. 4. When impending ruin forced him to close *Weekly Register* (see below) in December 1845, Governor Gipps (whose attempted liberal land reforms Duncan had supported against the squatters) rewarded him – despite accusations of jobbery – with a government post as customs officer at Moreton Bay (Brisbane), then still part of NSW. Duncan accepted in May 1846. In time, he would rise to become collector of customs for NSW, a position he held until 1881: see p. 227 n. 5.

Shortly after Mr. Harpur's death, some gentlemen, who knew my early interest in him, asked me to join in getting up by subscription a collected edition of his works, for the benefit of his family. To this I readily assented, but the matter seems to hang fire.[1] I trust, however, it is not too late to do justice to one who, if he had the eccentricities and faults of a poet, was not destitute of a poet's genius.

W. A. DUNCAN.

150. Henry Parkes to Mary Harpur, 11 September 1875

Text: ML MSS 947

Ashfield[2] near Sydney Sept 11th 1875

Dear Mrs Harpur

I have lately turned up a number of your late husband's letters written to me, some of them thirty-two years ago. Many of these letters have the true charms of genius—come upon the spirit with a freshness which is inaccesible to the ravages of time. The reading of them has recalled much of our long-past intimacy & has set me thinking of what poor Harpur has left behind him.

I was speaking to Mr T. S. Mort[3] yesterday and I gather from him that you possess all your late husband's manuscripts carefully preserved. I should be glad if you would write to me & inform me how the matter stands as to the Poems and also whether Mr Harpur's correspondence has been preserved especially the letters of Mr Deniehy, Mr Kendall and my own letters of the time to which I allude. I do not know whether Mr Harpur kept copies of his own letters.

I think a work might be produced under some such title as the following— "The Poetical Works of Charles Harpur with Particulars of his Life and Selections from his Correspondence",—which while doing honour to his memory might be of some benefit to his family.

Yours very sincerely
Henry Parkes[4]

---

[1] See Letter 145.

[2] Inner suburb of Sydney, eight km south-west of the city. 'Milton House', sitting among vines and an orange orchard, had been purchased for Parkes in 1873 by a political admirer. The family would live there until 1877. The house still stands, in Blackwood Avenue.

[3] See p. 215 n. 10.

[4] In parliament, Parkes was in opposition at this point.

151. Mary Harpur to Henry Parkes, 18 September 1875

Text: ML A888

Euroma Eurobodalla Sept 18th 1875.

Dear Mr. Parkes

I feel much gratified to know that my late gifted husbands memory is still cherished by you; one of his oldest and once best beloved friend, The falling away of your kind feelings for each other caused poor Chas. many an heart ache; hence his beautiful poem "Fallen Away".[5] I am so pleased to hear you have some of his old letters and that their perusal has revived old pleasant memories (I hope) of the past, and a wish (I trust) to do something towards establishing the fame of the neglected first Australian Poet.[6] How well I remember poor C. bringing to my Fathers your first *beautiful* letter with, Shellys Poems, your gift;[7] how proud and delighted the young Poet was. I will not repeat his high compliments on your genius; As for the coolness in after years *I* never blamed you; and ever had a kind word for you when he heard aught to vex him. Poor C. knew not all, and expected too much. Some of his detractors have since come to the end they deserved;[8] who endeavoured to make you think so ill of him.

I have the greater part of C.s poems ready for the press, if there was only a reading public to appreciate fine poetry. I am sorry to say I cannot see any of yours or Deniehys[9] letters, or any copy of his own. There are a good many of poor Kendalls recent letters well worth publishing they are the letters of a man of genius. He C. loved poor Deniehy greatly. D. thought C. a great poet and fully returned the feeling of Affection. Chas alway called him of late years

---

[5] This poem about forsaken friendship appeared in *PA* on 3 May 1851, p. 6 as 'Song' (h126a), a few years before CH's serious rift with Parkes, though his letter to Parkes of 22 August 1850 (Letter 22) seems to foresee it. Mary Harpur's apposite choice of poem suggests an easy familiarity with CH's poetry MSS, still at Euroma and 'ready for the press'.

[6] See Introduction, pp. xxvi–xxvii.

[7] When, in November 1843, an admiring Parkes had sent CH, then keeping the post office at Jerry's Plains, a gift of the *Poetical Works of Percy Bysshe Shelley*, Mary – then Mary Doyle – was living nearby at her parents' property; the pair were still in their long courtship: see Letter 3 and p. 5 n. 7.

[8] Their identity remains a mystery, but they may have been diggers or goldfields officials. If so, Adolphus Norblad or Nordblad, Clerk of Petty Sessions at Nerrigundah where CH was Assistant Gold Commissioner, and who had died in April 1875, is a contender: see Norblad to CH, 18 July 1862 (in *Suppl. Letters*), where he implicitly chides CH (still at Araluen) for failing to attend a 'Special Meeting for granting licences' in Nerrigundah. Policeman Martin Brennan remembered, in a 1909 article, that, at Araluen, CH 'rarely visited the stringy-bark hut designated a police court. He was a gentleman of education' ('Looking Backward over Fifty Years: The Golden Valley of Araluen', *Freeman's Journal*, 30 September 1909, p. 57). See also Letter 106.

[9] Whatever CH–Deniehy correspondence there may have been has not survived.

The blighted child of promised Genius.[1] Poor Kendalls downfall[2] would have grieved him terribly had he lived. Chas. had a high opinion of him but never thought him a great poet.[3] The only letter of Chas here is one to *Bennett* a frightfully severe one, so severe that Kendall said it would be unwise to give it.[4] Gentlemen here say Bennett *deserved* it.

Your kind letter has partially removed the painful feeling that my late husbands life long endeavours; his toil even to death; may not have been in vain, that his works may yet take the stand they merit and his fame be established as a man of genius poor as I am I would cheerfully submit to loss for this, instead of expecting help.

I am endeavouring to get from the Gov. partial compensation for the ruin of this once valuable place[5] by a road having being cleared and cut along the soft river bank causing road after road to be washed away by floods utterly destroying my place and the open road leaving the remaining part of my place worse than useless. Had a private company done it (against Cs will too) they would have had to pay £1000. I have asked only £500. If they will be just and give it I am determined much as I need it, I shall donate what is necessary to publishing poor Cs book: That will be the fittest memorial I can give, as I have been unable yet to place a stone over his grave or my childs.

[*continued next page*

---

[1] Others called Deniehy a 'child of genius'; 'promised' may have been CH's qualification: the phrase was proverbially applied to English poet Thomas Chatterton. e.g., Mary Robinson's *Walsingham; or, The Pupil of Nature*: 'Poor boy! ill-fated child of genius and of sorrow!' (London: T. N. Longman, 1797; II.63); and Coleridge's 'Monody on the Death of Chatterton' (1794). See also Letter 65 and p. 126 n. 6; and CH's 'Memo. The Sorrows of Chatterton' (h151-ac).

[2] In the face of impending bankruptcy and dismissal Kendall had resigned from the NSW public service in 1869. Unable to support his family with his pen in Melbourne or Sydney – his celebrated *Leaves from Australian Forests* (Melbourne: George Robertson, 1869) was a failure financially – near destitute, drinking heavily, ill and depressed, his baby daughter Araluen recently deceased, he was charged in December 1870 with forging and uttering a cheque. He escaped gaol only with a plea of temporary insanity. His wife Charlotte left him and he became a derelict, spending time in 1871 and again in 1873 in the Hospital for the Insane at Gladesville (see *ADB*, and Ackland, pp. 155–89).

[3] In the draft of a probably unpublished review (ML A87-2, p. 756) of the *Australian Monthly Magazine* for November 1867, CH wrote: 'This November number opens with a poem by Mr. Henry Kendall ['Mountain Moss'], in which torents *moan* (though after a somewhat roaring fashion no doubt), shades are dreamy, suns *slumbrous*...noons *burn mute* &c., &c. with that fatal alacrity which all such matters always attain to, when in his hands...But the vital defect of the piece is the nothingness of its subject; which indeed, is so inferior to the treatment, that even *it* is thereby degraded.'

[4] See Letter 126.

[5] The Harpur farm had suffered terribly in the floods of May 1870 and April–May 1871. Mary was still petitioning for assistance fifteen years later: see Mary Harpur to Henry Copeland (Lands Minister), 29 June 1886 (in *Suppl. Letters*).

Trusting I have not trespassed to much on your patience

I am dear Sir
Yours respectfully
Mary Harpur

152. Henry Kendall to Mary Harpur, 8 October 1879
Text: Kendall papers, ML C199

Camden Haven[6] 8th October 1879.

My dear Mrs Harpur,

Charles Harpur was the first and greatest of Australia's sons of genius; and his *name is not forgotten*. From year to year I have written of him. In Melbourne I published several articles on him in the leading journal there;[7] and since my return to this colony, I have cast abroad my opinion that he was immeasurably greater than Deniehy or myself. I have been more successful because I have pandered more to the popular taste.

Only twelve months ago, I expressed myself strongly, on the subject of Charles Harpur and his claims, in the *Freeman's Journal*. My article was entitled *Old Manuscripts*.[8] By applying to the proprietor of the *Freeman* you could get a copy of the paper.

With regard to the manuscripts in your hands, I do not think it would be advisable to publish them now—that is to say, in a book form. The leisured and lettered class here is very small yet; and your gifted husband's writings are only for minds of the highest order. Therefore, as things *are*, you would only lose money over a volume. Still, you ought to let his writings see the light, from time to time, through the metropolitan newspapers.

---

[6] A small timber settlement and harbour on the mid-north coast of NSW, south of Port Macquarie. In 1875, the Fagan family of Gosford gave Kendall employment as storekeeper and bookkeeper at their timber outlet there.

[7] Kendall wrote for and helped edit various journals in Melbourne during his time there in 1869–70, including *Australasian*, *Argus*, *Melbourne Punch*, *Humbug*, *Touchstone* and *Colonial Monthly* (see Ackland, p. 170; McLaren, *passim*). His 'About Some Men of Letters in Australia' [CH, Deniehy and Dalley] appeared in *Australian Journal*, 1 October 1869, pp. 84–5. McLaren (item 1147) attributes to Kendall the unsigned article 'Australian Literature: (No. III.) Charles Harpur', *Colonial Monthly*, 1 February 1869, pp. 447–54. Authorship is uncertain of 'The Late Mr. Charles Harpur' (*Argus*, 25 May 1869, p. 6), with its intimate description of CH's last hours and not published elsewhere.

[8] *Freeman's Journal*, 17 November 1877, pp. 17–18 – Sydney's Catholic weekly from 1850, named after the leading Irish nationalist newspaper. It appealed to a wide reading public with literary articles by William Bede Dalley, Deniehy, Frank Fowler, Joseph Sheridan Moore, Kendall and others.

14. Henry Kendall as an older man (after c. 1872), photographer S. Milbourn Jnr

I have gone through much suffering since I saw you.[1] The sorrow which walked side by side with Charles Harpur ha[s] attended his friend and successor, Henry Kendall.

Thanking you for your letter I am, my dear Mrs Ha[rpur]

> Your Sincere Friend
> Henry Kendall

I live at Camden Haven 300 miles north of Sydney.

153. Henry Kendall to Mary Harpur, 3 April 1881

Text: Kendall papers, ML C199

Cundletown[2] April 3rd 1881.

My dear Mrs Harpur,

I am much obliged to you for your kind letter;[3] and you may be sure that

---

[1] Possibly in Sydney in August 1867: see Letter 125.

[2] Small town near the mouth of the Manning River, mid north coast of NSW. When in 1881 Parkes appointed Kendall as the first Inspector of State Forests (see p. 247 n. 12), he left isolated Camden Haven moving south to Cundletown (near Taree), where there were significant forest reserves and direct access by sea to Sydney. See Ackland, p. 274.

[3] Not located.

I deeply sympathize with your touching efforts on behalf of your gifted husband. Book or no book his fame is imperishable. Whatever I can do in the cause of the projected volume shall be done; and the work of course will be a labor of love. I do not like however the idea of bringing a volume out by subscription: 1000 copies of a volume containing 250 pages would cost about £110—printing and binding. If your relatives knew this, perhaps they would advance the money. It would come back to them in a very short time.

The book should be edited by some competent and loving hand. I have so many children, and so many troubles, that I could not, in justice to my dead friend, undertake the work. Mr Philip Joseph Holdsworth[4] of the Colonial Treasury is the most competent gentleman I can think of; and I feel sure that he would be only too glad to act as editor. At your distance from Sydney you could not be expected to read proofs. I am too far also.

Keep your head up. Your loyalty to your great husband is very touching

Yours ever
Henry Kendall.

Your letter arrived today.

Perhaps you had better use my name at the head of the subscription lists. Don't print more than 50 lists. Send one to every good man you can think of

Letter to my Mother..
.MM. BALDWIN..[5]

CHARLES HARPUR'S POEMS.[6]

Subscriptions are hereby asked in aid of a projected volume of the late Charles Harpur's poems. It is not necessary to say who Charles Harpur was. He was the first and greatest of Australian poets; and the publication now in view would not only add lustre to our young literature, it would also shed glory on our national life. It is emphatically the duty of Australia to rescue the works of this masculine poet from oblivion.

HENRY KENDALL.

Dear Mrs Harpur

State price and size of book at foot of the above

[4] Sydney public servant and writer (1851–1902); Holdsworth would contribute a preface to the 1886 memorial edition of Kendall's poems (online at HathiTrust).
[5] Typed annotation by Mary Harpur's daughter Mary Araluen Baldwin.
[6] Kendall's text here is the one used for the printed subscription form.

154. Subscription lists for *Poems*, [after 3 April 1881]

Text: ML MSS 827

CHARLES HARPUR'S POEMS.[1]

Subscriptions are hereby asked in aid of a projected Volume of the late Charles Harpur's Poems. It is not necessary to say who Charles Harpur was. He was the first and greatest of Australian Poets; and the publication now in view would not only add lustre to our young literature, it would also shed glory on our National life. It is emphatically the duty of Australia to rescue the works of this masculine Poet from oblivion.

HENRY KENDALL.

Size of Volume, about 300 pages; price, 10's.

Copy

Subscription List
towards
Charles Harpur's Poems.

Subscriptions are hereby asked in aid of a projected volume of the late Charles Harpur's Poems. It is not necessary to say who Charles Harpur was. He was the first and greatest of Australian poets; and the publication now in view would not only add lustre to our young literature, it would also shed glory on our national life. It is emphatically the duty of Australia to rescue the works of this masculine poet from oblivion.

Henry Kendall.

The volume will contain about 300 pages. Price 10/-.

John Howe (Singleton)[2]	£5 ·· 5
John Keys (Bengalla)[3]	5

---

[1] With this printed subscription form Mary Harpur launched her venture to publish a collected edition of her husband's poetry. It represented the third attempt at publication by subscription, following the efforts of CH in 1857 and Lang and Stenhouse in 1871. The text of the form is Kendall's (see Letter 153). The forms were sent initially to Mary's relatives in the Hunter region and northern NSW and to her Sydney and South Coast social circle, with a request to gather subscribers. The two attached lists (both headed 'Copy') are in the handwriting of James Doyle and Mary, with annotations by Doyle recording payments he received. They represent the subscriptions gathered over the following year.

[2] John Kennedy Howe (1812–90) of Redbournberry near Singleton, elder brother of James Doyle's mother Catherine Broughton Howe. With his nephew James, Howe would end up bearing most of the cost of producing *Poems*.

[3] John Hudson Keys (1811?–87), magistrate, settled in the upper Hunter in the 1840s with an extensive landholding, Bengalla, *c.* 15 km west of Muswellbrook. See Keys to Mary Harpur, 24 May 1881 (in *Suppl. Letters*).

James H. Doyle (Scone)[4]	[£]5
W C Doyle (Upper Hunter)[5]	2
Mrs S & G Dight (Hunter)[6]	2
Dr Fortescue[7]	2 - 2
W B Dalley[8]	2
R Doyle (Cowhill)[9]	1
Rev Mr & Mrs Evan Jones (Bega)[10]	1
W Coman[11]	1
A L Mc Dougall (Grafton)[12]	2 .. 10
Recd. JHD. May. 25' /per Thomas Parnell (Welbendungah)[13]	3 .. 3
Recd. JHD. May 25' /per J K Doyle[14] (Tamworth)	4 .. 0
„ „ „ „ Mrs Geo Bowman[15]	1 - 0
„ „ „ „ Mrs Wm Bowman[16]	1 - 0.
Received J.H.D. May 25' /per Roscoe Doyle[17]	£3 .. 3 .. 0

[4] James Henry Doyle (1844–1921), pastoralist of Invermein (or Invermien) near Scone in the upper Hunter region, and Mary Harpur's first cousin once removed, who, with his uncle John Kennedy Howe, underwrote the publication of *Poems*. See further, Doyle's obituary in *Scone Advocate*, 19 August 1921, p. 2.

[5] Possibly Mary's brother Willie, Cyrus William Doyle (1837–1922), grazier, of Goorangoola north of Singleton.

[6] Sisters Emma Dight, née Howe (1815–85), wife of early Singleton settler Samuel Billingsley Dight, and Elizabeth Ann Moore Dight (1823–1908), widow of Samuel's brother George Dight.

[7] George Fortescue, M.B. (1838–85), Sydney surgeon. He treated Mary's relatives and may also have treated CH, whose poetry he appreciated; see Fortescue to Mary Harpur, 29 November 1877 (in *Suppl. Letters*).

[8] See p. 168 n. 3.

[9] Robert Doyle (1848–1924), a brother of James Henry Doyle with grazing interests in NSW and Queensland. Cowhill or Cow-Hill Paddock is near Lochinvar, between Branxton and Maitland in the Hunter Valley.

[10] The Reverend David Evans Evans-Jones (1838–1901), Anglican vicar of Bega 1880–85, and his wife Emily Jane, née Pentland (1835–1914).

[11] See p. 222 n. 3.

[12] The McDougall brothers were cousins of Mary's, sons of her aunt Louisa, née Doyle. Andrew Louis McDougall (1819–1900) was a police magistrate in Grafton, northern NSW.

[13] Thomas Liverpool Parnell (1829–99), grazier, of Welbendungah station between Moree and Mungindi in northern NSW, husband of Mary's sister Isabella.

[14] John Kennedy Doyle (1840–1907), of Glengarvon, near Tamworth, grazier, auctioneer and stock and station agent, James Doyle's brother and husband of Mary's youngest sister Emily Maria Doyle.

[15] Probably Eliza Sophia Bowman, née Pearse (1797–1884), widow of George Bowman of Richmond, whose family held land on the Hunter at Arrowfield, Archerfield (opposite Granbelang) and Skellatar at Muswellbrook.

[16] Probably Elizabeth Bowman, née Arthur (1798–1885), of Richmond, widow of George Bowman's brother William, former Member of the Legislative Council and magistrate.

[17] Mary's youngest brother Roscoe Rienzi Doyle (1849–1908).

[Received] James Tom[1]	[£]1 .. 1
" " " " Ed Doyle[2]	1 .. 1
Malcom McDougall[3]	2 - 0 .0
E. A Doyle[4]	2 - 0 0
Jas R Doyle[5]	2 - 0 0
F. Clode[6]	1 - 0 0
W Harpur[7]	2 - 10 0
Richardsons'[8]	
[Limb?[9]]	[2?] - 0 0 pd
	34 . 12 0

Copy

Charles Harpur's Poems.

Subscription's are hereby asked in aid of a projected volume of the late Charles Harpur's Poems. It is not necessary to say who Charles Harpur was. He was the First and greatest of Australian Poets; and the publication now in view would not only add lustre to our young literature, it would also shed glory on our national life. It is emphatically the duty of Australia to rescue the works of this masculine poet from oblivion.

Henry Kendall.

Price of volume 300. pages. 10s

List of subscribers

John Howe. Singleton	£5 .. 5 Pd
John H. Keys. Bengalla	5 - - Pd
James H. Doyle Scone	5 Pd
A. L. McDougall. Grafton	2 . 10 Pd
W. B. Dalley. Sydney	2 -

---

[1] Probably James D. Tom of Bundabulla station, Bokhara River north of Brewarrina, a neighbour of the Doyles.

[2] Probably Mary's cousin Edward Norris Doyle (1840–82) of Yarriari, Quipolly, near Quirindi.

[3] One of the McDougall brothers (see p. 241 n. 12). Malcolm Septimus McDougall (1833–82) was a pastoralist at Lyndhurst near Warwick on the Darling Downs, south-east Queensland.

[4] Mary's brother Edmund Adolphus Doyle (1831–99) of Radfordslea, at the junction of Black Creek and the Hunter River, Branxton.

[5] Mary's brother James Rowland Doyle (1828–1900) at Walgett.

[6] Possibly Frederick E. Clode (1856–1923) of Walgett. The Clodes were relatives of Mary through her grandfather Andrew Hastings Doyle.

[7] Probably Washington Harpur (1851–1938), son of CH and Mary, recently married and living at Walgett.

[8] Not identified. This and the next name are late additions, written slantwise.

[9] Not identified.

Dr Fortescue Sydney	[£]2	
Rev. Evan Jones Bega	1	
Mrs. S. & G. Dight	2	Pd
Robert Doyle. Lochinvar	1	Pd
W. C. Doyle.[10] Hunter	2	Pd
Mallcolm Mc Dougall. Queensland.	2	Pd
J. R. Doyle – Walgett.	2	
Clode Walgett	1	
John McDougall Rosalie Plains[11]	2 . 2	
Recd. JHD May 25 /per Thomas Parnell Welbndungah	3 . 3 –	Pd
„ „ „ „ John K. Doyle Tamworth	4	Pd
F. Stennett (Cobargo[12]	10	
P. Brock (Bodalla[13]	10	
R. Campbell Clyde River[14]	10	
Dr. King[15] (Moruya)	1 ..	
E. A. Doyle	2. –	Pd
Received JHD. May 26' /per Mrs Geo Bowman.	1. –	Pd
„ „ „ „ Mrs Wm Bowman	1.	Pd

155. Mary Harpur to James Henry Doyle, 21 April 1881

Text: ML MSS 827

Euroma Eurobodalla April 21st 1881

My dear Cousin[16]

I enclose a circular[17] earnestly requesting you will use your influence in forwarding the proposed publication of a volume of my late husbands poems.

---

[10] Not identified with certainty.

[11] John Frederick McDougall (1820–96), pastoralist of Rosalie Plains, Jondaryan, Queensland, and Member of that colony's Legislative Council. He was brother of Andrew and Malcolm McDougall.

[12] Frederic Stennett, J.P., farmer, of Woodlands, Dry River, Cobargo, father-in-law of Rodolph Campbell (see n. 14 below).

[13] Not identified with certainty. There was a family of Brocks at Bodalla; this may be Patrick (1860–1936).

[14] Rodolph Archibald Clarence Campbell (1854–1905), schoolteacher at Tomakin, a friend of the Harpur family when his father W. A. M. C. Campbell taught at Eurobodalla, 1868–70. The Campbells later moved north to make their home on the Buckenbowra River, Clyde River. See Mary Harpur to Rodolph Campbell, 29 August 1881 (in *Suppl. Letters*).

[15] Henry Kirwan King (1844–1920), doctor at Moruya 1878–85 and, on return from his visit to England, at Nowra. See King to Mary Harpur, 8 August 1885 (in *Suppl. Letters*).

[16] Mary gives Doyle's address as 'Walgett'. He would, in September 1881, purchase the Invermein homestead near Scone along with 2,900 acres of rich farmland to use as a fattening property for sheep from his station Ulumbie near Walgett in northern NSW: see *Maitland Mercury*, 21 December 1895, p. 15. He then lived at Invermein for the rest of his life.

[17] See Letter 154.

His claim's have been so frequently urged by the leading papers, and his works so often enquired for that I feel it a duty to do my utmost to bring out some of his works, The size of the book will depend on the amount subscribed, if sufficient a Book of high class literature could be published as large as Byrons works,[1] Surely his Countrymen who are so proud of, so generous to their athletes will not be less proud of, or less generous to their their men of genius.

If my large and influential family will only aid the good work as I am sure they will there will be no doubt about the book being published. I have written to my brotherinlaw John of Tamworth[2] and many others of the family Will you James see, or send to your brother Robert[3] and all you think will help me. I have asked all to return me the lists in about a month or six weeks. My late husbands friends Sir H Parkes & John Robertson[4] I know will do a great deal to further the publication I have rec. several kind letters from the former about it. He is most anxious to see the works published. It is a matter of surprise that the family did not publish the book long ago, as the outlay would soon be returned.

I only regret I am not in a position to do it now.

I suppose James you have quite forgotten me. Do you remember your visit to me at Granbelang with your dear Father[5] who was alway like my own brother. I remember you so well.

With love to you and your family and hopes that you will take a warm interest in the matter of the publication

I am dear James
Yours affec.
Mary Harpur

---

[1] The Harpurs had a single-volume Byron, now at NLA: *The Poetical Works of Lord Byron* (London: John Murray, 1859; shelf-mark FERG/760), with CH's signature and date 'Euroma 1866' pasted in twice on the half-title, apparently cut from the title pages of other books, and a leaf apparently in CH's hand pinned to the endpaper. J. A. Ferguson purchased the book from Mary Araluen Baldwin (née Harpur) in 1927.

[2] John Kennedy Doyle: see p. 241 n. 14.

[3] Robert Doyle (1848–1924), with grazing interests in NSW and Queensland.

[4] Parkes was at this time Premier of NSW and Colonial Secretary; Robertson, a former political enemy, was Minister for Public Instruction.

[5] Andrew Doyle (1815–78), Mary's cousin.

156. Sir Henry Parkes to Mary Harpur, 2 May 1881 *Text:* ML C376

Sydney May 2. 1881

Dear Mrs Harpur[6]

I shall be very happy to assist in any way within my power to bring a collection of your late husband's Poems before the Public The best way I think would be to induce Mr Robertson the publisher[7] to bring out the volume under some guarantee[8]

I have already taken a step towards seeing what can be done[9] When I see the result I will write to you again. Thank you much for your kind enquiries after Lady Parkes.[10] We are both rapidly going down into the Vale of Shadows[11]

Yours sincerely
Henry Parkes

157. George Robertson to Sir Henry Parkes, 11 May 1881

Text: ML A904

GEORGE ROBERTSON
33, & 35, Little Collins Street West, and 1,3,&5, McKillop Street,[12] *Melbourne*
11th May *1881*

Dear Sir Henry,

I enclose with this memo. of the cost of producing 500 copies of Harpur's

---

[6] This letter responds to: Mary Harpur to Parkes, 24 April 1881 (in *Suppl. Letters*). The torn envelope located with the present letter (in ML C376, p. 417) is stamped 'JU 81', with the day of the month missing, apparently because of the removal of the cancelled stamp. The envelope must have originally enclosed a different, later letter, possibly Letter 161 (now located in ML MSS 947; 'JU' was the abbreviation for June, 'JY' for July).

[7] George Robertson (1825–98), Melbourne publisher, bookseller and the largest book importer and wholesaler in Australia, with a London buying office. The firm had published Parkes's *Speeches* (1876), Adam Lindsay Gordon's *Sea Spray and Smoke Drift* (1867), Kendall's *Leaves from Australian Forests* (1869) and, in the 1870s, works by G. G. McCrae, James Brunton Stephens and Arthur Patchett Martin. A leaflet of January 1875 entitled 'Mr. George Robertson's Terms for Publishing Books on Commission, for Authors, Booksellers, etc.' specified that the author must meet all expenses of printing, paper, advertising etc., and that Robertson would receive a commission of 15 per cent on all copies sold – see Parkes papers, ML A927, vol. 57, p. 23.

[8] See p. 216 n. 2.

[9] Parkes had evidently written for an estimate of printing costs: see Letter 157.

[10] When Parkes was created Knight Commander of the Order of St Michael and St George, an Imperial order, in 1877, his wife Clarinda became Lady Parkes.

[11] A common expression, from Psalm 23: 'Yea, though I walk through the valley of the shadow of death, I will fear no evil: for thou art with me.' Clarinda Parkes, an invalid in her last years, suffering from gout, kidney disease and a weak heart, would die in February 1888. Parkes, who had not yet reached the height of his fame, would outlast a second wife and marry a third.

[12] In 1872 Robertson moved from his Elizabeth-street premises to an imposing new four-storey book manufactory and wholesale warehouse on the corner of Little Collins and McKillop-streets, Melbourne: see *Argus*, 3 May 1872, p. 6.

Poems.[1] It would scarcely be worth while to print any smaller number. If 200 copies were subscribed for @ 10/. each it would cover the cost.

I think the association of Mr Kendall's name with the book would not be of any advantage—perhaps the reverse[2]

Yours faithfully
Geo Robertson

MEMORANDUM

From George Robertson,
Importer of Books & Stationery,
PUBLISHER & MANUFACTURING STATIONER,
33 & 35 Little Collins St. West, and 1, 3 & 5, McKillop Street,
MELBOURNE.

May 9th *1881*

To
Harpur's Poems, 1 Vol. *cr.* 8vo[3] Similar to specimen page attached—
19 sheets = 304 pp. in best cloth binding, gilt lettering[4]
    Cost of edition of 500 Copies   £95 : 0 : 0
    Each 16 pp of printed matter addl say   4 : 0 : 0
    Corrections & all publishing changes extra—

158. Henry Kendall to Mary Harpur, 13 May 1881

Text: Kendall papers, ML MSS 957

Cundletown Friday 13th May 1881.

My dear Mrs Harpur,

I have been absent travelling, and did not see your letter[5] before this morning. I have never been within 200 miles of your district. The circular[6] will do; but it would look better on foolscap. Do not however incur extra expense. Send a copy of the list to every leading man in Sydney, and write to

---

[1] This quotation responds to an enquiry from Parkes – see Letter 156.

[2] In 1869 Robertson had published Kendall's *Leaves from Australian Forests* under a profit-sharing arrangement and at the publisher's expense. He lost about £100 on the venture.

[3] Single volume, crown octavo. For octavo and the sheet–page calculation, see p. 228 n. 2.

[4] *Best cloth*: a binding of cloth (usually cotton) glued over 'mill-board' covers became common in the mid-19th century, a cheaper alternative to leather. *Gilt lettering*: the title, ornamentation etc., impressed onto the spine in gold leaf: see further, *SMH*, 26 May 1856, p. 3.

[5] Not located.

[6] Kendall had provided the text (Letter 153), but the printing was mismanaged: 'The printed lists are all out they were such absurd things too printed wrongly on small note paper instead of foolscap' (Mary Harpur to Rodolph Campbell, 29 August 1881; in *Suppl. Letters*).

Messrs Garnet Walch[7] and Marcus Clarke[8] of Melbourne. Get Mr Robertson the bookseller of Sydney[9] to print and publish for you. As to editing and correcting proofs, you may depend upon either Mr Thomas Butler[10] of the *Freeman's Journal* York Street Sydney, or Mr Philip Joseph Holdsworth[11] of the Colonial Treasury. If I were not constantly on the move travelling from one place to another I would gladly do the work myself. As it is, I will, of course, assist your noble endeavour in every possible way. You are aware that I am Chief Inspector of State Forests. My late journey has completely knocked me up;[12] but I have lost no time in answering you. You are a good brave woman; and your efforts on behalf of your great husband ought to bring about the assistance of every educated member of the Australian community.

> I am, my dear Mrs Harpur,
> Yours faithfully,
> Henry Kendall.

Mr Marcus Clarke is to be found at the Public Library—Melbourne. Mr Garnet Walch is a member of the Yorick Club,[13] Collins Street Melbourne. Get from Robertson an estimate of the cost of printing and binding When the subscription lists shall have been returned to you, send them to Robertson and he will, no doubt, proceed with the work without troubling you for money.[14]

---

[7] Garnet Walch (1843–1913), prolific journalist, dramatist and author of two volumes of light verse, known for his pantomimes, burlesques and comediettas as well as his long-running stage adaptation (1890–1914) of Rolf Boldrewood's *Robbery Under Arms*. Kendall would have known him on the staff of *Sydney Punch* in the 1860s and as one of the Melbourne bohemian circle during Kendall's time there in 1869–70.

[8] Marcus Andrew Clarke (1846–81), Melbourne journalist, editor and novelist, best known for his novel *His Natural Life* (1874), previously serialised, in a longer form, in *Australian Journal* – which he edited for part of the serialisation. Clarke was at this time Clerk to the Trustees of the Public Library of Victoria: see *His Natural Life*, ed. Lurline Stuart (St Lucia: University of Queensland Press, 2001), pp. xxi–xxii, xxix–xxx.

[9] I.e., Melbourne publisher and bookseller George Robertson (1825–98), who had a Sydney branch at 361 George-street. Robertson's younger namesake and future competitor (1860–1933) did not settle in Sydney until February 1882, and would commence publishing six years later.

[10] Thomas Butler (d. 1910?), editor and proprietor of the Sydney Catholic weekly *Freeman's Journal*, in which he printed Kendall's satirical prose and verse pseudonymously.

[11] See p. 239 n. 4.

[12] In May 1881 Parkes had Kendall appointed as first Inspector of State Forests, with a colony-wide remit to report on systems for conserving timber and supervising timber cutting and collecting revenue. This involved almost constant hard travel around central and western NSW, with Kendall in deteriorating health (see Ackland, pp. 278–86).

[13] A club for the literary and artistic bohemians of Melbourne, founded 1868. Early members included Marcus Clarke, Adam Lindsay Gordon and, later, Kendall and George Gordon McCrae. See Kendall's 'A Colonial Literary Club', *ATCJ*, 18 February 1871, p. 18, attributed to 'A Wandering Bohemian'.

[14] I.e., provided the promised subscriptions covered the costs of production.

159. Sir Henry Parkes to Mary Harpur, 24 May 1881

Text: ML MSS 947

Colonial Secretary's Office Sydney May 24th 1881

My dear Mrs Harpur[1]

I have communicated with Mr George Robertson the publisher as to the cost of bringing out a volume of your late husbands' Poems[2] & I should be disposed to take the work in hand if I could see my way in respect to the selection & supervision Do you know any person of taste & sound judgment who would make the selection & edit the volume

I need hardly say that it would be impossible for me to undertake any labour in the matter myself[3]

Very sincerely yours
Henry Parkes

160. Mary Harpur to Sir Henry Parkes, 28 May 1881

Text: ML A887

Euroma Eurobodalla May 28th 1881

My dear Sir

Your truly generous, nay, noble intentions[4] have removed a mountain of anxiety from my mind, With you at the helm the book will be a success; It is the wish of my children as well as mine that it shall be dedicated to our good, our great Premier Sir Henry Parkes. The names of Harpur, Parkes will again be associated in an immortal wreath of poesy.

I enclose the last letter I had from my kind friend H. Kendall as it relates to the publication His good words of me are pleasant although I am only doing my duty. The Gentlemen he names[5] are no doubt competent but could not be expected to devote their time to the matter without remuneration perhape they would wait awhile until the sale of the book. I doubt my own ability else I would go to Sydney and correct the proofs myself, the expence too would be more than I could afford although I would do it if I thought the book would be spoiled by typographical errors I have so often seen poor Chas stamping

---

[1] See Mary Harpur to Parkes, 24 April 1881 (in *Suppl. Letters*) and Parkes's initial reply, Letter 156.

[2] See Letter 157.

[3] A reasonable objection: at this time Premier of NSW and Colonial Secretary, Parkes's time was monopolised by affairs of state.

[4] Mary was responding to Parkes's somewhat ambiguous offer 'to take the work in hand' (Letter 159). He clarified his offer in Letter 161.

[5] Thomas Butler and Philip Holdsworth are named in Letter 158: see p. 247 n. 10 and p. 239 n. 4.

mad about such *calamities*.[6]

As soon as I hear from you, I will take the poems to Sydney perhapse *you* could aid me in the selection although your duties are so manifold. I was looking over the works yesterday and felt shocked to see some of the letters and little words faded, almost obliterated.

Before I rec. Mr Kendalls letter I had distributed all but 2. lists amongst my relatives and personal friends mostly these two I sent to Marcus Clark and Mr Walch.[7] To day I rec. a brotherly letter from an old friend John Keys of Bengalla[8] with £5. sub. Last week another old friend and relative John Howe of Singleton[9] wrote most affec. and promises £5.5. Every one seems so rejoiced about the publication. Pray tell me what to do, *you* have the matter, thank God in your hands. Should I return the money? Your goodness has redeemed the publication from subscription

Awaiting your advice and wishes

> I am my dear Sir
> Yours respectfully
> Mary Harpur

161. Sir Henry Parkes to Mary Harpur, 2 June 1881

Text: ML MSS 947

June 2. 1881

Dear Mrs Harpur

I have your note of the 28th May

I should not return any money given towards the projected publication if I were you & I incline to the opinion that it will be best to get subscribers to cover the cost 200 would be sufficient [....] of [sub]jecting you to trouble in that matter

The great thing to be done is to place the poems in the hands of some one competent to select & revise I should not myself approve of the gentlemen named by Mr Kendall but I cannot at this moment think of a proper person The issue of 500 copies, @ 10/- would cost about £100 If 200 copies were subscribed for that would cover costs The other 300 copies if sold would give you £150 less circumstances & on the whole say £100 clear.

What I meant to convey to you was that if I could be satisfied that the book would be properly edited, I would see to raising the expense of publication

---

[6] A longstanding complaint: see Letter 112 and p. 190 n. 2.

[7] See p. 247 nn. 7, 8.

[8] See p. 240 n. 3 and Keys to Mary Harpur, 24 May 1881 (in *Suppl. Letters*).

[9] See p. 240 n. 2. See further, Howe to Mary Harpur, 2 May 1881, and her reply, 7 May 1881 (both in *Suppl. Letters*).

I will write to you[1] after making some further enquiries

Very sincerely yours
Henry Parkes

162. Mary Harpur to John Kennedy Howe, 4 June 1881
Text: ML MSS 827

Euroma Eurobodalla June 4th 1881

My dear Mr Howe

Your kind letter and generous subscription has pleased me very much at the same time I rec. another kind letter from another old friend Mr Keys, of Bengalla with his subscription £5.[2] it is so gratifying to me in every way

I'cant help thinking had such goodness been more common what years of pinching poverty I and my poor children would have been spared with works on the shelf that would have been a fortune in any land but this. In writing to Sir Henry Parkes I have mentioned yours and Mr Keys's kind sympathy and generosity. Since I wrote you I have received another letter from the Premier he will most generously, most nobly, take the matter of the publication in his own hands He Has seen Robertson the publisher about the matter so that all will be a *success* with such a man at its head. Thank God for all his mercies in raising up such good friends

I wish all the lists to be returned to me with names although the publication will not be by subscription still friends will just do the same as before in helping with the work I intended to send all my returned lists with subscribing names to Robertson (publisher) for *him* to collect. I am so busy putting the manuscripts in order for I am daily expecting a letter from Sir Henry to take them to Sydney. If it is published well and neatly it will be an honour to our Country the matter is of the highest class of its kind acknowledged by all. I have had such nice letters from W. B. Dalley & Dr Fortescue with kind promise of subscription. I wish H. Kendall were in Sydney to correct the proofs. Perhapse Sir Henry will manage to get some one of intelect able to do it, I fear I am not.

The Neglected poet's grave is still without a stone *Years ago* the highly gifted Stenhouse told me there would be a monument erected to the memory of so great a poet. It is lang lang a coming.

I fear I tire you John. Give my love to Emma & Betsy tell them I never forgot them or any dear old friend of my youth I think so much of them all

---

[1] Parkes did not do so. He took no further role in the publication of *Poems*.
[2] For Keys and others mentioned in this letter, see notes for Subscription lists for *Poems* (Letter 154); 'Emma & Betsy' are the Dight sisters (p. 241 n. 6).

that I never could care for the new friends and have made none

> I am dear Mr Howe
> yours sincerely
> Mary Harpur

163. Mary Harpur to Sir Henry Parkes, 12 June 1881

Text: ML A923

Euroma Eurobodalla June 12th 1881

My dear Sir

I cannot express my feelings of gratitude to you for your warm sympathy and kindness with regard to the proposed publication of poor Chas's works.

Believe me my sole wish is to see the *works safe* and in print In my endeavour to publish them *gain* (however desirable) is not thought of. Permit me to enquire if the greater part of the poems could not be published in one volume It would be so desirable if possible. There would still remain another volume of Lectures. *play* satires. unfinished poems. newspaper letters. &c. &c. Nothing he has written is undeserving of publication. I found amongst the papers a sonnet to your poor Robert when a child.[3] If I *counted* every sonnet there would be near 266. poems if not more ready for publication Allow me to send you a list, with this note.

> I am dear Sir
> Yours most respectfully
> Mary Harpur

List of Poems

Manu't. No. 1.

    Creek of the Four Graves.
    The Bush Fire

No. 2.

    A Storm in the Mountains
    The spectre of the Cattle Flat
    Dawn in the Australian Forest
    Midsummer in the Forest.

No. 3.

    Lost in the Bush
    The Murder of the Lamb.
    The voice of the Swamp Oak

No 4.

    The Glen of the Whitemans Grave.
    A poets Home

---

[3] 'To Robert Sydney Parkes, aged 10 Months' (1844; h626a), and published in *Weekly Register*, 29 November 1845, p. 258 (h626c). Robert died in 1880 aged 36, after a long and painful struggle with Bright's disease (nephritis) and dropsy (oedema).

No. 5.

    The Tower of the Dream
    The Cloud
    Humanity
    The Vision of an Angel
    The Spouse of the Infinitude
    A Coast View
    The Flight of Faith

No. 6.

    The Dream by the Fountain
    A Rhyme
    To. Henry Parkes.
    The Losses of the Past
    To an Echo on the Banks of the
      Hunter
    The Death of Shelly
    Happiness & Faith
    Monodies
    Autumnal Leaves
    Bits. Property is Funded Talent
    A Summer House Treat
    Luck out of Season

No. 7.

    The World & the Soul
    The Bard of Paradise
    The Vision of the Rock
    A Musical Reminicence
    Consolation

No. 8.

    Ideality
    A Lament
    To a Comet
    Love the Idealiser
    The Widows Boy
    The Snow Child
    A Combat
    To——
    Blindness of Merit
    Joshua

    A Basket of Summer Fruit
    The Death of Shylock
    Finish of Style
    Abed Ben Houran

No 9

    The Poet.)
    Outward Bound
    Diana
    Yon Green Wood
    Mary Arden
    Absence by the Sea Side
    To Mary
    Emblems
    Virginal Love
    Eva Grey
    Love and Song
    The Dream of the Orient
    An Aboriginal Mothers Lament
    Early Summer
    Love
    The Lost Voice
    Dora
    The Hunters Indian Dove
    Love to the Last
    To a Child Sleeping
    A Song of David &c &c.
    Death of Sisera
    Love. Friendship & Truth
    Nobility
    The Muses Ethic's
    The Battle of Life
    Cora's Sire
    Cora
    The Anchor
    Lines & Figures
    The World Birth of Love.
    To a Girl
    Contempory Praise
    Compensation
    In the Past
    Ecce Homo
    Ineffable

No 10.

> The Flight of Peace
> To the Moon
> Lifes first Despair
> The Night Bird
> Life and Death
> Onward
> Eden Lost
> What's Poetic.
> Love Dreaming of Death
> The Past
> A Thought Sting
> Asking in Vain
> No Mean Dwelling

No 11.

> Sonnets

No. 12

> The Slave Story
> The Forgotten
> Emigrants Vision
> Forward Ho!
> Yearnings
> A Political Gospel
> Hope On

No. 13.

> Kangaroo Hunt. & Morning in the
> Mountains

No 14

> The Witch of Hebron
> Castle Carnal
> The Forging of Achille'ss Armour
> The Rose of Albana
> The Infinate

No 15.

> To Poesy
> War Song of the Australian League
> Elegiac verses
> Educational Matters
> The Devils own Glee
> Three Thousand Years Ago.
> A Song of Manhood
> The one thing Needful
> Valadictory Bunkum
> A Charactistic Epitaph for an Able
>   Dealer
> The Babalonian Captivity
> A Keen
> Both Sides of the Medal
> A Burley Beast
> A Character
> Honest Poverty
> The Knight of Bunkam
> Change & Death
> God's Man
> Similies from Homer
> The Famous Night seen in VIII. Iliad
> Domestic Sonnets
> To the Lyre of Australia

No 16.

> Genius Lost

No. 17

> Rhymed Criticisms & prose notes
> on Chaucer. Shakespere. Milton.
> Waller. Dryden. Pope. Grey.
> Collins. Burns. Byron. Moore.
> Wordsw[orth.]
> Coleridge. Shelley.
> Critical Rhymes on some of the
>   Critical Reviewers of the Last Age
> House of Folly

164. Henry Maydwell Martin[1] to James Henry Doyle, 3 January 188[2]

Text: ML MSS 827

Adelaide SA January 3rd 188[2][2]

Dear Jim

Your favour of 26th ulto[3] duly reached me on New years Day and deserves more notice & comment than I shall be able to give it now, owing to the abnormal pressure of business at the end of the year limiting my leisure. To begin with, I am much interested in the poetry of the late Charles Harpur and will very gladly superintend the revision of the MS and the correction of the press. I would undertake the whole work gratuitously (looking upon it as a mental medicine and alterative[4]) very gladly, but that I believe I could get it better done (and still exercise a control) by a literary friend and relative[5]

---

[1] Henry Maydwell Martin (1846–1936), Adelaide-based co-editor of the 1883 edition of CH's *Poems* and an old friend of Doyle's. An accountant and business manager who turned to winemaking, he was from a well-known liberal Adelaide family of Unitarians. See further, the family history, *Hatbox Letters*, pp. 89–98; State Library of SA notes on the Martin family papers (PRG 550); an interview, in *Observer* (Adelaide), 1 January 1927, p. 16; and a brief obituary in *Advertiser* (Adelaide), 26 September 1936, p. 25.

[2] '1881' in MS is a turn-of-year mistake for 1882. Letter 165 is otherwise the first letter to suggest Martin as editor.

[3] Doyle's (lost) letter of 26 December 1881 must represent the first formal step in the enlistment of Martin as editor of CH's *Poems*. The two were old comrades, as appears from Martin's reminiscences of droving days in western NSW and his enquiries after mutual friends (e.g., Martin to Doyle, 6 November 1881: in *Suppl. Letters*); and Martin seems to have been a dependable family friend to the Doyles: see p. 286 n. 1.

[4] Medicine or remedy that acts by altering the body's processes.

[5] Previously unidentified, Martin's older sister Annie Montgomerie Martin (1841–1918) is the most likely candidate. Martin had several relatives with a literary bent: his brother Frederick; Frederick's wife Catherine Edith Macauley Martin, poet and novelist; his sister Lucy Martin (married to *SA Register* proprietor-editor John Howard Clark); and his sister Annie, teacher and headmistress of liberal and progressive schools for girls in Adelaide. In Martin to Doyle, 19 March 1883 (in *Suppl. Letters*), Martin reports he laboured over the preface ('almost the only unaided work of mine, and not entirely that' – Letter 187), 'my mate having gone off to Europe as soon as the other work was finished'. Adelaide passenger departures for Europe the previous six months include three ladies: Misses A. M. Martin, E. H. Clark and A. Balk, per *Natal*, 11 February 1883 (*SA Advertiser*, 13 February 1883, p. 4). Miss E. H. Clark is probably Ellen Howard Clark, daughter of John Howard Clark and Lucy Martin. Misses Martin and Clark arrived back in Adelaide from Europe per *Salazie* on 10 July 1884 (*Evening Journal*, 11 July 1884, p. 2). Around this time Miss Martin was advertising herself available for 'literary work and teaching', suggesting she had competency in both areas (*Evening Journal*, 2 July 1884, p. 1). While Annie's travelling companion Ellen Howard Clark (1861–1936) is also a possible candidate, she was only 20 years old when Martin took on his task, and we have no indication of any literary interests. He may have been reluctant to name a female co-editor (hence 'mate'), something unlikely to be welcomed by the Doyles or, perhaps, by Mary Harpur.

15. Henry Maydwell Martin, undated, photographer unknown

16. Annie Montgomerie Martin, undated, photographer unknown

who would see it through for £20. This is the amount which Bruce[1] insisted on giving me—much against my will, but it was either take it or quarrel with him—for what I imagine will prove in the end to have been a much greater work. In regard to the deceased Poet requiring no alteration[2] to be made by his editor, this is usual and quite understood. It applies to the introduction of foreign matter as a so-called improvement and is a just requirement,—but the right of *excision must* remain with the representatives of the publisher, and of course mere verbal correction, as of spelling or omission of syllables, is always necessary and can fairly be entrusted to an intelligent and *sympathetic* editor. As I have heard of Chas Harpur, not alone from your family but from the pens of contemporary writers, I am inclined to think that a small edition of the best of his poems might find a sale, though the fine arts are *not* in such request in the colonies as they should and will be. Of the intrinsic merit of the poetry I shall be better able to judge when I see the M.S. if you decide to chance it. Bruce's poems have not been a financial success by any means. Out of an edition of 700 paper & 300 cloth printed at a cost of £125. without including me there are 127 paper and 177 cloth remaining, and Bruce has *given away* about £50 worth out of what have gone to the public. The selling price of his books is 5/. and 3/. respectively and what with advertising, wood engravings, agency, and other charges he has really only had back about £30 cash to represent his outlay of £145. !! This is, however, not a fair criterion,— for in the first place the work itself—(which if you remember I described as "Bullock driver's poetry"[3]—and aggravated you by adding that perhaps you would enjoy it, meaning thereby, as I may now explain, that you (and I) being familiar with the scenes & incidents pertaining to the class alluded to might take more interest in the subject matter than ordinary City folks or than pure literati with fastidious tastes,—) the work itself is not one to recommend it to a general reading public. Again Sydney being an older community and a larger one has probably a better educated taste and a larger buying and reading class than we can yet boast, to say nothing of patriotism & the fact of the author being dead rather than living. Doubtless Harpur was pretty well known, and his friends would exert themselves in the matter?

What I would suggest is that a small and well selected volume be first printed and not in too-expensive a form. Then if this took we could have

---

[1] SA pastoralist-poet Robert Bruce (*c.* 1836–1908). Martin edited Bruce's *A Voice from the Australian Bush* (1877; online at Internet Archive), as can be seen from the details in his letters; for an advertisement, see *Illustrated Adelaide News*, 1 December 1877, p. 2. Bruce referred indirectly to Martin in his Preface as 'a friend who understands punctuation, and is a severe, though kindly critic'.

[2] The poems were to be 'printed *verbatim*': see Letter 135.

[3] Bruce's collection contains ballads and descriptions of bush life, 'true stories' of droughts, floods, dingo hunts and 'The Life of a Working Bullock', along with much comic and incidental verse. *ADB* considers that 'His poetry has rhyme and rhythm but lacks true poetic force.'

a second & complete edition according to circumstances, the cost of which would be less in proportion to the first one by the amount of matter already in type. Apprentices can set type from printed matter—only first class expensive hands from M.S. hence the difference in cost. I suppose it is a rule of the guild[4] Now for figures—printers & binders.—700 paper & 300 cloth similar to Bruce's herewith but type printed closer up—not so much margin & waste room would cost £125. but without the pictures. The very best paper. 700 paper & 300 cloth similar to "Experiences &c"[5] as regards paper & type about £50.

500 paper & 200 cloth like Bruces as above say £105. But a very good edition of 700 & 300 could be done for about £80. intermediate quality of paper &c. Say sell @ 4/. & 2/6 = 142/10/. gross Probably the whole of Harpur's works could be got into the same span as Bruce's 200 pages without detriment. But if you like to send me the whole of the M.S. without prejudice I will gladly go through it and reckon it out and report on it generally whether it is to go back or go on. If you decide to send it please "register" the package and if advisable, insure it. Do not be in the least afraid of trespassing on my leisure, for though this is certainly scanty I object to no employment for it which does not take me away from home, and this you[r] offer would I believe be simply healthy for me, for a change of work is notoriously as good as play and this would be an unusual and a welcome change.

It is perhaps premature to say anything relative to a memoir of the author or a preface,—but if you will have me supplied with data & detail I could get this well and gracefully done by my second. The particulars supplied in your last, tho' graphic are meagre, and certainly not suited for a public notice of an "in memoriam" notice, in which the old maxim "De mortuis nil nisi bonum"[6] must always be held in view.

I shall write to Peberdy[7] at once. I can only now thank you for your friendly confidence, and with best wishes for the happiness of you & yours in the new year

> I remain Dear Jim
> Yours faithfy
> H.M. Martin

---

[4] By the 1880s, Typographical Associations – printers' and compositors' unions – were well established in Victoria, NSW and SA. An apprentice worked for a fraction of the journeyman's wages, but tended to be used for easier jobbing tasks.

[5] Possibly *Experiences of a Colonist Forty Years Ago...* (Adelaide: Frearson & Bro., 1879; J. Williams, 1880) by George Hamilton (1812–83), farmer and police commissioner.

[6] 'Speak no ill of the dead', a Latin maxim attributed by Diogenes Laërtius to the sage Chilon of Sparta.

[7] Pastoralist W. K. Peberdy (1848?–1904), who married a niece of Mary Harpur's, Maria Wentworth Doyle.

P.S. I am a bachelor just now. My wife and children have gone to Port Elliot (60 miles) for a month.[1] all been ill—better now.

Sample volumes posted herewith, shew difference between "paper" & "cloth"

165. James Henry Doyle to Mary Harpur, 23 January 1882

Text: ML A1528

Singleton Redbournbury[2] January 23rd/82

My dear Mary

At Uncle Johns[3] request I write you respecting the contemplated publishing of your late husbands poems. Have you been able to arrange anything definate in the matter: if not we think we can propose a feasable plan of having something done

I have a friend in adelaide a Mr H. M. Martin who is no mean poet[4] himself a gentleman of education & honor & one that I would trust implicitly, and one who has already assisted in placing some literary works before the public[5]

I have written to Mr Martin and asked him if he would assist us in this matter: and he has replyed saying yes most willingly He offers to find a literary friend that he says is in every way competent to arrange the papers & put them in order for the publisher and also says he will himself supervise his friends work & to see that it is placed before the Sydney & general publick in an attractive form.

He also appears to quite understand the objections made by your late Husband to any alterations being made & says that such are usual in such cases.

John & your Sister Emily[6] both know Mr Martin and if you wish for their opinion of his fitness write them at once & let me know your decision upon receipt of their answer.

Mr Martin says justly that he can say nothing of the prospects ahead for the book until he sees the M. S. but he offers to receive it & go thro it carefully & report whether he thinks it is likely to be a success by selling well when

---

[1] Town on the south coast of the Fleurieu Peninsula, 80 km south of Adelaide. Once a seaport for the Murray River trade, it had become popular as a seaside resort.

[2] See p. 262 n. 2.

[3] John Kennedy Howe: see p. 240 n. 2.

[4] See p. 254 n. 1. Martin had a reputation among family and friends as a poet, although the love poem 'She and I' attributed to him in *Hatbox Letters*, p. 94, is by English writer and critic James Ashcroft Noble (*The Pelican Papers*, 1873).

[5] See p. 256 n. 1.

[6] John Kennedy Doyle (see p. 241 n. 14) and his wife Emily Maria Doyle (1842–1926).

published and he also says that perhaps it might be better to first place a portion of the poems (In a selected form) some of the best before the publick in a small volume & if that sold then a complete edition could at once follow but of all this he would advise us upon receipt of the M. S. & as soon as he could go carefully over it.

If you are inclined to let the M. S. go to Mr Martin: & will consen[t] Mr Howe & myself have determined to go thro with the publication ourselves[7] finding sufficient in addition to the Subs providing Mr Martins report is favorable & he thinks the publication will be even moderately successful or deserv[in]g So will you write Mr Howe & say what your ideas are on the matter & also let him know what you have been able to do since you wrote him last & if any further Subs have come in to Increase the list you sent to Mr Howe in November last.[8] also state what Subs you have recd paid up Mr Howe has not received any more since writing you If you decide upon letting the M. S go to adelaide it might be packed carefully and registered & if need be insured so as to prevent all possibillity of its being lost and if not all published I am sure would be returned safely to you if no unavoidable accident happened.

Mr Martin says that if he is supplied with the necessary data or information he will also have a neat preface arranged as an inmemmorium of Biography if you desire it but that information could be supplied later on if publication is gone on with: of which I have little doubt.

I hope you will lose no time in writing Mr Howe & letting us know what you decide upon & trusting all your circle are quite well

believe me your affett
Cousin
James H Doyle

Write Uncle John in answer to this—

166. Mary Harpur to John Kennedy Howe, 28 January 1882

Text: ML MSS 827

Euroma Eurobodalla Jan. 28th 1882

My dear Mr Howe

I have just received Cousin James's most kind letter,[9] I c'ant express how grateful I feel to you and James for the warm sympathy you are manifesting

---

[7] It must have been clear by this time that subscription alone would not suffice. Doyle's offer is an early indication of the family support that would make publication possible.

[8] See Mary Harpur to Howe, 1 November 1881 (in *Suppl. Letters*).

[9] Letter 165.

in the matter of the proposed publication of poor Chas's poems. My three children and self think it so good so noble of you, There was *clapping* of hands and *praise* of *relatives* after all when J's. letter came. I shall most gratefully accept your generous offer. Your word and James's is gaurentee sufficient for Mr Martins competency and honour Do you think when the time comes the post would be the safest way to send the manuscripts *registered*, at intervals; too. I think it would be safe.

I must tell you all that I have done (not much) since I wrote to you. I wrote to W. B. Dalley asking him to edit the work, His answer is that his engagements are so numerous also that he does not feel competant to undertake such an honour. He is competant but I suppose 'dont like the trouble. Robertson the publisher also wrote regreting I could not get a suitable person to edit the work an absolute necessity they all say. It is very kind of Mr Martin to undertake the work If it is brought out nicely, & neatly the work will sell and will repay for all trouble. Yours and James's kind generousity can not be paid by mere money. Sir H. P. forgot his promises and is just the *professor*[1] C. used to say he was. Robertson the publisher I fancy will be vexed but he has not used his influence as he ought to have done Hence he cant complain.

I believe there is about £60. altogether subscribed.[2] I have only £11. paid and in hand Will now have more heart in the work and remind subscribers to pay up. Will send it to you. I asked my brother James to send his collections to you. Isabella the same.[3]

I fear dear Mr Howe that it is giving you too much trouble I feel quite ashamed of doing so. It is well for the world there are some good unselfish spirits in it. What a dreary world it would be else.

We are having a severe drought here, I regret to see by the papers it is general. The grass and vegatables is so burnt up, and bush fires plentiful.

With kind regards
I am dear Mr Howe
Yours sincerely
Mary Harpur

[1] Parkes had shown interest in seeing *Poems* published, but Mary Harpur's letter to him of 12 June 1881 (Letter 163) apparently got no response. Cf. Mary Harpur to Howe, 1 November 1881: 'I am beginning to think him [Parkes] a great professor and little doer as poor Chas said he was when he used to say he loved him like a brother' (in *Suppl. Letters*).
[2] See Letter 154.
[3] Brother and sister of Mary: James Rowland Doyle at Walgett and Isabella Sophia Parnell, née Doyle (1829–87) at Welbendungah (north of Moree).

167. Henry Kendall to Mary Harpur, 22 March 1882

Text: Kendall papers, ML C199

Warroo Station Lachlan River[4] 22nd March 1882.

My dear Mrs Harpur,

I have only just received your letter[5]—having been on the back blocks of the Darling River for some time past. When I tell you that my official duties[6] compel me to travel all over the colony, and that I have not seen my home for the last six months, you will hardly wonder at what may have appeared to you my strange silence. One of my children died in January last;[7] but I was far away.

I need hardly say that I deeply reverence your noble devotion to your gifted husband. I wish to God it were in my power to edit his wonderful poems. I am so rushed with work that Sunday is no Sunday to me. You speak of a South Australian publisher and ask me if manuscripts can be sent safely through the post. Of course they can. By leaving the parcel open at each end, and marking close to the address "*manuscripts only*," you will escape heavy postage.[8] You also ask me—will the book pay? Judiciously looked after, it *will*; but you must remember that colonial printers and publishers will get [all] they can out of authors. With a view to success, send the first copies printed to the leading English journals—one to the *Athenæum*, one to the Spectator, one to the *Saturday Review*, and one to that great magazine, the *Nineteenth Century*.[9] Send one also to Algernon Charles Swinburne—the most liberal-minded of living English poets.[10] I wish you could persuade Mr Dalley or Archbishop Vaughan[11] to write the preface: if either of them did it, the book would go off at once. When it is fairly started I shall do my very best in every way to push it. Amongst other work, I will see to the reviewing of it in the leading Sydney and Melbourne papers.

[4] Extensive sheep station on the Lachlan River 50 km west of Forbes, proprietor Charles Smith MacPhillamy. Kendall was apparently based there for his inspections in this part of central NSW.

[5] Not located. This reply suggests it informed Kendall of H. M. Martin's role in preparing CH's poems for publication.

[6] See p. 247 n. 12.

[7] His son Orara died in convulsions on 21 January 1882 at the family home at Cundletown, aged seven months.

[8] Under the Post Office's Book Packet Regulations of 1878 a book packet (which could include written material other than a letter) could be sent more cheaply than the letter rate, provided it could easily be opened for inspection.

[9] Four of the main literary periodicals – weekly, monthly or quarterly – of the 19th century, all published in London.

[10] See p. 162 n. 8.

[11] Roger Bede Vaughan, Catholic Archbishop of Sydney (1834–83), noted for his scholarship (e.g., his *The Life & Labours of S. Thomas of Aquin*, London: Longmans & Co., 1871, the first English biography of Aquinas).

You will be sorry to hear that, for some time, I have been in very delicate health. It is not at all improbable that, before the year be out, I shall see Charles.[1]

Believe me to be,
My dear Mrs Harpur,
Yours sincerely,
Henry Kendall.

168. James Henry Doyle to Mary Harpur, 12 April 1882

Text: ML A1528

Redburnbury[2] Singleton April 12th / 82

My dear Mary

Uncle John & I have been talking over the matter of going on with the publication of Mr Harpurs poems this morning and we have finally decided to proceed at once without any further delay

I now give you a statement shewing how matters generally stand 1st from the list you sent Uncle John The following names[3] have not paid up so far viz

W B Dalley	£2
Dr Fortescue	£2
Revd Evan Jones	1.
J. R. Doyle	2
Clode	1.
John McDougall	2/2 –
Thos Parnell	3.
John K Doyle	4
J. Stennett	10/–
J. Brock	10/–
R. Campbell	10/–
Dr King	1– 0

We have decided to go on with, or without more but if you collect any more send it to uncle John as you get it and we will also accept any Subs that may be sent us and pass it Credi[t] of the publishing acct

I have read Kendalls letter[4] and his remarks about the greed of publishers

---

[1] Kendall died of phthisis (tuberculosis) on 1 August 1882.

[2] Doyle was staying with his uncle John Howe. (The spelling of the estate – Redbournberry – varied.)

[3] For the names, see notes to Letter 154. For 'J. Stennett' read 'F. Stennett' and for 'J. Brock' read 'P. Brock': Doyle has misread Mary's hand.

[4] Letter 167.

in the Colonys but with regard to Mr Martin I may say, he is not a publisher nor do I think he is interested in publishers work in any way he is simply a well Educated Gentleman, and no mean poet himself and acquainted with some literary people[5] and as he feels an interest in your husbands poems from what he has heard of them & would like to see them brought out he consented when I asked him to supervise the work for us & have it done as reasonably as possible

We would therefore wish you to send him the M.S. as soon as you like and in what ever way you think best: The Cheapest way is as Kendall suggests and I think it would be quite safe but if you decide upon sending it more closely and safely packed and in a way that would be more expensive we think it would be only fair for you to pay the expenses upon sending it out of the subscriptions that you may get in the future from those now promised. but this is a matter we leave to yourself

Mr Martins address I give you herein viz Henry M Martin c/o Simpson & sons King William Street *Adelaide*.[6]

This is the address I always put to my letters I write him abt 5 or 6 letters in the year and have never had one go wrong so far

When Mr Martin receives the MS he will go carefully over it & write us what he thinks of it & in what way he thinks it would be best to have it published and he will I am sure attend to any suggestion made by me as coming from you as regards your wishes as to style of volume Expence in binding & so forth that you may express for it seems to me that by the heading of the request for subscriptions that all subscribers who give 10/- are to receive a volume of the Poems when printed

Mr Martin also says that if supplied with the requisite information he can have the preface neatly .&. gracefully written and I have every confidence in the ability of his friend[7] to do it but still think that the more eminent the name of the writer of the preface the more beneficial to the prosperity of the work after edition[8]

Will you now forward the M S to Mr Martin: and write me any wishes and instructions that you would like to express or give any which I will have attended to if possible

Mr Martin has suggested that a small edition of the best of the poems should be printed and that if they should take favorably then a full & complete edition could be printed at a comparatively less cost than the 1st edition but

---

[5] Martin came from a cultured Adelaide circle that included a novelist, newspaper editor and noted teacher, and he had edited a poetry collection: see p. 254 n. 5 and p. 256 n. 1.

[6] Martin was at this time working as managing clerk (accountant) for A. Simpson and Son, ironmongery and hardware manufacturer, at Gawler Place, Adelaide.

[7] See p. 254 n. 5.

[8] I.e., publication.

of this he will be better able to report when you send him the M. S.

I am undertaking the Corresponde[nce] with regard to Uncle Johns & my share in this business. So in future will you write me your wishes and instructions relative to the publication & I will attend to them My address is James. H. Doyle Invermein Scone

I am sending Mr Martin Mr Kendalls letter that he may profit by Mr Kendalls ideas of what is best to be done to assist the prosperity of the work and I can assure you should the work not be a success it shall be from no wilful neglect or mismanagement as we will (and I promise for Mr Martin) do all in our power to make it prosperous but I do not say we may not make mistakes.

Mr Howe desires to be kindly remembered and trusting that all your circle are quite well

I remain
Your affect Cousin
James. H. Doyle

169. Mary Harpur to James Henry Doyle, 15 April 1882

Text: ML MSS 827

Euroma Eurobodalla April 15th 1882

My dear James

I rec. your kind letter this morning and according to your wish have dispatched the poems to Mr Martin, as the P. Office is next place to this I posted them and registered the parcle; May they bear good fruit, and may *you* and good kind Mr Howe have cause to rejoice over your generous kindness. I have sent 13 manuscripts 12 of which Chas copied out in his last illness to get published in England as Mr T. S. Mort promised to be the bearer Mr Martin will see his preface in the first leaf of No 1. mnscp sealed together.[1] (As Mort never went as he intended) It was to be dedicated to the people of England as he felt so disgusted with the neglect of his country. Do you think it would be well to dedicate the book to the people of Australia[2] I shall leave the matter intirely in your hands feeling sure of success, Mr Martin too knows more about the matter than I and will do all for the best He may think I have sent too much for the vol. I feel sure he will be pleased with all It would be well to have the book neatly bound and poems not *crowded*. I ought to have sent the

---

[1] CH, 'To the English Reader', now in ML A87-1, p. 17; 'mnscp' for *manuscript* is an afterthought, squeezed into the available space. For the 'manuscripts', see p. 266 n. 1.

[2] *Poems* (1883) was dedicated thus: 'This book, the work of one of the earliest of our national poets, is dedicated to The Australian People, in the belief that, while it has a special claim to their regard, it will be found not unworthy to take a place in the literature of every English-speaking community.' Signed 'Mary Harpur' but written by Martin (see Letter 187).

poets likeness[3] will enclose it to you. I wrote to Archbishop Vaughn to write a preface[4] if he *will* I will forward it to you If not Mr M. will most kindly do so. You cant think how deeply grateful I feel to *you* for your great kindness & sympathy, as well as your dear Uncle's. I shall do all in my power to collect money as I could not bear the idea of your suffering loss. I sent a list last week to Judge McFarland as he paid me a few visits here he is not a stranger.[5] I am sure he will subscribe

The likeness was taken in the last stage of consumption the beard looks white that was quite yellow as was his hair[6]

I have another likeness taken in health[7] but it is one of the framed old fashioned style I could not enclose. You are perhapse not aware that C. poetry has often rec great praise in English papers[8] and that *Deniehy* made the poems a subject to lecture on in Sydney & Melbourne Kendall has also lectured on its beauties and power Stenhouse told me he intended also to do so as Chas was a great poet. I shall be so anxious to hear of the safe arrival of the manuscripts.

With love to yourself wife and little ones[9] in which I am joined by my children

I am dear Cousin
Yours affc
M Harpur

170. Henry Maydwell Martin to James Henry Doyle, 29 April 1882

Text: ML MSS 827

Gawler Place Adelaide April 29th 1882

My dear James

Since receipt of yours of 18th bearing on the subject of the m.s. poems

---

[3] This photograph (presumably a copy of the Lomer studio *carte de visite*: see Introduction, n. 20) has not surfaced.

[4] Kendall had suggested that politician W. B. Dalley and Catholic Archbishop Vaughan of Sydney be invited to write a preface to *Poems*. Mary followed up but to no avail: see Letter 167 and Mary Harpur to John Howe, 28 March 1882 (in *Suppl. Letters*). The preface, signed only 'M.', would be the work of Henry Martin: see Letter 187.

[5] Alfred McFarland (1824–1901), District Court judge on the southern NSW circuit. For one visit and the friendship, see Letter 173, and McFarland to Mary Araluen Baldwin, 8 September 1883 (in *Suppl. Letters*); 'not bear' reads 'not be / bear' in MS.

[6] This is the first (and only) indication we have that CH was blond, with a golden tinge.

[7] Not identified and presumed lost.

[8] CH was known a little in England: see p. 61 n. 8. Four poems appeared in Douglas Sladen's 1888 anthologies: see p. 294 n. 1. Fifty copies of *Poems* went to London (Martin to Doyle, 4 April 1884; in *Suppl. Letters*); but only 15 had sold by 1 April 1890 (George Robertson sales account, 29 May 1890, ML MSS 827: in *Suppl. Letters*).

[9] Doyle's wife was Rebekah, née McDonald (1848–1919); the children at this point were Margaret Emma (b. 1875) and James Hilton (b. 1881).

of the late Chas Harpur I have the packet you mention as being sent by Mrs Harpur direct to me, to hand per Thursdays mail. The m.s. are numbered I notice 1 to 12 and then 15.[1] Do you know if it was intended to send me the two numbers (13 & 14) which are not included? I should be glad of any more in order to extend my power of selection as it will take 12000 lines to make a book of 300 pages of same size as Bruce's.[2] It is therefore better to have too much than too little.—

Perhaps Kendall's "Leaves from Austn Forests" is a prettier and handier style & size than Bruce? It would only take about 7500 lines to make 300 pages of this. I shall be glad to have your views on this point and also what number you would think it wise to print? Perhaps Mr Kendall, if you are sufficiently intimate with him, would advise you on this point? At any rate, I will proceed with the selection & preparation of the m.s. and as soon as I can get an idea of the quantity of suitable matter available, I will see what number of lines and let you know. Meanwhile you had better let me know the style you prefer and then I will get alternative prices from two different printing establishments for that description of book with "so many" pages, whatever it comes to.

From the cursory perusal which I was able to take in a few hours on Friday, I am not in a position to say much of the poetry itself—I only know that without getting beyond No 4 I found very much that was interesting to *me*; but then of course I have already acquired a personal bias in favour of the venture,— which must, to some extent, warp my judgment. It will be necessary for me to go twice through the whole before I can make any estimate of the extent of the probably valuable portion of the work. The m.s. has been taken possession of by the friend[3] who is to assist me with the editorial—or rather who has undertaken the editorial work for the sum I named in my last and who is far more competent & enthusiastic than I—(in fact I think is anxious to wait for payment by results.)——When I can recover it, I will master its content & write you again.

Can you obtain any data for fixing the ages of any of the poems? Or must I separate the earlier from the later entirely by instinct? Or is there any advantage in doing so? The m.s. altho' apparently prepared by the author

---

[1] During 1867–68 CH transcribed 11 collections of poems he intended for English publication; a twelfth was completed by Washington Harpur after his father's death. These are presumably the manuscripts '1 to 12' noted by Martin. Known as the 'major' Harpur manuscripts, they have been preserved (haphazardly) in ML A87-1, A92 and A97 (see Holt, p. 220). After CH's death Mary and Washington drew up a list of poems in 20 groupings (ML C381, pp. 290, 315–21: see Holt pp. 221–5). The titles in the first 12 groupings follow the content of the 'major' manuscripts closely but not exactly. At least four poems from group 15 ('To Poesy', 'The Babylonian Captivity', 'Change & Death' and 'The famous Night Scene in VIII Iliad') appear in *Poems*, suggesting it may list the content of Martin's manuscript 15. Omissions 13 and 14 are explained in Letter 171.

[2] See p. 256 n. 1.

[3] See p. 254 n. 5.

himself for publication (in England) is by no means ready for the printer (It is written on both sides of the paper for instance)—but the order of the poems is no doubt that which the poet himself had selected,[4] though not perhaps the most judicious.

Of course, if the preface is to be written here, we must draft one and submit it to Mrs Harpur for her approval or correction, but then we must be supplied with details. I think Mrs Harpur's suggestion as to dedicating to the Australian People is a good one and if any of the great names she mentions will do the preface[5] so much the better.——

I am afraid this letter is rather incoherent if not obscure, but I will not rewrite it as my eyes are none of the best and the hour is late.

With kind remembrances to Mrs Doyle & the little ones in which my wife joins

I am Dear James
Yrs faithfy
H. M Martin

171. Mary Harpur to James Henry Doyle, 16 May 1882

Text: ML MSS 827

Euroma Eurobodalla May 16th 1882

My dear James

I rec your kind letter to day informing me of the safe arrival of the manuscripts I felt so anxious about As you desire, I enclose two lives of Chas. in a book I will register for safety[6] I advise you to do the same when you forward them to Mr Martin: as with such data the preface had better be written in Adelaide[7] I send the book merely to ask you if you approve of the style of *printing* and binding which I think is so neat and so carefully printed. The typographicl errors so few too. (Tis a pity such care was spent on such stuff) Of course C's book will be much larger. The manuscripts I sent were copied by the Author for publication in England he was called away in the midst of his writing the "Slave Story"[8] No

---

[4] The ordering was secondary to CH: he required mainly that they be published in their integrity – see Letter 135.

[5] See p. 265 n. 4.

[6] Mary Harpur sent Doyle two newspaper cuttings slipped into a book, itself sent as an example of typography and binding. The 'lives' of CH were from *ATCJ*, 14 March 1874, p. 13 (retrospective 'Charles Harpur', with engraved portrait) and, probably, *Sydney Mail*, 5 March 1881, p. 366 (article 'The Brothers Harpur' by Alciphron Jones) – see Martin to Mary Harpur, 17 June 1882 (in *Suppl. Letters*).

[7] See p. 265 n. 4.

[8] See 'The Slav's Story' (h514c; ML A97). A note at p. 82 in ML A97 (apparently in Mary Harpur's hand) reads: 'Copied by the Poet to the 9th line in part II. Continued the copy by his son after his Fathers death'. The last line CH penned, 'Save in that Isle so summer-bright!', is at p. 85.

13. & 14 are long poems too long for the present publication. No 16. is also a long poem not copied yet for the press.[1] I sent no satires thinking it unwise. *All* the poems I have sent are of the highest order.

Do you not think it would be better to follow Sir H. P.s suggestion of pub. 500 copies. The expence would not be so great and as Kendall says judiciously managed my kind friends will not be loosers by their generosity[2] I hope your goodness with your Uncles[3] will be honourably mentioned in the publication. My rich brotherinlaw T. Parnell[4] had not the soul to do such an act of grace as you are doing.

Do not trouble Mr Martin about sending me a copy of the preface I have no doubt it will be elegantly written. I had a kind letter from Judge McFarland[5] with his name for £1. As he generally calls he will pay next circuit They dont like the work being published in Adelaide C. was an *Australian* not a Sydnite[6] I fancy there will be a petty jealousy Never mind! Glory to Adelaide! and I hope her book will be a credit and glory to her Ask Mr Martin to be careful of *typographical errors*.

I can think of no more I ought to say respecting the work in hand There will be trouble in distributing advertising &c &c. to push the thing, the greatest writers never succeeded without it.

You would feel very sorry for the death of our dear Uncle John[7] although his affliction was great: He is the last of my Uncles and was always a great favourite of mine. Poor Aunt Ellen has had sore trials[8] indeed

With love to you and your family

I am my dear Cousin
Yours affc
M Harpur

---

[1] The listing of poems Mary Harpur and Washington drew up after CH's death (ML C381, pp. 290, 315–21; Holt pp. 221–5) may provide a guide as to the content of 13 and 14: 'Kangaroo Hunt or Morg in the Mountain', 'The Witch of Hebron' (long poems), and four other poems. No. 16 lists another long poem, 'Genius Lost', and various 'Rhymed Criticisms'. However, 'The Witch' did appear in *Poems*, probably based on one of the two versions in ML A97 (h689d).

[2] See Letter 167.

[3] I.e., John Kennedy Howe's.

[4] See p. 241 n. 13.

[5] See p. 265 n. 5.

[6] I.e., *Sydneyite* (the end-of-line word is squeezed into the available space); 'they' probably means subscribers – most of whom lived in NSW – and perhaps some of her South Coast acquaintance.

[7] John Frederick Doyle senior (1809–82), brother of Mary's father Edmund Doyle. His estate Dartmouth lay a few kilometres north of Muswellbrook, on the Hunter River.

[8] Ellen Ann née Fitz (1813–91), wife of John Frederick Doyle, had borne 13 children, the eldest son John Frederick predeceasing his father by two years.

172. Henry Maydwell Martin to James Henry Doyle, 17 June 1882

Text: ML MSS 827

Adelaide June 17th 1882

My dear Jim

I received yours of 6th[9] today together with all its enclosures. It did not previously occur to me that it was intended to publish Harpurs likeness and I thought the photo[10] (which I returned) was merely intended as a personal solace for myself. As a work of art the photo was a failure, but I own I admire the engraving in the "T&C"[11] and if this happens to be flattering, what matter? I thought to save time and write Mrs Harpur direct as per letter enclosed,[12] but on reflection I decide not. If I once open communication with the widow, my freedom of action may be interfered with, for I dont mind being candid with you and saying that it would be a *great mistake* to publish *all* the m.s. I have—both financially as regards the widow and posthumously as regards the author's fame. (In point of grammar the above sentence won't stand analysis,—but no matter.) It is far better to publish too little than too much for a really qualified critic, or even an aesthetic-minded poetaster,[13] opening on a clumsy or halting stanza might close the book in disgust. And I do think we shall have plenty of material for an interesting and valuable work without bilking[14] the subscribers, and without running the risk of hanging fire[15] by reason of making the thing too tedious. Therefore you will please understand that altho the letter is addressed and signed I d[o not w?]ish her to see it but you will do for me what I have asked and ascertain her wishes as indicated. Thus I transfer my trouble to you to some extent.

Printing and binding in what I consider a suitable & attractive style will cost (for 300 pages) as follows

500 Copies, bound green cloth, gold lined,		49 . 9 . 6
500 ,, ,, paper		46. 15. 0
		96. 4 . 6

---

[9] Not located. Mary Harpur and Martin were dealing with each other indirectly, through Doyle – an awkward arrangement, particularly given the postal distances between the far south coast of NSW, the upper Hunter Valley and Adelaide.

[10] I.e. the 'likeness' mentioned by Mary in Letter 169: see Introduction, n. 20.

[11] The woodblock engraving of the photograph of CH in *ATCJ*, 14 March 1874, p. 13, reproduced here on the half-title page.

[12] Martin to Mary Harpur (but recipient revised to 'James' [Doyle]), 17 June 1882 (in *Suppl. Letters*).

[13] Writer of poor or trashy verse; a mere versifier.

[14] Cheating or defrauding.

[15] Being slow to take effect (from delayed ignition in firearms).

of course if we get into more than 300 pages it will be extra on the printing, but *not* on the binding. And less,—less. You will see in the other letter my ideas on the point of issue. The "1000" Edition would cost, as above, under £*100* but then this is exclusive of extra copies, of advertising and of my mate's fee. I suppose an edition of 250 each cloth & paper = 500 would cost for printing & binding about £*65.* while advertising &c would be the same—So if you have anything like 2 or 300 subscribers it might be well to strike off the whole 1000— though, mind you, the *ordinary* bu[y]ing public are not likely to take up more than 5[o]o copies unless the thing is vigorously pushed in all three markets.[1] However, my theory is that the subscribers whoever they are, are most likely *not* the people that would buy in any case (like myself) and that therefore the *actual* market will not be much diminished. I myself have been victimised with[2] all sorts of darn nonsense in the course of my brief career! But I should be glad to have a volume of Harpur's on my shelf—he tops *Bruce* altogether, but Bruce you see, licked him at making money so that squares that account.—(You will look upon all my enclosures as simply addressed to you)

Another reason for not sending my letter to Mrs Harpur is that she might form an unfavour[a]ble opinion of her Editor's style—*and this would involve [a] gross injustice to my mate* (whose style you have had a sample of).[3] I can not write well in these days. I am rusty and stick for words to properly express my thoughts unless I take long & painful labour to the task and then I fear the labour is too apparent. However I need not fear that you will act the scornful critic,[4] but simply bear in mind your caution "especially widows." By the way is not Mrs Harpur a sister of Mrs John?[5] It haunts me that she is.—Reverting to your letter.—We are all well except Emily[6] who has a slight eruption which interferes with her temper. I trust you & yours are thriving and remain

Dear Jim Yrs faithfy H. M. Martin

173. Mary Harpur to James Henry Doyle, 24 July 1882

Text: ML MSS 827

Euroma Eurobodalla July 24th 1882

My dear James

I rec. your letter[7] early yesterday and at once packed off to Mr Martin a

---

[1] Martin probably means the three largest colonies at the time: NSW, Victoria and SA.
[2] I.e., prevailed upon to subscribe to.
[3] Unidentified, but 'sample' suggests something small.
[4] 'But lo! What tumults rise? what bustling throng / Provokes the scornful Critic's angry song?' – William Boscawen, *The Progress of Satire: An Essay in Verse* (1798).
[5] Mary's youngest sister Emily Maria, née Doyle (1842–1926), was married to Doyle's brother John Kennedy Doyle of Glengarvon, Tamworth.
[6] The Martins' eldest child, Emily Rose Martin (b. 1875).
[7] See Doyle to Mary Harpur, 20 July 1882 (in *Suppl. Letters*).

large pacle of Manuscripts Nos 13. 14. 16.. 17.. 18. 19. 20. (registered) I wrote also to Mr M. explaining my reason for not sending them before The fact was some were not prepared for the press However he will superintend the matter He has a great work in hand If *all* could be published our country would have a book to be proud of A *Selection* will be difficult when every poem is good. As I shall be very anxious until I hear of the safety of the packet I have asked Mr M. to write as soon as he receives it.

Please give my kind regards to your Uncle John and say I wrote to Dr Fortescue[8] and W. B. Dalley to send their subscriptions to him I fear I shall be put to the trouble and pain of hav'g to write to many to *pay* their promised sub. for I have rec. no money since I wrote you yet all are good names.

I wrote to Sir J. Robertson last week and mentioned your kindness in the matter of the pub. as well as your Uncle John's He will applaud you both Years ago Mr T. S. Mort told me it should be a family matter and brought out by them: as it was well known the family was very large and influential. Judge McFarland stayed here a day and night on his circuit from Moruya to Bega he thinks highly of Chas's works His sub. is sure but I did not like to ask a *visitor* for it. So do not think I am getting subs in and using the money.

We are having a very severe winter more like frosts for weeks past; no abatement.

The Hunter I hear is in a sad state Nothing but sickness and trouble I am very anxious about my sister Fanny[9] and Cousin Edward and Robert[10] who have been suffering such severe, long illnesses.

How is it you tell me nothing about your own family in whom I am so interested

How I would like your portraits, I remember *you* perfectly as you were when I saw you.

My children join me in love to you and yours

I am dear Cousin
Yours affec
Mary Harpur

Does the old splendid estate of Invermein[11] belong to you

[8] Probably Dr George Fortescue: see p. 241 n. 7.

[9] Mary Harpur's younger sister Frances Doyle (1840–1910); she married Andrew John Doyle in 1857.

[10] Probably Edward Norris Doyle (1840–82) and his brother Robert Raworth Doyle (1846–1937), sons of Mary's uncle James George Doyle.

[11] See p. 243 n. 16. The name, conferred by original grantee Francis Little, is said to commemorate a Scottish river.

174. Henry Maydwell Martin to Mary Harpur, 3 August 1882

Text: ML A1528

Gawler Place Adelaide August 3rd 1882

Dear Mrs Harpur

Your letter of 23rd,[1] together with the package of M.S. advised, reached me yesterday—and I can well understand that you will be glad to hear at once of their safety

The book you enclose—which bears the stamp of age—was too roughly got up[2] to create much impression, as well as being too crude in itself to stake any permanent place in the literature of the day. I suppose however it was a fair sample of what the colonial press could produce 30 yrs ago in regard to printing and binding. With the mass of material I have now, and the type and press available in these latter days, I am really encouraged to hope that the publication now in hand will not only be worthy of your late husbands reputation but a source of profit to yourself. Still, this latter hope is more uncertain of fulfilment because as Kendall says, "the leisured & lettered class" here is still small altho' increasing.[3] I have tried to get Robertson to publish, but as he insists on printing in Melbourne as a condition, I am precluded from doing so, for I must retain the power of correcting the press.[4]

As regards the date of issue I must write you later on,—but no time is being lost in the matter. There are many things that it would not be wise to publish in the first instance because if the volume is cumbered with any thing mediocre, the critics might go no further; and on the verdict of these "free lances"[5] success, unfortunately, so much depends.

Of course rewriting the Manuscript involves much care and thought. Mere literal errors that occur to any one with much writing—spelling or punctuation—are only mechanical in correction—but where there is any slip in the grammar you will readily conceive that the work of a conscientious editor is not light and cannot be hurried—the substitution or omission of any word necessary to restore the *sense*, must be so done as not to interfere with the poets *thought*.

I thank you for your kind expression of confidence in me—and as far as the

---

[1] Not located, but see Letter 173.

[2] Probably *Bushrangers* (1853); Martin had requested copies of CH's two published collections (Martin to Mary Harpur, 17 June 1882 [enclosed with Letter 172]; in *Suppl. Letters*); for him, appearance and marketability of *Poems* would be key.

[3] In Letter 152.

[4] I.e., the Melbourne publisher and bookseller George Robertson. Martin would overcome his reservations about printing at such a distance from Adelaide, though it would cause delay and anxiety.

[5] Controversialists, mavericks. *OED* quotes journal editor Samuel Carter Hall (1883): 'The band of literary free-lances that...made *Fraser's Magazine* a name of terror'.

desire to do justice to the trust reposed in me is concerned, it is deserved. As far as the ability to undertake the task is concerned I can assure you that my adviser here is *thoroughly competent*. Kendalls hints and suggestions[6] as regards the different home and colonial magazines are wise, and shall have attention.

I was sorry to notice in the telegrams today the death of Kendall[7] is announced. I had hoped for his assistance at any rate with the preface, but this cannot be. The draft of the preface, when ready, shall be submitted to you before printing it.

Our mutual friend James Doyle is trying to get me another copy of the "Town & Country Journal" of the date you sent me, and will also enquire about the engraving.[8] I want this copy for myself.

With best wishes (& endeavours) for the success of the volume

I remain my dear Mrs Harpur
Yrs faithfully
H. M. Martin

175. Henry Maydwell Martin to James Henry Doyle, [after 7 November 1882][9]

Text: ML MSS 827

Gawler place, Adelaide

Dear Jim

I shall let Robertson[10] do the publishing—and enclose you a copy of his reply to mine so that you may see his views. I asked him for a quotation for a book of 300 pages each 26 lines printed & bound exactly similar to the green cloth edition of Tennyson's "Queen Mary" (crown octavo, King & Co, 1875)[11] He quotes *£80* for the printing and *£45* for binding an edition of 1000 which comes to exactly 2/6 per volume. Add to this *£20* for my mate[12] and sundries say *£150* in all or about 3/. per copy. The selling price,—say 7/.,—would bring you in 5/3 nett, as the booksellers stick to *25%*!!![13] so that you would need to sell 600 copies to reimburse yourselves. Then any further number sold would be actual gain. I

---

[6] In Letter 167.

[7] Kendall had died in Sydney on 1 August 1882.

[8] Mary had sent Martin a 'mutilated' copy of this article (see Martin to Mary Harpur, 17 June 1882; in *Suppl. Letters*). He was now pursuing a fresh copy and the engraved block for the portrait.

[9] The letter is undated but Martin enclosed George Robertson's quotation of 7 November 1882.

[10] See p. 245 n. 7.

[11] Alfred Tennyson, *Queen Mary: A Drama* (London: Henry S. King & Co., 1875; online at Internet Archive).

[12] See p. 254 n. 5.

[13] Publishers allowed booksellers a discount off published prices: see Letter 197 for Martin's calculation of actual prices and returns.

think there is no doubt this number will be sold having in view the numerous markets that Robertson commands, hence I am sanguine that you will not lose, financially, by your benevolent enterprise. It is however, consoling, to know that if you *do*, it won't break you. Robertsons idea in respect to advertising, agrees with my own. The *Reviews* are the only channels through which to get at the reading and artistic section of the community. The "Saturday Review" the "Nineteenth Century" the "Athenæum", "Harper's", the "Quarterly"[1]—and a few similar ones will hit the people who will buy if they are advised to by these authorities,—and the people who will as soon give 7/. as 5/., too! On the other hand no amount of simple "*advertising*" would produce the slightest impression on the people who wanted to buy Farm's, houses, Horses, Pigs, or Portable property or otherwise of any sort! Because *business* is altogether distinct from *Poetry*—and hence disaster always follows the unfortunate who is *compelled* to try to unite the two. Inasmuch as you have *not* gone into this affair as a business matter, the chances are you will lose nothing!

I asked Robertson to give me an idea as to how many these markets could take, but in the absence of any knowledge of the Poets best efforts, he prudently gives a non-committal answer. I *suppose* he paid Kendall a lump sum for the "Leaves" and printed the 1500 on his own responsibility.[2] Otherwise Kendall wouldn't have been so set up about it. In any case it is always better to print too few than too many, the former error being more easily repaired than the latter; so that, tho' I think the book we are producing can lick the "Leaves" clean out of sight, we will stop at the 1000 for the present. Should the reviewers help us—and I think I can answer for the local ones[3]—and the book sell right out,—then we can print a *Second Series*—and no doubt get it done free of expense too! But it is the *English Reviews* we have most to hope from or dread, as they are read all over these Colonies, as well as through the rest of the English speaking world, and reach every one of the class we want to hit. Robertson says it will take 8 weeks to run it through the Press, and a little extra time will be involved by sending me the proof sheets & having them returned. We are of course preparing the m.s. still but shall not forward any till we are near enough to the end of it to ensure no stoppages. My mate is rather hard up, so if you like to trust me with £*20* on a/c I will see to its proper application.

Yrs faithfy
H.M. Martin

[1] Five of the main literary periodicals of the 19th century, all published in London apart from *Harper's Magazine* (New York).
[2] See p. 246 n. 2.
[3] *SA Register* had been edited and part-owned (1870–77) by Martin's brother-in-law, John Howard Clark (1830–78). Pre-publication articles about *Poems*, probably based on text provided by Martin, appeared there on 23 March 1883, p. 6, and in its weekly stablemate *Adelaide Observer*, 31 March 1883, p. 41. Both papers carried generous reviews post-publication.

Robertson discourages the idea of having 2 forms of binding [and 2?] prices perhaps it will be better not to *bind* more than 600 in the first instance. This will save *£18.* in case of failure.

Copy of Letter received from George Robertson

Melbourne Nov 7 1882

Dear Sir I enclose estimate for printing Harpur's Poems as described. I could not advise Paper Covers[4] for a book of the size—and the cost of printing a neat wrapper (for a small number) would come to nearly as much as the cloth. As to the number to be printed, I should say *not* more than 1000, but I really have no indication of any demand for the work that would guide me in offering an opinion. I printed 1500 of Kendall's "Leaves" and it was an absolute failure i.e. commercially.

Proofs can be forwarded to Adelaide for revise,—if this is done, the time of printing will depend on this delay. As for price, to leave a fair margin of profit the volume should sell at say 6/. or even 7/6 retail. For books of this sort I would not advise much outlay on advertising. Review copies, well placed, should serve to bring it before probable buyers

Yrs obediently
George Robertso[n]
(signed) p R [R][5]

176. Henry Maydwell Martin to Mary Harpur, 29 December 1882

Text: ML A1528

Gawler place Adelaide December 29 1882

My dear Madam

By this post but under separate cover I return Dr Breretons poems[6] which as an autograph copy to your late husband is doubtless of special value

---

[4] Early term for paperback binding. Plain paper covers were used as cheap bindings from the 18th century. In 1899, William Dymock would reissue *Poems* cheaply in paper covers.

[5] I.e. *pro* [for] R[ichard] R[aymond]: see p. 283 n. 4.

[6] The Harpurs possessed at least two volumes of Brereton's poetry – probably the two issued in CH's lifetime: (1) *The Travels of Prince Legion, and Other Poems* (London: Longman, Brown, Green, Longman & Roberts, 1857: ML holds a copy inscribed 'Charles Harpur with the author's kind regards', at A821/B841.1/1A2); and (2) *Poems* (London: Sampson Low, Son, and Marston, 1865: also at ML, inscribed 'With the author's kind regards', at DSM/A821/B841.1/4A1). Mary would subsequently offer them to Angus & Robertson (Letter 195).

In regard to my own work we are really making substantial progress. The actual printing will not take long We had intended to publish *extracts* from the "Creek of the Four Graves"[1] but not to print it in its entirety on account of a few bad lines here and there which my critic[2] would not pass. It is very undesirable to have any lines printed which may serve as a handle for carping criticism. When we found that you had a special value for the poem we reconsidered the question, and found that the weak parts could be excised[3] without injuring the plan of the whole. This has been done and we feel satisfied that it is much better now than the extracts alone would have been The *descriptive* portions of this poem have always excited our warm admiration

With best wishes for yourself for the new year, and with the hope that the years to come shall have more knowledge and appreciation of your late husbands genius

I am
Yrs very truly
H. M. Martin

177. Henry Maydwell Martin to Mary Harpur, 25 January [1883]

Text: ML A1528

Gawler place Adelaide January 25th 188[3]

Dear Mrs Harpur

You will I know be glad to hear that the book is now rapidly approaching completion. The first half is already in type and the proofs are being corrected. Meanwhile the second parcel of M.S. has gone to Melbourne (two days since) to be set up. I hope to forward the remainder of the M.S. (finally) towards the end of next week.

I should like to explain that though our task in copying, revising proofs, selecting, and arranging has not been really as arduous as the time we have been over it might lead any one to suppose, the facts are that both my coadjuter[4] and myself, are very fully employed in other ways, so that our scanty leisure

---

[1] See p. 139 n. 11.

[2] Martin's literary assistant.

[3] Martin's excisions were first noticed by Henry Gyles Turner and Alexander Sutherland in *The Development of Australian Literature* (1898) when they compared the text of 'The Creek...' in *Poems* with that in *Bushrangers*. In 1951, Harpur scholar Cecil Salier showed that Martin's editing had reduced the poem by about one third from 410 to 270 lines, mainly by the wholesale omission and telescoping of lines ('Harpur and his Editor', *Southerly*, 12.1, March 1951, 47–54). Martin was working from ML A87-1 of 1867 (ho8ol); a textual comparison with *Poems* (ho8om) reveals the extent of his surgery (the Compare function in CHCA visualises the differences).

[4] Assistant. The letter's date is a turn-of-year mistake.

leaves us very little time to call our own. And at the same time, the task with which we are entrusted requires for its performance, at least some season of *uninterrupted quiet*. This has been a matter of difficulty to both of us, and especially difficult to obtain it *simultaneously*. Hence the apparent tardiness with which we have got thus far. I need not say how anxious I am in regard to this publication. Robertson will send me a second "proof", so that it shall be almost impossible for any mechanical errors to pass.

I hope to forward the preface[5] for your approval and criticism next week in which case please return it to me, with any needful or advisable corrections suggestions or alterations, with as little delay as convenient I think you will be pleased with the form and arrangement of the matter. The "Iliads" have gone in[6] and so has the "Creek of the Four Graves" The Satires, we agreed with you, were too dangerous in their nature to run any risks with[7]—especially in a posthumous work. We shall have over 300 pages. I am writing to James now, & remain

my dear Mrs
Harpur
Yrs faithfy
H. M. Martin

178. Henry Maydwell Martin to Mary Harpur, 20 February 1883

Text: ML A1528

Gawler place Adelaide February 20th 1883

My dear Mrs Harpur

I am at last able to send for your approval my draft of the preface for the volume of your late husbands Poems, which latter I am glad to say will be rapidly approaching completion by the time this reaches you. Will you therefore kindly return this to me as soon as you possibly can with any needful corrections or alterations or any additions you may wish made. I need not tell you how anxious I have been over this, fearing to put in too much on the one hand and not enough, on the other, and my difficulty has been enhanced by reason of the fact that I had no personal knowledge of the man. But I

[5] Martin laboured over the preface of *Poems*: see Letter 187 and p. 254 n. 5.

[6] As 'Translations', *Poems* printed (1) 'The Famous Night Scene from the Eighth Book of the Iliad' in four forms: 'Paraphrased in Homeric Hexameters', 'More closely rendered in Blank Verse', 'In Heroic Rhyme' and 'Very Literally' (h127-aj etc.); and (2) 'Battle Piece from the Eighteenth Book of the Iliad' in two forms: 'More closely rendered in Blank Verse' and 'Very Literally' (h575-af etc.)

[7] Cf. 'I sent no satires thinking it unwise' (Letter 171). Whether loss of topicality or risk of offending the powerful was the concern, or both, some of CH's sharpest and funniest verse was thus omitted from *Poems*.

have obtained some insight into his character from his writings and hence I am led to hope that I have fallen into no serious errors in that which I have written. After all, the merit or otherwise of the preface from a literary point of view cannot affect the reputation of any but the unknown writer of it. But nevertheless, as we hope to introduce our poet to english readers and foreign countries where his name has been hitherto unknown, some particulars of his life and character are required to satisfy the interest we must create. In the first instance I thought of bringing in to the preface as many well-known names as I could possibly associate with the poet—Stenhouse Lang Robt Lowe Henry Parkes Sir John Robertson Deniehy & Kendall[1] but as we may reasonably expect our author to stand on his own merits and it seemed to me that any such "reflected glory" would be contrary to the self reliant prideful spirit of the Poet himself (and further, implied a mildly snobbish sentiment on the part of those now interesting themselves), I abandoned this line. Nor was I sure of the amount of intimacy or friendship existing in any single case. And I have judged it better to leave out all allusion to or comparison with Kendall, as "comparisons are odious", we know.[2] Not that I dread comparison in the least.

You will soon be able to see the results of our labours, and I hope and trust they may be such as will satisfy and gratify us all.

Yrs faithfully
H. M. Martin

179. Henry Maydwell Martin to James Henry Doyle, 5 May 1883

Text: ML MSS 827

H. M. Martin
c/o *Joseph Crompton, Freeman St. Adelaide*. May 5th *1883*

Dear James

The heading of this paper will give you my new address.[3] Crompton's wife and my wife are sisters[4] and I hope the new arrangement is going to last Bob[5] met him when he was over here, but I don't think you did. I am still very busy

---

[1] Well-known comrades or associates of CH (consult Index for glosses).
[2] Traditional, much-repeated saying, originally from the 14th century: here, comparison of CH with Kendall, whose popularity was high in the early 1880s, particularly after his death in 1882. His *Songs from the Mountains* (1880) had been a critical success.
[3] In 1883 Martin joined the firm of his relative by marriage Joseph Crompton (1840–1901), a merchant with interests in vineyards, olive plantations, soap and export of skins and hides.
[4] Martin's wife Ellen Rosa, née Clark (1837–99) was sister to Crompton's wife Susan Mary (1846–1932). All three families were from the Unitarian Church community in Adelaide.
[5] Probably Robert Raworth Doyle (1846–1937), of Dumble Station near Goodooga – John Howe's grandson and Mary Harpur's cousin.

so I will only write now what is absolutely necessary and leave detail for a little while longer.

On the first instant I drew out the balance of your Bk L/C[6] = £100 This I did because that was the last date on which I could operate on it, and I thought it better to draw the balance at once rather than ask for a fresh credit because I think Robertson will be ready for more money by the end of May or soon after. I explained that I paid Robertson £50 when I was in Melbourne and this will probably have the effect of expediting matters, which I am sorry should have been so long in hand. They tell me now that the engraved block[7] you took so much trouble to obtain is not good enough and much too large for the purpose, but suggest that photos might be put in at an extra cost of about 6d on each book. They suggest also that a list be supplied them of those entitled to subscription copies—that is of the number of Half guinea subscribers[8] already promised, and that we keep them to their money and give them an extra handsome binding and gilt edges,[9] so as to make a nice drawing room volume. This could be very handsomely done for about 1/6 or 2/. extra, so that would leave a nice margin of profit on a given quantity and in a perfectly legitimate way. Will you confer with Mrs H. on these points and send me a list of the promised subscribers. We shall have a little over the 300 pages so that we can keep our promises. Robertsons recommends that only 500 be bound in the first instance, the remaining 500 being left in "sheets"[10] till wanted. The subscribers copies would be a good advertisement, too, for the plainer ones.—I must write you again shortly in regard to our other point of interest. Meanwhile with kind regards and regret that I did not get up to your "town" I am

Yrs faithfy

H.M. Martin

PS Better luck next time. I am still very busy, learning a new trade.[11]—

---

[6] Letter of credit with a bank.

[7] See p. 269 n. 11.

[8] Those who had subscribed (at least) 10s. 6d. for one copy: see Note on Equivalences.

[9] Applying gold leaf to the edges, and black and gilt tooling to the front cover, would give the special issue of *Poems* a luxury appearance. ML has a copy at A821/H295/5A3; title-page owner's signature is 'Cyrus W. Doyle / Goorangoola. 1883'.

[10] Sheets printed and folded in the required format but not yet bound.

[11] Martin later recounted: 'Then Mr. Henry Dunstan bought Stonyfell quarry, and in the same year Stonyfell vineyard as well (about 1886), and I was practically put in charge of both. That meant that I was tar-paving Adelaide with one hand, and running vineyard and cellars with the other' – interview, *Observer* (Adelaide), 1 January 1927, p. 16.

180. Henry Maydwell Martin to Mary Harpur, 27 June 1883
Text: ML A1528[1]

William St Norwood[2] June 27th 83

Dear Mrs Harpur

Your letter of 20th,[3] which reached [me] today, makes me feel vexed [th]at I have allowed so long a time to elapse without writing. The fact is I have been hoping every steamer[4] would bring the final section of proof, and that I might announce the advent of the volume; which I beg you to believe is now scarcely less interesting to me than to yourself. The disappointing delay has arisen partly through a misunderstanding with the printers—mostly my own fault—as when I was in Melbourne in the end of April I thought I had left every thing definite, whereas Robertson understood that I was to call again, and stopped the type, pending my visit. I wrote some what urgently [ju]st a fortnight after my return, and [then] found out that they supposed I [had] gone on to Sydney and was not [rea]dy to proceed. However the next [bo]at brought me the concluding section but one; and the alterations necessary were so numerous that I had to ask for a second revise[5] to be certain that no mistakes shall pass into the Book, and this I have today returned to Melbourne as correct. The difference between print and manuscript for purposes of revision is greatly in favour of the former, as when the m.s. becomes type the eye readily detects faults of punctuation, profusion of capitals, and similar technical errors which are apt to escape notice [....]d which, even if trivial in themselves, would [make?] a permanent blemish in the work itself if left. Hence I have had a second revise of nearly every section, and the course of post has thus protracted the work. I hope in a fortnight's time however that Robertson will be able to post you an advance copy direct.

I have reluctantly decided that the wood cut portrait is too rough[6] for a book of the class we are bringing out. Robertson was against it from the first, insisting that it would do no credit to the Poet, to his friends, or his publishers—and those whom I am able to confer with here whose opinion & taste are valuable agree. It would add about 6d each to the cost of the volumes to have a photographic likeness prepared and inserted, and even then I doubt if any existing photograph could be successfully copied after this lapse of

---

[1] MS is damaged (see facsimile image in CHCA), requiring the supply of many editorial readings, some of them uncertain.

[2] The Martin family home; Norwood is an inner suburb east of the Adelaide city centre.

[3] Not located.

[4] Martin, based in Adelaide, was over 800 km by sea from publisher George Robertson in Melbourne. The steamship service took two to three days: see Letter 181.

[5] A proof sheet that includes corrections made in an earlier proof.

[6] See Letter 172.

years. I am glad you liked the notice I sent you. It was compiled by a friend mainly from a first draft of my own,[7] which I had intended for the preface but afterwards abandoned.

James has instructed me about the copie[s] for the subscribers. We will have at leas[t] 25 *extra* bound,[8] to sell at 10/. There w[ill] be about 312 pages. In regard to th[e] Copyright,[9] Robertson advises that it [is] not necessary to take any steps. It would involve several months more delay after the book is ready for issue, considerable expense, and no security as against America or the Continent—while in these colonies the love of poetry is so lacking that *no* local publisher would think of printing any book of poetry *at his own risk.*[10] Speaking [to him?] he said he would sell Kendall's "Leaves["]"[11] now @ 6d per copy!! It seems he bought the m.s. from Kendall, and it is his last experiment, and will be. This is perhaps not very encouraging for us, but Kendall, as he himself very well knew, is a very long way indeed behind our poet, and I am much more sanguine than Robertson. In reg[ard] to the manuscript, I have every sheet of it carefully put away in safety, and with your permission I would like to keep it a little while after the book appears, as there are several pieces—which—though my Coadjuter would not pass as fit for the book while we had so much more material to use and the critics in front of us—I should like to cull out and insert now and then one by one in the local or the Melbourne papers.[12] This will take some little time & care, which I cannot well devote at present. I have left my old appointment with Messrs Simpson and taken service in a new direction and much of the detail of my present work is new to me, so that I would rather keep this pleasant task back for a little until I can command a little more leisure. And I may then be able to keep alive, or create, some amount of public interest in the matter, with a tangible result. Meantime, the m.s. shall suffer no injury—The advance copies of the book will be sent to the Reviewers as soon as possible; to A C Swinburne and the "Athenaeum" "Spectator" "Nineteenth Century", as suggested by Kendall—but I have not quite decided as to the "Saturday Review"?[13] The

---

[7] Probably the pre-publication article 'Charles Harpur', in *SA Register*, reprinted in *Adelaide Observer*: see p. 274 n. 3.

[8] See p. 279 n. 9.

[9] Mary Harpur would register copyright in *Poems* in 1890 in Melbourne – see J. McL. Abernethy to Mary Harpur, 23 September 1890 (in *Suppl. Letters*). C. W. Salier reported seeing a certificate of registration in the possession of Mary's daughter in 1946 (ML A98-2, p. 57).

[10] See p. 216 n. 2.

[11] See p. 246 n. 2.

[12] There is no indication in Victorian and SA newspapers that Martin succeeded in this.

[13] Kendall's suggestions (Letter 167). Brief notices of *Poems* appeared in *Spectator*, 18 October 1884, p. 21, and *Saturday Review*, 6 December 1884, p. 733.

Melbn Review[1] & the leading colonial newspapers[2] of course. Robertsons knowledge & experience will be valuable to us here—

I hope to write again soon & meanwhile with kind regards I remain

Yrs faithfy
H. M. Martin

181. Henry Maydwell Martin to James Henry Doyle, 31 July 1883

Text: ML MSS 827

Adelaide July 31 / 83

Dear Jim

You will think me dilatory or neglectful in the matter you have intrusted to me, but such is not the case. The delay arises in the distance I am from the printer & the loss of time in sending documents to & fro. If I cannot get ready for 1 steamer I have to wait then perhaps 3 days, and the same at the other end. Copy of letter I send Robertson today, however, is as follows

"Herewith I return the final sections of the book, and I am glad to think the matter is so nearly completed. I like the cover very much indeed, and hope that my part of the work done will redound as much to the credit of the volume as will yours—in which case nothing has been left undone to secure success. Altho' I am most anxious to avoid any further delay I do not wish any blemish to appear in the volume betokening want of care, and as so much pains have been already bestowed it will be best for me to ask you for one more revise of these sections. On receipt of this I will telegraph to you if it is clear, in which case I want you to oblige me by binding and sending one copy as speedily as possible by post to Mrs Harpur Euroma Eurobodalla NSW, and then let the reviewers have their copies as early as may be. You will be good enough to let me know the amount of my indebtedness and when and how you

---

[1] Literary quarterly, est. 1876 by Arthur Patchett Martin, Henry Gyles Turner, Alexander Sutherland and others. It carried articles on general and literary topics, and original poetry. Contributors included Marcus Clarke and George Gordon McCrae. It ran until 1885, when dwindling circulation led publisher George Robertson to withdraw financial support. Sutherland's review of *Poems* appeared on 1 October 1883, pp. 457–61.
[2] Early reviews and notices appeared in *SA Advertiser*, 6 September 1883, p. 5; *Sydney Mail*, 8 September 1883, p. 437 (by 'F. H.' – possibly Frank Hutchinson – who recalled meeting CH with Kendall, presumably in early 1868); *SA Register*, 10 September 1883, p. 6; *Australasian* (Melbourne), 15 September 1883, p. 8; *Adelaide Observer*, 15 September 1883, p. 41; *SA Register*, 17 September 1883, p. 6; *Maitland Mercury*, 22 September 1883, p. 4; *SMH*, 26 September 1883, p. 3; *Weekly Times* (Melbourne), 29 September 1883, p. 4; *Brisbane Courier*, 5 October 1883, p. 5 (unsigned, but believed to be by Brunton Stephens); *Queenslander*, 13 October 1883, p. 594; *Leader* (Melbourne), 20 October 1883, p. 35; *Freeman's Journal*, 20 June 1885, p. 17. For a thoughtful New Zealand review by Henry Lapham, see *Otago Witness*, 17 May 1884, p. 25 and 24 May 1884, p. 26.

would like to have it settled; and I shall be glad to learn that the book is fairly launched, and to have your views as to price and other matters referred to in my last. Mrs Harpur's advance copy I am particularly solicitous about"

Now you will see the position, & can reassure Mr Howe or Mrs Harpur if either of them doubt the bona fides of your unknown friend. Mrs H. was good enough to thank me for the preface, and I am glad she was pleased with it for it was a delicate & responsible task to throw upon an unknown writer, and I recognised it as such. I have got to be as nervously anxious about the book as Mrs H. herself, almost—and I do hope it will go.

I will not write more now as it is very late, but I am not unmindful that your last requires a thoughtful rejoinder & the subject-matter of it continues to receive my attention in various ways. I will write fully later on. You will be shearing soon? Where shall I address? Kind regards from self & wife to all your circle

Yrs

H. M. M.

182. George Robertson to Henry Maydwell Martin, 16 August 1883

Text: ML A1528

GEORGE ROBERTSON

33, & 35, Little Collins Street West, and 1,3, &5, McKillop Street. Melbourne

August 16th *1883*

Dear Sir

The Cost of Printing, &c 1000 Harpur's Poems and binding 500 only will come to say £112, or binding the whole £134.10.0. Advertising say £5. This makes the cost of the 1000 about 3/. per copy.

In the hope that the volume will secure a fair share of public attention I would advise the selling price to be 6/. trade 4/9 less commission, *say* 4/.[3] this would leave a margin of profit if we sold into the second 500.

Your instructions as to distribution shall be attended to, and no time lost in getting the volume befor the public

Yours obediently

R. P. Raymond[4]

Pro. MJB

[3] Publishers allowed booksellers a discount off published prices. In addition, George Robertson deducted his commission on each sale to cover agency, freight and other charges. On his calculation this would return Mary Harpur around 1s. per copy sold to the trade. Even with subscriptions the venture never covered costs. Half of the original 500 remained unsold in 1890, and Doyle and Howe were still owed over £50 (see documents dated 29 May 1890 and 31 December 1890 in *Suppl. Letters*). Sales then all but ceased: see Letter 197.

[4] Richard Powell Raymond (1843–1918), publishing manager for Robertson.

183. Mary Harpur to James Henry Doyle, 24 September 1883

Text: ML MSS 827

Radfordslea Branxton[1] Sept 24th 1883

My dear James

I received a vol. of poems from Robertson publisher,[2] also a letter from
Mr Martin I answered from Tamworth[3] but fear he may never get as he
has removed[4] and failed to give me his address, I am much pleased with the
manner the book has been brought out It is very beautifully printed and all the
criticisms[5] I have yet seen are *wonderfully* favourable The only thing I regret
is the alterations[6] in some of the poems *all* regret who has read them in the
original It was so averse to the poets wishes who *studied* and restudied every
line so often. However it was done for the best, and the original manuscripts
remain. I do not think above one third of the manuscripts are printed I sent
Mr Martin and I have no end more in my home at Eurobodalla I hope yet
will be given to the public. You, and my kind friend J. Howe[7] has done an
act of kindness you are so honoured for and Mr. Martin editing the work so
carefully is receiving much praise It is my desire that he will receive something
more substantial out of the profits when expences of the work are paid even if
nothing comes to me Let *him* be remunerated for his trouble. I shall ever feel
grateful to him, to you, and John. H[owe] Esq. I wrote to Robertson to send a
book to the Editor of Maitland Mercury[8] and am glad to see such a favourable
review in last Saturdays paper I shall write to Robertson to day to send a vol.
to other leading papers Freemans Journal Town & Country and the *Bulletin.*[9]
John is having it reviewed in Tamworth.[10] I hope I shall see it. The Melbourne
papers are sure to review the work. I fear I shall miss seeing them.

T[he] books ought to be distributed freely amongst the booksellers How

[1] Estate of Mary Harpur's brother Edmund Adolphus Doyle (1831–99).

[2] *Poems* by CH was published by George Robertson in Melbourne in August 1883 – also the
date of the preface. The earliest publisher's advertisements appeared in Melbourne papers:
Herald, 29 August 1883, p. 2; and *Argus*, 30 August 1883, p. 12 ('Now ready').

[3] Town in northern NSW. Mary had been visiting her sister Emily Maria and husband John
Kennedy Doyle, of Glengarvon near Tamworth.

[4] Martin had changed employers, but the family was still at William Street, Norwood.

[5] See p. 282 n. 2.

[6] Although aware that 'The Creek of the Four Graves' would incur 'a little alteration of a line
or a few lines that did not please him' [H. M. Martin, the editor], she would, after publication,
repeat the more general complaint: contrast Mary Harpur to Doyle, 6 January 1883 (in *Suppl.
Letters*) and Letter 186. For Martin's self-defence, see Letter 185.

[7] John Kennedy Howe.

[8] See review, *Maitland Mercury*, 22 September 1883, p. 4.

[9] *Freeman's* waited two years to review the book (*Freeman's Journal*, 20 June 1885, p. 17);
neither *ATCJ* nor *Bulletin* noticed it.

[10] Neither *Tamworth Observer* nor *Tamworth News* carried a review.

is it to be done James? The subscribers should now pay up, their volumes are gilt edged and more elegantly bound. Lipscombe[11] says he never knew a first publication so cheap before. Write to me here if you think I can or ought to be of any service in the matter. I only hope I have not taken too much on myself already

    I am waiting here and at Clare Cottage[12] until poor Edwin Parnell[13] recovers from a dangerous illness inflamation of lungs in Sydney

    Isabella[14] does not want me to go to Sydney yet awhile or until he is better

    With love to you and yours whom I should so liked to have known

I am dear Cousin
Yours affe
M Harpur

excuse haste as the boy is waiting

184. Henry Maydwell Martin to James Henry Doyle, 3 October 1883

Text: ML MSS 827

Adelaide Oct 3/83

Dear Jim

The Book is now fairly before the Public, and has cost so far

Editorial services	20. 0. 0
Pd Geo Robertson a/c enclosed	111. 2. 6
	131. 2. 6

This includes Binding 500 in cloth 25 of which are extra bound, and 500 copies are still in sheets and can be bound for 90/. per 100 as required. I suppose about 25 or 30 "review" copies will be given away, and the Publishers charge these to me.

    You sent me £20 and I drew under L/C[15] £150 = £170. but I have spent about £50 on the other account since April so that you owe me about £10. As

[11] Probably William Griffin Lipscomb (1840–1913), West Maitland bookseller, stationer, chemist and seedsman. He stocked CH's *Poems*: see *Maitland Mercury*, 3 May 1884, p. 19.

[12] The (extensive) home of Mary Harpur's cousin and brother-in-law Andrew John Doyle (1833–1913), near Lochinvar between Maitland and Branxton.

[13] Mary Harpur's nephew Edwin Arthur Parnell (1855–1929), son of her sister Isabella and Thomas Liverpool Parnell.

[14] Mary Harpur's sister Isabella Sophia Parnell (1829–87).

[15] Letter of credit.

I shall have to pay the usual quarter[1] in a few days I should like you to send me say £25. the first time you are near the Bank. as it will cost £9. to bind 200 *more copies* it will take the sale of

25 @ 10/. =	12. 10. 0
650 " 4/. nett	130. 0. 0
25 Reviewer gratis	—.—.—

to put you in funds.[2] I suppose Robertson will furnish account of sales, and money whenever demanded. I hope we may sell the lot. Mrs Harpur is pleased with the book.

I will write you again shortly with actual statement of a/c & vouchers. In haste

Yrs faithfy
H M Martin

56. 1
43– 3. 2
12.17.10
6. 9

1500
8
12000
60.0.0[3]

185. Henry Maydwell Martin to Mary Harpur, 20 October 1883

Text: ML MSS 827[4]

William St, Norwood, near Adelaide, October 20/1883

My dear Mrs Harpur

Your kind letter of Sept 12th dated from Glengarvan has not yet been acknowledged, and I have also read your last, dated from Sydney. I was glad to

[1] Martin may be referring to quarterly school fees, remitted by Doyle, for George James Kennedy, a boarder at Prince Alfred College, Adelaide, for whom Martin acted as guardian during 1882–84. George's exact relationship with the Doyles is unclear and references to him are always discreet.

[2] To cover your outlay. Martin's calculations are approximate: the sale of 650 copies will bring in £142 10s. less publishing costs of £131 2s. 6d.

[3] These calculations may relate to Doyle's sale of livestock: see *Maitland Mercury*, 18 August 1883, p. 6.

[4] This letter copy is on an absorbent copying paper, the forerunner of carbon-paper copying for handwritten materials. Defective in places, the text is also blurry. It was probably enclosed in Martin to Doyle, 21 November 1883 (in *Suppl. Letters*).

hear that you had spent a pleasant month with my valued friends at Tamworth, of which Mr Gainor (of the Opera Company now here),[5] is still to give me some particulars. I was also much pleased with your expressions of approval of the result of my work; and although this praise is a little qualified by your later views,[6] I still hope you will return to your first opinion, and I trust you will believe that the reputation of the dead poet has been the one thing which I have had before me throughout the delicate and responsible task which was confided to my care and judgement.

No man is perhaps ever competent to judge fairly of either the merits or demerits of his own work. Your late husband, gifted though he was, owing to the untoward circumstances which beset his whole life—hailed on the one hand by the unqualified admiration of those who were dear to him, and on the other by the unreasoning censure of his would-be critics—was, I feel certain, less able to rightly distinguish his own defects than is his unknown but sympathetic editor. I should feel more uneasy about making this assertion *to you*, were it not for the specially gifted assistance I have fortunately been able to secure I feel sure also, that were it possible, we should have received the poets sanction—in the main—for what has been done editorially in regard to his literary remains. But while *I* feel certain of this, I cannot expect *you* readily to concede that any alteration must necessarily mean improvement— for I do not undervalue that devoted loyalty to which your whole wife-hood and widowhood bear witness.

You, however refer to "the reviewers" as complaining of my editing down various passages and "wrecking" the poems generally. This I think is unjust to me. I am waiting with anxiety for the English reviews, but meanwhile have collected all the Colonial notices I could, and shall be glad if you will name all those you have yet seen, that I may procure copies of such of them as I have not got. The only review which has [ye]t come before me in any way supporting your statement, is that published in the "Maitland Mercury" of Sep 22nd.[7] The writer of this is evidently one who was acquainted with your late husband, and that therefore acquired what Herbert Spencer calls "the personal bias".[8] And he is also necessarily much more behind the times than is the ordinary reader or the average reviewer. This writer refers regretfully

---

[5] R. Warwick Gainor was a baritone with the Montague–Turner Grand English Opera Company (or the London Opera Bouffe Company for comic opera); it toured New Zealand and eastern Australia (including Tamworth) during 1881–84. By October 1883 it was in Adelaide.

[6] Mary's letters to Martin from Tamworth and Sydney are lost, but her disappointment with his editorial freedoms is evident in Letters 183 and 186.

[7] Unsigned review, *Maitland Mercury*, 22 September 1883, p. 4.

[8] Herbert Spencer (1820–1903), English philosopher, social theorist and sociologist. For the various kinds of personal bias that thwart scientific knowledge about society, see his *The Study of Sociology* (London: Henry S. King, 1873; 3rd edition, 1874, online at Internet Archive).

to the omission of pieces[1] which *I have never had the opportunity of seeing—* but adds, in regards to [various] of them, "in many respects crude x x x x x perhaps the Poet himself condemned it, and his widow and editor are loyal to his wish". And further on, though he quotes passages which he remembers, and is sorry to miss, he says—"here we see that Mr Harpur before his death applied the pruning knife judiciously on the whole. We have before us a copy of the poem as it first appeared, and note that some moral reflections, rather clumsy in character, have been wisely excised".

Further, the same writer says—"but we have not noticed a single puerile sentence".—I think the review under notice, notwithstanding the personal bias, justifies me more than it finds fault with me?

But it is not an editor's duty to study the tone of any foolish review, or of any class of reviewers. The aim I kept before me the whole time was,—to do justice to my author and prevent his doing injustice to himself. If this was not my task, then what was it? Any intelligent Monkey could have corrected the press, and taken care of mere mechanical errors on the part of printers. But to cut out passages when prolix or ineffective, and superfluous words, or syllables which wreck scansion destroy the rhythm—and to correct accidental errors of grammar—requires an educated and appreciative skill, so as to restore the poem after any necessary deletion without interfering with the current of the poet's thought, or marring the unison of his language. If I have overstepped the lines, it is through lack of skill, not lack of love.—

I did not for a moment suppose that [we] sen[d] to print the whole of what you sent me just as I received it. Had this been made clear to me, I should certainly not have undertaken the task. The book would have been too costly to sell and too bulky to read; and the fine thoughts and eloquent language by which this Poet himself hoped to attain a place in English literature, would have been buried and lost in much matter of an ephemeral Nature, of a merely [local?] interest, or of an [injurious?] and faulty construction.

That there is much more of your late husband's well worthy of publication, none can be more ready to believe than myself, but I am sorry I had not the opportunity of a wider selection than was afforded me. If the present volume "takes" with the literary world, it will not be a difficult thing to publish a second. If it does not, I am quite willing that the blame shall be considered mine. [....], and hope that your first impressions of the little green volume I almost know by heart may be borne out by subsequent experience.

I have all the M.S. here. It has not been out of our possession. The printers

---

[1] *Mercury*'s reviewer regretted the absence of a delightful pastoral whose title he could not recall, some rhymes in praise of tobacco that had once appeared in *Mercury* ('The One Thing Needful,' h363a) and some of CH's essays for *SMH*: 'We are sorry also to miss the drama of "The Bushranger," a production in many respects crude, but which contained some very excellent verse. Perhaps the poet himself condemned it, and his widow and editor are loyal to his wish. Still, we regret the absence of that piece...'.

in Melbourne set the type from transcripts. I will post the ms and register it at an early opportunity.

Meanwhile I remain my dear Mrs Harpur

Yours faithfully
H M Martin

186. Mary Harpur to James Henry Doyle, 27 October 1883

Text: ML MSS 827

103 Pitt Street Sydney[2] 27th Oct 83

My dear Cousin

I received your kind letter a few days since and quite agree with you about all Subscribers who have not paid up. Robertson tells me the book is selling but not so fast as if more attention were called to it by friends you know some of our greatest *Poets* have written letters and reviews on their own works (under fictitios names of course) in order to draw *public* attention to their works *some* have *condescende[d] so* far all for fame and *money too*, the most essential after all, The Town & Country Journal did not review the book[3] The Freemans Journal[4] would, I am certain, have reviewed it splendidly had a copy been sent to the Editer They always had such a high opinion of C. Harpurs poetry. I sent the volume you gave me to the *Governor*[5] knowing that if the snobs[6] *saw* the book on his table *they* would buy at once if it had been the veriest trash.

There is no doubt I think that you and my generous old friend your uncle will be repaid for your goodness. Poor as I am, that is what troubles me most.

Robertson publisher tells me that all the manuscripts he had has been *returned* to Mr Martin I have asked Mr M. to *return* me *all* I sent him through the post first registering them and I will return all the cost I am most anxious to have them back and beg dear James *you* will request that it may be done as soon as possible I have a list of all I sent I could never think of allowing Mr M. to edit any thing more of C. Harpurs works.[7] for notwithstanding

---

[2] Address of John McGarvie Smith, metallurgist and bacteriologist, second husband of Adelaide Elizabeth, Daniel Deniehy's widow – suggesting a link that may have survived the deaths of CH and Deniehy.

[3] *ATCJ* carried CH's poems (rarely) and Robertson's advertisements for *Poems*, but did not review the book. Two biographical pieces appeared: 14 March 1874, p. 13 and 20 May 1893, p. 17.

[4] *Freeman's Journal* reprinted part of *SA Register*'s pre-publication article on CH's poetry on 23 June 1883, p. 20; its review of *Poems* appeared 20 June 1885, p. 17.

[5] Lord Augustus William Frederick Spencer Loftus (1817–1904) was Governor of NSW during 1879–85. Mary presumably sent him an extra-bound copy passed to her by Doyle.

[6] See p. 184 n. 2.

[7] This is the clearest expression of Mary's dissatisfaction with Martin's work, complicated by her desire for him to 'receive something more substantial out of the profits...Let *him* be remunerated for his trouble. I shall ever feel grateful to him' (Letter 183).

your instructions; mine; and the *Poets written* orders, that his works should be published as *he* left them even to *italics* and *punctuation* Mr M. has destr[o]yed and weakened *all* published by *alterations* even leaving out whole *verses* and putting in *his* words in other poems *always* to the *detriment* of the poem. Harpur has long been pronounced a man of genius M. has neither taste or genius and has taken a deal of trouble to *hurt* the *long studied works* of poor C. It is like altering a will Dr Fortescue who knew some of the poems by heart thinks M. has acted most *presumptisly*

You are a near relative of mine and *one* I feel *proud* of *Help* me to get *all* the Manuscripts as soon as you can for Mr M. does not answer my letters; and if the book now published sells to pay expences a full volume of all H's works can be published (as *all* authors works are) as the *poet wrote them*, not a word not a line of C. poems but have been studied & restudied half a doz times; Instead of feeling grateful to Mr M. I am indignant at his not acting according to *your instructions* as well as mine own.

However we must be silent and when the book is sold *all* the works *prose* and poetry shall be given to the world [without] alterations and *cutting* away the best parts;

With kindest regards and gratitude for your kindness Not forgetting your good generous Uncle John Howe

> I am dear James
> Yours affec
> M Harpur

I intend leaving for home very soon now. All is well there else I should have gone sooner

187. Henry Maydwell Martin to James Henry Doyle, 9 April 1884

Text: ML MSS 827

Freeman St Adelaide April 9th 84

Dear Jim

The enclosed[1] speaks for itself. I only acknowledge it as an act of courtesy to the sex. If any male relation of the house write to me, into the fire goes the

---

[1] Martin's comments suggest that the sender of the enclosed letter, not identified, was female and a resident of Eurobodalla, and that the subject was connected with the publication of *Poems*. CH's newly married daughter Mary Araluen Baldwin, perhaps incited by her husband from whom she later separated, is the most likely candidate. Doyle presumably burnt the letter and Martin's draft reply as requested.

letter. You will see my pencil copy of reply, after perusing which, please burn the lot. I only wait your reply to my last[2] as to disposal of the "sugar"[3]—and I am writing to Robertson so that he may not compromise any one by giving unnecessary particulars. At present I suppose Robertson knows no one in the matter, financially, beyond me, and I do not want to transfer my position to yourself until I know your wishes, for by doing so I might accidentally give offence to Mr Howe,[4] who is a stranger to me. But Robertson should know the real owner to prevent complications in case of my death, as the thing is likely to extend over some time yet. I shouldn't be surprised (or annoyed— but merely amused) if the local Dodson & Fogg[5] of Eurobodalla doesn't send me a lawyer's letter some day—in which case, into the fire it goes. But in anything of this sort a masterly inactivity[6] is the correct front. They shall not get at my principal behind me in any shape or form. At present they cannot, for I do not know what I am expected to do with the funds—or by whom, in fact, I am really employed. The extent of my knowledge on this point is set forth in "the preface"—and I have a general undefined idea that it is a case of "heads I win tails you lose" so far as Mrs H. is concerned. But you will observe I do not sign the preface[7] (modesty, however, not fear) so that there is nothing legally to connect me with the "sugar", while Robertson understands that I am merely an agent, though he can at present recognise no one else as having any direction over him. Therefore till I get your instructions I am passive. In regard to correspondence with ladies, do not allow yourself to be entrapped. If you feel compelled to reply at any time to anything of a doubtful tenor—admit nothing, deny nothing, assert nothing, suggest nothing. If this is also the value of my good advice, it is likewise the charge for it.

You never told me how you liked the preface?[8] That and the dedication are almost the only unaided work of mine, and not entirely that.

Mrs Harpur writes in friendly strain and sends me some m.s. that I asked to be permitted to look over. But it would not have done to print.

I see they have had partial rains on the Darling. I hope you & John have had some[9]

---

[2] Martin to Doyle, 4 April 1884 (in *Suppl. Letters*).

[3] Money, funds (slang – 1862, *OED*).

[4] John Kennedy Howe.

[5] The unscrupulous lawyers in Charles Dickens's *Pickwick Papers*.

[6] 'The Commons, faithful to their system, remained in a wise and masterly inactivity' – Sir James Mackintosh, *Vindiciae Gallicae* (1791).

[7] The preface to *Poems* was signed 'M.' Martin's connection with the book was not common knowledge until 1946 when revealed by Cecil Salier in 'The Life and Writings of Charles Harpur', *Royal Australian Historical Society Journal and Proceedings*, 32.2, pp. 8–105 (online via NLA).

[8] See Martin to Doyle, 18 January 1884 (in *Suppl. Letters*).

[9] Darling River in western NSW, in severe drought in 1884; Doyle had properties in north-western NSW, as did his brother John Kennedy Doyle.

Kind regards to Mrs Doyle[1] & yourself in which my wife joins

Yrs faithfy
H M Martin

188. Joseph Graham O'Connor to Mary Harpur, 4 September 1885

Text: ML C 376

Express Office, Sydney,[2] 4th Sept '85.

Dear Mrs Harpur,

Your kind note to hand. You had no need to thank me for a defence of the dead poet.[3] When the works (?) of others shall have faded into the dim obscurity from whence they sprung, the poems of Charles Harpur will live and be appreciated by Australians yet unborn.[4] 'Tis many a long year since I first read poor Charles's poems—his first collection, printed by Barr and published by Piddington;[5] and it was one of the pet projects—and he had many—of poor Joe Harpur to bring us together.[6] However it was not to be, and he (Charles) departed before such a consummation could be accomplished. Until Mary Harpur—Mrs Jas. Hackett[7]—sent me the *Herald* criticism[8] of the Volume of poems some 18 months ago I did not know they had been published. I knew, of course that the late T. S. Mort was to have seen to the matter, and that Dr Lang had the *MS* in hand for some time, and there I lost sight of the subject. John Lucas[9] spoke to me on one or two occasions about the publication of the work—but he said or did nothing practical. I hope the

---

[1] See p. 265 n. 9.

[2] *Express*, a weekly established in 1877 as *Catholic Times* by Joseph Graham O'Connor (1839–1913), Irish-born journalist and politician. It was a rival to *Freeman's Journal*, but debt forced its closure in 1891. In 1885 the offices were at 84 Clarence-street.

[3] See article 'Critics and Critics', *Sydney Express*, 27 August 1885, p. 13 and p. 14.

[4] *Express* printed several CH items around this time. 'Absence by the Sea Side' (h004i) appeared on 10 September 1885, p. 1, the first number of *Express* after this letter. Not in *Poems*, its text is very close to late manuscript versions h004g and h004h. Another three were obviously taken from *Poems*: 'Onward' (6 August 1885, p. 3), 'The Battle of Life' (3 September 1885, p. 1) and 'The Forgotten' (1 October 1885, p. 3).

[5] CH's second collection, *Bushrangers*, was published by W. R. Piddington in 1853. Robert Barr, jobbing printer of York-street, Sydney, printed the early issues of *Empire* for Henry Parkes. In later years he ran newspapers at Kiama, NSW – *Examiner, Independent* and *Pilot* (the last employed CH's brother Joseph).

[6] CH's older brother Joseph (d. 1878) had edited (short-lived) newspapers for O'Connor including *Sydney Times*, which published several of CH's poems (1864), and *Balmain Reporter* (1867): see p. 198 n. 3. He and O'Connor were interested in the Lang–Stenhouse subscription proposal of 1871 – see O'Connor to Lang, 4 April 1871 (in *Suppl. Letters*) and Letter 147.

[7] See p. 137 n. 6.

[8] 'The Poems of Charles Harpur', *SMH*, 26 September 1883, p. 3.

[9] Probably John Lucas (1818–1902), politician and pamphleteer.

sale has been a good one. The article *Critics & Critics* was written, at a few moments notice, by a lady friend of mine—Miss E. A. Martin—Deneihy's Historian[10]—from the few facts I could supply her with on such short notice. I see this week's *Bulletin*[11] credits me with the authorship—Well, I shall not disavow it; and while I have life and a printing press, or the command of one, I shall miss no opportunity of seeing justice done to the memory of our first— in every sense—Australian poet—notwithstanding the critics. Many thanks for the poem—it will appear in next issue.

Very faithfully yours,
J. G. O'Connor

189. Douglas Brooke Wheelton Sladen to Mary Harpur, 10 July 1887

Text: ML C 376

c/o Griffith and Farran.[12] St Paul's Churchyard London. E.C. July 10th 1887

Madam.[13]

I have been commissioned by Mr Walter Scott[14] to prepare for his *Canterbury*

[*continued next page*]

[10] Elvira A. Martin (d. 1905), journalist. Her *The Life and Speeches of Daniel Henry Deniehy* (Melbourne: George Robertson, 1884; online at Internet Archive) provided a biographical memoir, a selection of Deniehy's speeches and contributions to *Southern Cross* and *Freeman's Journal*, and Deniehy's celebrated satire 'How I Became Attorney-General of New Barataria', with a key to the personalities involved.

[11] *Bulletin*, 5 September 1885, p. 6 quoted from the *Express* article but mistakenly credited O'Connor.

[12] London mass-market publishers, later Griffith, Farran, Okeden and Welsh. They published several books by the prolific Sladen – his own poetry and prose, as well as his anthology *Australian Poets, 1788–1888: Being a Selection of Poems upon all Subjects Written in Australia and New Zealand during the First Century of the British Colonization with Brief Notes on their Authors and an Introduction by Patchett Martin* (1888). Sladen (1856–1947) developed a lasting interest in Australian poetry – particularly that of Adam Lindsay Gordon – during his years there in the early 1880s.

[13] The addressee is given as 'To Mrs Harpur (wife of the Poet / Charles Harpur.) / Sydney'.

[14] Walter (later, Sir Walter) Scott, English civil engineer and publisher (1826–1910), acquired the bankrupt Tyne Publishing Company in 1882, his output focussing on inexpensive reprints, issued monthly, such as the Camelot Classics prose series (edited by Ernest Rhys of Everyman fame) and the one-shilling Canterbury Poets.

Poets Series a volume of extracts from Australian Poets.[1] Your husband has one of the foremost claims to be represented, indeed I am not sure if his "Cloud" is not the finest thing in Australian poetry.[2]

I write to ask your permission to include a few extracts from his poems. Of course Mr Scott will pay nothing—even Tennyson[3] is paid nothing for his poems appearing in selections—but on the other hand the poems will get a splendid advertisement for nothing in England as Mr Scott's books sell by tens of thousands; and I shall insert a footnote saying where they may be procured,[4] so that readers struck with Mr Harpur's poems in the selection may go and buy his volume for themselves. I have been doing what I could to familiarize Mr Harpur's poems with the British public by quoting lines from them (with his name given) in a dictionary which I am preparing with Monsieur Barrère, Hans Breitman (C G Leland) & Charles Mackay.[5]

I am yrs obediently
Douglas B W Sladen.

190. Mary Harpur to James Henry Doyle, 27 July 1891

Text: ML MSS 827

Euroma Eurobodalla July 27th 1891

My dear James

I wrote to Robertson[6] telling him that you had authorised me to apply to him

---

[1] Published as *Australian Ballads and Rhymes: Poems Inspired by Life and Scenery in Australia and New Zealand*, ed. Douglas B. W. Sladen (London and Newcastle-on-Tyne: Walter Scott, 1888; online at Internet Archive). Sladen advertised in Australian newspapers for contributions – e.g., *Australasian* (Melbourne), 27 August 1887, p. 42. In his Introduction, Sladen dubbed CH 'the grey forefather of Australian poets' (p. xxiii), a much-repeated tag. For two British reviews, see *Academy*, 11 February 1888, p. 89 and *London Quarterly Review*, 6.1 (July 1901), pp. 121–3; for Australian reviews, mainly dismissive, see, e.g., *SA Advertiser*, 6 April 1888, p. 6; *Freeman's Journal*, 7 April 1888, p. 17; and *SMH*, 28 April 1888, p. 9. Walter Scott also published another anthology compiled by Sladen, *A Century of Australian Song* (1888), an expansion of *Ballads and Rhymes* but with the same CH items: 'The Cloud' (h067o), 'The Creek of the Four Graves' (h08on), 'A Storm on [sic] the Mountains' (h571g) and 'An Aboriginal Mother's Lament' (h003h).
[2] CH marked the earliest versions of this poem 'Imitated from the German'. His source was a translation by Margaret Taylor (which he appends to h067b) of the children's tale 'Die Wolke' by Richard Reinick. Note also Shelley's 'The Cloud' (1820), translated into German by 'P. H.' (Paul Haugwitz) in 1830 as 'Die Wolke'.
[3] See p. 141 n. 9.
[4] 'Volume published by George Robertson & Co.' appeared under each CH title in Contents.
[5] *A Dictionary of Slang, Jargon & Cant*, ed. Albert Barrère and Charles G. Leland ([London]: Ballantyne Press, 1889–90: Vol. I. A–K, 1889; online at Internet Archive). No CH items appeared. For a sharp contemporary assessment of Sladen and his contribution to this project (he loaded the dictionary with quotations from his own works), see *Bulletin*, 18 September 1897, Red Page.
[6] I.e., the Melbourne George Robertson.

for the proceeds of the sale of the book now in hand also to deal with me *direct* in the matter for the future. *He* says in answer that Mr. Martins (Editor of book) *order* is *necessary* before he can comply as he has had all the business in hand. I have sent Robertsons letter with a few lines from myself to Mr Martin. Will you kindly write to Mr. M. authorising me to deal with the publisher direct, It seems to me that an order signed by *you* as well as Mr. Martin is necessary to satisfy the *greedy* publisher who has mismanaged the affair being sure of his payment there must be by far the greater part of the books in Melbourne,[7] I have found great difficulty in buying a vol. in Sydney indeed few know that the book is published. Sir H. Parkes calculated the book would cost £100. for publishing & would bring £100. to the authors family.[8] He then thought of becoming gaurenter for the publication. but had to go to England,[9] When my late lamented kind old friend John Howe[10] (whom I have known from girlhood) undertook in connection with you to take Sir H.Ps place in the hope I am sure of helping me and my children: I feel dissapointed at the result of your attempt so kindly given and feel very grateful to all who have so generously helped in the matter If the book were distributed amongst booksellers it would soon sell.

You now know Robertsons answer and I feel sure you will act for the best. I thought he would require written authority from Martin as well as yourself; before dealing with me.

With best love to you and all enquiring friends

I am my dear Cousin
Yours sincerly
Mary Harpur

Copy of second letter from Sir H. P.

I have communicated with Mr George Robertson the publisher as to the cost of bringing out a volume of your late husbands poems and I should be disposed to take the work in hand if I could see my way in respect to the selection and supervision. Do you know of any person of taste and fine judgement who would make the selection and edit the work. I need hardly tell you that it would be impossible for me to undertake any labour in the matter myself.

Mrs Harpur July. 1891[11]

[7] I.e., the unsold bound copies of *Poems* held by publisher George Robertson in Melbourne, plus the 500 unbound, in sheets.
[8] For this calculation, see Letter 161.
[9] Parkes sailed for England via America in December 1881, returning in August the following year.
[10] John Kennedy Howe had died the previous September.
[11] Annotation by an unknown hand.

191. Sir Henry Parkes to Mary Harpur, 7 May 1892 *Text:* ML C376

Balmain Sydney[1] May 7th 1892

My dear Mrs Harpur

I am thinking of publishing in London a Book under the title enclosed.[2]

I possess something more than 20 of Charles Harpur's letters extending over several years from 1841 and I have a large number of J. J. Harpur's letters. My personal acquaintance with your husband terminated some years before his marriage but my recollections of him are very distinct. Many of the Sonnets addressed to yourself were written under my roof.[3]

I see by the Volume published in 1883 that your husband was born in 1817[4] so that if he was still living he would be a younger man than I am. On the 27th of this month I shall myself be 77 years of age. Yet mine has been a toilsome and weary life full of failures and great sorrows. It is possible that my success in political life may have been envied by on-lookers; but little do they know of the suffering heart-burning & bitterness of spirit which amidst it all I have borne in secret. My time has never been my own and my load of work has been enough for many shoulders.

I write to you to ask if you can assist me with material—letters or memoranda or possibly some unpublished poems.

I trust your own health keeps fairly good.

Sincerely
Henry Parkes

I purpose beginning my projected book in about two months. Until then my

---

[1] In the late 1880s Parkes moved from Faulconbridge in the Blue Mountains to a rented house with harbour views and extensive grounds, Hampton Villa in Grafton-street, Balmain (still standing). His wife Clarinda died there in 1888, and two sons were born there to the second Lady Parkes, Eleanor Dixon. The family left in late 1892.

[2] The enclosed slip, in Parkes's hand, lists 'Gifted Australians', recollections of CH, Deniehy, Kendall and William Bede Dalley, by 'Sir Henry Parkes G.C.M.G. – London'. For press reports, see, e.g., *Daily Telegraph*, 8 July 1892, p. 4; *Barrier Miner*, 6 December 1892, p. 3. The plan was not new: Parkes had resigned as Premier in October 1891 and, in January 1892, he recorded reading 'some old letters of mine 40 years old' (Martin, *Parkes*, pp. 409, 467n.). The envisaged book was never published but Parkes did complete 'his great apologia', *Fifty Years in the Making of Australian History* (London: Longman, Green, 1892). He died in 1896.

[3] See p. 9 n. 8: in 1895 Parkes annotated this copy of *Thoughts* (now held at ML C378): 'The writing on the first page of these "Sonnets" was made by Charles Harpur who at the period very frequently visited my house Some of the sonnets had been written in my house. I can well remember poor Charles reading the one on page 16 entitled "Absence" to me after he had composed it and going into raptures about the subject of it – Mary Doyle. "Rosa" is still living though the poet has been in his grave many years. H.P. 8/6/95'.

[4] The date given in the preface to *Poems* approved by Mary Harpur. CH was actually born in 1813. Rawling (p. 321, n. 10) notes: 'It is hardly credible that he believed it, but Harpur always gave his age as four years under what it really was.'

hands are quite full.

Have you any photograph? or copy of his little Volumes "The Bushrangers" &c?[5]

192. Mary Harpur to David Scott Mitchell, 8 July 1895

Text: David Scott Mitchell correspondence, ML A1461

Euroma Eurobodalla via Moruya July 8th 1895

Sir[6]

Permit me to enquire if you would purchase a number of H. Kendalls letters (about 30 more or less) to his brother poet Chas. Harpur[7] my late Husband. The letters are such as a man of genius would write on literary topics including criticisms on the leading writers of his day

The subject of one letter is the sad end of my late Husbands dear friend D. H. Deniehy.[8] There are several letters to me about literary matters and his own sufferings are very pathetic shortly before my lamented friends death.[9] In any country but this the letters would be greatly valued, time alone will enhance their value. Should you decide to purchase the letters and require a gaurentee as to their genuinness I can send you one from my friend the Revd J. H. Archibald[10] who has read them & seemed so pleased, Several book sellers

[5] In reply (24 May 1892: in *Suppl. Letters*), Mary Harpur undertook to copy some poems for Parkes and recalled events of September 1859 when the Harpurs – en route to Braidwood – stayed in Sydney, possibly at the Sydney Boarding Establishment, 2 and 3, College Buildings, Jamison-street, run by a Mrs R. Byers who advertised in country papers (e.g., *Maitland Mercury*, 21 December 1858, p. 1): '[P]ermit me to recall to your mind the fact of you and Miss Parkes calling on Mr. Harpur & myself at Jamison Street long ago, of your kind invitation to us all to spend the day with you at Millers Point. You and Mr H. after dinner went to Parliment House. Your poor Robert (then approaching manhood) showing my little boys the wonders of the City. We saw freqntly our old, kind, true hearted friend J. Robertson…Poor Deniehy & Stenhouse were our frequent visiters then.' (See Index for names.)

[6] Mary Harpur gives the addressee, in error, as 'J. S. Mitchell Esqr / Sydney'; this Mitchell, James Sutherland (1819–93), was a wealthy Sydney merchant, head of brewers Tooth and Co., and a supporter of charities. Mary meant David Scott Mitchell (1836–1907), prominent Sydney book collector and public benefactor. His collection of fine English literary editions and Australasian material, bequeathed in 1907 to the Public Library of NSW, formed the core of the Mitchell Library collection.

[7] ML holds 27 of Kendall's letters to CH, 25 of them at ML C199 (Kendall correspondence), and one each at ML *D19 (CH papers) and ML C198 (Kendall poems). C199 also contains 7 letters from CH to Kendall.

[8] I.e., Letter 97.

[9] Kendall's five letters to Mary Harpur are preserved in ML C199 and ML MSS 957 (Kendall papers).

[10] The Reverend John Howard Archibald (1839–1902), Presbyterian minister at Moruya.

want them but will not buy as they *sell* their *book unread first*.[1]

Your well known fine taste & love of literature has prompted me to make you an offer of the above letters

Yours respectfully
Mary Harpur

193. Mary Harpur to David Scott Mitchell, 14 July 1895

Text: David Scott Mitchell correspondence, ML A1461

Euroma Eurobodalla July 14th 1895

Sir

I have consulted several friends re the value of Kendalls letters[2] who all agree that £70 is a reasonable price to ask If you are disposed to buy please let me know

Yours truly
M Harpur

PS. I could let you have a few books.[3] I would *sell* the copy right of my late Husbands work[4]

194. Mary Araluen Baldwin (née Harpur)[5] to David Scott Mitchell, 2 March 1896

Text: David Scott Mitchell correspondence, ML A1461

82 Flinders St Moor Park[6] March 2nd 1896

Dear Sir

Refering to your offer[7] to purchase the letters of the late Henry Kendall to

---

[1] Obscure, but perhaps meaning that booksellers were reluctant to buy Kendall's letters because they could not sell their copies of his published poems. George Robertson was still advertising Kendall's *Poems* at 7s. 6d., in 1895 (as well as CH's at 6s.) – see *Age*, 30 November 1895, p. 16.

[2] See the offer in Letter 192.

[3] Probably books from CH's library. Several titles are listed in Letter 195.

[4] This offer runs counter to Mary's refusal 14 years previously: 'Overtures have been made to purchase the copyright but as Chas. always spoke strongly against the fruit of his brain going to enrich book sellers, I would not think of going against his often expressed wishes' (Mary Harpur to John Howe, 7 May 1881: in *Suppl. Letters*). Mary's change of heart may reflect the financial difficulties she faced in her last years. For the copyright registration, see p. 281 n. 9.

[5] Mary Araluen Baldwin, née Harpur (1861–1945), daughter of CH and Mary. By this time she had divorced Thomas Baldwin (who, it is thought, had left the country) and was supporting their surviving children Florence (b. 1888), Dora Araluen (b. 1890) and Cecil Charles Harpur (b. 1893). Her sister Ada had died in 1895 aged 38 at Mary Araluen's house in Crown-street, Surry Hills, with a cerebral haemorrhage.

[6] Moore Park, an inner suburb three km south-east of the Sydney city centre.

[7] See Letters 192 and 193. She asked £70; we do not have Mitchell's counter-'offer'.

my late father, I have to say that I have submitted same to my mother, she has decided that she will not sell.

I am Sir
Your respectfully
M. A. Baldwin

195. Mary Harpur to Angus & Robertson, 12 April 1896

Text: Angus & Robertson records, 1888-1932, ML MSS 314

Euroma Eurobodalla April 12th 1896

Sir[8]

Permit me to enquire if you would purchase gift books to the late poet Chas Harpur (my lamented Husband) from his admiring friends 2 Homers Iliad with note from the Poets dear friend D. H. Deniehy.[9] Vol of Murmers of the Stream with note from Sir H. Parkes[10] J. Nortons essays. Breartons poems 2. vol. pamphlet of Michiels life[11] odd Col. magazines Monthly. I have some old books Bishop Berkelys works.[12] With most of the greatest poets works. I should like to sell 5 large vol. of Carlyles Frederick the Great[13] (cost Mr Harpur £10. years ago) also Isaac Disraeli works[14] & many more

[8] Sydney booksellers and publishers founded in 1886 by George Robertson (1860–1933; no relation to his Melbourne namesake and competitor) and David Mackenzie Angus (1855–1901).

[9] The volume(s) may have been a translation, or included one. CH produced several translations from the *Iliad*: see p. 157 nn. 9, 10.

[10] Henry Parkes, *Murmurs of the Stream* (Sydney: James W. Waugh, 1857), probably the copy at ML (shelf-mark DSM/C479) inscribed 'Charles Harper with the author's love and admiration. Not published August 18th 1857'. (The book was being advertised as 'Just Published' in *SMH*, 1 September 1857, p. 1.) Parkes died at his home Kenilworth, Annandale, on 27 April 1896.

[11] Probably Joseph Sheridan Moore, *The Life and Genius of James Lionel Michael: With Fifteen Years' Experience of Literary Life in Sydney* (Sydney: Ferguson, 1868: 31pp.), though this must have been published shortly after CH's death. For Michael, see p. 127 n. 10. For 'Nortons essays', see p. 77 n. 4; for 'Breartons poems', see p. 275 n. 6; and for 'odd Col. magazines Monthly' (next item), see p. 212 n. 3.

[12] George Berkeley, Bishop of Cloyne (1685–1753), Irish philosopher, propounder of the theory of Immaterialism. His collected *Works* (various editions from 1784) appear in Australian bookshop advertisements from at latest 1839. Tegg of London published a single volume in 1837 and a two-volume edition annotated by the Reverend G. N. Wright in 1843. See also CH's 'Bishop Berkeley' (h046a) of 1855.

[13] Thomas Carlyle (1795–1881), Scottish philosopher, writer, historian. *History of Friedrich II of Prussia, Called Frederick the Great* was his final major work (6 vols.: London: Chapman and Hall, 1858–65). NLA holds CH's copy of Carlyle's *Sartor Resartus* (London: Chapman and Hall, 1858; shelf-mark FERG/6548), purchased by J. A. Ferguson from Mary Araluen Baldwin.

[14] Isaac D'Israeli (1766–1848), English writer and scholar, and father of British politician and novelist Benjamin Disraeli. His multi-volume *Curiosities of Literature* was immensely popular. Seven volumes of his works edited by his son were published 1849–59, variously by Moxon, Henry Colburn, and Routledge, Warnes and Routledge.

I trust you will let me know if you are inclined to buy any of the works mentioned & at what price

Yours truly
Mary Harpur

P.S My daughter Mrs Baldwin mentioned your offer to buy pamphlets & few of w[hic]h I am sorry to say remain after so many years.

I have lecture[1] delivered of Sydney school of Arts on poetry by my late Husband also an oration on Tetotalism,[2] beside many prose articles to newspapers &c &c.

M H

196. Mary Harpur to George Robertson, 3 June 1896
Text: Manuscripts and correspondence of Australian authors, NLA MS 3605

Euroma Eurobodalla June 3rd 1896

Sirs[3]

I request you will without *further delay* return through the bearer Mrs. Baldwin the parcle of manuscripts with papers & list[4] you after keeping them .3. months although you *agreed* to *answer promptly*. Your delay in the matter has seriously injured me

I also request you will furnish me with an account of the sale of Chas. Harpurs poems and that within one month from the present date you will

---

[1] See p. 112 n. 1. No manuscript or printed text of the lecture itself has surfaced.

[2] CH's 'An Oration on Teetotalism' appeared anonymously in *Australian Home Companion, and Band of Hope Journal* in six parts, 6 April – 15 June 1861, but written much earlier. A manuscript essay 'Teetotalism', dated 10 February 1848, in ML C382, pp. 109–31, may be the text (or a copy of it) from which the *AHC* article was set. At ML A87-2, p. 453, is a single-page manuscript introductory note to 'An Oration on Teetotalism. By Charles Harpur', which Holt dates to 1860–65; this does not appear in *AHC*. CH also left handwritten amendments, dated Euroma, 16 February 1865, on cuttings of the *AHC* article – see ML C376, pp. 500–17. He added his name beneath the title, then struck out both. We have no evidence that the oration was ever printed as a pamphlet.

[3] The Melbourne George Robertson, but addressed to Robertson's Sydney branch at 361–363 George-street.

[4] George Robertson had set *Poems* of 1883 from Henry Martin and his assistant's transcriptions, and Martin had returned the manuscripts to Mary Harpur. It seems she sent further material to Robertson's Sydney branch *c.* March 1896 for possible publication. Perhaps this was the material – poems by CH and letters from Henry Kendall – also turned down by Angus & Robertson the following month (see Angus & Robertson to Mary Harpur, 11 July 1896: in *Suppl. Letters*).

deliver to my agent in Sydney the *whole* of the *unsold edition*[5]

Yours truly
Mary Harpur

197. Henry Maydwell Martin to Mary Harpur, 27 August 1896

Text: Manuscripts and correspondence of Australian authors, NLA MS 3605

William St Norwood August 27th 1896

Dear Mrs Harpur[6]

Robertson in the first instance printed 1000 copies of which 500 were bound, and James[7] paid him for the work done up to that point. There are still I suppose 250 volumes bound and unsold. It might be well to reduce the price of these to say 3/6[8] and of course you are at liberty to either arrange this with GR & Co or take the whole of the remainder bound and unbound out of their hands and place them for sale with any other house with whom you can make suitable arrangements. My own impression is that you will do better by remaining with Robertson who perhaps would make another effort if the selling price were reduced though they might require a higher comn[9] for selling? But I know nothing of the standing & reputation of any publishing or book selling firms in Sydney and am therefore in the dark as to which course may be best for you. The volume should be in every railway book stall and stationer's counter.[10]

If you think of no better way it will be well to consult GR & Co and ask their advice as to the reduction in price and their actual terms. Then I would suggest that the "500 in sheets"[11] be cheaply bound in paper covers and sold say @ 2/6 but not until the first lot now remaining is cleared off. GR & Co would give you a price at which this could be done and if you thought it excessive you could get an alternative price from some Sydney house. But you must on no account quarrel with Robertson unless you see your way to

---

[5] George Robertson had printed 1000 copies of *Poems* (1883), binding half of the print run and leaving the remainder (516) unbound, in sheets. These would eventually be sold (probably at a discount) to Sydney bookseller-publisher William Dymock (1861–1900) for his cheap 'popular' paper-covered edition of 1899. Mary Harpur's 'agent' may have been her daughter Mary Araluen Baldwin.

[6] We do not have the letter from Mary Harpur to which this responds, but it must have sought Martin's advice on what to do about unsold stocks of *Poems* and raised concerns over payments for sales from its Melbourne publisher George Robertson ('GR & Co', below).

[7] James Henry Doyle.

[8] *Poems* retailed at 6s.

[9] Commission.

[10] Bookstalls at railway stations and stationery shops were outlets for cheap popular literature.

[11] See p. 301 n. 5.

take the whole matter out of their hands. I think I am right in saying you can do this if you choose, and you must remember that any publisher will require payment in advance for the expense of binding the remaining 500 whenever the time arrives to have this done. GR & Co will be able to advise you as to how much reduction in the price of the present volume will be advisable as a preliminary to clearing it and the sale of this will give you ample funds for the other.—Clarke should not have charged you 8/6[1] and I would mention this to G.R & Co for investigation. The price is fixed at 6/- and GR & Co charge the trade 4/9—which is the recognised scale—and surely 1/3 is an ample profit. 6/- is the retail price and 4/9 the wholesale or trade price upon which GR &Co charge 15% comn[2] to cover their agency freight & other charges

   With kind regards and best wishes believe me

Yours truly
H. M. Martin

198. Mary Harpur to Mary Araluen Baldwin (née Harpur), 17 July 1898

Text: Mary Araluen Baldwin papers, ML MSS 5643

Euroma Eurobodalla July 17th 1898

My dear Mary[3]

   It is some time since I wrote to you. my seeming neglect is not want of affection but really a dearth of pleasant news to tell you. It is a fortnight to day since Harold[4] came home looking very ill after a rough cold passage[5] *worse* in mind than when he left for Sydney He seems unable to do his business, will go out to gather milkers[6] and come home without any although cows with young calves are so often seen. We have not milk enough to use I am truly miserable and know not what to do. I want you to tell me truly if Harold ever made any complaints to you about me treating him unkindly as I feel I never did and was alway fond of my good son the foul lie repeated here by a mischief maker is troubling me I have enough *beside* to drive me mad I will show your

---

[1] Probably J. W. R. Clarke (1850?–1911), Sydney bookseller and stationer, of the Market buildings, George-street.

[2] 15 per cent commission. Thus Robertson paid only around 4s. on the sale of each 6s. copy of *Poems* – and the family had met the cost of production (about 3s. per copy: see Letter 182.

[3] Mary Araluen Baldwin's address in early 1899 was 31 Surrey-street, Darlinghurst, an inner suburb immediately to the east of the city. This was the home of her relative Frederick Milton Harpur, Lands Department officer and cricket writer.

[4] Harold Harpur (1856–1940), youngest of the Harpur boys.

[5] Before railways and highways the quickest way to Sydney from the far south coast of NSW was by sea. The Moruya Steam Navigation Company's *Koonya* ran weekly services between Sydney, Moruya and Wagonga (see Map 3), carrying passengers and produce.

[6] Cows in milk.

letter: I will ask Amy[7] too the same question. Harold says he *never* said an unkind word of me in his life. To think I have been so self sacrificing denying myself common necessaries to give both Ada[8] & Harold change and pleasure yet all I have done & suffered. I am scandalized by the vile wretches I *keep at a distance.*

The children are very well Cecil I have taught to spll & letters & say his prayers.[9] I think it was a mistake not to send him to England where he could be educated cheaply and well.

Dora[10] does not go to school regularly the long cold wet walk and wet weather is much against it.

Harold is nearly rid of his cough and looks much better he does not laugh now yet he is *worse* What will the end be. I think he never would be better no cure for the brain[11] my energy too has forsaken me and made me feel unable to bear my misery & difficulties. If poor H could only get the cattle together & sell. I fear he never will. He is out every evening until late playing cards & draughts with the Barlows[12]

I think the Dr here was right when he advised H. not to go to Sydney or any large noisy Town

I hope you are doing well and have some chance of getting a comfortable settled home

Do you ever see Mr Mitchel or Fitzpatrick[13]

All join in love to you and Florence.[14] You ca'nt think of how jealous my two children are of one another kissing me Cecil dare not love me without

[7] Not identified; possibly a domestic servant at Euroma.

[8] Mary and CH's daughter Ada Emily Harpur (1857–95).

[9] Mary was looking after her two younger grandchildren, Cecil and Dora, at Eurobodalla. Mary Araluen had divorced her husband Thomas George Baldwin in Sydney in November 1894 on the grounds of his habitual drunkenness and cruelty. He did not contest, and a decree nisi was granted, made absolute in 1896. Mary Araluen was given custody of the children. Cecil would be killed in action near Bapaume, northern France, in March 1917.

[10] Dora Annie Baldwin (1890–1960), daughter of Mary Araluen and Thomas Baldwin, her naming perhaps inspired by CH's love poem 'Dora' (h098). She would have attended school at Eurobodalla.

[11] Harold Harpur (see p. 232 n. 2) suffered from mental-health problems and, as his mother neared death, he would be committed to the Hospital for the Insane, Callan Park, Sydney, in February 1899. He likely spent the next four decades there before being transferred to the Kenmore Mental Hospital near Goulburn in 1937. He died there in 1940.

[12] Possibly the family of Reginald Heber Barlow, architect, surveyor and dairy farmer. Barlow was well known in the Moruya district, contributing articles to newspapers as 'Wolrab'. He was writing from Eurobodalla in 1899, and is recorded there in the Sands Directory for NSW, 1903.

[13] Probably John Charles Lucas Fitzpatrick (1862–1932), politician and journalist, editor of *Windsor and Richmond Gazette*, trustee of the Public Library of NSW and a supporter of Mitchell's bequest. He was a champion of CH, and knew both Mary and Washington (see, e.g., his account of a meeting with the latter in *North Western Courier* (Narrabri), 17 May 1926, p. 2).

[14] Florence Baldwin (1888–1969), daughter of Mary Araluen and Thomas Baldwin.

Dora claiming double Cecil is a fine boy but for one thing that gives us much trouble and makes himself uncomfortable

I am my dear Mary
Yours affec.
M Harpur[1]

199. Cecil Walter Salier to Mary Araluen Baldwin (née Harpur), 11 April 1943

Text: Rawling papers, ML MSS 1326, Box 3

"Avon" 33 Parkes Rd Artarmon[2] 11 April 1943

Dear Mrs Baldwin,[3]

I am still collecting matter about your late Father, and report progress,—

Joseph J Harpur. I looked up the Freeman's Journal about the date of Joseph's death but there was no obituary notice,[4] and, unhappily, the file of the journal is not indexed. Perhaps I will come across references elsewhere, by accident.

W.A. Duncan[5] Publisher of Harpur's first volume (Sonnets, 1845). Did you ever hear about him, from your mother?

"Euroma" My friend, H.M. Green, Fisher Librarian,[6] is still harping on the point whether "Euroma" was a successful farm when managed by or for

---

[1] Mary Harpur (b. 18 October 1820) died at Euroma on 2 June 1899, the cause recorded as senile decay and syncope (loss of consciousness) brought on two hours previously. She was buried on the hill at Euroma between her husband and son. Brief press notices appeared in, e.g., *Evening News*, 3 June 1899, p. 5 and *Windsor and Richmond Gazette*, 17 June 1899, p. 6. Her estate, valued at £234, was left to Mary Araluen.

[2] Suburb on Sydney's lower North Shore.

[3] Addressee of this typed letter is: 'Mrs M Araluen Baldwin / 12 William St / TURRAMURRA', a suburb on Sydney's upper North Shore. Mary Araluen was 81 at this point; the address was the home of her daughter Florence Araluen Griffiths (1888–1968).

[4] Joseph Jehoshaphat Harpur, CH's brother, died from 'a fit of sanguineous apoplexy' on 2 May 1878. He was a Catholic convert, and this may have steered Salier to *Freeman's Journal*, Sydney's long-running Catholic newspaper. However, the death was reported elsewhere – see notice in *Evening News*, 3 May 1878, p. 2; inquest report in same issue, p. 3; and obituary in *SMH*, 10 May 1878, p. 8.

[5] See p. 8 n. 4 and p. 233 n. 9.

[6] Henry Mackenzie ('Harry') Green (1881–1962), journalist, lecturer, librarian and literary historian. He succeeded John Le Gay Brereton (son of CH's correspondent) as librarian at the Fisher Library, University of Sydney, 1921–46. Green wrote on CH in his *Outline of Australian Literature* (Sydney: Whitcombe & Tombs, 1930) and discussed his work in his wartime ABC radio broadcasts: *Fourteen Minutes – Short Sketches of Australian Poets and their Work, From Harpur to the Present Day: Based on Wireless Talks Delivered for the A.B.C. in 1942* (Sydney: Angus & Robertson, 1944).

your father.[7] Rather a bothersome question, but perhaps you may be able to add to the facts you formerly gave me on the point.

Editor of edition of "Poems," (1883). This question looms more importantly the more I see the differences between versions of poems in this collection and versions published while your father was alive. My impression is that the latter versions, while in many instances rougher, as poetry, are stronger and more virile, frequently more simple, than the versions issued later, wherein also the tone of religious resignation, even sometimes of personal despair, is strongly marked.[8] I suspect that latter feeling was, in part at least, a result of his disease. Will you please allow your mind to wander among your early memories, perhaps then you will recall some facts about this "Editor," (a Mr Martin, of Adelaide, I think you said) which will help me to identify him and clarify his share in the emendations to the several poems.

Portrait[9] Among the papers in possession of the Genealogical Society I came across a small photo, labelled "Mr Harpur," and indexed as "Charles Harpur." Could you help me to decide if it be an early photo of your father, if I brought it to you for inspection? It presents a vigourous man, full bearded, and full faced, of about 40 to 50, I judge. I am asking the Genealogical Society to let me have the loan of it for a few weeks, for your inspection and identification: if it be one of your father, I shall have it copied.

When I have got the picture, I will arrange, with your consent, to visit you again. Meantime, this letter does not require an answer—unless you have something important to reply that would be better for me to know *before* we meet.

---

[7] This question had been aired before in *ATCJ*: '[CH] might have saved money [from his Gold Commissioner's salary] if he had been a shrewd man of business, and, in the event of losing his place, could betake himself to trading for a livelihood. But, however clever in other respects, poor Charles Harpur was not over-charged with worldly wisdom. By way of making provision for his young family he free-selected a farm at Eurobadalla, in the improvement of which he expended, from year to year, the major part of his salary. The improvement of his little estate, however, was – it is easy to guess – far more expensive to him than profitable. It exhausted the means in his possession, without providing for a proportionate recompense in the future' (14 March 1874, p. 13). In 'Daughter's Memories', Mary Araluen countered: 'My father left no debts, an unencumbered farm, a well-furnished, comfortable home, which I am sure was much better than most would have done on the same salary, although he was a poet' (*SMH*, 24 August 1929, p. 11). In his wartime radio talks Green said 'he seems to have been fairly successful as a farmer also, though accounts differ about that' (*Fourteen Minutes*, p. 10).

[8] Salier was not the first to favour earlier versions of some of CH's poems over those published in *Poems* (1883): e.g., unsigned review, *Maitland Mercury*, 22 September 1883, p. 4, and Turner and Sutherland (1898), pp. 33–4. But Salier's scrupulous work on the Harpur manuscripts at ML and his interviews with family members would lead to the identification of *Poems* editor 'M.' as Henry M. Martin, and provide evidence of the extent to which the texts, previously accepted as authentic, had been altered. See his 'The Life and Writings of Charles Harpur', *RAHS Journal and Proceedings*, 32.2 (1946), pp. 89–105, online at NLA.

[9] Photograph not located but presumably another of the *cartes de visite* of early 1868: see Introduction, n. 20.

With kind regards to yourself and Mrs Griffiths,

Yours sincerely
C W Salier[1]
(C.W. Salier)

200. Mary Araluen Baldwin (née Harpur) to Cecil Walter Salier, 13 June 1945

Text: Rawling papers, ML MSS 1326

12 William St., *Turramurra.*[2] 17th August . 1947.

Dear Mr. Salier,

In answer to your questions about my mother's family—I will try to put things down as plainly as possible, as our families are so intermarried that one is likely to get things slightly mixed, unless I am very careful. My mother the wife of Charles Harpur, was the eldest daughter of Edmund Doyle of then "Eulengo," Jerrys Plains.[3] My mother said at about that time my grandfather Doyle was left a legacy. He had the property at Jerry's Plains enlarged, and a new stone house built. As my mother was the eldest daughter, she was given the honour of naming their new home. She was just then reading Sir Walter Scotts novel "Montrose"[4]—that was the name she chose.

I visited my grandfather Doyle's old home at Jerry's Plains about twenty eight years ago. It was in good order, and is still known as "Montrose".

My mother had eight brothers, and four sisters. Two of my mother's sisters married their cousins Doyles. Her sister Fanny married her cousin Andrew

[*continued next page*

---

[1] A finance adviser by occupation, Cecil Walter Salier (1880–1949) undertook the earliest serious research on CH's poems. His first article, 'The First Australian-born Poet Charles Harpur, 1817–1868' appeared in *Publicist*, later the organ of the stridently nationalist Australia First movement, in August 1936. During the next decade Salier would closely examine the ML's Harpur manuscripts, publishing articles and lecturing on his discoveries. He edited *'Rosa': Love Sonnets to Mary Doyle by Charles Harpur* ([Melbourne]: Hutchinson, 1948) from manuscripts at ML.

[2] Mary Araluen lived there in the 1940s until her death in 1945; her children also lived there at various times. For the date, see end of letter.

[3] Mary Ann Doyle (1820–99) was the daughter of Irish-born Edmund Doyle (1799–1871) and Frances, née Smith (1802–68). She was born at Lower Portland Head on the Hawkesbury River, north-west of Sydney. The family moved north to Jerry's Plains on the Hunter River in the later 1830s. Doyle's grant there was subsequently known as 'Eulengo'.

[4] Montrose Park abutted Eulengo on the east, the properties sitting not far east of the village of Jerry's Plains. The reference is to Scott's historical novel *A Legend of Montrose* (1819).

Hamilton Doyle, of then "Claremont" station, Lochinvar.[5]

My mother's kinsmen who helped to publish my fathers book of poems were her first cousins James Hume Doyle of then "Invermenes," Scone,[6] and John Kennedy Howe, of then Redburn-Berry, Singleton. John Howe's mother was a Doyle.[7] I suppose it is not necessary to say that they were named after their kinsmen, the Australian explorers, Hume and Kennedy.[8]

Mr. Martin. When my uncle John K. Doyle, owned "Moorabilla," Mr. Martin came there to gain station experience. He was a very young man then, and they made a strong friendship that lasted all their lives.[9] I am referring to the Mr. Martin who edited my fathers book of poems. When my mothers sister Emily was in her eighty fourth year, she had a very severe illness. Mr. Martin was then living in Tasmania, and came over to visit her.[10] He was then himself an old man.

Was Charles Harpur temperate? From my mothers account Charles Harpur was neither a teetotallor nor a "tippler." He could drink a few glasses, with friends, when the occasion warranted.

My father was always fond, and very proud of his wife. Although she was not a beautiful woman, she was very graceful and elegant looking. I believe he said of her—"that he never saw her in an ungraceful attitude;" "Even if she swept a room, she did it gracefully."

---

[5] Mary Araluen is unreliable on some details of family history. Mary Harpur's sister Frances ('Fanny') Doyle (1840–1910) married her cousin Andrew John Doyle (1833–1913) at Patrick's Plains in 1857. He was the son of James George Doyle, younger brother of Mary and Frances's father Edmund Doyle, and was owner of 'Claremont' at Lochinvar in the Hunter Valley between Maitland and Branxton. There are no records of a related Andrew Hamilton Doyle. However, in some genealogies Andrew John Doyle appears as Andrew John Howe Doyle. Perhaps Mary Araluen confused the names of two early explorer-settlers, Hamilton Hume and John Howe. Mary Harpur's sister Emily Maria Doyle (1842–1926) married her first cousin once removed John Kennedy Doyle (1840–1907) at Jerry's Plains in 1861. He was the grandson of Cyrus Matthew Doyle, brother of Edmund Doyle.

[6] I.e., James Henry Doyle (1844–1921): see p. 241 n. 4.

[7] John Kennedy Howe (1812–90): see p. 240 n. 2. His father was John Howe (1774–1852), explorer and early settler on both the Hawkesbury and Hunter rivers, and his mother was Jane Kennedy (c. 1782–1859), daughter of early Windsor settler James Raworth Kennedy. The Doyle and Kennedy families were, however, related by marriage.

[8] I.e., Hamilton Hume (1797–1873), early explorer of southern NSW and Victoria, and Edmund Besley Kennedy (1818–48), surveyor and explorer, speared to death on the Cape York Peninsula in far north Queensland. They were not kin, though Hume was a cousin of Howe's mother Jane Kennedy.

[9] John Kennedy Doyle (1840–1907): see p. 241 n. 14. With Ross R. Doyle, he owned Morabilla, a sheep station on the Bokhara River 48 km north of Brewarrina, north-western NSW. Based at Tamworth, and a grazier, auctioneer, and stock and station agent, John was James Henry Doyle's brother and husband of Mary Harpur's youngest sister Emily Maria Doyle. Henry M. Martin worked on Doyle properties in north-western NSW in the early 1870s.

[10] This places Martin's visit in 1926, the last year of Emily's life. He may have been visiting Tasmania at the time, but it is unlikely he was living there, as his winery company H. M. Martin & Son Ltd. at Stonyfell was newly established in Adelaide. Martin died in 1936 aged 89.

My mother was also most devoted to her husband. She kept his memory green, by speaking of him so often when we were children, growing up.

Washington. My brother Washington's wife's maiden name was Mary King.[1] Of his children, the ones I used to know are dead, years ago,[2] any that may be alive I have lost touch with. Washington had two loves in his life, which I am sure is the reason others mattered so little to him. His love for his cousin Annie Doyle;[3] Washington and Annie were in love with each other for years. It was always called the family romance. And his great affection for his cousin Morice Doyle, of then, "Wirriston" Station, Moree.[4]

Washington and Morice were about the same age and were inseparable companions for years. Annie was the daughter of my mother's brother Andrew Doyle, of then, *"Woolooman" station,[5] near Tamworth. "Woolooman" was the station to which my father Charles Harpur, took his son, Washington, to gain station experience.

My father, and other near relatives, were very much against the cousins marrying, as there had been so much intermarrying in the family recently. I suppose they thought it right to interfere, but it spoilt both their lives.

I always admired my brother Washington, he was a man's man, and led a man's life. Very prosperous at times, fond of sport, especially horse-racing, which I have no doubt kept him from becoming too prosperous. He came down to visit us in Sydney when he was well over seventy, and went to Randwick[6] whenever he could obtain a chance, and enjoyed himself immensely. He died at the age of eighty-seven. I was shown a cutting from one of the Queensland papers, it said,—as near as I can remember,—"So passed a picturesque personality, who in his heyday was one of the cleverest all-round men in this

---

[1] Washington Harpur (1851–1938), the first child of CH and Mary Harpur, left Euroma after his father's death to settle in northern NSW where his Doyle relatives had properties. He married housekeeper Mary Agnes King (1865–1935) at Walgett in 1880. They would have seven children (five surviving infancy) before their divorce in 1896.

[2] Ada Emily (1881–1930), Stella Ruby (1883–1903), William James (1885–1916), Lillie Frances (1887–87), Mary Ethel (1889–1982), Charles Harold (1891–92) and Florence Isabel Gertrude (1893–1966).

[3] Annie Isabella Doyle (1853–1941), daughter of Mary Harpur's brother Andrew Doyle. Two years younger than Washington, she was born at Jerry's Plains and did not marry.

[4] Neither Morice Doyle nor 'Wirriston' near Moree has been identified. Werriston, a sheep station near Werris Creek, 45 km south west of Tamworth, was owned by Robert Fitz Doyle (1838–91), a cousin of Mary Harpur, and subsequently by his sons. However, Maurice Doyle (1868–1940), son of Mary's cousin Cyrus Edmund Doyle and therefore second cousin to Washington, owned Werrina, between Moree and Mungindi on the NSW–Queensland border. This is the district in which Washington lived and died. It is likely that Mary Araluen was wrong about the age difference and misremembered the name of the property, and that the transcriber of this letter misspelt Maurice's name.

[5] Andrew Doyle (1824–98) was a brother of Mary Harpur. Woolomin or Wooloomon was on the Peel River, 25 km south-east of Tamworth.

[6] Racecourse in the eastern suburbs of Sydney.

territory."[7]

The love of Washington's life, Annie, never married. She lived to be a very old woman. They corresponded, all through the years, almost to the end.

Yours sincerely,
(signed by M. A. B—Mary Araluen Baldwin.

From original in possession of C. W. S.—Dictated to me by Nar[8]—Wednesday, June 13th, 1945.

* "WOOLOMIN"

---

[7] Washington Harpur died at Mungindi, on the NSW–Queensland border, on 13 July 1938. Brief death notices appeared in several newspapers, e.g., *SMH*, 19 July 1938, p. 17, and *Wingham Chronicle*, 26 July 1938, p. 2. The item Mary Araluen mentions has not been located.
[8] This letter was originally dictated to a third party – presumably her grandson Cecil Beverley Griffiths – on 13 June 1945, four months before her death. It survives as a copy, made in 1947, presumably by Griffiths, preserved among copies of Salier's correspondence in the Rawling papers at ML. 'Nar' was the affectionate name for Mary Araluen used by her grandchildren (see her memorial notice, *SMH*, 20 October 1948, p. 20). The process of dictation may explain misspelt place names. Minor annotations and corrections in ballpoint pen appear to be by Griffiths.

MAPS

Maps

1. New South Wales

□ Indicates rural property, station

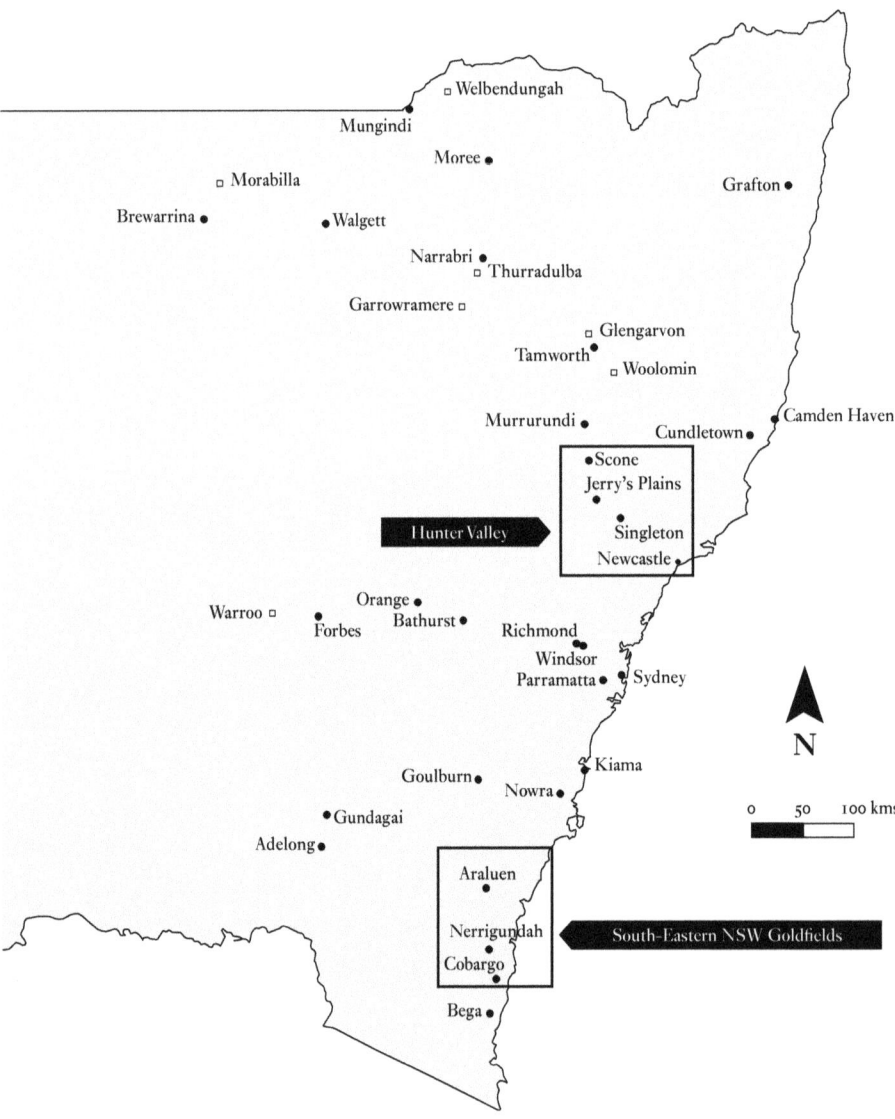

2. Hunter Valley

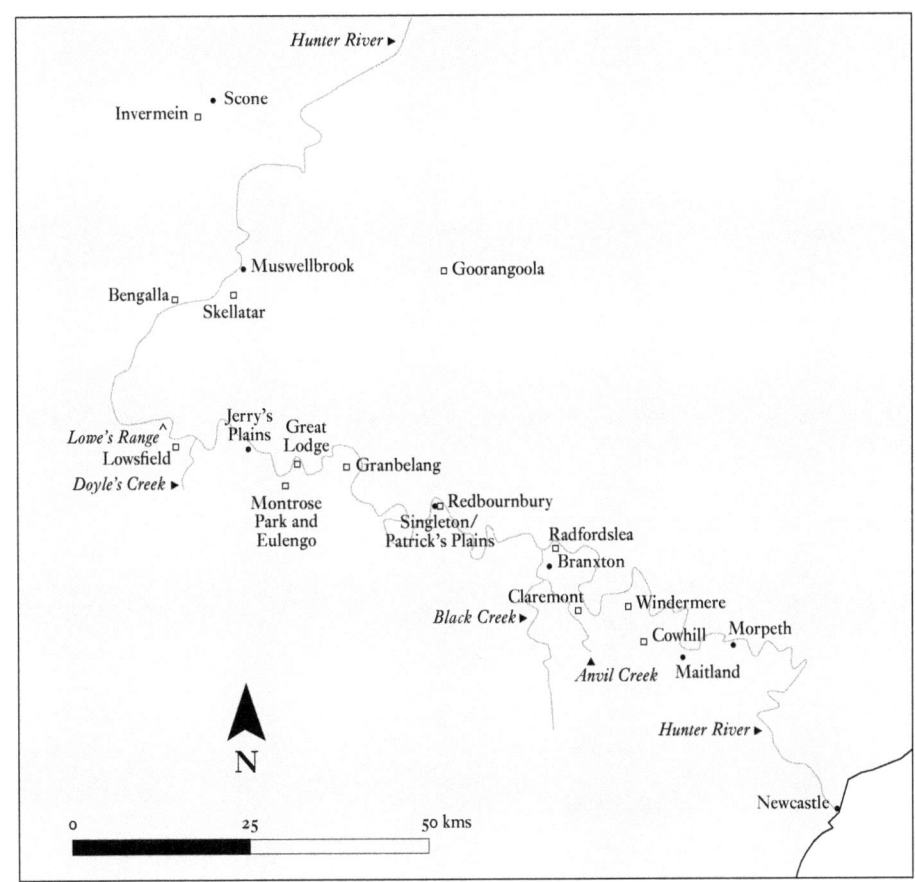

Hunter River ▶

• Scone

Invermein □

• Muswellbrook

□ Goorangoola

Bengalla □

□
Skellatar

Jerry's
Plains

Great
Lodge

Lowe's Range ^
Lowsfield □

□ Granbelang

Doyle's Creek ▶

□
Montrose
Park and
Eulengo

◨ Redbournbury
Singleton/
Patrick's Plains

Radfordslea
□
• Branxton

Claremont
□

□ Windermere

Black Creek ▶

□ Cowhill

Morpeth

▲
Anvil Creek

• Maitland

Hunter River ▶

Newcastle •

N

0   25   50 kms

3. South-Eastern NSW Goldfields

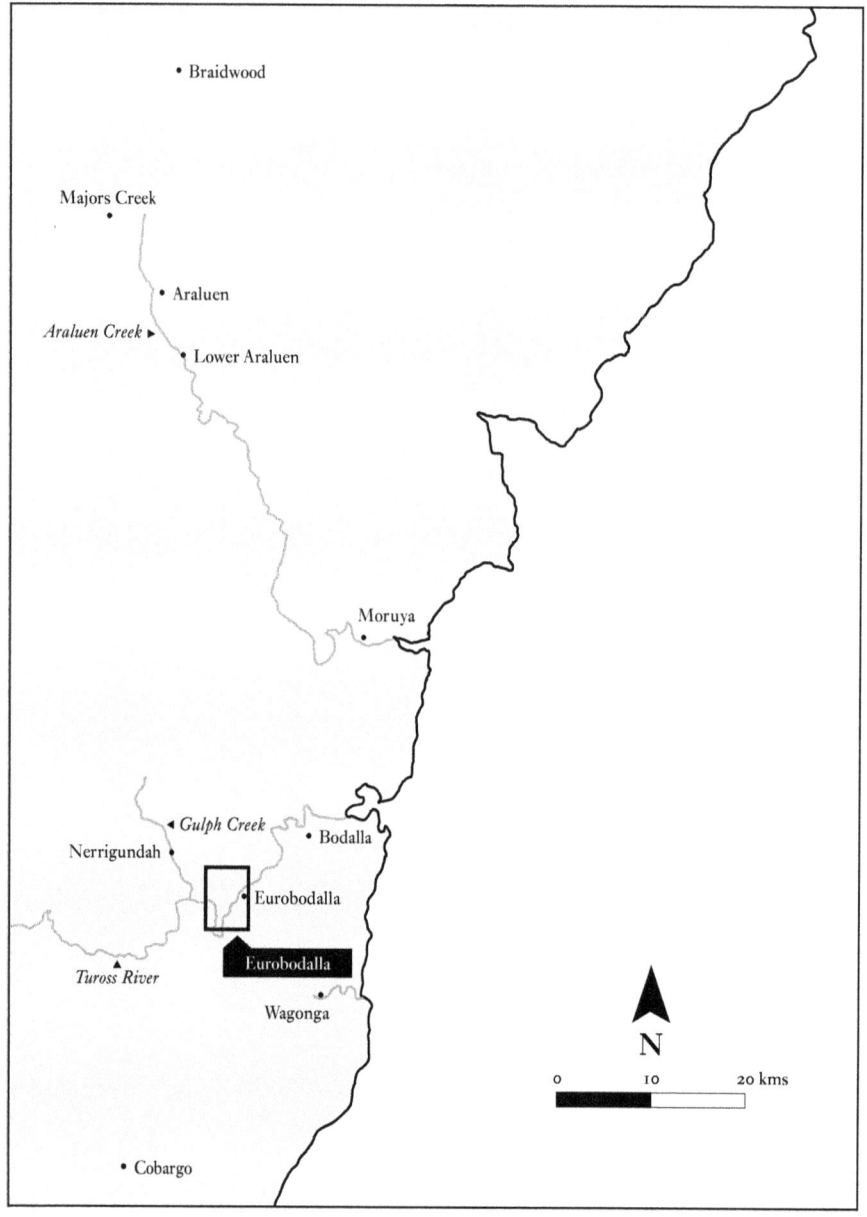

4. Eurobodalla

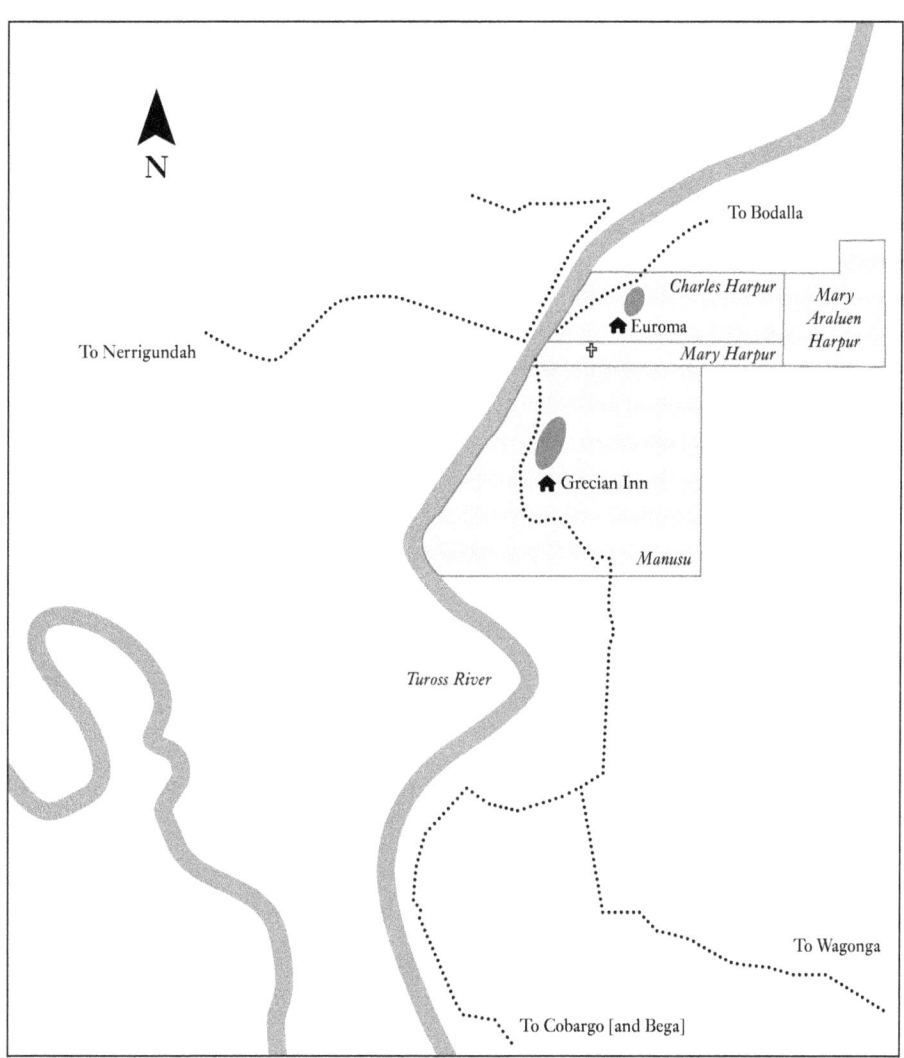

Source: Parish map, Parish of Urobodalla, Second Edition (1896), NSW Land Registry Services

INDEX

This is a name and subject index. Its largest entry 'Harpur, Charles' divides into CHARACTERISTICS AND CONCERNS, LIFE and WORKS. In addition to these groupings, the following subject entries are relevant to colonial and literary print cultures: 'book publishing and bookselling, colonial'; 'book publishing, British'; and 'literary culture in Sydney'. Individual newspapers and magazines are grouped under 'newspapers as literary publishers'. Those with other, usually political, roles relevant to Harpur are also listed separately by title. Literary figures (influences, sources, commentary on, etc.) are gathered under 'poets, dramatists and essayists: literary references'; those with personal roles in Harpur's life such as Henry Parkes, Henry Kendall and Henry Halloran, or with other relevance, are also given separate name entries. Bolded references (e.g. **123n**) indicate the page on which the main footnote may be found.

www.ingramcontent.com/pod-product-compliance
Lightning Source LLC
Chambersburg PA
CBHW041642010726
47507CB00012B/427